CAMBRIDGE STUDIES IN EARLY MODERN HISTORY

Editors

J. H. ELLIOTT   OLWEN HUFTON
H. G. KOENIGSBERGER

Neighbourhood and community in Paris, 1740–1790

CAMBRIDGE STUDIES IN EARLY MODERN HISTORY

Edited by Professor J. H. Elliott, The Institute for Advanced Study, Princeton, Professor Olwen Hufton, University of Reading, and Professor H. G. Koenigsberger, King's College, London

The idea of an 'early modern' period of European history from the fifteenth to the late eighteenth century is now widely accepted among historians. The purpose of the Cambridge Studies in Early Modern History is to publish monographs and studies which will illuminate the character of the period as a whole, and in particular focus attention on a dominant theme within it, the interplay of continuity and change as they are represented by the continuity of medieval ideas, political and social organization, and by the impact of new ideas, new methods and new demands on the traditional structures.

Neighbourhood and community in Paris, 1740–1790

DAVID GARRIOCH

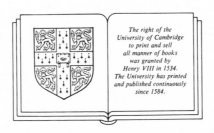

The right of the
University of Cambridge
to print and sell
all manner of books
was granted by
Henry VIII in 1534.
The University has printed
and published continuously
since 1584.

CAMBRIDGE UNIVERSITY PRESS

Cambridge

London   New York   New Rochelle
Melbourne   Sydney

Published by the Press Syndicate of the University of Cambridge
The Pitt Building, Trumpington Street, Cambridge CB2 1RP
32 East 57th Street, New York, NY 10022, USA
10 Stamford Road, Oakleigh, Melbourne 3166, Australia

First published 1986

Printed in Great Britain at the University Press, Cambridge

British Library cataloguing in publication data
Garrioch, David
Neighbourhood and community in Paris, 1740–1790. –
(Cambridge studies in early modern history)
1. Paris (France) – Social life and customs – 18th century
I. Title
944'.36034   DC715

Library of Congress cataloguing in publication data
Garrioch, David
Neighbourhood and community in Paris, 1740–1790.
(Cambridge studies in early modern history)
Bibliography
Includes index.
1. Paris (France) – Social conditions. 2. Neighborhood – France –
Paris – History – 18th century. 3. Paris (France) – Economic conditions.
4. Paris (France) – Social life and customs. I. Title. II. Series.
HN438.P3G37 1986   306'.0944'35   86-2290

ISBN 0 521 30732 5

CE

For E.F.M., F.E.G.,
and my parents

Contents

Contents

Illustrations

Tables and graphs

Acknowledgements

Many people have helped me in my research, and I cannot thank all of them individually. However, I would especially like to thank my D.Phil. supervisor, Dr Colin Lucas, for his constant help, encouragement, and friendship. I am grateful to Dr Alison Patrick and Dr Chips Sowerwine, of the Melbourne University History Department, who introduced me to French history; to Professor George Rudé, who first suggested that I look at the Y series in the Archives Nationales; and to Professor Richard Cobb, for early guidance. My thanks also go to Monsieur Denis Richet, for allowing me to attend his most stimulating seminars; to Dr Michael Sonenscher of Middlesex Polytechnic for many useful documents and helpful suggestions; to Drs Marian Aveling, David Chandler, and Bill Kent of Monash University History Department, and to Professor Olwen Hufton of Reading University, for their suggestions; to Sue Tomlins, Vicki Tipping and Tony Miller of Monash University Geography Department for the maps and photographic work; and to the staff of the Archives Nationales in Paris for their friendly assistance. Thanks to Dr John Rowett and Dr Geoffrey Ellis for their encouragement, and to Liz Loden for help with the photos. Special thanks to Jan Pinder for her constant support and encouragement, to Paulette Schmidt for typing a seemingly endless manuscript, and to Mary Baffoni for her extremely careful and patient sub-editing. Needless to say, while all of these people have contributed much to this book, its flaws and inaccuracies remain entirely my own responsibility.

I would like to acknowledge financial support from the Gowrie Trust, Sydney; the British Council; the British Institute in Paris; the Zaharoff Fund of the Taylor Institute, Oxford; the Oxford–Sorbonne Exchange Scheme; Balliol College, Wolfson College, and St Anne's College, Oxford.

Abbreviations

A.H.R.F.   *Annales historiques de la Révolution française*
A.N.   Archives Nationales
Annales: E.S.C. Annales: Economies, sociétés, civilisations

A.P.P.   Archives de la Préfecture de Police
Bast.   Archives de la Bastille, Bibliothèque de l'Arsenal, Paris
B.H.V.P.   Bibliothèque Historique de la Ville de Paris
B.N.   Bibliothèque Nationale, Paris
B.N. Ms. fr. Bibliothèque Nationale, Manuscrit français
interr.   interrogation
J. de F.   Joly de Fleury Collection, Bibliothèque Nationale
Lam.   Lamoignon Collection of Edicts, Archives de la Préfecture de Police
opp.   opposition (to *scellé après décès*)
Orléans   Bibliothèque Municipale d'Orléans
Seine   Archives de la Seine
wit.   witness

All manuscript references are to the Archives Nationales, Paris, unless otherwise specified. To avoid unnecessary repetition in the notes, the years and quarters of the *cartons* most frequently cited are listed here:

Y10994	Faubourg St Antoine	1752
Y11239	Halles	1752
Y11705–Y11706	Place Maubert	1775
Y12596–Y12597	Place Maubert	1752
Y13290	Place Maubert	1788
Y13751	Palais Royal	1746
Y13760	Palais Royal	1752
Y13816	St Germain des Prés	1788
Y14078	Luxembourg	1752
Y14436	Faubourg St Antoine	1788
Y14484	Halles	1789
Y15099–Y15100	Grève	1788
Y15350	Grève	1752
Y15402	Halles	1788

Introduction

The existence of local communities in eighteenth-century Paris has been both assumed and largely ignored by historians. P. Ariès, writing about 'the family and the city', speaks of large seventeenth-century cities as composed of separate neighbourhoods, each with its own community and its own character, and claims that in eighteenth-century Paris this pattern was upset by the arrival of a more transient population.[1] There is nevertheless plenty of evidence to suggest that, however reduced, local loyalties remained strong. G. Rudé has shown the extent of local participation in many of the revolutionary riots. Many writers, following Mercier, have stressed the social particularities of individual quarters: the inhabitant of the Faubourg St Marcel is 'more turbulent, more quarrelsome, more disposed to rebellion than that in the other quarters': the Marais is a hundred years behind, old-worldly, *triste*. A study by A. Farge has shown how the neighbourhood would often unite to protect beggars from arrest.[2]

Yet only a few studies have taken local ties into account when discussing events in Paris or looking at Parisian society. R. Andrews' unpublished thesis on the revolutionary sections stresses the particular character of the quarters and the pre-revolutionary career of the political leaders within them. R. Cobb has constantly emphasized the idea of the urban village and pointed to its importance in sectional politics: the prominent terrorists of the Year II were all well known in their own quarter and for this reason were as much pushed into politics as deliberately choosing the role. The failure of the *sans-culotte* 'movement' was largely due to its being composed of people whose angle of vision and whose loyalties were local rather than city-wide, much less national.[3]

These, however, are exceptions. Most works on eighteenth-century Paris

---

[1] P. Ariès, 'The Family and the City', *Daedalus*, 106 (1977), 227–35 (p. 231).

[2] G. Rudé, *The Crowd in the French Revolution* (Oxford, O.U.P., 1959). L. S. Mercier, *Tableau de Paris*, new edition, 12 vols. (Amsterdam, 1782–8), vol. 1, p. 272; vol. 2, pp. 277–8. J. Godechot, *La Prise de la Bastille, 14 juillet 1789* (Paris, Gallimard, 1965), pp. 75–8. J. Kaplow, *The Names of Kings* (New York, Basic Books, 1972), ch. 1. A. Farge, 'Le Mendiant, un marginal? Les résistances aux archers de l'hôpital dans le Paris du XVIIIe siècle', in *Les Marginaux et les exclus dans l'histoire* (Paris, Union Générale d'Editions, 1979), pp. 312–29.

[3] R. Andrews, 'Political Elites and Social Conflicts in the Sections of Revolutionary Paris: 1792 – Year III', unpub. D.Phil. thesis, Oxford University, 1970. R. Cobb, *The Police and the People* (Oxford, O.U.P., 1970), pp. 122, 198–200, and *Reactions to the French Revolution* (Oxford, O.U.P., 1972), pp. 116–21.

ignore geographical differences and take no account of local ties in their assessment of events. Recent studies of the city, concentrating on its social composition, have uncritically used the socio-professional categories elaborated by A. Daumard and F. Furet, classifying Parisians according to the place they are assumed to have occupied in the economic life of the capital.[4] Yet emphasizing economic function and occupational status to the exclusion of family, friendship, and neighbourhood is to ignore the reality of everyday life in the city. Most people felt themselves to belong to a particular area, and even a master artisan might well identify more closely with his next-door neighbour, of a quite different occupation, than with another master of the same trade elsewhere in the city. His wife was even more likely to belong to the local community: men and women had different social networks and could have different allegiances. It is therefore vital to take account of gender divisions when discussing social organization. Other factors could also play a role, of course: for example family ties, age and marital status. Social divisions cannot be traced simply by measuring wealth, professional status, or area of economic activity. This study, in exploring the role of various social bonds within the local community, attempts to show how different combinations of these factors affected social organization in the city.

Studying 'communities' in a city the size of eighteenth-century Paris, however, is hardly the same as in a rural village or even a small town. Where the society under discussion is relatively isolated, geographically and socially, where it falls within a single parish and administrative area, and where the economic and social interdependence of its members is obvious, as in most rural villages, the use of 'community' can lead to no confusion. Works as important as M. Spufford's *Contrasting Communities* or Y. Castan's *Honnêteté et relations sociales en Languedoc* rely heavily on the concept, yet make no attempt to define it and indeed have little need to do so.[5] In a city, however, the meaning of 'community' is much less clear. It is extremely difficult to define its limits, either topographically or socially. Geographic mobility tends to be higher than in rural areas; there is greater contact with outsiders and with strangers; and the different quarters are heavily interdependent. No part of eighteenth-century Paris formed a single economic unit, and few areas were in any sense physically distinct. The various administrative divisions used by different authorities rarely coincided. It was impossible, given the density and the mobility of much of the population, for anyone to know everyone else even in the same street. The city's population was mixed and mobile, the range of occupations, wealth and life-styles in any one area enormous, the web of daily contacts across the whole

---

[4] A. Daumard and F. Furet, *Structures et relations sociales à Paris au milieu du XVIIIe siècle* (Paris, Armand Colin, 1961).

[5] M. Spufford, *Contrasting Communities* (Cambridge, C.U.P., 1974). Y. Castan, *Honnêteté et relations sociales en Languedoc, 1715–1780* (Paris, Plon, 1974).

city infinitely intricate. In this context the term 'community' requires careful definition.

Community studies have proliferated in recent years and there have been many attempts to find a definition which is applicable in different places and cultures, as well as at different periods.[6] There have however been few studies of 'communities' in early modern cities, although the idea of the quarter as an 'urban village' enjoys some acceptance.[7] On the other hand there has been considerable work on nineteenth- and twentieth-century cities, nearly all of which uses 'community', implicitly or explicitly, to refer to a group of people in a given area who are strongly linked by one or more social bonds such as kinship, work, race or origin, religion, culture, socio-economic status.[8] The obvious difficulty of defining the exact geographic limits of urban communities has led to attempts at 'social area' analysis and to the idea of 'factorial ecology', which tries to use a combination of socio-economic indices in order to map the implantation of particular groups in the urban environment.[9]

This approach is unsatisfactory in a number of ways. The extent and the nature of the 'community' thus mapped depend very much on predetermined categories, and will vary according to the specific criteria chosen. In other words, one to some extent finds the sort of community that one is looking for or that the records available dictate. The use of parish registers for family reconstruction, for example, privileges kinship; that of taxation records makes economic and occupational status seem more important.

But there is a weightier objection both to social area analysis, and to the 'area plus social bonds' definition of 'community' on which it is based. Tracing the particular social bonds which have been selected as significant still does not bring us closer to identifying an urban community. In Victorian cities it is often possible to find out where people lived, how often they moved and where, with whom they socialized, where they worked and with whom, to whom they were related. But none of this necessarily provides evidence of community life, and nor

---

[6] C. J. Calhoun, 'Community: Toward a Variable Conceptualization for Comparative Research', *Social History*, 5 (1980), 105–29. G. A. Hillery, Jr, 'Definitions of Community: Areas of Agreement', *Rural Sociology*, 20 (June 1955), 111–23. A. Macfarlane, *Reconstructing Historical Communities* (Cambridge, C.U.P., 1977). P. H. Mann, *An Approach to Urban Sociology* (London, Routledge and Kegan Paul, 1965), ch. 7. D. E. Poplin, *Communities. A Survey of Theories and Methods of Research* (New York, Macmillan, 1972).

[7] M. Garden, 'La Vie de quartier', *Bulletin du Centre pour l'histoire économique et sociale de la région lyonnaise*, 3 (1977), 17–28.

[8] H. Gans, *The Urban Villagers* (New York, Free Press of Glencoe, 1962). U. Hannerz, *Soulside. Enquiries into Ghetto Culture and Community* (New York, Columbia University Press, 1969). M. Young and P. Willmott, *Family and Kinship in East London* (Harmondsworth, Penguin, 1957).

[9] On 'social area' analysis see Poplin, *Communities*, pp. 100–2, and R. Dennis, 'Community and Interaction in a Victorian City: Huddersfield, 1850–1880', Ph.D. thesis, Cambridge University, 1975, pp. 10–20. The method has only recently begun to be used in France: M. Demonet and G. Granasztói, 'Une Ville de Hongrie au milieu du XVIe siècle: analyse factorielle et modèle social', *Annales: E.S.C.*, 37 (1982), 523–51.

does it tell us anything about community structure.[10] It does not allow for the way people actually behave. Family ties may or may not be significant. Social homogeneity, while it may be a basis for social interaction, is not necessarily so. Nor does simply tracing different social bonds take into account the subjective element of community: people's sense of belonging and of collective identity. This may be connected with living or working in the same area, with similar socio-economic status, or with family ties, but it is not necessarily concomitant with any or all of these.

A final objection to defining 'community' in terms of area and social bonds is that residence in one particular place is not indispensable. Admittedly a certain degree of proximity is essential, especially in an early modern city without rapid means of transport, but the possibility of a non-territorial community is widely accepted.[11] It may be based, for example, on religion and ethnic origin: the adherents of the French and Dutch churches in London in the sixteenth century did not all live in the same area yet many had a strong sense of collective identity and maintained close ties with each other.[12]

Much recent work has recognized these difficulties and has sought to define 'community' in terms of social interaction, based on social bonds (of which neighbourhood may be one) but not dependent on any specific bond.[13] Communities are seen as networks of individuals, not closed and mutually exclusive, but bound together more closely than they are linked to outsiders. The emphasis is therefore placed not on the type of bonds but on their quality and multiplicity. This is much more satisfactory, for, while recognizing that social ties such as kinship, neighbourhood, religion, or economic interdependence are potentially significant in the formation of a community, it allows that none is necessarily so. It also makes the concept a much more relative one, for it acknowledges that degrees of community are possible, according to the relative strength and quality of the bonds between individual members. If these are weak in relation to the ties that each individual has outside the community, then the community itself is weak. According to the strength and quality of the links between members, too, one community may have less cohesion, resistance to change, or control over its members than another.

This concept of community, however, raises enormous methodological problems. What criteria do we use to discuss the quality of interaction? What observable characteristics indicate the existence of a community, particularly in a

---

[10] R. Dennis and S. Daniels, '"Community" and the Social Geography of Victorian Cities', *Urban History Yearbook 1981*, 7–23 (p. 8).

[11] Dennis, 'Community and Interaction', pp. 4, 7, 21. J. Gusfield, *Community. A Critical Response* (Oxford, Blackwell, 1975), p. xvi.

[12] A. Pettegree, 'Stranger Communities in London', unpublished paper communicated to Early Modern History seminar, Oxford, 19 Oct. 1981.

[13] Macfarlane, pp. 16–19. Dennis, 'Community and Interaction', pp. 21–30.

historical context? I shall suggest a number of such characteristics which are applicable to the study of an early modern urban society.

The first criterion is that there must be social bonds between members of a community, such as kinship, neighbourhood, occupation, although no one of these is indispensable. The more such relationships are shared by the members of a community and the more the links between the same people are multiplied, the stronger the community is likely to be. Of course the bonds between members of a community must be significant ones within that society. In the case of cousins for example, kinship is a significant bond only to the extent that the relationship of cousin is recognized and is important in social organization. It is therefore vital to look at what each social relationship actually meant to people.

Secondly, there must obviously be interaction, based on such social bonds, between the members of the community. Yet clearly the interaction must be of a certain kind, for strangers or mere acquaintances may have things in common and meet, perhaps drink together, yet do not necessarily belong to a single community. It is not the frequency or the regularity of contact that is important, either: neighbours in a block of flats might see each other on the stairs every day, yet scarcely know each other. 'Community' assumes a certain quality of human interaction which is not directly related to frequency of contact. It is not necessarily friendly contact, for although friendship is a bond that can be significant it is not indispensable.

The essential characteristic of community interaction is that it conforms to certain unwritten rules which do not apply to outsiders. Of course all human relationships are to some extent governed by general norms of behaviour and those observed in different communities in the same society, in the same area, or in the same status group, may well be the same. But the behaviour of people towards members of the same community will differ from the way they react to those of another community. Thus, for example, when a husband in eighteenth-century Paris beat his wife other members of the family could and would intervene readily; neighbours and others who knew the couple well would frequently step in, depending on the circumstances. Strangers or casual acquaintances would very rarely do so: two women who had witnessed an assault on a fishwife whom they knew only vaguely later testified that they hadn't gone to her assistance because they thought the man beating her was her husband. Those who did intervene in this case were the others in the market who knew the woman well. Membership of a community involves both familiarity with the others who belong and acceptance of certain norms and behavioural expectations to which all the members generally conform.[14] This of course is the essential element of collective identity. The necessity for a degree of familiarity further implies that a community must be limited in size, although without

---

[14] Archives Nationales, Paris, Y11239, 18 September, wit. 5 and 6. All MS references are to Archives Nationales unless otherwise stated. Calhoun, p. 117. Poplin, p. 22.

requiring it to be of any particular size: the larger it is the more difficult it will be for all the members to recognize each other and to fulfil their mutual obligations, and the weaker the community is likely to be.

The existence of behavioural norms also requires a degree of self-regulation, for the community's survival depends on continued observance of its internal rules. There must be some incentive to conform to them, either through the benefits gained or because of the penalty incurred if they are breached or ignored. Degrees of community are therefore possible: communities may be able to enforce their rules with differing degrees of success.[15] Some members may be able to appeal to an outside authority – the police for example – to override community sanctions. In other contexts, particularly in the urban environment where for some people it is relatively easy to move, the social cost of non-conformity may not be as great as in a rural village where there is no escape from community disapproval. Escape may also be possible through social as well as geographic mobility. It is this possibility which accounts for the inability of local communities during the Industrial Revolution to enforce traditional moral obligations on many manufacturers.[16] This too is more likely to occur in a city, where people whose ties to a particular community are relatively weak have the possibility of joining an alternative community, perhaps with different behavioural expectations (for example in another status group). Indeed it is quite conceivable that an individual could belong to more than one community at a time: if we are talking about local communities, for example, a person may live in one area but work and spend leisure time in another.

In order to identify a community, then, we need to pick out the behavioural conventions which influence the interaction of individuals in different ways according to whether they belong to the community or not. We can look for evidence of self-regulation and of community sanctions against those who do not conform to the norms. Such a definition is admittedly very fluid and very relative, but community is a very fluid and relative thing. It is only in studying the way people behaved in a particular historical, social, and geographic context that we can attempt to define it more precisely, to distinguish the extent and the structures of a community in action.

It is with the extent and structures of a particular sort of community – local communities in eighteenth-century Paris – that this book is primarily concerned. It looks first at the bond of neighbourhood and at the day-to-day functions of the local community, then seeks to define the social limits of the community, to evaluate its wider role in social organization, and to examine the interaction of neighbourhood with the bonds created by kinship and gender, work, religion, and recreations. The final section considers the eighteenth-century Parisian local community in a wider historical context, in relation to long-term changes in social organization.

[15] Calhoun, p. 111. [16] Calhoun, pp. 112–13.

Some aspects of community life have had to be neglected for lack of space, notably the important relationship of *pays*: common geographic origin. Few people lost touch either with their birth-place or with fellow countrymen and women in the capital, and the bond of *pays* is evoked time and again in the documents. It is nevertheless clear that people's place of origin never excluded them from the local community in the way that their work or family background might. Membership of the community depended primarily on adopting certain forms of behaviour and of sociability, and wherever in France a newcomer arrived from he or she seems to have been sensitive to these forms. Acceptance was not dependent on origin.

The principal source used is the papers of the *commissaires au Châtelet*, preserved in the Y series at the Archives Nationales in Paris. There were forty-eight *commissaires*, two or three in each of the twenty quarters into which the Châtelet divided the city. Their functions have been described elsewhere, and I will therefore discuss them only briefly.[17] As the local police officials of Paris, the *commissaires* had a wide range of functions: civil, criminal, and administrative. Of these civil matters were the most remunerative, and foremost among them the apposition of *scellés après décès*: wax seals placed on the effects of a deceased person in order to ensure that nothing was removed before a full inventory could be drafted by a *notaire*. As an added safeguard the *commissaire* drew up a summary description of the premises and its contents, often a valuable indication of the way of life, if not the wealth, of the individual concerned. The *scellés* could only be removed by the *commissaire* himself, and a list of those present – the heirs and any creditors or their representatives – is always included.

Also profitable were *comptes*, the checking of the account rendered by an executor or by a child's guardian of his handling of the affairs with which he was charged; and *partages*, the division of property or money, normally after the sale of an estate or of a debtor's property ordered by a court. All of these documents cost a great deal and concern only the more affluent sections of the population: D. Roche estimates that *inventaires après décès*, which normally followed the removal of the *scellés*, were drawn up for ten to fifteen per cent of those who died in the capital.[18]

The civil functions of the *commissaires* also included statutory declarations, among them the *déclarations de grossesse* (declarations of pregnancy) which all single women who became pregnant were supposed to make. There were in

---

[17] M. Chassaigne, *La Lieutenance générale de police de Paris* (Paris, A. Rousseau, 1906), ch. 3. S. Kaplan, 'Note sur les commissaires de police de Paris au XVIIIe siècle', *Revue d'histoire moderne et contemporaine*, 28 (1981), 669–86. A. Williams, *The Police of Paris* (Baton Rouge, Louisiana State University Press, 1979). A. Gazier (ed.), 'La Police de Paris en 1770', *Mémoires de la Société de l'histoire de Paris et de l'Ile de France*, 5 (1879), 1–131 (pp. 42–61).
[18] D. Roche, *Le Peuple de Paris* (Paris, Aubier, 1981), p. 60.

addition formal complaints, in theory the first step in a civil proceeding. They were undertaken entirely voluntarily; and whereas after about 1750 declarations cost nothing, complaints were quite expensive: three *livres* for the *commissaire* and fifteen *sols* for his clerk, which represented two or three days' income for a labourer.[19] Despite this the plaintiffs come from a very wide range of socio-economic groups, even including unskilled workers. Few complaints were taken further, however, for civil enquiries, the next step, could be very expensive.[20] They were usually restricted to well-off people but concern a wide range of matters and include *enquêtes en séparation*: proceedings brought by a woman against her husband.

The only other civil matters to produce many documents were those in which the presence of the *commissaire* was required to authorize entry into private property: to inspect and describe the state of repair of a building; in order to seize the possessions of a debtor; or when the different trades corporations wanted to search for illegally made goods.

Criminal functions were more straightforward: receiving declarations of theft; interrogating suspects brought in by the *garde* (the city militia) or by the *inspecteurs* (subordinate police officers); hearing witnesses in the criminal enquiries which were undertaken before a case came into the courts of the Châtelet. The witnesses were named by the victim or by the *procureur du roi au Châtelet* (police prosecutor) and were obliged to attend, but their testimony was supposed to be given in private.[21]

Finally, as the local representatives of the *lieutenant général de police*, the *commissaires* were supposed to enforce all the police regulations of the Châtel-et.[22] This they did with varying degrees of enthusiasm but with increasing efficiency towards the end of the eighteenth century. It was a side of their work which left few documents except the reports of the *garde* which, twenty-four hours a day, brought in people arrested for disorderly behaviour or because they looked in some way suspect. The special jobs for which certain *commissaires* were responsible, such as arresting beggars, inspecting carriages, supervising the book trade, the prisons, the gaming-houses or the markets, keeping watch on Jews or Protestants – the list goes on and on – generally leave some trace, although the reports made to the *lieutenant général* have rarely survived. A few may be found among the Bastille papers in the Arsenal library.

The bulk of the archives are in more or less the condition in which they were handed over in 1791 by the last incumbent of each office, only one of the forty-eight failing to surrender them. The system of classification is therefore

---

[19] Chassaigne, p. 165. The figure of about 30 *sols* a day is used by Rudé, *Crowd*, p. 21, and by Roche, *Peuple*, p. 60.

[20] Y10944, account book of *commissaire* Thiérion. See table 1, p. 14.

[21] Jousse, *Traité des fonctions, droits et privilèges des commissaires-enquêteurs-examinateurs* ... (Paris, 1759), pp. 14–15, 101.

[22] N. de Lamare, *Traité de la police*, 4 vols. (Paris, 1705–38), vol. 4 by Le Cler du Brillet.

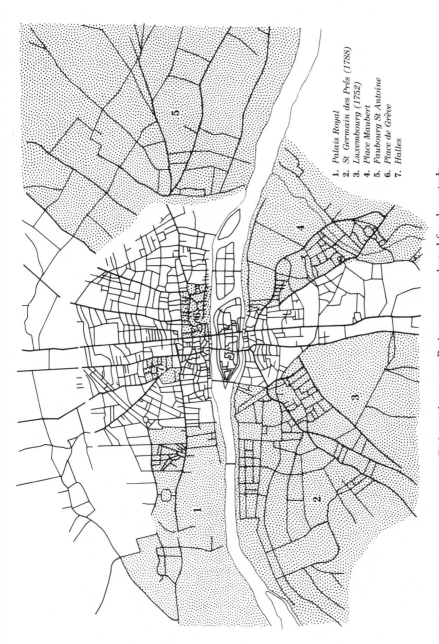

1. Palais Royal
2. St Germain des Prés (1788)
3. Luxembourg (1752)
4. Place Maubert
5. Faubourg St Antoine
6. Place de Grève
7. Halles

1. Eighteenth-century Paris, quarters selected for close study

that used by the *commissaires* themselves, usually chronological. The documents are not individually numbered and can therefore be cited only by box number and date. Each *commissaire* inherited his predecessor's papers and clearly weeded them out, for, although some of the offices went back to the sixteenth century, documents earlier than the end of the seventeenth century are rare. The later years are consistently better documented, with the records for the second half of the eighteenth century almost complete, to judge from the surviving inventories drawn up by the *commissaires* from year to year. Occasionally there are references in complaints or enquiries, or in outside sources, to documents which are no longer there and it is usually the less remunerative matters which have disappeared: there are a few boxes which contain only *scellés*.

The bulk of the series – some 6,000 boxes, each containing on average two to three hundred documents – made careful selection necessary. As the documents reflect the character and social composition of the area in which each *commissaire* was stationed, six quarters were chosen for close study: firstly the central market area because of its economic importance, its central position, and its place in events in the city; the quarter of the Place de Grève, at the crossroads of Paris; and the Faubourg St Antoine, also important during the Revolution, semi-rural yet home to a very large number of artisans, a useful contrast to the inner-city area. There is the Place Maubert quarter, containing the second-largest market in the city and harbouring a large seasonal and immigrant population, but also including the Faubourg St Marcel with its tanning and brewing trades, its horse-market, and its ancient village centre. The Luxembourg–St Germain des Prés area was included because of its relatively recent development, its large population of domestic servants, and its great extremes of rich and poor. Finally the Palais Royal quarter, prominent in the early years of the Revolution, offered a very mixed collection of people: foreigners, for there were many hotels; bankers and wealthy merchants; the rich noble families of the St Roch parish; shopkeepers along the busy rue St Honoré; and pockets of a humbler character, particularly in the back-streets behind St Roch. Choosing areas at both ends of the city and on both banks of the river was important in order to get an idea of movement around the city and of the personal ties which stretched across it.

It was necessary, since the papers are chronological, to decide which years to look at. Because each sort of document contains different information, it was preferable to read every one in each box rather than to select any particular type. Similarly, in order to gauge the effect of the seasons on the type of documents and the life of the city it was necessary to follow each *commissaire* throughout the year. After a preliminary survey one year at each end of the period was picked out for close study. 1752 was a year of peace when, if prices rose fairly high, they by no means reached crisis point. 1788, at the end of the regime yet before the Revolution dramatically changed the role of the *commissaires* and the quality of their papers, began as a relatively normal year but ended with a particularly severe winter and a developing political crisis. One box from 1775 and one from 1789 were included by way of contrast. In addition to this main sample a range of other years and quarters was studied in less detail to check for any major variations in the source and in order to look at documents arising from the special functions of particular *commissaires*. All in all, therefore, nearly two hundred cartons of *minutes* were looked at and some fifty more containing letters, personal papers, and reports. Surprisingly, the economic situation had little effect on the number or character of the documents, hard times being marked by many more declarations of theft but with little change in the incidence of complaints or other material. A vastly greater impact was made by the momentary preoccupations of the police, notably the crack-downs on beggars in 1750 and 1768.

The papers of the *commissaires* do not on the whole lend themselves well to quantification. The documents are too diverse and above all too subjective. Yet it is precisely these qualities which make them invaluable in answering questions about social behaviour. Studies based on quantitative sources are often afflicted by what has been called 'the problem of meaning': they may show us how people behaved but are no help in explaining why, or what that behaviour actually meant to people at the time.[23] The papers of the *commissaires*, on the other hand, present artisans and unskilled workers actually describing their own behaviour and that of others.

The problem of meaning is not entirely eliminated, of course, for we still need to interpret what people say. The information, furthermore, is partly filtered and potentially deformed by its being written down by men whose ideas and values were not necessarily those of the speaker. Not everything witnesses or plaintiffs said was necessarily recorded, and their words were framed in legal language. However this remained largely a matter of form, for despite the use of judicial formulae and the translation of testimony into the third person there remains considerable variation of content, of vocabulary, and of tone. For instance some complaints are visibly drafted from written models provided by the plaintiff, examples of which sometimes turn up, and in such cases the description of events is ordered, and repetition and inconsistencies are largely eliminated. More usual is the document drafted from an oral account, frequently repetitious, with a confused and disorderly presentation which the clerk does his best to sort out. There are often afterthoughts noted in the margin or added at the end. Names may not be spelt consistently and occasionally do not correspond to the signature at the end, the difference in these cases often a result of mishearing: 'Belanger' for 'Boulanger' or 'Bastien' for 'Sebastien'.[24] Clerks were paid by the document and therefore did not spend overmuch time on each one. It was often

---

[23] M. Anderson, *Approaches to the History of the Western Family, 1500–1914* (London, Macmillan, 1980), p. 34.
[24] Y14078, 23 Dec., wit. 5, 8, 9.

easier for them simply to write down what people said without worrying too much about its clarity or style. Thus we find popular words and expressions jostling with high-flown legal terminology, and all the more so as in some contexts they were relevant to the legal process. Insults and threats are listed in vivid and often hilarious detail. On occasion direct speech is reproduced by witnesses and recorded by the clerk. There are even examples of direct speech, not always of immediate relevance!

The problem of the consignment to paper of oral testimony is therefore not too serious. More so is the possible influence of the *commissaire* on the way people presented themselves and spoke of their actions and motivation. In interrogations this influence was very great, for the *commissaire* asked all the questions and the suspect was able to do no more than reply. In declarations, complaints, or enquiries, however, his role was more discreet: indeed in enquiries everything a witness said was supposed to be noted and the *commissaire* was formally forbidden to ask questions.[25] The frequent irrelevancies of many testimonies suggest that on the whole these instructions were followed. His presence and that of the clerk remains a distorting factor of course, for people presented themselves as they wished to be seen, in some cases trying to influence the authorities in their favour. Thus, as in eighteenth-century Languedoc, institutions are never attacked, only individual abuses of authority.[26] Motives of revenge or of personal antipathy are not mentioned, the emphasis being placed on a plaintiff's concern for public order or on potential damage to his or her livelihood or reputation. The view we get of family relationships is often stereotyped.

This does not mean, however, that all we have is a faithful reflection of the dominant value-system. On occasion there is a surprising disregard for it: for example an unmarried textile worker comes to complain of the brutality of the man she lives with; a prostitute explains that she had quarrelled with the man with whom she was living because she continued in her trade: 'He asked her why she behaved thus, she replied that it was because it pleased her.'[27]

In fact the degree of distortion caused by the judicial context varies according to the purpose of the document and the situation and interest of the speaker. More often than not, as we shall see, a complaint was less directed to the authorities than to the tribunal of the local community, and the need to impress the judges was correspondingly reduced. But even where the attitude of the

---

[25] A. Farge, *Délinquance et criminalité: le vol d'aliments à Paris au XVIIIe siècle* (Paris, Plon, 1974), pp. 143–50. Y13728, *procureur du roi* to *commissaire* Guyot, 12 Dec. 1786. Jousse, *Traité*, pp. 14–15.

[26] Y. Castan, *Honnêteté*, p. 101. On this and what follows see Y. Castan, 'Les Procès criminels, sources d'étude des mentalités rurales', *Bulletin du Centre pour l'histoire économique et sociale de la région lyonnaise*, 4 (1978), 1–5.

[27] Y15099, 13 May. Y13819, 21 Apr. 1788. I have translated all quotations and give the original only where the exact words used are important.

police was important its effect on what people said varied. The way a man described his own treatment of his wife in reply to a complaint she had made against him, for example, is hardly to be seen in the same way as a passing reference to the relations between husband and wife made by a witness in an enquiry into a theft. Among the best indications of popular attitudes are casual remarks of this nature, made more to set the scene than with any didactic aim. But even an individual who appealed directly to the police and who chose the words accordingly could not completely shake off his or her own assumptions and adopt a different set of values. W. Sewell has shown the way that during the Revolution the journeymen printers, while able to master perfectly the new political language of the 1790s, were incapable of escaping from the corporate mentality of the old regime, anathema to the National Assembly. Y. Castan has observed in using judicial material in Languedoc that there is a tendency for people to regard their own rules of conduct as universal.[28] The actions they approve or disapprove, the expectations they express, all provide an indication of the models and the rules of conduct to which they subscribe. When people made complaints they were concerned to demonstrate how far their opponent fell short of his or her duty, obligations, the behaviour others expected. The way people speak of their own actions is equally instructive. When a 'commis marinier' (shipping clerk?) explains that through consideration for his wife he had taken in his mother-in-law 'to live and be kept by them, given her state of poverty', we know that the poverty of the older woman was a socially acceptable reason for taking her in and can assume, since the explanation is offered, that it was not the rule in this social context for parents to live with their married children.[29] The problem of meaning does not disappear but the source has the rare merit of telling us how people behaved, while at the same time providing their commentary or that of their peers on that behaviour.

But just how representative are these documents? I have pointed out that some of them concern primarily affluent people. Criminal matters, on the other hand, brought in delinquents and those who for one reason or another seemed suspect. However, those members of society best represented – in complaints, in enquiries, and in reports of the *garde* – were artisans and shopkeepers, less often semi-skilled and unskilled workers: precisely those who, statistically, were 'average' Parisians (see table 1).[30] Nevertheless the variety of the documents and the fact that many of them introduce witnesses who just happened to be passing, allow us to reach people from a very wide social range. A few bodies largely escaped the jurisdiction of the Châtelet: the enclosed clergy, the University, the

---

[28] Y. Castan, *Honnêteté*, p. 48. W. Sewell, Jr, *Work and Revolution in France* (Cambridge, C.U.P., 1980), pp. 97–8.
[29] Y10994, 3 Nov.
[30] Kaplow, *Names*, ch. 1. G. Rudé, 'The Parisian Wage-earning Population and the Insurrectionary Movements of 1789–1791', 2 vols., Ph.D. thesis, University of London, 1950, ch. 2.

Table 1. *Occupations of plaintiffs, Grève and Faubourg St Antoine quarters, 1752*

Occupation (or that of husband or parent)	Men		Women	
	Faubourg	Grève	Faubourg	Grève
Master artisans or *marchands*	32	33	7	14
Journeymen[a]	8	8	2	0
Artisans of unspecified status[a]	30	9	18	3
Rural trades (excluding *maîtres jardiniers*)	14	1	4	0
Stall-keepers	4	0	7	2
Itinerant street-traders and street-labourers	4	5	5	1
Servants	1	1	3	6
Textile workers	4	0	3	2
Chirurgiens	2	3	2	0
Waggoners, coachmen	2	3	1	0
Soldiers	1	1	0	1
Laundry trades	0	0	3	0
Marchands forains	2	1	1	0
Workers in manufactories	2	0	0	0
Bourgeois de Paris	3	1	0	0
Nobles	1	0	0	1
Unskilled workers in corporate trades	0	0	0	2
Other (*Garde magasin, archer, commis, huissiers, notaire, avocat*, teachers)	9	10	1	2
No occupation given	1	0	2	1
Total	120	76	59	35

[a] Journeymen's wives generally had a trade of their own, and are classified accordingly.

Parlement, and the inhabitants of the few remaining seigneurial jurisdictions, but even so nearly everyone who spent any time in Paris would sooner or later come in contact with one of the *commissaires*. Women appear as plaintiffs less often than men, but are still well represented in the documents. Old people often come before the *commissaires*. Children are gravely under-represented and rarely testify, although they are frequently mentioned.

This is not to say that the source is equally good for studying all areas of society. Minorities appear less frequently, so that in looking at the habits and attitudes of the court aristocracy, for example, there are relatively few cases to go by. Furthermore many groups appear only or predominantly in certain types of documents and our view of them is therefore partial. Wealthy people turn up mostly in *scellés* and in civil enquiries; beggars and prostitutes appear in interrogations; soldiers tended to be brought in by the *garde*. Domestic servants rarely made complaints and were most likely to appear as witnesses, as suspects, or in *scellés*. We therefore have different sorts of information about each of these groups. In some cases this is not very important because of the type of questions being asked: the aristocracy for example were almost entirely outside the local community and I have looked at them only briefly in order to determine what sets them apart from it. For other groups I have wherever possible used other sources as well.

The further problem of how to classify people in a big city is shared by most sources. Individuals rarely appear in the documents more than once. The papers of the *commissaires* do not tell us much about people's wealth, and an occupation or title may hide as much as it reveals. We generally know something about a person's way of life but nothing systematic. In almost every case, however, we do have details about the individual's relationships with other people and this reveals as much, if not more, about his or her place in society than the most accurate income figures.

Police records put a premium on the individual. They introduce real people and immobilize them for an instant in brown ink on yellowing paper. The incidents they recount are often trivial yet their myriad words and gestures recreate the shared ideals, assumptions, and aspirations of their society.

The primacy of neighbourhood and the local community

In Paris, wrote L. S. Mercier in 1782, 'one is a stranger to one's neighbour'.[1] For Mercier the city was vast, anonymous and unhealthy, the individual lost in a maze of streets, stranded in an ocean of humanity. It is a theme which flourishes in literature, in the writings of eighteenth- and nineteenth-century observers, and which still has some currency. Yet in Mercier's own work, as D. Roche has recently remarked, there is much evidence to the contrary.[2] Take for example this description of popular behaviour in the Faubourg St Marcel:

There all private quarrels become public; and a woman displeased with her husband pleads her case in the street, brings him before the tribunal of the populace, gathers the neighbours into a riotous assembly, and recites her man's scandalous confessions.[3]

This illustrates a relationship between neighbours which was rather different from that in his earlier picture of a city full of strangers. It suggests a society where neighbours knew each other well and where there was a lively street life – what the French call *vie de quartier*.[4]

This chapter explores what *vie de quartier* meant. It looks first at the supportive role of neighbours, materially and emotionally, and at the forms and locations of neighbourhood sociability. It then examines how most eighteenth-century Parisians perceived their environment, as revealed in the way they spoke about it, and argues that the neighbourhood lay at the centre of their mental as well as their physical world. Finally, the way people acted in their dealings with neighbours enables us to pick out some of the norms and constraints – the informal rules – which I have suggested characterize a community. Their behaviour in disputes reveals the self-regulating and self-perpetuating mechanisms of the local community.

The key to neighbourhood relations is familiarity. Indeed the French word for neighbour, *voisin*, itself implied familiarity. Literally of course it referred simply to those who lived in the vicinity and could also be applied to those who worked there. There are certainly examples of Parisians who did not know their neighbours or who knew them only by sight. But when people talked about the

---

[1] Mercier, *Tableau*, vol. 1, p. 64.
[2] Kaplow, *Names*, p. 70. Roche, *Peuple*, pp. 49–51, 253. Farge, *Délinquance*, pp. 187–8.
[3] Mercier, *Tableau*, vol. 1, p. 270.   [4] Garden, 'Vie de quartier'.

2. Rue de Lappe, Faubourg St Antoine

relationship they felt it to imply familiarity. 'The said Jamin, domestic servant, and his wife were then living there', explained a seamstress, 'so she had often had occasion to be in their company.' A man explained that his affair with a young woman had developed because 'as neighbours, being accustomed to seeing each other had led them to form a more intimate relationship'. Being neighbours did not necessarily imply real friendship: a *marchande mercière* described her encounters with the wife of a master mason 'as a neighbour, but nevertheless without for her part ever having had any particular connection with the

3. Old houses in the rue Laplace (formerly rue des Amandiers)

aforementioned lady'.[5] The relationship did however suggest free and frequent association: it was normal for neighbours both to know each other and to be found together.

The papers of the *commissaires*, like Mercier's tomes or the novels of Restif de la Bretonne, illustrate the importance, variety, and frequency of contact between neighbours.[6] In any emergency they were invariably the first ones turned to for

[5] Y15350, 17 Aug., wit. 2. Y13290, 23 Oct. Y15100, 10 Sept.
[6] I have classed as 'neighbours' those who (a) are termed *voisins* in the documents; (b) live in the same street (unless it is a very long one), in an adjacent street, or who appear from the evidence in the document to live within a few doors.

help or protection. When a master turner living in the rue de la Cordonnerie suddenly felt ill his wife called the two men who lived opposite. An innkeeper, attacked by a man to whom he owed money, called for help and was rescued by about twenty neighbours![7] In sickness or old age it was only their help which enabled poor people to survive. A woman who sold coal in the rue de la Tannerie explained that as one of her sub-tenants, a printing-worker sick with venereal disease, had no one to look after him, 'she as well as several other neighbours took care of him and from time to time took him soup and other assistance'. After an old woman in the rue Comtesse d'Artois had had a bad fall, it was a man living in the same house who discovered her dead in her room when he brought in some washing for her.[8]

Neighbours also afforded protection, especially for women. There are many examples like that of Anne Marguerite Lagrange, living in the rue de Bercy near the Cimetière St Jean, whose neighbours threw out a weaver who had been courting her but who refused to leave her alone. There was also a degree of protection for property: a fifteen-year-old girl, hearing someone at the door of the family who lived opposite, went out to see what the man wanted then watched out of the window for him to leave.[9] Admittedly this did not always happen, and there are many examples of burglaries where the neighbours heard nothing or even where they saw the robbers but apparently suspected nothing. Nevertheless their vigilance could afford a considerable measure of security.

Assistance could also take more banal, everyday forms. People frequently borrowed household items: a stove, a broom, some dishes. More common still was getting a light from a neighbour: the nine-year-old son of a shoemaker, a witness in an enquiry, mentioned that their neighbour, widow of a *procureur au Parlement*, had come to ask for a light on her way in one evening.[10] It is just mentioned in passing, a prelusive detail to the discovery of a theft, yet it was a necessary daily contact between neighbours.

The most eloquent testimony to the extent of neighbours' role in everyday life is their intervention in family affairs. As in revolutionary Rouen, neighbours – and female ones in particular – would intervene in disputes, enlighten deceived spouses, sometimes offer refuge to a woman expelled by her husband. They often stepped in to stop a man from seriously injuring his wife, like those of a *marchand épicier* in the rue Jean de l'Epine who rushed to prevent him from hitting her with an iron bar; or those of a *frotteur* and a female linen-worker near St Benoît who came right into the bedroom to rescue her. They might equally

---

[7] Y15402, 30 July. Y15350, 11 Dec.   [8] Y15100, 30 July. Y15402, 25 Nov., wit. 4.
[9] Y15350, 23 July. Y14078, 10 Nov.
[10] Y12597, 10 Oct., wit. 1. See glossary for terms not translated in the text.

4. Well and courtyard, rue du Four, Faubourg St Germain

take the husband's part, although examples of this less often reached the *commissaire*.[11]

On the whole neighbourly ties were built up through chance meetings in the house or in the street outside, meetings which provided the opportunity for an exchange of pleasantries and of news. The normal, open sociability of the eighteenth-century city required that neighbours stop for a chat no matter how busy they were: a *revendeuse* in the rue St Etienne des Grés took offence when a journeyman printer living in the same street passed by several times without speaking to her.[12] Witnesses often mention standing on their doorstep ('sur le pas de leur porte') talking with the neighbours. This especially applies to shopkeepers but neighbours on their way in or out would stop to chat. One lengthy enquiry of 1752 gives us a glimpse of the Grande Rue du Faubourg St

[11] R. Phillips, *Family Breakdown in Late Eighteenth-Century France. Divorces in Rouen, 1792–1803* (Oxford, Clarendon, 1980), pp. 129, 180–7. Y15350, 12 Sept. Y11705, 23 June. Y15350, 21 July is an example of neighbours taking the husband's part.

[12] Y12596, 29 June, wit. 9. See Y11239, 4 Sept.

5. Narrow stairs, 6 rue Princesse, Faubourg St Germain

Antoine at ten o'clock on a Thursday night in September. A *marchand épicier* and his two *garçons* are standing at their door; the son of another shopkeeper is outside his father's shop; a *praticien au Châtelet* is at another door; a *marchande lingère* and her two shop-assistants are chatting with the daughter of a *huissier* living in the same house. Other documents reveal people gossiping in the courtyards and on the stairs.[13]

Actually in the house, or right outside, were the most common locations of neighbourhood contact, as the evidence of disputes clearly shows, for it was there that the overwhelming majority of those between neighbours occurred. But there were other centres of sociability. A frequent meeting place was a common well or fountain. When in 1765 repairs were necessary to a public well in the rue St Jacques, near the Val-de-Grâce, a list was made of the owners of the nearby

---

13 Y10994, 21 Sept., 12 Oct. Y12596, 25 July. Y13819, 15 Nov. 1788.

houses so that they could be asked to contribute. Seventeen houses are mentioned, of which three had their own wells: the occupants of all the rest relied on the public water supply.[14]

One would expect the churches to figure prominently in the documents as centres of neighbourhood sociability, especially for women, but in fact they are very rarely mentioned. They were commonly used as landmarks in giving addresses, but people very rarely refer to meetings or conversations in or in front of the churches. I will suggest some reasons for this in chapter 4. In fact the most prominent places for exchanging news and gossip were the local shops. Most people did their shopping in the area where they lived, patronizing nearby shopkeepers who knew them both as clients and as neighbours and who would extend credit. After the death of a *fruitier-oranger* in the rue Mondetour, and that of his wife ten months earlier, his creditors made themselves known to the *commissaire*: a fishmonger, a cobbler, a joiner and a *rôtisseur*, a glazier, and a spicer, all in adjoining streets. He also had accounts with no fewer than three *marchands de vin* and two *limonadiers*, all within a few minutes of his home. Only for less common items had he gone further afield: to a stonemason in the rue de Bourbon Villeneuve, to a roofer in the rue du Grand Hurleur, to a clockmaker in the rue St Antoine and a jeweller on the Ile de la Cité. This example is unusual in its completeness, for local debts were usually settled by the family, but wherever shopkeepers do appear to claim small sums they are nearly always from the immediate vicinity.[15]

Going shopping was not simply a chore: it was an opportunity to catch up on all the local gossip. The shopkeepers themselves, in any given area, all knew each other and would swap news regularly. A *garçon marchand de vin* in the rue d'Avignon near St Jacques de la Boucherie reported a theft and the capture of the culprit, describing his conversation with the man and his discovery of the theft when the *garçon* of a nearby wood-yard came 'as was his custom' to get change. He had gone to enlist the help of a fruiterer opposite, but when the thief reappeared went to get his brother who was in the shop of a neighbouring *perruquier*. A similar network was described by a *marchande limonadière* in a complaint against a neighbour who had insulted her first while she and another *limonadier* just around the corner were comparing the customs of their respective provinces, then again two days later as she exchanged news with a cobbler across the road.[16]

Certain trades were particularly important in neighbourhood sociability and in the communication of news. The *revendeuses* and *fruitières* who had stalls right in the street, at the doors of houses, on street corners and on the bridges, were at the heart of the whole network. They saw everything that went on in the street, gossiped with everyone. They were the obvious people to ask for directions or for

[14] Y12830, de Sartine to *commissaire* Roland, 18 May 1765.   [15] Y11239, 7 Jan., 8 Nov.
[16] Y15099, 17 Apr. Y15100, 6 Sept.

news of someone. After a theft in the Grande Rue du Faubourg St Antoine, the victim, wife of a sawyer, was told by a flower-seller at the Porte St Antoine that a man had been seen carrying a large bag. Setting off in search of this individual, whom someone had recognized, she found his house but was told by the woman selling fruit at the door that he was not at home.[17]

Other trades were also prominent in the local network. In an enquiry into the death in a house in the rue de la Harpe of a woman who had been in the area only a short time, the police received information from a number of people who had had contact with her. A laundryman was able to tell them her previous address in the same quarter, and that she had been living with a *perruquier*, but that they had paid separately. An innkeeper in the rue St Séverin also knew her previous address and had seen her with the *perruquier*, having provided them with meals on numerous occasions. Much the same information was given by her baker in the rue St Jacques.[18] All of these trades were important in the life of the quarter. A visit to the baker's was a daily affair for all Parisians or their servants, and it was one of the best places for exchanging news.

Another shop women visited regularly was that of the *pâtissier*, who according to Mercier would cook the family meal for two *sous*. People could buy their meals ready-cooked from a *rôtisseur*, a *pâtissier*, or a *traiteur*. A census carried out in the Year III for food-supply purposes revealed that in the Grange-Batelière Section nearly a quarter of the population got their meals from *traiteurs*.[19] And eating places, as in France today, were very important centres of sociability.

Except for the shopkeepers themselves, the markets and food shops tended to be meeting places primarily for women, for it was usually they who did the shopping. Similarly because women tended to spend more time at home than men they were more often to be found chatting on the stairs or in the courtyard. Other centres of neighbourhood sociability, however, were almost exclusively for men. The local *perruquier* was a masculine meeting place, a regular port of call for many men in a wide range of social groups. A gardener in the Faubourg St Antoine accused an engraver living in the same house of spreading stories about him, notably in the shop of the *perruquier* they both went to. *Perruquiers* also turn up frequently in enquiries, especially in court cases brought by women against their husbands, in which a detailed knowledge of business transactions and habits was required.[20]

Even more important than the *perruquier*, and also principally for men, was the wineshop (*cabaret*). Although not closed to women it was little used by them. In

---

[17] Y10994, 10 Aug.   [18] Y15350, 28 June.

[19] Mercier, *Tableau*, vol. 5, p. 14. 'Etat de la population d'après les subsistances', pluviôse an III, F[7] 3688[4], cited in A. Goeury, 'La Section Grange-Batelière pendant la Révolution française', in M. Reinhard (ed.), *Contributions à l'histoire démographique de la Révolution française*, 3rd series (Paris, Bibliothèque Nationale, 1970), pp. 93–153 (p. 109).

[20] Y10994, 9 Sept. Y14078, 11 Jan., wit. 3; 8 May, wit. 3. Y12597, 15 Dec., wit. 3. Y14436, 22 Mar., wit. 1.

the papers of the *commissaire* de Courcy in 1752 there are mentions of fifty-four men in wineshops, but only eighteen women, twelve of them accompanied by other members of their family. In the documents for the Faubourg St Antoine for the same year, there appear seventy-three men and eight women.[21] A woman going to a wineshop alone risked being taken for a prostitute, and to say that she 'courait les cafés' (ran around the cafés) was tantamount to calling her a whore.[22]

Like present-day cafés, wineshops varied enormously in size, décor, and clientele, but in each neighbourhood there were those which served as a regular rendez-vous for the locals. Men tended to go regularly to the same place: when a *bourgeoise de Paris* near St Eustache wanted to contact her hairdresser she sent a note to the café where he usually went. Similarly, after the inhabitants of a house in the rue Mondetour discovered one of the doors open and clothing strewn about on the stairs they knew exactly where to find the victim of the theft: in a nearby wineshop where he was waiting for his wife.[23]

Men frequented wineshops for a variety of reasons. A *garçon chirurgien* is stated to have gone regularly to one near the Place de Grève in order to read the *petites affiches* (a sort of private-notices sheet). Men working nearby would often have their midday meal there. Journeymen printers in the vicinity of the rue du Mont St Hilaire were in the habit of taking their meals at an establishment in that street.[24] In the evenings wineshops were pleasant places to pass the time, providing comfortable surroundings, warmth and light in winter. Cafés, wrote Mercier, were 'the refuge of the indigent. They warm themselves there in winter to save wood at home.' There was company, for the ordinary eighteenth-century Parisian preferred to eat and drink (and travel or work) with other people.[25]

The pleasant atmosphere of the wineshop made it the normal place for people to go if they met someone in the street. Indeed refusal to share a bottle and pass a few minutes together was usually taken as an affront.[26] Drinking together, on the other hand, cemented a friendship, sealed an agreement, capped a reconciliation. In an enquiry into a dispute between a journeyman mason and a beer-seller a witness recalled that the two men had, after an initial refusal on the part of the mason, drunk a bottle of beer together. Yet the very next day, he pointed out with obvious disapproval, the mason had again picked a fight.[27]

Partly because of this ritual of the shared drink and no doubt because the atmosphere of the wineshop was most suited to discussion and agreement, many

---

[21] Excluding the *guinguettes*. This does not reflect a preference for men as witnesses, for the proportions are quite different in events occurring in the street or in the house.
[22] Y10994, 17 Mar. On the use of 'café' and *cabaret* see chapter 5, section IV.
[23] Y14484, 2 Sept., 17 Mar.
[24] Y15100, 27 Aug., wit. 2. Y13290, 6 Sept. Y12826, report of *commissaire* Dupuy to Chambre de Police, 18 Oct. 1776.
[25] Mercier, *Tableau*, vol. I, p. 227. Y15350, 7 July. Y15402, 10 Feb. See Roche, *Peuple*, pp. 256–74.
[26] Y11239, 31 Oct. Y14484, 30 Nov., wit. 5. Y11239, 19 June.
[27] Y15350, 21 July. See Y11239, 5 Aug.

business transactions were concluded there.[28] But *cabarets* were above all centres of leisure and were well organized as such, often providing games for their clients: dominoes, draughts, chess. Games of chance were particularly popular and one known as 'petit pallet' crops up frequently. It was in fact illegal for *marchands de vin* to allow gambling on their premises but apart from periodic crackdowns the police seem to have largely ignored it. Other games such as bowls or skittles were also commonly provided for clients, especially in establishments which had a garden at the back or an open space in the street in front.[29]

The use of wineshops by those who lived or worked in the vicinity, together with people's propensity for conversation, all the greater under the influence of alcohol, made them one of the best places to plug into the informal news-circuit, which in a city without any real press constituted the principal source of information. In a neighbourhood wineshop gossip was rife and many complaints specifically mention them as the scene of damaging calumnies. It was possible to pick up a lot that was not said openly in the street: in an enquiry into the alleged misappropriation of part of the estate of a *marchand mercier* in the Grande Rue du Faubourg St Antoine, several of the neighbours remembered being in a nearby wineshop about a month earlier when a local locksmith was boasting that he had some of the things at his place. The police, at times of crisis, were concerned about what people were saying in drinking places and kept an eye on them.[30]

But the role of the wineshop extended much further than providing a shelter and a casual meeting place. The *marchand de vin* himself fulfilled a range of functions for his clients and neighbours. The example has already been given of a man from a wood-yard going to a nearby *cabaret* to get change. A coachman presented with a gold coin by a client went to the nearest *marchand de vin* to have it changed. People would leave objects in his charge, like two bookbinders who, having a lot to carry, left a piece of meat with a *limonadier* in the Place Maubert, returning to collect it some hours later. Another man who sold fruit in the streets of the Faubourg St Germain was in the habit of leaving his merchandise in the care of a neighbouring *marchand de vin* every night. In a slightly different case and admittedly one not likely to occur in the city centre, a herdsman who found someone else's sheep grazing on his land took one of them to a wineshop and refused to return it until he received compensation.[31]

A *marchand de vin* would even lend money to regular customers. One man arrived after the death of a client to claim 1,200 *livres* he had lent her and which

---

[28] Y15350, 7 Oct., wit. 2. Y13819, 13 Apr. 1978.
[29] Y15099, 28 Mar. Y15117, 2 Mar. 1788. Y12596, 3 Apr. Y15350, 17 Jan. Y10994, 17 June, 18 June, 23 June. Y12469, Ordonnance de police, 24 Dec. 1773. Y12469, 'procès-verbaux pour la police des jeux', 3 Mar. 1774. Y12830, Ordonnance de police, 26 July 1777.
[30] Y10994, 19 Jan. S. Kaplan, 'Réflexions sur la police du monde de travail, 1700–1815', *Revue historique*, 529 (Jan.-Mar. 1979), 17–77 (p. 65).
[31] Y15099, 17 Apr. Y12597, 20 Sept. Y12596, 28 Mar. Y13819, 13 Apr. 1788. Y10994, 1 July.

he had little chance of getting back as he had no receipt. On a much humbler scale, a water-carrier pawned two buckets for twenty-four *sols* in a wineshop in the rue des Carmes. It is also possible that *marchands de vin* sometimes helped clients, through their contacts in the neighbourhood, to secure jobs or accommodation. There is certainly one example of a *limonadier* finding positions on several occasions for one of his customers, a language teacher.[32]

The wineshop – or sometimes the local *traiteur* – was also the natural centre for almost any kind of organized gathering. Most people had little room at home and there were few other places available. Weddings and special celebrations involving catering were often organized by the *marchand de vin*, usually in association with a *traiteur*. This was apparently the arrangement at the wedding breakfast of a female blanket-maker and a journeyman shoemaker held in 'Le Petit St François', a wineshop in the rue St Victor. Another couple married at St Sulpice had a celebration with about thirty guests in a first-floor room at 'Le Sabot' in the rue des Boucheries St Germain where the meal was provided by a *rôtisseur*, the *marchand de vin* furnishing wine and lettuce.[33]

Some *marchands de vin* and *traiteurs* organized dances on Sundays and holidays, setting aside a large room behind or above the shop. One *marchand de bière* in the rue du Cherche Midi, in whose establishment dances were held regularly, even hired out instruments. It was more usual to hire musicians to play, although not always qualified ones![34] Those present at such dances were not necessarily always locals but it is likely that in many cases they were. At a dance at 'L'Ecu d'Orléans' near the Luxembourg the proprietor assured the *commissaire* that the assembly of thirty-odd people was composed solely of neighbours, including the musicians. This was an attempt to justify holding a function which infringed on the monopoly of the *maîtres traiteurs* but the *marchand de vin* presumably thought it a likely enough story. In the case of informal gatherings those present were almost certainly locals. Ten or twelve neighbours and friends of a *marchand de bière* on the Port de Grève naturally chose his shop to get together to celebrate the feast-day of St Martin. A cab-owner whose son was briefly home on leave from the army assembled his family in 'Le Barreau Jaune' in the next street from where he lived. Someone played the violin while the others danced.[35] On such occasions the wineshop was of course open to women, although always accompanied by another member of the family.

The multiple uses of the *cabaret* made it one of the foci of neighbourhood life, the natural place for people to turn in all sorts of situations. There are many examples of the public arresting someone and taking them into the nearest wineshop to await the arrival of the *garde*. It was also the obvious place to go if

---

[32] Y15100, 20 Sept. Y12597, 24 Dec. Y15350, 14 Oct.   [33] Y15363, 23 Nov. 1750, 4 Sept. 1754.
[34] Y15364, 1 Dec. 1743, 29 Sept. 1743, *procès-verbal* dated only Nov. 1743. Y15363, 26 Dec. 1753.
[35] Y15363, 26 Nov. 1758. Y15350, 12 Nov. Y11239, 2 Oct.

someone was injured in the street: when an old man tripped and fell in the rue du Foin, near the rue St Jacques, two booksellers from a shop opposite helped him up and took him into a nearby *cabaret*.[36] The wineshop was thus more than just another shop: it was an extension of the street, more private and protected yet in some way belonging to the public. It became a sort of neutral common territory. This can also be seen in its occasional use as a local forum for ironing out differences. A master shoemaker in the rue des Sept Voyes near St Victor was requested by two journeymen to go with them to a wineshop in the rue des Amandiers 'to hear the explanation of some remarks made by a certain Monbillard, another journeyman shoemaker, against the said Bourguignon'. There are several similar examples where the *cabaret* served almost as an informal court where a person suspected of a theft was confronted with the victim and with witnesses. After a labourer was robbed of all his money in the lodging-house where he slept with fourteen others, he suspected one of them who suddenly appeared to have a lot of cash, and led him to a *cabaret* near the lodging-house where five or six of the others searched and questioned him. Almost in the same way as the market-place or the street, the wineshop belonged to the local community: what M. Agulhon has called 'la sociabilité diffuse du cabaret' was one of the most important of all local ties.[37]

Neighbourhood sociability was essentially diffuse and unorganized, based on shared space and shared habits, to a large degree fashioned by the constraints of the urban environment. Neighbours could not help meeting each other on the stairs, in the street, in the shops: a female linen-worker made a complaint against a needlewoman who insulted her each time they met, 'which happens frequently given the proximity of their homes'.[38] For many Parisians the neighbourhood was where they knew most people and were themselves known. It lay at the centre of their preoccupations.

Nowhere is this clearer than in the way they described the city. The landmarks used, for example in giving an address, were often local ones, things which were noticed and which remained in people's memories because of their significance in everyday life. Very often they were familiar primarily to the locals. Neighbourhood markets for instance were felt to dominate the surrounding area even though they were rarely physically prominent and in some cases not held every day. A woman indicated the shop of a goldsmith 'rue de Bucy près du petit marché' and an *archer* gave his address as 'petit marché de laport' (a small market at the river end of the rue St Denis). The same is true of fountains and wells, also important centres of neighbourhood sociability: 'the plaintiffs went into "La Croix d'Or" near the Ponceau fountain'.[39] Other local landmarks included the

36 Y15350, 1 Jan. Y12596, 6 Mar. Y15100, 5 Sept. See Y15350, 22 Sept.
37 Y12596, 27 Feb. Y13290, 27 Jan. See Y10994, 3 Mar. M. Agulhon, *La Sociabilité méridionale* (Aix-en-Provence, La Pensée universitaire, 1966), p. 428.
38 Y13819, 27 May 1788.
39 Y15350, 25 Nov., 5 June, wit. 5. Y12597, 21 Dec. Y11239, 27 June.

écoles de charité (charity schools) of whose impact on ordinary people very little is known.[40] The statues of the Madonna scattered around the city were often mentioned in addresses, and the *corps de garde* (guard-posts) in each quarter were likewise prominent in descriptions, a testimony to the important role played by the *garde*.

Most common of all local landmarks however, were shops – and among them wineshops: 'behind the butcher at the sign of "Le Bras d'Or"'; 'rue St Denis opposite the big house called the Hôtel de la Trinité'; 'in front of a *rôtisseuse* Grande Rue du Faubourg near "La Boule Blanche"' (a large wineshop); 'r. St Martin near St Nicolas cemetery . . . at the "Café du Rendez-vous"'. Very often the name of the proprietor was given, sometimes alone, sometimes with the shop sign: 'opposite the wineshop of Sieur La Cloche'; 'at Doucet's, at "La Tête Noire"'; 'above and next to Bordau, baker'.[41] In the rue du Faubourg St Antoine in 1752, after a battle between the *garde* and a group of musketeers, the witnesses located different stages of the fight in front of various houses: the carriage commandeered by the musketeers was stopped outside 'Le Tambour Royal', then went on as far as 'the house of Sieur Gervais *marchand tapissier* at "La Toison d'Or"'. Another witness had seen it go as far as 'Sieur Claret's door'. Yet another mentioned the shop of the same Sieur Gervais, but gave its sign as 'La Barbe d'Or': in this case at least, the name of the owner was a better indication than that of his shop. Sometimes, however, only the occupation was given. 'She was at present living with her father and mother, pin-makers, rue Ste Marguerite . . . near the saltpetre manufacturer in the house of a *fruitière*.'[42]

Many of these details required a comprehensive knowledge of the area which outsiders could not be expected to have. Within each individual quarter there was a host of purely local landmarks: the statues of the Virgin; the wells, often placed against the buildings and not always obvious. Perhaps on arrival on the Quai de la Tournelle 'la maison rouge' (the red house) and 'la maison blanche' (the white house) were clear landmarks. But even the clearest name could be difficult to find amid the jumble of shop signs and symbols lining the streets. And if the owner's names alone were given, the only way someone who was not familiar with the neighbourhood could find the spot was by asking the locals.[43]

This could apply even to finding the street itself. In theory the names were indicated at every corner, but repeated police ordinances encouraging the owners of corner houses to put up clear street names suggest a certain reluctance

---

[40] The principal study of the charity schools, by M. Fossoyeux, does not tackle the question of who actually used them: 'Les Ecoles de charité à Paris sous l'ancien régime et dans la première partie du XIXe siècle', *Mémoires de la Société de l'histoire de Paris et de l'Ile de France*, 39 (1912), 225–366. Y14436, 8 July.

[41] Y12596, 3 Jan. Y15350, 14 Oct. Y15100, 28 July. Y10994, 24 May, wit. 9. Y13816, 10 Jan. Y12597, 9 Oct.

[42] Y10994, 21 Sept., 12 Oct. Y14436, 19 May.

[43] Y12597, 24 Oct. Mercier, *Tableau*, vol. 3, p. 204.

to comply.[44] Most people certainly knew the names of the streets they frequented: in cases where someone was unsure of the name, the street was almost always outside the quarter where they lived, except for the occasional temporary lodger who could not give his address.[45] But it is likely that this knowledge was by word of mouth rather than by reading the signs. If, in an interrogation, one man was able to claim that he couldn't remember the name of a street because he couldn't read, on the other hand the occasional use of variations on the official names suggests the existence of an independent oral tradition. For example the street near the Halles which on some maps and in common use was called the rue de la Grande Friperie was also known to the locals as the rue du Petit St Martin and the rue du Puits.[46]

The whole system of addresses and descriptions was based on familiarity with the neighbourhood, designed for locals and not for strangers. Eighteenth-century Parisians had no use for north and south, left or right, or for numbers in order to define a place. They preferred purely local landmarks: objects and very often people. Even after the houses of the capital were numbered most people continued to use the old methods of description, and those few who did use the number often gave other indications as well. In one case even the clerk of one of the *commissaires*, indicating a house that his employer was called to, wrote down the number but added the shop sign just to be on the safe side.[47] Admittedly the numbering of the houses was a symptom of change, a manifestation of a new preoccupation in official circles with classification and ordering, and reflecting a new way of looking at the urban environment. Even at the end of the eighteenth-century however, the old parochial descriptive system still worked perfectly well, an indication of its continuing relevance to people's everyday lives and of the good health – indeed the pre-eminence – of local patterns of sociability.

For many of the inhabitants of eighteenth-century Paris, therefore, the neighbourhood was the hub of daily life. They relied on neighbours for material and psychological support; among them they found human contact and companionship; and their vision, shaped by day-to-day sociability, was parochial. But more than that, they were aware of belonging to a community, geographically circumscribed although without fixed boundaries. As D. Roche has recently observed, people were divided into those who belonged to the quarter and those who did not.[48]

The identification of people and place emerges in the use of spatial terms.

---

[44] Arrêt du Conseil d'Etat, 10 Oct. 1752, in J. Peuchet, *Collection des lois, ordonnances et règlements de police*, 2nd series, *Police moderne de 1667 à 1789*, 8 vols. (Paris, 1818–19), vol. 6, p. 113. Ordonnance de police, 27 May 1763, Peuchet, vol. 7, p. 224. Ordonnance de police, 1 Sept., 1769, Peuchet, vol. 8, p. 238. Cf. Mercier, *Tableau*, vol. 2, p. 203.

[45] Y15100, 30 Nov. Y15350, 20 Sept. Y12597, 31 Aug.

[46] Y11239, 18 May. Y15350, 22 Nov., 24 Nov.

[47] Y14484, 9 Mar.   [48] *Peuple*, pp. 255–6.

Probably the most common was *le quartier* (the quarter), employed officially to refer to a specific division of the city. But in everyday use it was essentially an area of familiarity where it was considered normal for most people to know each other, at least by sight. A journeyman printer arrested for theft said that he knew the hatter with whom he was accused of complicity 'pour être du quartier' (to belong to the quarter). When a body was found on the Port de la Rapée, no one recognized it 'pour être du quartier'. Sometimes the association of people and place was closer still: after a theft in the rue des Prêcheurs, near the Halles, a *négociant* said that he had learned 'dans le quartier' (in the quarter) that there had been several such crimes. The widow of a domestic servant complained about a prostitute who had moved into her house, causing a scandal 'dans tout le quartier'.[49] In this usage *le quartier* refers as much to the place itself as to the people. It is as much a social unit as a physical one.

Other terms were also used in this way, even *la maison* (the house, apartment building) and *la rue* (the street) which applied to definite physical objects. Two neighbours explained that a man had taken in a woman to live with him, causing a scandal 'dans la maison'. Or when a *marchand de vin* in the rue St Louis, in the Marais, beat up his *garçon*, 'l'on disoit dans la rue que c'étoit pour avoir embrassé sa femme' (they said in the street that it was for kissing his wife).[50]

But the spatial term in which the identification of people and place was most complete was *le voisinage* (the neighbourhood). The very existence of the word is significant, for unlike *la maison*, *la rue*, or *le quartier*, it never applied to a clearly defined object or space. It always retained some sense of *voisin* (neighbour) from which it was derived. Like the other terms it could be used ambiguously to mean both a place and a group of people: a journeyman mason complained of having been insulted in the street, which caused great scandal 'dans tous [*sic*] le voisinage' (throughout the neighbourhood). The wife of an innkeeper, speaking on behalf of her former servant, said that she had found out 'dans le voisinage' that the girl's new master robbed his employees.[51] Unlike any of the other spatial terms used, however, *le voisinage* could refer explicitly to the people who lived there. The wife of a *maître sculpteur* living in the rue du Faubourg St Antoine claimed that her husband's brutality to her 'scandalise tout le voisinage dont ledit Ledain dit se moquer' (scandalizes the whole neighbourhood, whom the said Ledain says he doesn't care about). When three men appeared outside a house in the rue de Charenton armed with swords, *le voisinage* had them arrested. *Le voisinage* was indignant when two or three young men sang obscene songs in the rue de Loursine in the Faubourg St Marcel.[52] In this usage the physical sense of the term disappears completely. Even more than *le quartier*, which always retains something of its physical reference, *le voisinage* was a social description; no

---

[49] Y13290, 8 July, wit. 1; 8 Oct. Y10994, 26 May. Y15402, 29 Feb. Y15350, 10 Jan.
[50] Y12596, 15 May. Y15350, 28 Sept., wit. 3.
[51] Y11239, 3 Sept. Y15350, 18 Sept.   [52] Y10994, 8 July, 16 Sept. Y12596, 24 July.

longer an area but a group of people who acted and reacted as one, a single social unit.

The neighbourhood, therefore, was the social context which was foremost in people's consciousness. It was an entity based on proximity but created by daily contact between neighbours: by relationships and interaction, not by simply living within certain boundaries. Contact alone, however, was not enough. What ultimately defined people as part of the community was adherence to certain norms of social behaviour. Belonging depended on a primarily local investment of attention and energy, on commitment to the neighbourhood, and on an overriding concern for its reactions and opinions.

Any local event, however minor, excited great curiosity. 'She saw a lot of neighbours going to visit the widow Rivet to learn of the misfortune which had just befallen her', said the wife of a *bourgeois de Paris* who had herself heard of the theft from a woman who sold meat at the door of the house.[53] Afterwards the matter could be discussed at length and witnesses in enquiries very often recount what others have told them, frequently distinguishing little between fact and opinion. The extent of local interest is reflected in the speed with which news travelled and in the extraordinary detail in which it was reported. Take for example this entry from the journal of the bookseller Hardy:

Towards midday four fairly well-dressed individuals, who were suspected of being the journeymen tailors who that morning had gone to [the wineshop of] Fournier, *marchand de vin* in the rue Gallande on the corner of the rue St Julien le Pauvre ... according to the general rumour escaped with 500 gold *louis*, several pieces of silver and many other goods ... The popular rumour, which always deforms events and exaggerates things, put the value of this theft as high as 50,000 *livres*.[54]

There are innumerable similar entries in Hardy's journal concerning such events as thefts, arrests, and fires – throughout the city but especially in his own quarter. The precision of his record reflects both the extent of his own interest and that of those who passed on the information.

Almost any event provided material for discussion. Two witnesses called in an enquiry into a fight in the rue des Cordeliers had been away that day, but on their return had heard all the details. An arrest by the police always aroused interest: a waggoner robbed of two sacks of goods had no trouble finding out that the *garde* had picked up a man sleeping in the street with two such sacks beside him.[55]

Less common in police records but probably predominant in everyday conversations were events of even more parochial interest: weddings, births and deaths, romances, domestic disputes, local scandals. Four years after the marriage of the daughter of a *marchand épicier* in the rue de la Montagne Ste Geneviève, several of the neighbours were still able to give all the details of the

[53] Y14436, 4 Jan. [54] B.N. Ms. fr. 6682, p. 112, 28 Aug. 1775.
[55] Y14078, 23 May, wit. 6 and 9. Y14078, 9 Mar.

31

dowry. Most of the neighbours of a recently deceased *marchand mercier* in the Grande Rue du Faubourg St Antoine had heard that a certain amount of the silver and other goods had been surreptitiously removed before the inventory was drawn up.[56]

Much of the gossip exchanged was, to judge from numerous complaints of calumnies, rather more harmful. People were quick to pass on any story they heard and there was always an eager audience, intensely interested in goings-on in the neighbourhood. At the source of a great deal of the gossip lay an extraordinary vigilance facilitated by thin walls, narrow streets and crowded lodgings. Some people displayed an almost pathological interest in the lives and doings of those who lived around them. A midwife in the rue de la Coutellerie complained that two women in her street were spying on her, watching everyone who came in, and that this might put off her customers. Usually the vigilance was more discreet, sometimes almost unconscious: concluding from the sound of voices that a neighbour had company; knowing the time the man on the floor above got up and went to work. Or noticing who came in and out of the house, almost automatically: two women going to see a friend first checked with a neighbour whether their friend's husband was at home.[57]

But as soon as anything the slightest inhabitual happened the attention of the neighbours was immediately attracted. The non-appearance of someone whom they were used to seeing frequently would provoke concern, especially if the person were old or known to have been unwell.[58] Anything even more out of the ordinary, of course, instantly aroused the greatest curiosity. After being woken by voices in the middle of the night, a poultry-seller and her son followed with enormous interest the doings of the woman in the next room: she had come in late accompanied by two men carring a large trunk containing lots of paper which they had burned. At four in the morning they had all gone out carrying a large package. At five they returned, drank some *eau-de-vie*, then took another package out, the man going to the door first to see if anyone was coming. The following Thursday the woman had put new sheets on her bed but had not spent the night there, appearing the following morning with new clothes. On the Saturday night one of the men had slept with her, and again on the Sunday when they had both come home drunk.[59]

As in eighteenth-century Languedoc people sought an explanation for anything out of the ordinary, and however harmless it really was seemed invariably and instinctively to hit upon a sinister motive. A man suddenly appeared to have more money than usual: he must have stolen it. A domestic servant left her master for a while then returned: she had had an illegitimate child. A stream of visitors to the room of a tenant at all hours of the day 'indicates

[56] Y13290, 1 Dec. Y10994, 19 Jan.
[57] Y15350, 26 May. Y15402, 24 Nov., 7 May, 18 Dec., wit. 3.
[58] Y13290, 30 May. Y12596, 1 Apr.   [59] Y14436, 4 Jan., wit. 1 and 12.

most unacceptable misbehaviour'. The smallest change was noted. An innkeeper spread the word that one of his tenants, a journeyman joiner, was a thief:
'He must certainly be a thief because he had previously worn a suit of clothes,
and he no longer had it and he must assuredly have stolen that suit of clothes.'[60]

Frequently the neighbours' vigilance was betrayed only by some chance
remark or by a retort let fly in a moment of spite or anger. 'He would do better to
pay her than to dress his wife in *folbales* [?] and a watch', burst out a *marchande
fripière* during a dispute with a client over the amount he owed.[61] The
surveillance was unremitting, the curiosity of the neighbours insatiable, although
in normal relations masked by a formal politeness and a familiar cordiality which
made it tolerable.

It was gossip therefore, based on familiarity and on a degree of vigilance
requiring a considerable local commitment of interest and energy, which more
than anything else defined the boundaries of the community. People gossiped
primarily with and about people they knew. What they said could have little
impact on outsiders, but for those who belonged to the community the way
neighbours spoke of them and behaved towards them was a constant preoccupation. Because the neighbourhood, socially and materially, was central to
people's existence, the place they occupied in it was vitally important to them. It
is this which explains the huge number of disputes over individual rights and
over reputation, often seemingly petty, yet treated with absolute seriousness by
the parties and by the authorities. Such disputes must be examined in detail, for
they were more than individual differences: they were a form of collective
behaviour and the very mechanism of community self-regulation.

A dispute could of course be over almost anything. Failure to pay a debt, some
minor damage to property, disagreement over a contract, the smallest slight, real
or imagined, could culminate in a noisy, sometimes even a bloody quarrel and
ultimately in an expensive complaint to the *commissaire*. In September 1752 the
wife of a bell-ringer at St Eustache came to the *commissaire* to complain that her
nephew and brother-in-law, meeting her on her way back from the market, had
called her names, slapped her, taken her husband's wig and hat and thrown them
at her, and finally broken some eggs she had just bought. For this she was
prepared to spend over two days' wages on a complaint.[62] It is only when such
quarrels are seen and understood in the context of the local community that their
real significance becomes clear, for it was not the particular object at issue which
was important but what it represented in terms of the way people were seen and
treated by their peers. Occasionally this was quite explicit. A fight erupted at a
fountain in the rue de Baffroid when one water-carrier tried to push in front of
another and the second man objected 'primarily to prevent the said Picard from

---

[60] Y. Castan, *Honnêteté*, p. 149. Y15402, 10 Feb. Y10994, 21 July. Y15350, 13 Oct., 7 June.
[61] Y15350, 24 Nov.
[62] Y11239, 30 Sept.

boasting that he was master of the other water-carriers rather than through obstinacy'. On another occasion a female servant caused a rumpus when she told the owner of the house where she lived, who was in front of her at the well, to hurry up: 'the plaintiff who owns the said house told her that if she were in a hurry she could go elsewhere, that for himself he was free to pump the water at his leisure'.[63] In both cases it is a question of precedence: one party tries to do something which, if permitted, would make him or her appear superior, and the other reacts to oppose this pretension. There was no virtue in being conciliatory.

The concern with precedence was not usually as openly expressed as in these two examples. Status was concretized in a great many privileges and rights, all of which were jealously defended. But in the urban environment where ownership of one's lodgings was rare, where people had common use of entrances, stairs, courtyards, and of facilities such as wells and toilets, the exact limits of each person's rights and territory were ill-defined and many disputes resulted. Quite a number concerned the use of some place or object, one side claiming exclusive rights, the other contesting them. For example a fight developed when a man tried to prevent a group of domestic servants from playing bowls in front of his house, in an area which he claimed to be by convention attached to his property and which they maintained to be a public square. Another dispute arose between the co-proprietors of a house in the rue de la Muette, when one of them, without consulting the other, removed the doors of a shared passage-way.[64]

Such conflicts were especially common and particularly bitter when one side had effective control but without clearly higher status. The relationship of principal tenant and sub-tenant, for example, was a potentially stormy one. Most Paris houses were let to one person, often the shopkeeper who used the ground floor, and he or she would sub-let to others. The principal tenant could refuse to renew a lease or, more often, because poor people rarely had a formal lease, could simply give them notice. Some of the disputes thus caused were extremely acrimonious. A gardener-florist complained that a female porter whom he had expelled but who was still in the neighbourhood was insulting and threatening his wife every time they met in the street, lying in wait for her, and even physically attacking her. Another woman, told to leave by the principal tenant, picked a fight with the man's daughter and, so it was claimed, pushed the girl down the stairs.[65] The violence of such disputes is to some extent explicable by the fact that the sub-tenant was losing his or her lodging, but in most cases the notice was only a manifestation of existing friction, a weapon used by someone in a position of minor authority.

The principal tenant's position was admittedly in some respects an unenviable one. Rent was normally paid in arrears and without any bond, and if people

[63] Y10994, 26 June. Y11239, 8 Mar.
[64] Y15350, 21 July and Y13760, 8 June, 21 July. Y10994, 27 Oct.
[65] Y10994, 5 June. Y14078, 17 Aug., 23 Dec.

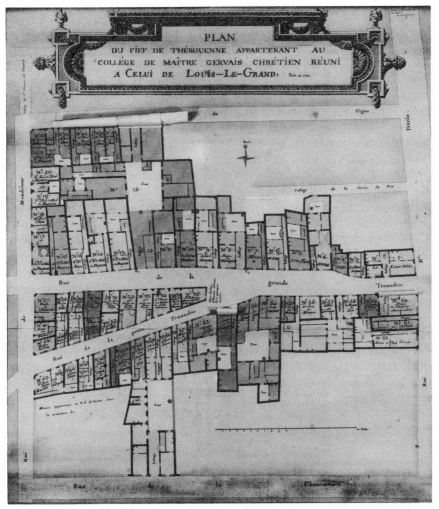

6. Map of houses in Halles quarter showing floor plans: Fief de Thérouenne, 1782
(*A.N. NII Seine 105. Photo. Service Photographique des Archives Nationales*)

moved out without paying or seriously damaged the property he or she suffered the loss. The principal tenant was also held responsible by the police for the good order of the house and could be fined if prostitutes used it or if the door onto the street was found open after dark.[66] The famous *concierges* began to appear in ordinary Paris houses only during the late eighteenth century, and until then it

---

[66] Ordonnance de police, 29 Oct. 1760, in Peuchet, vol. 6, p. 466. Y12830, Ordonnance de police, 26 July 1777.

was principal tenants who looked after the premises. They were therefore anxious to know what the occupants of the house were doing, particularly anyone new or whom they suspected might be disorderly or financially unstable. This could naturally lead to tension, and those who abused their position could make life rather unpleasant for their victims. The widow of a master gilder living in the rue de la Vannerie complained that since taking over the lease of the house two months earlier the new principal tenant – an innkeeper and journeyman mason – had insisted on closing the main door so that everyone had to go through his shop. When the widow announced her intention of leaving he began searching her and all her visitors in case she tried to move anything out before she had paid the full rent. In another case a 'bourgeois', coming home at ten thirty at night, found the entrance of the house closed. He objected to having to pass through the shop and tried to force the door open, which caused a violent confrontation. There had already been some conflict between him and the principal tenant over payment of the rent and he quite correctly assumed the early closing of the door to be specifically directed against him.[67]

Whether or not in such cases the principal tenant was being deliberately provocative, the fact remains that the relationship was not an easy one. People naturally resented the surveillance of their lives and the interference with their freedom to come and go as they pleased, and were particularly sensitive to any attempt, real or imagined, to lord it over them. The occupations of principal tenants rarely gave them any significant social superiority, so their power over their neighbours, which some did not hesitate to use quite maliciously, could arouse considerable resentment.

Any attempt on the part of a colleague or a neighbour to dictate to someone what they should do provoked a similar reaction. The gardener of a country house in the Faubourg St Antoine attributed an attack on him by a labourer to his having rebuked the man for not working. Considerable resentment was likewise provoked when the wife of a *chirurgien* told some neighbouring bakers to move their drying-racks from in front of her door. 'We would put our racks in front of the doors of grander gentry than you', they retorted.[68]

Refusal to take orders from those who were felt to have no right to give them also underlay many disputes over the activities of the officials of the corporations. A *juré fruitier-oranger* complained that, wanting to inspect some butter being offered for sale in the Halle, its owner had cried out: 'What are you doing, don't touch that basket of butter, it's mine.' The *juré* replied that no one could stop him from examining it, at which the man retorted 'who does that b... think he is'. Two *jurés* ropemakers, supervising the sale of two waggon-loads of rope of varying quality, insisted that all the masters take some rope of each quality. Several protested, and one man refused to obey: 'Scoundrel what do I have to do with you, get f...' Like the power of the principal tenant over the other occupants of

[67] Y15350, 4 Sept., 13 Oct.   [68] Y10994, 9 Oct., 6 Nov., and 22 Nov.

his house, the authority of the *jurés* was not backed up by any significant social superiority. Some of them certainly abused their power, or were suspected of doing so, and could be fairly high-handed in asserting their authority.[69]

A great many disputes therefore had to do with the way people were treated by their peers, with their position among those around them, the respect they felt to be due. Complaints stress the insolence with which an action was done, the 'hauteur' (haughtiness) of tone: a gilder addressed a neighbour 'with an imperious and insolent tone'; a *huissier* demanded payment of a debt 'with an insolent air'.[70] This is not to say that the immediate cause of the dispute was not important in itself. Real persecution by a principal tenant or by the *jurés* could cause loss of clients, even material damage. Apparently minor privileges could be vital to people's livelihood. But small rights and perquisites, the freedom to come and go without taking orders from anyone, the personal independence of the humblest artisan or unskilled worker, were essential to people's self-esteem and to their ability to associate with those around them on equal terms. Many disputes were ultimately struggles for recognition and respect from other members of the local community, for the same 'tribute of esteem' which Y. Castan speaks of in eighteenth-century Languedoc.[71]

Nowhere is this clearer than in the constant references to reputation. Damage or potential damage to reputation was the commonest reason given for complaints to the *commissaire*. A market porter accused of theft by his workmates pointed out indignantly that he had worked there for twenty years, 'and that he has an interest in preserving the reputation of *honnête homme* which he has always enjoyed'. The widow of a saddler in the rue de Reuilly complained that the wife of a *marchand de vin*, one of her tenants, kept insulting her, had punched her in the face and had thrown stones through her window, but put the emphasis on the damage all this might do to her reputation.[72] As in this example, material damage was used wherever possible to lend weight to a complaint and sometimes it was obviously the prime motive, but its normal role was a supplementary one. It was quite legitimate in eighteenth-century Paris to make a formal complaint just about calumnies or about insults, and to justify it entirely in terms of reputation: quite the opposite to what Y. Castan describes in Languedoc where neither official nor public opinion regarded attacks on the honour of humble folk as sufficient reason to make a complaint.[73]

There were sound practical reasons for this concern with reputation. Witnesses in enquiries frequently assessed people not on the basis of individual value-judgments or personal knowledge, although these are often implicit, but in terms of how they were considered locally. When in June 1752 a young man

---

[69] Y11239, 29 Mar., 29 Nov. *Fruitier-orangers* sold butter and eggs!
[70] Y11239, 17 Oct. Y14078, 21 Mar.
[71] Y. Castan, *Honnêteté*, p. 13.   [72] Y11239, 28 Oct. Y10994, 18 Sept.
[73] Y. Castan, *Honnêteté*, pp. 260–1.

hanged himself in the cellar of a house in the rue de la Harpe, the *commissaire* was told by the neighbours that he was known as a drunkard. He had lived with a widowed relative and the locals were quick to exculpate her: 'The wife Dupuis is highly esteemed in her quarter and is known as an *honnête femme* full of religion and esteemed by all'.[74] It could be dangerous to have any flaws in one's reputation. Witnesses would repeat stories often long past but never quite forgotten, in order to justify suspicions for which there was no other foundation. A water-carrier, learning of a theft in the rooms which his wife kept in the rue des Boulangers, at once suspected a blanket-maker who had supposedly once been arrested in Reims. After a burglary in the rue Ste Marguerite, Faubourg St Germain, a *marchand de vin* assured the victim 'that only the said Mille and his wife could have committed the said theft because he Mille had once stolen the sum of ten thousand *livres* from a man in the rue St Honoré [but] had got away with it because there was no proof'. Before the *commissaire* the same *marchand de vin* repeated this story, which he had had from someone who had heard it from someone else![75]

Local opinion of people very often determined the attitude of outsiders who did not know them. After a woman standing at her door in the rue des Arcis was insulted by a man who obviously took her for a prostitute, two passers-by took her part, even accompanying her to see the *commissaire*, when they were assured by several people that she was an *honnête femme*. The same criteria were used by the authorities. The *inspecteur* Dumont, investigating a petition from a locksmith against his step-daughter, reported to the *lieutenant général* that 'for about eighteen months people in the neighbourhood had noticed that the said Teil treated his wife badly and that he beat her and that this divorce arose over the said Pottier his step-daughter'. The *curé* (parish priest) of the Gros Caillou, replying to police enquiries about one of his parishioners, said 'that he always had the most favourable reports of her ... and that she is known throughout this place to have always been of regular and irreproachable conduct'.[76]

Reputation therefore really did influence people. Part of the reason lies in the things upon which it was based; best seen in attacks on it, for reputation was something which could be damaged rather than enhanced. These concentrated on two main areas, those guaranteed to have maximum effect in the conditions which prevailed in eighteenth-century Paris.[77] The first was sexual, used almost entirely against women, and playing primarily on the themes of sexual promiscuity, prostitution and venereal disease. The second main accusation, more often directed against men, was that of dishonesty and criminal activity, most commonly theft. Dishonesty in business was a common theme, especially

[74] Y15350, 20 June.   [75] Y12596, 5 Feb., wit. 5. Y14078, 10 Nov., wit. 9, 10.
[76] Y15350, 18 May. Y13377, dossier Teil, May 1752. Y15402, 14 May.
[77] An expanded version of the following discussion can be found in D. Garrioch, 'Verbal Insults in Eighteenth-Century Paris', in P. Burke and R. Porter (eds.), *Essays in the Social History of Language* (New York, C.U.P., forthcoming).

selling by false weights, and others were accused of fraud and bankruptcy. A journeyman asserted that his former master had written false promissory notes in Bavaria![78] Another common technique was to suggest some criminal conviction or association: that the person had been publicly shamed or that they had been whipped and branded. Such accusations are more common against men, but were sometimes directed at women.[79]

A related theme was the claim, also principally made against men, of practising some dishonourable profession, such as pimp or brothel-keeper, and the implication of shady activity was also present in insults like 'night-prowler', 'spy', and *mouchard* (police spy).[80]

These themes reflect the major fears and obsessions of eighteenth-century Parisians. People were haunted by the possibility of theft, for lodgings were rarely secure and there were no banks for valuables or cash. Business agreements were often verbal and credit was extensively used, so that the slightest rumour of financial instability or fraud was very worrying. It was particularly so when so many artisans and shopkeepers relied on the payment of debts in order to be able to pay their own creditors.

Another obsessive fear which insults played on was that of vagabonds and brigands. Insults like 'night-prowler', *gueux* (beggar), *fripon* (rogue), and the socially equivalent female ones, *gueuse*, *putain* (whore) *coureuse* (loose woman), played on the themes of rootlessness and lack of scruples. 'Spy' awoke fears of denunciation.

The different insults used against men and women reflect their different social roles. Men were more open to accusations of professional dishonesty because they were more often in trade. They were also more likely, statistically and in contemporary stereotyping, to be accused and convicted of criminal offences.[81] For a woman a reputation for sexual purity could be vital to her chances of finding a good husband, and hence to her very existence. Insults against women reflect contemporary ideals of female behaviour, whose observance provided a symbolic guarantee of loyalty to her husband or future husband, and to the family unit which it was so often the wife's task to hold together.[82]

---

[78] Y15100, 25 Nov., wit. 2. Y10994, 1 Nov. Y13290, 14 Oct. Y12596, 29 June. Y13290, 6 Sept., wit. 5. Y12597, 29 Dec., wit. 5; 31 Dec. Y10994, 31 July. Y15350, 31 Aug., 11 July. Y10994, 20 Sept., 16 Oct.

[79] Y11239, 13 Oct. Y10994, 16 July, 29 Sept. Y15099, 16 Feb. Y13290, 15 June, wit. 8. Y15117, 13 June 1788. Y12596, 2 July.

[80] Y10994, 29 Nov., 29 Sept. Y15100, 1 Dec. Y15117, 16 June 1789, 31 July 1789.

[81] N. Castan, *Les Criminels de Languedoc* (Toulouse, Université de Toulouse-Le Mirail, 1980), pp. 26, 34–5. P. Petrovitch, 'Recherches sur la crimialité à Paris dans la seconde moitié du XVIIIe siècle', in A. Abbiateci *et al.*, *Crimes et criminalité en France sous l'ancien régime* (Paris, Armand Colin, 1971), pp. 187–261 (pp. 234–5).

[82] O. Hufton, 'Women and the Family Economy in Eighteenth-Century France', *French Historical Studies*, 9 (1975), 1–22. U. Hannerz, in his study of a black area of Washington, D.C., describes the way that the role of women in the family economy, very similar to that among ordinary people in eighteenth-century Paris, contributes to an image and an expectation of women as virtuous,

The values on which reputation was based were therefore essentially those that were necessary for survival in the particular social and economic context in which people found themselves, and if the listeners actually believed insults or calumnies then the victim's livelihood could suffer. This is a possibility frequently evoked in complaints. Calumnies by the wife of a nearby innkeeper, said a journeyman baker, could prevent him 'from in future finding ... another master because of the impression that they could make on those who know the plaintiff only imperfectly'. Public insults against a tailor were likely, he claimed, 'to make him lose the greater part of his clients'.[83]

On the other hand there is a certain element of rhetoric in complaints which dwell on the damage that insults might cause. People's preoccupation with reputation frequently seems out of all proportion to its possible practical significance. For example, when a strange man insulted the wife of a chemist and followed her right into her house in the rue des Quatre Vents she and her husband made a formal complaint 'to protect their reputation', despite the fact that all the witnesses had taken her part. The glazier and his wife who kept the shop in the same house, and who had had words with the man, felt obliged to add a complaint of their own, 'having likewise an interest in safeguarding their honour and their reputation'.[84]

There are many similar examples in which it is difficult to see what conceivable damage insults could do. The apparent over-reactions make more sense, however, if we look at them in the context of a local community. Insults were not necessarily to be taken literally. They were a symbolic casting-out of the victim, individual expressions of rejection and contempt which if left unpunished could affect the attitude of other people. They were a blow to the victim's self-esteem, a public humiliation which both the adversary and the witnesses would delight in recounting. The wife of a *bourgeois de Paris* complained indignantly that 'she had had the disgrace to hear herself treated ... as if she had all her life led the most scandalous existence'. A stream of insults directed against a locksmith's wife quickly attracted all the neighbours, 'in whose eyes the plaintiff's wife now passes for a woman of loose morals'. The public nature of insults and stories is constantly emphasized: they were 'heard by the whole neighbourhood', spoken 'publicly in the slaughterhouse', 'in the midst of all the populace of the quarter'. A butcher and his wife, accused of theft by the son of their employer, did not take the accusation seriously until he spread the story around.[85] Insults normally gave rise to complaints only when third parties were present.

Behind people's preoccupation with reputation therefore, just as in their

particularly with regard to sex and drink. *Soulside* (New York, Columbia University Press), pp. 74–6, 95–7.
[83] Y10994, two complaints of 28 Feb.   [84] Y14078, 24 May.
[85] Y12597, 29 Aug. Y14436, 2 Feb. Y12597, 29 Aug., 17 Oct. Y11239, 8 Aug.

concern with rights, privileges, and precedence, lay an awareness of belonging to a community which could through the recognition and respect it accorded an individual offer security and comfort. But it could equally, by its condemnation or rejection, withhold them. The group thus had a strong hold over its members and this was in turn vital to its own survival. People's concern to win respect and recognition from their peers pushed them to conform to its dominant values: first of all to the moral ones of honesty and, for women, of sexual fidelity. Thus when people insulted someone by calling them a thief or a whore they were reaffirming the basic values whose general, if not necessarily total, observance was essential to the continued existence of the community.[86]

Furthermore, people's quest for the esteem and recognition of those around them meant that they needed the rest of the community. By striving to preserve their place within it they were in turn recognizing and affirming its authority, thus helping to preserve it.

There is an apparent paradox in this explanation, however, for people's anxiety to win recognition pushed them into competition with others, forcing them to defend their position strongly and to combat the pretensions of those around them. While in other ways the process helped to preserve and maintain the community, in this respect it caused tension and division, a multiplication of conflicts which N. Castan sees, in southern French towns at the same period, as evidence of destructuration.[87] Furthermore, it sounds rather like the law of the jungle, every individual against every other, and this also seems quite the opposite of what we normally associate with a sense of community.

In fact it was not the law of the jungle and nor did the admittedly numerous disputes divide or weaken the local community. On the contrary they served to strengthen it further, for people's behaviour followed clear patterns and rules which permitted the expression and resolution of grievances with the minimum of damage both to them and to the group. We must, in order to see how this happened, turn to the form of disputes and look at the way they were conducted, at the weapons used, and at the reaction of the rest of the community to them.

A typical example of the disputes recorded in the papers of the *commissaires* took place in the rue Tiquetonne near the Halles, between the wife of a public writer and a pawnbroker from whom she had borrowed money. Seeing her in the street he had greeted her and stopped to talk. After a brief chat about his recent absence from Paris and his return, she said that she would like to reclaim the things she had pawned. They had been sold long ago, he replied. Well, he would have to get them back. 'Old tarts like her', he retorted, 'can go to hell.' She should have reclaimed them before. But this had not been possible, she

---

[86] As Y. Castan points out, prostitutes were not social outcasts because their presence helped to reinforce the dominant value of female sexual fidelity. *Honnêteté*, p. 81.

[87] N. Castan, *Criminels*, pp. 14–21.

retaliated, during the two years he had been in the Bicêtre prison.[88] This was too much: she had dared to insult him. 'He had women at her place whenever he wanted ... she had been in the hospital [where prostitutes were imprisoned] ten times, she was known for it, if her husband got what he deserved he would be in irons.' At this she turned and walked off down the street with him following, keeping up a string of insults at the top of his voice. He put his clenched fist in front of her face, she pushed it away, he slapped her. At this point a soldier of the *garde* who was going past intervened to break up the dispute, and she went to the *commissaire*.[89]

Each move in this dispute was staged for maximum effect. The voices were gradually raised, a signal for the passers-by to gather round. Their attention attracted, open insults broke out, many of them fixed expressions: 'she had been in the hospital ten times' is just one of a whole arsenal of standard phrases. Although not mentioned here, it is at this point that the parties usually begin to use the familiar (and in this context insulting) *tu* to each other. Her moving off down the street was both a sign of contempt and a measure of prudence, but it also provided the maximum audience possible and gave her the appearance of the innocent victim, pursued by the aggressor. Then there is the threat of violence as he shakes his fist under her nose, and pushing the fist away provides the actual physical contact which permits the escalation to the next stage, the *soufflet* (slap). Each move is open, theatrical, carefully timed.

Nearly all reported disputes follow this pattern. There is maximum emphasis on noise and publicity: disputes occurred, with the sole exception of family quarrels, in the street or the market-place, in the courtyard or on the stairs of a house, in wineshops, but very rarely in rooms or workshops. If they did erupt inside, one or both of the parties would invariably step out into the street. In one example in the rue de la Grande Friperie a *fripière* was standing in front of her door when her attention was attracted by a heated discussion in the shop opposite, and a minute later a woman came out and began to shout insults at the shopkeeper. 'You louse-ridden scoundrel, pay me.'[90]

A dispute was a public performance, noisy and animated. It contained a strong element of ritual and symbol which the audience recognized and knew how to interpret.[91] There were set phrases like those in the above example. There were also gestures. It was common for men to try to seize each other by the collar, a symbolic act of superiority. Another frequent action was seizing an adversary's hat, bonnet, or wig. 'The said street-sweeper having insulted him without reason,' admitted a shoemaker, 'he had indeed thrown his bonnet into the water.'

---

[88] Bicêtre was where convicted criminals were sent. There was also a treatment centre for those suffering from venereal disease.

[89] Y11239, 30 Apr.   [90] Y15350, 24 Nov. Y10994, 16 Apr.

[91] Very similar behaviour, on an island off the Irish coast, is described by R. Fox, 'The Inherent Rules of Violence', in P. Collett (ed.), *Social Rules and Social Behaviour* (Oxford, Blackwell, 1977), pp. 132–49.

When a laundrywoman refused to pay one of her *ouvrières* the latter tried to grab her bonnet.[92] More than other items of clothing, head-gear had great symbolic significance. Wearing a wig was often indicative of a certain social pretension. A decorated hat could also be provocative: a complaint by a *marchand limonadier* recounts that, some days after a dispute in his shop, his adversary had come back looking for trouble and wearing a cockade and a feather in his hat.[93] Doffing a hat, on the other hand, was a sign of deference, so that seizing an opponent's headcovering while continuing to wear one's own was a symbolic gesture of superiority.

There were other common gestures : shaking one's fist in the other's face has already been mentioned. A slap in the face (*soufflet*) was used by both men and women – and against both men and women – as a sign of contempt: in a dispute between the wife of a dyer and a bird-seller she called him a 'f... scoundrel'; he retored that she would do better to pay what she owed, whereupon she gave him two *soufflets*. When an engraver met a *colporteur* at the door of their house and asked him not to lock it the *colporteur* snapped at him: 'Say, *jeanfoutre* [ne'er-do-well], why don't you raise your cap to me.' The engraver replied in surprise that he was 'un insolent', at which the man slapped him in the face.[94] There are innumerable such examples and a whole vocabulary of insulting gestures. The wife of a *nattier* (maker of straw mats) complained that when she went to get her pet sheep (named Martin) back from a neighbour whom she suspected of taking it, the woman '[reached out and] lifted her nose with her hand and pushed her out of the house'. A woman who sold pork, rebuked by a neighbour for interfering in his business, told him 'that he was a *jeanfoutre* and double *jeanfoutre* and made horns at him'. The *garde* arrested a tailor for refusal to pay his rent 'and for having bared his bottom when the said Cretté asked him for money'.[95]

All these gestures, and the streams of insults, served to prolong the encounter, attracting the maximum public attention and at the same time giving the adversary as many chances as possible to back down. For the aim in a dispute was not usually physically to punish or to injure one's opponent so much as to force him or her to give way by drawing public attention to one's grievance and if possible by publicly humiliating him or her. Very often the actual confrontation was preceded or followed by a veritable publicity campaign similarly designed to win over public opinion. A market-gardener in the rue Plumet, Faubourg St Germain, said that he was being slandered by the owner of the house where he lived who blamed him for damage to the garden. This had been going on for six months but especially over the preceding three weeks, with threats to have him arrested. Whether the aim of the owner was to get compensation or whether he wanted his tenant to move out is not clear, but a few days later he brought in a

---

[92] Y14078, 21 Mar. Y13290, 28 May. Y11705, 21 Mar.   [93] Y14436, 19 Jan.
[94] Y15350, 2 Oct., wit. 3; 17 June.
[95] Y15350, 4 June. Y11239, 24 June. Y15117, 28 Apr. 1789.

bailiff to expel the gardener. His publicity campaign had presumably been intended to avoid legal action, but when this had not succeeded it at least served to prepare public opinion and to justify the expulsion in advance. In another case, this time in the rue Royale near St Paul, the wife of a master rope-maker told everyone that her husband was a *débauché*, with a view, according to him, to seeking legal separation.[96]

Many of the threats used were extremely extravagant. 'The Sieur Denniere will not die except by his hand,' predicted a master baker, 'he will blow his brains out with a pistol.' The attack would be made 'at the moment he expected it least and they won't let him live long'. 'He wanted to draw swords with the plaintiff and would break his arms and legs.' Such boasts and threats were not really to be taken at face value, however, for promises 'to break his arms and legs' or to 'lui donner des coups de canne' (hit him with a cane) or 'des coups d'épée' (run him through with a sword) were part of a standard vocabulary of bravado. The expression 'il ne mourra que de sa main' (he won't die except by his hand) is mentioned by Y. Castan as common in eighteenth-century Languedoc.[97] Their real significance is as signals: a challenge to the opponent; and a sign to the local community that one has a grievance and that it is up to the other to seek conciliation. The extravagance of many of the threats is a show of force designed to impress the audience, to indicate that the individual concerned is not someone to be trifled with, and of course to intimidate the adversary when he or she hears of it.

And hear of it he or she soon would. The passing-on of the aggressor's words was an essential part of the process, ensured by the choice of place, time and audience. A journeyman goldsmith complained that his adversary 'never stops saying, especially to the plaintiff's acquaintances, that he wanted to draw swords with the plaintiff'. Several people had 'charitably' informed a gardener of calumnies against him by an engraver living in the same house.[98]

A similar form of publicity, and even more clearly an appeal to community opinion, was the institution of *tapage*, or *bacchanale* as it was more often called. This consisted of an aggrieved party – nearly always a man – stationing himself outside his opponent's door or window, shouting out insults and generally creating a nuisance, often for quite some time. After a boatman was given notice by the owner of the house where he lived in the rue Contrescarpe, Faubourg St Antoine, 'he made a horrible *bacchanale*' at four o'clock in the morning, then again all the following afternoon. In January 1788 in the rue du Four, Faubourg St Germain, it was the owner of the house who from twelve thirty at night until half past one bashed on the door of one of his tenants, shouting out insults and threats. Two police observers complained that a laundrywoman and her son had

---

[96] Y14078, 15 June. Y10994, 31 Oct.
[97] Y14436, 7 Feb. Y15099, 28 Jan. Y15100, 7 July. *Honnêteté*, p. 167.
[98] Y15100, 7 July. Y10994, 9 Sept.

'fait tapage' outside their door in the rue des Lyonnais, Faubourg St Marcel, and had attracted a large crowd.[99]

Bacchanale or *tapage* was an imitation on an individual level of the social sanction of rough music or *charivari*, an attempt to bring community pressure to bear on someone in order to make them redress a grievance. In one case it was designed to make a *compagnon ébéniste* pay his part of drinking expenses. In another a *maître limonadier* was trying to get his wife, who had left him and gone to live with her step-father, to come back. Strikingly close to the *charivari* was the *bacchanale* by four women, all of the same family, which began at three on a Sunday afternoon and continued until eight, then was repeated the next evening from seven thirty until nine, the reason apparently being that the victim was in the habit of beating his wife.[100]

Like insults of any kind, such scenes always reflected on the person attacked and never on the aggressor: a *tabletier* in the rue de la Mortellerie complained that *tapage* by a neighbour was causing 'a scandal most injurious to him and his wife'. The *vacarme* created by a horse merchant in the rue des Marais, Faubourg St Germain, was likely to damage 'the honour and the credit' of a *bourgeois de Paris* against whom it was directed.[101] Furthermore, whether or not local opinion did support the aggressor, the neighbours appear to have recognized the legitimacy of the exercise for although they suffered from the disturbance, often late at night, it was only ever the victims who complained. Plaintiffs were rarely able to point to the reaction of witnesses in support of their case: the onlookers are simply not mentioned.

Just as much part of the public campaign as *tapage*, slander, or the actual physical confrontation, was recourse to the police. This could take several forms. The easiest and cheapest was a verbal complaint, and references in the documents and in the correspondence of the *commissaires* indicate that these were a current practice. It was also possible to send a petition to the *lieutenant général*, and quite a number can be found in the police archives.[102] But it is written complaints to the *commissaires* which survive in the greatest number. These were officially the first step in a judicial proceeding but very few are followed by enquiries, which were much too expensive for most people. Going to the *commissaire* was primarily a statement for the benefit of the local community, a public response and a refutation of the opponent's claims, for if these remained unanswered people would assume them to be true. 'If they were to remain silent any longer without taking action over this calumny they would in a sense be showing themselves to be guilty'.[103]

---

[99] Y10994, 12 July. Y13819, 29 Jan. 1788. Y12596, 5 June.
[100] Y10994, 16 June. Y11239, 29 Jan. Y10994, 13 Sept.
[101] Y11239, 21 Aug. Y14078, 23 June.
[102] Y11239, 3 Oct. Y13760, 21 Jan., wit. 5. Y11267A, petition and letter from *lieutenant général*, 2 Apr. 1776. Y13163, petition of Aug. 1777. Y11243B, letter from *lieutenant général*, 22 Dec. 1756. Bast. 12399, petition of 5 June 1769.
[103] Y10994, 2 Dec., 28 Feb.

Always in the back of the plaintiff's mind was the effect of the complaint on a wider audience. A tobacco seller claimed that two neighbours had come into her shop and insulted her, and that it was important 'to have them spoken to (*leur en faire imposer*) ... to prevent other evil individuals from the said rue Ste Marguerite from assuming that if she did nothing they could insult her in future'. A former servant of the Calas family, some time after the affair had blown over, even had her complaint printed in order to dispel persistent rumours that she had confessed to being a Protestant and to having been an accomplice to the killing of Marc-Antoine Calas.[104] Going to the *commissaire* was a public gesture, an indication that the plaintiff did not intend to give in and that he or she had confidence in the justice of his or her cause.

It is true that this was not always the sole purpose. Complaints were appeals to an outside authority and often contain explicit appeals for the intervention of the police. Requests to 'leur en faire imposer' are common and some complaints, stating that the plaintiff does not intend to take the matter to court, request 'the participation of the public prosecutor'. To this end various techniques are used to try to make what is clearly a civil case into a criminal one. Police regulations are evoked to condemn insults by a journeyman against his master: 'it is a type of insubordination'.[105] The accusation or suggestion of theft is added to those of insults and violence: during the altercation the plaintiff's wallet was stolen; after a fight between a shoemaker and four coal-haulers two pairs of shoes were found to be missing. Other complaints seek to exaggerate and criminalize violence by claiming that it was premeditated, that the plaintiff is in danger of his or her life. Potential risk to public order is emphasized: 'the said Bolagnie associates with a troop of dangerous individuals who are not only suspect but capable of anything'.[106] Sometimes such appeals worked. If one side seemed clearly in the wrong the *commissaire* might administer a rebuke and put pressure on them to make good any damage. The *commissaire* Desmarest even imprisoned a *chirurgien* who had insulted a jeweller, 'the said individual having failed to give a satisfactory account and the said Prevot [the jeweller] in view of the damage that his affair did to his reputation having been unable to obtain adequate satisfaction'. A butcher in the rue de la Montagne Ste Geneviève recalled past complaints and 'the injunctions that the *commissaire* had several times made to the said wife Le Neveu not to insult the plaintiff and his wife again'.[107] Such action by the *commissaires* seems to have been quite common.

Even here, however, their intervention was important only because of its local repercussions. The satisfaction of the plaintiff in seeing his or her opponent rebuked, or even better forced to apologize, was considerable. It was presumably

---

[104] Y10994, 26 Sept. Complaint of Jeanne Viguiere to *commissaire* Hugues, 29 Mar. 1767, printed copy in B.H.V.P. MS 704 f. 9.
[105] Y10994, 9 Oct. Y15100, 7 July, 5 Sept., 28 July. Y10994, 16 Oct., 16 Apr.
[106] Y10994, 29 June. Y15100, 27 Nov., wit. 4. Y10994, 9 Oct.
[107] Y13377, June 1752. Y15117, 20 Feb. 1788. Y12597, 31 Dec.

pressure from the *commissaire* which forced a gardener at Bercy to retract his insults against a neighbouring family, and even sign an act before a *notaire* declaring that 'he recognized the above-mentioned as people of honour and beyond reproach'. Both parties had made complaints, two days apart, and the retraction was only a few days later. Best of all, of course, was to get one's opponent arrested by the *garde*, for this was a public humiliation. He was 'led like a criminal', said one man, who subsequently sought compensation for this 'public insult'. A rebuke from the *commissaire* was already a slap in the face for one's enemy, and even the fact of having him summoned was something of a triumph. There is a note of satisfaction in the words of a *maître tabletier* who had come to the *commissaire* 'to obtain an order from us in order to summon the said Marigny senior, that hardly had the latter received the said order than he came and requested the plaintiff to come down [from his apartment]'.[108]

Whether or not the *commissaire* himself intervened, simply going to him was a powerful weapon in a dispute and sometimes the mere threat was enough to force the adversary to back down. After a quarrel between two *maîtres oiseliers* on the Quai de la Mégisserie one of them turned away saying that he was going to a *commissaire*, but the other's mistress came after him: 'Don't make a complaint, I will expect you for lunch tomorrow and we'll settle this matter.' It didn't always work though: 'her purse was too thin for that,' retorted the wife of a shoemaker.[109]

Once made the threat had to be carried out, but even then the opponent was not always impressed. Receiving word of a complaint against him one man went round to his enemy's house to beat him up. Sometimes the opponent would counter-attack with a complaint of his own, and in this case it was considered an advantage to be first.[110]

A complaint did not necessarily end the dispute. Like the parade of insults, the bravado and boasting, the threats and even violence, it was primarily a gesture for the benefit of the local community. It was not available to everyone: in a dispute between people of significantly different rank – between master and servant, for example – a complaint would usually be made only by the person of higher status, sure of a more favourable hearing from the *commissaire*. In such cases the humbler party was forced to use other methods: *bacchanale*, calumnies, insults, violence (if he or she dared).[111]

On the other hand, women often had recourse to complaints in disputes with men in order to compensate for their physical inferiority. They could hold their own as long as the quarrel remained verbal, but the only way most women could retaliate against men who attacked them was by appealing either to another man

[108] Y10994, 13 Apr., 15 Apr., 2 Oct. Y13290, 12 Aug.
[109] Y15350, 2 Oct., wit. 2. Y12597, 6 Sept., wit. 2.
[110] Y15100, 25 Sept. Y10994, 15 Apr., 17 June, 18 June, 23 June, 5 Oct.
[111] Y10994, 30 Mar., 9 Oct.

Table 2. *Use of violence in disputes, by sex (Grève and Faubourg St Antoine quarters, 1752)*

Use of violence[a] (man/men = M, woman/women = W, both = B)	Violent disputes	Total disputes	% of total which are violent
M against M	67	103	65.0
M against W[b]	25	32	78.1
W against M[b]	9	19	47.4
W against W	16	23	69.6
B against M	2	5	40.0
B against W	6	12	50.0
B against B	3	5	60.0
M against B	9	22	40.9
W against B	0	6	0.0
Total	137	227	*Average* 60.4

By men	101
By women	25
Against men	78
Against women	47

[a] The vast majority of disputes involve only two people. 'Violence' includes any physical contact, but usually means slaps, blows, or kicks.
[b] Excludes disputes between husband and wife.

– husband, brother or son – or to the *commissaire*. Thus, whereas the proportion of complaints of violence in disputes is similar when only men or only women are involved, it is greater when the altercation is between male aggressor and female victim (see table 2).

The use of complaints was also different in quarrels between strangers, which were hardly ever reported until they became violent (see table 3). Public retraction or reparation of insults was not effective if the incident occurred outside one man's own quarter, the most likely place to meet strangers, nor indeed was the damage as great. The memory of the insults was not continually jogged by the presence of the unpunished offender, and a successful plaintiff was in any case unable to parade his or her victory as satisfactorily as if it were over someone who lived locally and whom everyone knew. Where violence was concerned the damage was more quantifiable and monetary compensation more important.

In a number of different respects, therefore, disputes provide clear evidence of community-oriented behaviour governed by unwritten but almost universally observed rules. But if this behaviour constituted an appeal to the local community, what of the response? If we first of all examine the audience reaction to a fight in the street, we find that it too was an actor in the drama. The onlookers were never passive: always attentive, they enjoyed the repartee and the

Table 3. *Disputes in Grève and Faubourg St Antoine quarters, 1752, showing relationships and use of violence*

	No. of disputes		% of total[a]		No. with violence		% with violence[b]	
	Grève	Faub.	Grève	Faub.	Grève	Faub.	Grève	Faub.
Neighbours: total	*40*	*67*	*32.8*	*48.2*	*12*	*29*	30.0	43.3
only	18	42	14.8	30.2	7	14	38.9	33.3
and same trade	5	11	4.1	7.9	3	8	60.0	72.7
and seller–client	1	4	0.8	2.9	0	1	0.0	25.0
principal tenant	16	10	13.1	7.2	2	6	12.5	60.0
Seller–client: total[c]	*13*	*13*	*10.7*	*9.4*	*7*	*6*	53.8	46.2
only	11	9	9.0	6.5	7	5	63.6	55.6
Same trade: total[d]	*13*	*18*	*10.7*	*12.9*	*6*	*13*	46.1	72.2
only	7	6	5.7	4.3	3	4	42.9	66.7
Master–Journeyman	9	11	7.4	7.9	6	4	66.7	36.4
Master–Servant	3	2	2.5	1.4	1	1	33.3	50.0
Acquaintances	8	5	6.6	3.6	5	2	62.5	40.0
Friends (includes former lovers)	7	2	5.7	1.4	5	2	71.4	100.0
Workmates	3	5	2.5	3.6	1	4	33.3	80.0
Strangers	23	11	18.9	7.9	20	9	87.0	81.8
Family: total	*11*	*21*	*9.0*	*15.1*	*5*	*12*	45.5	57.1
siblings	0	1	0.0	0.7	0	1	0.0	100.0
husband–wife	5	8	4.1	5.8	3	5	60.0	62.5
in-laws	6	9	4.9	6.5	2	4	33.3	44.4
parent–child	0	3	0.0	2.2	0	2	0.0	66.7
Total	122	139	100.1	100.0	65	72	53.3[e]	51.8[e]

[a] Percentages are rounded to one decimal place and therefore do not always add up to 100.
[b] Within each category.
[c] Includes neighbours in seller–client relationship.
[d] Includes neighbours with same trade.
[e] Average.

play-acting, bore witness to the humiliation of one side and the victory of the other. The raising of voices, the violence of gestures at once drew a crowd, for people were always ready to drop what they were doing so as to miss nothing of the performance.

By their very presence the crowd encouraged the escalation of the dispute, for neither party would want to give way in front of witnesses. Sometimes, however, the onlookers took a more active role, encouraging or goading. When a woman beat up a girl in the entrance of their house in the rue de Charenton, 'several persons told her to return the blows'. In another case, after a battle of words, a locksmith told one of the participants 'that she shouldn't worry, that she had given her a good seasoning'.[112]

Although the audience would encourage the disputants in this way, they very rarely took sides in the quarrel. There were a limited number of people who were

[112] Y14436, 17 July, wit. 5. Y12597, 19 Sept., wit. 1.

permitted, and in some cases even expected, to join in: members of the same family, servants, workmates and close friends. Neighbours and other onlookers, however, would normally refuse to take one side or the other, a convention which was as we shall see essential to the survival of the community. There were a few situations, however, in which the crowd did take sides, and these are worth looking at more closely because they too reveal something of the nature of the local community.

One such case occurred in May 1752. A *chirurgien* in the rue de Seine had bought two puppies from a *marchand de vin* some blocks away in the rue des Cordeliers, who assured him that they were poodles, but when they turned out to be something else he refused to pay the full price. The *marchand de vin* came to demand the rest of the money but was promptly shown the door, according to a witness, and 'advised by the neighbourhood to go away'.[113] Here the audience came out clearly in favour of the local man, against the outsider.

The same happened in another more violent dispute which took place in the rue du Faubourg St Denis in 1788. A domestic servant was leading a horse to the fountain when he was insulted, so he said, by a group of waggoners. He asked them not to touch the horse, as it was highly strung, so they struck at it with their whips. The owner of the horse then appeared, a man named de Crest de St George whose rank and address are not given but who had just dined with the secretary of the Duc de Tonnere and who was accompanied by the director of the *coches d'eau* (ferries) on the Marne. He rebuked the waggoners and was in turn abused, so he struck one of them with his whip. An hour later, when he came to leave he found a crowd of thirty or forty people armed with sticks waiting for him and on trying to escape in a carriage was attacked and severely injured.[114] This incident was treated by the police as a riot rather than a dispute, but it was essentially the same as the example given above. One of the locals had some quarrel with a person who did not belong to the community – in this case removed both by place of residence and by rank – and the onlookers sided against the outsider.

More common still were what the authorities termed 'rebellions', notably against bailiffs and against the officials of the corporations who came to expel someone or to seize their tools or possessions. When a bailiff came to seize the furniture of a baker in the rue du Faubourg St Jacques the baker ripped up the *procès-verbal*, shouting to his wife to call for help and 'à l'assassin' ('murder') knowing that the neighbours would support him. And this is what happened, for the crowd which gathered looked so hostile that the bailiff felt obliged to withdraw. In December 1752, when the officials of the needlemakers' corporation confiscated the merchandise of a brushmaker whom they found selling pins, the *commissaire* who accompanied them had previous experience of such

---

[113] Y14078, 30 May, wit. 5. See also 24 May.   [114] Y15099, 26 Jan.

events and 'observing that a large populace was assembling in front of the said stall we sent for a company of the *garde*'.[115]

The same sort of reaction was provoked by arbitrary arrests. A *huissier* charged with the capture of a *négociant* was beaten up by 'Dauphiné *crocheteur* and two shop-assistants of the rue Montmartre, three individuals carrying swords ... their servants and others unknown'. The *négociant*, siezed by the *huissier* and ten *archers*, had cried for help, 'à moy bourgeois, c'est pour dettes' (it's for debt), and had been rescued by passers-by while the crowd drove off his assailants with a hail of stones. The subsequent enquiry included nine of the *archers*, but only two other witnesses, one of whom knew of the affair only by hearsay – presumably none of the locals could be persuaded to testify. This is similar to rebellions studied by A. Farge, against the *archers de l'hôpital* who attempted to arrest beggars in the streets.[116]

While such revolts were often more violent than ordinary disputes in which the onlookers took a hand and certainly provoked greater passion because they threatened the very livelihood of the victim, like such disputes they show the local community mobilizing to defend its members against outside interferences. In these particular cases, however, the sense of outrage was so strong that people would sometimes react in exactly the same way even when it was a local who had initiated the action. When the principal tenant of a house near the Porte St Denis had a journeyman joiner evicted and his furniture removed, the joiner's wife

> began to call out and to break several pieces of porcelain, and to shout many insults at the said Delisle and his wife, which caused a large crowd to gather, therefore considering the distant quarter where we are, and that we find ourselves exposed to a rebellion, we sent for the *garde*.

In such cases the victims attracted as much attention as possible, knowing that the crowd would take their side. Not only did the community defend its members against strangers, but it also resisted the interference of outsiders in its internal affairs.[117]

In ordinary disputes the refusal of the onlookers to take sides was equally essential to the survival of the local community. By remaining apparently neutral they confined the dispute to those immediately involved, preventing it from developing into a serious split which might divide the whole neighbourhood, one person's supporters against the other's. Secondly their neutrality enabled the witnesses to act and be accepted as arbiters, preventing the quarrel from going too far and even in some cases resolving it. Intervention in disputes was a vital part of the role of the audience, illustrated in example after example from the papers of the *commissaires*. In the typical dispute discussed above, between the

---

[115] Y13290, 17 Mar. Y15350, 2 Dec.   [116] Y15350, 30 May, 5 June. Farge, 'Mendiant'.
[117] Y15350, 30 Aug. On very similar reactions in London before World War I see E. Ross, 'Survival Networks: Women's Neighbourhood Sharing in London before World War I', *History Workshop Journal*, 15 (Spring 1983), 4–27 (17–18).

wife of a public letter-writer and a pawnbroker, one of the onlookers stepped in to separate them after the first *soufflet*. When a *vendeuse de beurre* (woman who sold butter) came into a wineshop near the Halle to pick a fight with a fishwife the onlookers watched until the two came to blows, but then put an end to the quarrel.[118] They were content to sit and enjoy the performance but intervened to prevent serious injury.

This, indeed, was something expected of them. A witness in an enquiry expressed surprise 'that the worker who was with the said Hugain took no part in the dispute even to separate them'. Being with one of the disputants this man might have been excused for taking sides, but if he chose to remain an observer it was extraordinary that he should not intervene to separate them. The common expectation is expressed by a witness of a dispute outside the central market: one of the two women involved had gone off 'without anyone being obliged to intervene'.[119] The onlookers had a duty to prevent things from going too far.

Intervention was also expected, or at any rate accepted, by the participants themselves. It is very rare to find anyone turning against witnesses or passers-by who helped to break up a fight. A mason, seeing a man hit another over the head with a stick, took the aggressor by the collar, an action which had he been involved himself would have been highly provocative. It was quite often women who intervened: a slanging-match between a joiner's wife and a waggon-maker in the Faubourg St Antoine, culminating in a *soufflet*, was ended by a female neighbour 'who made the said Collet go inside and the wife Morel go on her way'. Women would even separate men who were fighting, with total impunity.[120]

There are, it is true, examples of quite serious injuries being inflicted in fights. Usually these occurred between strangers, often outside the area where either party lived. For example a gardener from the Faubourg St Honoré was quite badly injured in a battle with six or seven bakers from the Faubourg St Antoine, whom he met and quarrelled with outside the Barrière de Bercy. Neither side knew the other, although the gardener was able to find out the names of two of his assailants from a local *traiteur*. The boulevards and other *promenades* around the city attracted groups of young men, frequently flamboyantly dressed and often spoiling for a fight, and these were areas where few people lived and where the force of community presence and public opinion was largely absent.[121]

Occasionally the conventions would be broken and disputes within the community which would normally have resulted in little more than hurt pride could give rise to serious injuries. In most cases these were old quarrels which had perhaps lain dormant for some time, and there is often evidence of premeditation on the part of the aggressor. A farmer was driving through the

[118] Y11239, 30 Apr., 18 Sept., wit. 7.   [119] Y11239, 7 Aug., wit. 1. Y15402, 30 June, wit. 4.
[120] Y14436, 13 Dec., wit. 2. Y10994, 10 July, wit. 3. See Y12597, 19 Sept., wit. 4. Y13760, 21 July.
[121] Y10994, 15 May, 20 May, 1 Dec.

Faubourg St Antoine when two others – a man and his father – emerged from a shop and picked a fight with him, punched him several times and took his hat, then returned with a stick and hit him over the head. One of them later told another neighbour 'that it was a grievance he had had for over two years, and that it had to be done sooner or later'. This sort of violence broke the normal rules of behaviour and was generally condemned by the onlookers, but rarely left them time to take action.[122] In most cases however, the ready intervention of the audience, like the ritual of disputes, served as a safety-net, preventing serious injury. Disputes took place in a public forum, under the eye of the local community, and their gradual, predictable escalation allowed the maximum opportunity for one party to back down or for the audience to intervene.

But the physical confrontation did not necessarily mark the end of the quarrel, nor of the part played by the audience. The aim of public disputes was to make known a grievance and to force the opponent to give satisfaction. This might, indeed, be achieved through the use of threats or calumnies, through a show of force, or in a battle of words or blows from which one or both sides emerged feeling they had come out on top and that honour was satisfied. Very often, however, all this was inconclusive or else the loser went off nursing his or her wounds, but undaunted. Where something concrete was at issue, such as control over a place or object, victory in a public confrontation did not necessarily remove the object of the dispute. An outside initiative was therefore required and frequently this came from the local community. After the rights and wrongs of the issue had been thoroughly discussed, both parties having publicized their version of the story, friends or neighbours would put pressure on one or both to come to an arrangement. The widow of an *ébéniste*, hearing that the wife of another *ébéniste* had beaten up and injured a neighbour's daughter, went to see the aggressor's husband to urge him to make amends. A journeyman goldsmith tried to mediate between a neighbour and a workmate in a long-running dispute over a debt that the latter refused to pay.[123] Within a relatively confined space it was intolerable for a dispute to go on too long, and it was in the interest of the locals to attempt a reconciliation.

If the disputants refused to accept their advances however, a formal complaint was often the result. In this respect the *commissaire* undermined the position of the community, for he provided an alternative authority to which people could appeal. Sometimes it is clear from the attitude of witnesses that they had little sympathy with a complaint, even if they were neutral in the dispute itself. An example is provided by an enquiry into an 'insult' against an embroiderer by a butcher living in the same house. The embroiderer's son having come in one day wearing a new coat, the butcher began taunting him because his father owed fifteen *livres* for meat, then seized the boy and hung him by his collar from a

122 Y14436, 3 Dec., 13 Dec., wit. 1. See also 21 June, 17 July. Y13816, 2 Feb. 1788, wit. 3.
123 Y14436, 17 July. Y15099, 28 Jan., 11 Feb.

meat-hook, saying that he could stay there until the debt was paid. This incident provoked a noisy quarrel between the boy's mother and the butcher's wife, but eventually the money was paid and the butcher's wife apologized on her husband's behalf. The embroiderer, however, persisted with a civil enquiry, but the witnesses were not inclined to support him. Two of them described the interview which ended with the debt being paid; another two said they had been absent that day and knew nothing about it. One had heard the dispute between the two women, but 'had paid it no attention'. Another 'doesn't remember well', adding that when the dispute broke out 'the witness, who does not like interfering in his neighbours' business, went off'.[124] This is quite a contrast from the usual curiosity of the neighbours, who were normally able to recount every detail of a dispute, and who would in this case as in others have discussed the whole affair fully. They were simply anxious to see an end to it.

Recourse to the *commissaire*, therefore, could be an alternative to community arbitration although it was still to some extent dependent on local support: the embroiderer was unlikely to receive any satisfaction without the co-operation of his witnesses. The *commissaire* himself was in an ambiguous situation. Representing an outside authority, he was in certain respects a threat to the local community's control over its members. It had however adapted to his presence, so that his intervention was generally effective only because of its local significance. Paradoxically, complaints served to reinforce people's allegiance to the community.

The presence of the local community is thus reflected in people's behaviour and preoccupations. With their set forms, gestures and language, their strong element of performance, and the publicity which accompanied them, disputes were public expressions of grievance designed to win over the onlookers, appeals to the community to bear witness and to redress the injury done. The innumerable individual battles over minor privileges, points of honour and precedence, which were inevitable in the confined urban environment where the limits of people's domain – both physical and social – were ill-defined, were ultimately struggles for recognition and respect within the local community: for the 'tribute of esteem' which made life comfortable and secure. This whole process reflects a mentality dominated by collective values, as opposed to individualistic ones: the appeal was made to the community as the ultimate arbiter. The onlookers were expected to intervene, not simply pass on their own way, and the combatants were equally expected to respect their authority.

It was an extremely flexible system, displaying the same sort of built-in economy which Y. Castan refers to many times in his study of Languedoc. The public violence of disputes helped to preserve the community by channelling discontent and frustration into forms which the public could control with the minimum of damage to the individuals and to the group. It was flexible, too, in its

[124] Y11239, 1 Jan., 26 Jan.

ability to adapt to outside influences: the *commissaire* himself, an authority who did not belong to the community or come under its control, was nevertheless largely integrated into the system. Recourse to him, while it could be an alternative to collective arbitration, was more often used as a device to win public support and to reinforce someone's position within the community. Ultimately these outside influences, which imposed new patterns of behaviour, were to change the character of the local community, but in late eighteenth-century Paris it remained largely self-regulating, with its own rules and conventions of behaviour. And what forced conformity, above all else, was gossip. It was what made reputation and what made it important. Gossip created a sense of what was normal and of what was expected, helped to instil community values at the same time as it enforced them.

The local community was thus also self-perpetuating. Through their words and actions its members continually reinforced its authority and reaffirmed its values. Local patterns of sociability and the ready familiarity they betray, the regular communion of gossip and the less regular one of disputes, the repeated making and breaking and remaking of alliances and relationships, the constant jostling and realignments: all this was what created the local community. Like living tissue it can be understood only when observed in operation, and not by stopping it and breaking it down into its different parts.

2

The family

The relationship between family and local community has provoked much debate, some writers seeing them as complementary, others stressing the potential conflict between them. The question is rendered particularly difficult by the fact that almost every kinship term is emotionally and morally charged: our very use of language can therefore lead us to make unjustified assumptions about the nature of relationships in the past. A good example of this is the widespread assumption that kinship ties are antithetical to economic ones and that relations within the family are therefore qualitatively different from those outside it.[1] This is not necessarily so, and we must therefore try to see what the family meant to people at the time and what obligations and privileges kinship bestowed. If both local community and family involved obligations and shared interests, what was the difference between the morality of the neighbourhood and that of kin? And, if there was a difference, was it of degree or of kind?[2] Nor must we neglect the likelihood that the obligations involved in kinship varied dramatically within different relationships: those of siblings may not be the same as those of parents and children. Indeed even within these relationships there may be differences according to age, sex, and place in the family, and they may not be entirely reciprocal. There may also be variations in different social, economic, or occupational groups. Ideally, all of these variables should be considered before any generalizations are made about family ties and their role in social organization.

I. GROWING UP IN PARIS: PARENTS AND CHILDREN

For the bulk of the working population of eighteenth-century Paris, the local community was an indispensable aid in bringing up children. Babies affected the mother's working ability even before they were born, and looking after a small child meant time lost from work which might be crucial to the family's survival. The wet-nursing system admittedly helped many working parents over the most

---

[1] E. A. Wrigley, 'Reflections on the History of the Family', *Daedalus*, 106 (1977), 71–85 (81–2).
[2] O. Harris, 'Households and their Boundaries', *History Workshop Journal*, 13 (Spring 1982), 143–52 (145–7).

7. Courtyard, 28 rue Broca (formerly rue de Loursine)

difficult period of infancy, but many of the poor could not afford a wet-nurse.[3] They therefore depended on neighbours and on nearby friends and family: a woman working for a laundrywoman, wife of a labourer in the Faubourg St Marcel, left her three-month-old baby with a neighbour while she went down to

[3] P. Galliano, 'La Mortalité infantile (indigènes et nourrissons) dans la banlieue sud de Paris à la fin du XVIIIe siècle, 1774–1794', *Annales de démographie historique*, 1966, 139–77 (167–70). J. Ganiage, 'Nourrissons parisiens en Beauvaisis', in *Sur la population française au XVIIIe et au XIXe siècle. Hommage à M. Reinhard* (Paris, Société de démographie historique, 1973), pp. 271–90 (277–81). In Lyon, too, the very poor could not afford wet-nurses: Garden, *Lyon*, p. 137.

the river. A midwife practically adopted her god-daughter, child of a domestic servant whose job made looking after a baby virtually impossible.[4]

It is of course true that many men and women worked at home or in a shop where they could supervise a small child to a limited extent. Sometimes too limited: a tragedy occurred in the rue de la Grande Truanderie in March 1752 when the two-year-old son of a fruiterer was crushed by a carriage while his father was busy in the shop. When they went out, parents would often take their small children with them, and women often mention in complaints, as an aggravating factor, that they were carrying a baby or child when attacked.[5]

Even if the parents were present, however, they could not keep children confined in cramped lodgings or workshops. Small boys and girls spent a lot of their early lives playing in the semi-public areas of the stairs or courtyard and in the street outside the house where parents and neighbours could to some extent survey them.[6] They appear in the décor of the documents, in the corners of contemporary engravings: one by Saint Aubin portrays children skipping next to a stall. Chardin's *La Blanchisseus* shows a child sitting next to a big laundry tub, blowing bubbles through a straw. A police *sentence* of 1766 fined a man for burning a mattress in the street outside his house, adding that 'numbers of children, to amuse themselves, gather around these fires, jump over them, and fan the flames up into the air'.[7]

It was in the street and from neighbours, as much as at home, that children picked up values and social skills. Parents provided only one model of adult behaviour, whereas neighbours and passers-by furnished myriad others. Mercier describes how after the Corpus Christi processions

the children make *reposoirs* in the streets. They have candlesticks of wood, chasubles of paper, censers of tin, a canopy of cardboard, a little sun made from pewter. One is the priest, another the sub-deacon. They chant as they carry the host, say the mass, give benediction, and force their comrades to get down on their knees. A little *bedeau* gets furious whenever anyone commits the slightest irreverence.[8]

Every aspect of adult behaviour was observed and imitated, right down to the gestures and expressions used.

As children left infancy behind, the behaviour of boys and girls began to diverge noticeably. Boys quickly became part of neighbourhood bands, feed from the surveillance of their parents. In 1735 the police took action against 'a troop of children of all ages from the Faubourg St Marcel and primarily from the

---

[4] Y13290, 29 June. Y15350, 11 Jan.
[5] Y11239, 6 March, 18 May. Y15402, 30 June. Y12597, 1 Nov.
[6] Y14436, 3 May. Y15350, 23 July. Y15099, 5 June.
[7] Saint Aubin, reproduced in A. Farge, *Vivre dans la rue à Paris au XVIIIe siècle* (Paris, Gallimard/Julliard, 1979), illustration 12. Chardin, *La Blanchisseuse* (1737), Hermitage Museum, reproduced in *Apollo*, vol. 101, no. 160 (June 1975), 436. Sentence de police, 11 Apr. 1766, in Peuchet, vol. 7, p. 452.
[8] Mercier, *Tableau*, vol. 3, p. 80.

Place de l'Estrapade' who were throwing stones over the wall of the Abbey of Ste Geneviève. In 1741 a similar problem arose at St Lazare, where the *commissaire* was told 'that it was all the children [boys?] of the quarter'.[9] The friendships of the courtyard broadened into ones based on a number of streets around which small boys would wander, recruiting as they went, and generally making a nuisance of themselves. 'I amused myself by making crackers', wrote Ménétra. 'I went around with my friends playing tricks on the women who sold apples and others, sliding [the crackers] under them and under their chairs as a joke.'[10] It was at this stage, therefore, that boys growing up in Paris developed a sense of local identity, of belonging to a particular quarter which they would continue to regard as theirs even as they wandered further afield. Ménétra mentions the arrest, after he had himself moved on, of four young men 'who were of the quarter and among my former acquaintances'. Soon after, following some trouble, he had been obliged to 'expatriate myself from the quarter'.[11]

Girls, on the other hand, were much less visible and more likely to stay close to home. When they were very young they presumably played with their brothers in the courtyard or in the street outside the house, but as they grew older people identified them as 'petites filles' (little girls) and they parted company with the boys. Parents – especially mothers – kept a much closer eye on daughters than on sons, and there are no mentions of groups of girls in the streets, mixing with the bands of boys. Their childhood sociability was much more closely tied to the house and the immediate neighbourhood. When the wife of a journeyman founder went out briefly at seven one evening in June 1752, she did not take her nine-year-old daughter with her as she apparently would have done normally, but left the child playing in the house 'because she was playing with other little girls on the said stairs'. A ten-year-old girl disappeared for a whole week and was eventually discovered hiding with another girl, one year her senior, in the same house.[12] Small girls began working – helping their mothers with small chores – while their brothers were still out roaming the streets. They were often sent on messages in the vicinity, but did not compete with the adolescent errand-boys who would run anywhere in the city. Very early, therefore, girls began to observe taboos on their movements and to form ties within a restricted neighbourhood in whose affairs they were as women to play a central role.

Children did not learn simply from observation, however. They also had a role to play in adult affairs. Parents, not wanting to appear the aggressors, could use them to provoke quarrels or to harass enemies in small ways: by throwing stones through the window, shouting abuse, disturbing things left in the courtyard. Extreme youth granted a large measure of impunity, for children below working

---

[9] Sentences de police du Prévôt de Paris, 9 July 1735 and 1 Sept. 1741, AD I 26. See also sentence of 17 May 1726, in AD I 23B. *Enfant* could refer just to males, as in the expression 'enfant de famille'.
[10] B.H.V.P. MS 678, f. 9.   [11] B.H.V.P. MS 678, ff. 55, 58.
[12] Y15099, 5 June. Y14078, 24 Jan.

age were not considered responsible beings. Their actions are mentioned as aggravations but never as the principal cause of a complaint. Their testimony was considered of little value, and people never bothered to take the names of juvenile witnesses even if they were the only ones there.[13]

This irresponsibility allowed children a place, like that of women, as the voice of public opinion. Very sensitive to general feeling, they sometimes expressed publicly what adults were saying in private: after the arrest of a brewer in the rue de Charenton the neighbours began to talk, but it was a local child who said openly that 'the plaintiff was a tart and a whore and that they would have her put in the hospital'. With public opinion behind them their audacity could far surpass that of adults. Hardy noted after the 1755 riots that

the *commissaire* Desormeaux Place Maubert in whose house I lived was obliged to let the rabble enter ... a little boy of ten or twelve had the effrontery to go into his room, into his study, and right to the bottom of his garden to make a more thorough search.[14]

Children learned community norms through participation as well as through observation.

Among working people, therefore, family and community complemented each other in bringing up children. Parents undoubtedly had the primary responsibility, but the neighbours often helped, and in socialization they played a vital role, for the children of working people grew up largely in the public areas of the house and in the street: the centres of community life.

The rearing of children among the affluent was completely different. For the sons and daughters of high-ranking people the local community was completely irrelevant. They were wet-nursed, not in the country because of the risk involved, but at home in the private *hôtel*. Once they were a little older they were confided to servants or to a governess who might give them some preliminary instruction. At a slightly later age the girls were sent to a convent for their education, the boys to a boarding-school (*pension*), where they learned the basic skills which were deemed necessary for people of high rank: reading and writing; for girls, music, needlework, sometimes painting; for boys, fencing, dancing, perhaps languages. When they were older still the sons of the nobility might go to a seminary or to a military school.[15]

Children of less high-ranking but still affluent parents also led very sheltered lives. A household account-book kept by a woman living somewhere in Paris, probably in one of the *faubourgs*, gives a good idea of the sort of upbringing they

[13] Y10994, 30 Aug., 31 Oct. Y11239, 18 May. Y15099, 10 June.
[14] Y10994, 2 July. B.N. Ms. fr. 6682, f. 58, 3 May 1775.
[15] C.M. de Talleyrand, *Mémoires*, ed. Couchoud, 2 vols. (Paris, Plon, 1957), vol. 1, pp. 10, 19. See Lauzun, *Mémoires*, quoted in Talleyrand (ed. Couchoud), vol. 1, p. 15, note 1. Y15402, 24 Apr., 28 June, 5 July. V. Advielle (ed.), *Journal professionnel d'un maître de pension de Paris au XVIIIe siècle* (Pont-l'Evêque, 1868). M. H. Darrow, 'French Noblewomen and the New Domesticity, 1750–1850', *Feminist Studies*, 5 (Spring 1979), 41–65 (44–5).

had. She had two female servants, together with a cook and a gardener. The family ate well: the butcher's bill was one of the major expenses each month, and there are occasional mentions of luxuries such as cakes, coffee, and jam. Every so often she would go to the theatre, and the hire of a carriage cost several *livres* every couple of months. The family had a pet dog for which a collar was bought in 1790. There were two surviving children whose development can be plotted through the monthly expenses. In 1781 there are a cradle, six bonnets, and three babies' vests. In December 1781 216 *livres* – about a third of the usual monthly expenditure – went on portraits of the children. By 1784 toys had become a regular expense. A new baby was sent to be wet-nursed, and the mother appears to have accompanied it, for there are various expenses to do with the journey. Later there are shoes, a corset for the little girl and a suit of clothes for the boy. From 1789 onwards they are referred to as 'Mimi' and 'Coco'. A writing master was employed in that year and in August Coco was given three *livres* 'for the master's *fête*'. At the end of 1789 he was sent to a *pension*, then six months later transferred to another more expensive one in Vendôme: 800 *livres* per year. His mother accompanied him on the journey. Mimi apparently remained at home, for the salary of a tutor was paid periodically. In 1791 a drawing master joined the first, a French grammar was purchased, and the following year – just before the accounts finish – a language master appeared.[16]

This was a household which largely centred on the children: their prominence in the accounts, the expensive portraits of them, the frequent indulgences all suggest that. At this level of society parents surrounded the children with concern, sheltering them from contact with the world outside the family for fear of the physical and moral harm that might come to them in the rough-and-tumble of the street. It is the same attitude that J. Schlumbohm describes among the 'upper bourgeoisie' in Germany around 1800, and it is very much what we see in occasional glimpses of the home life of affluent people in eighteenth-century Paris.[17]

Among well-to-do people, therefore, the local community had little or no part in bringing up children. The rich employed servants, governesses and school-masters to look after and instruct them, and the neighbourhood was shut out beyond the walls of the *hôtel* or the *pension*. For less wealthy but still affluent people concern for the child's physical and moral well-being precluded participation in the rough-and-tumble of street life. Children were sent to be wet-nursed and returned to a life firmly based on the home. When they were older they were despatched to boarding school. Thus the family assumed functions of socialization which among working people were at least partly

[16] B.H.V.P. MS 696.
[17] J. Schlumbohm, '"Traditional" Collectivity and "Modern" Individuality: 'Some Questions and Suggestions for the Historical Study of Socialization. The Examples of the German Lower and Upper Bourgeoisies around 1800', *Social History*, 5 (1980), pp. 89–98.

fulfilled by the neighbourhood and by participation in collective activities. At home and at school the children were encouraged to conform to models and to develop aspirations far removed from the morality of the local community.

Much the same correlation between socio-economic position and the respective roles of family and community can be seen in relations between parents and their grown-up children. For the poorer sections of the population adulthood came early. Teenagers old enough to do serious work were considered to be grown up and were assimilated into the class of unmarried youth which extended until the mid or late twenties. They were described by witnesses in much the same terms as adults: 'un particulier' ('a fellow') saved from drowning in 1788 turned out to be aged fourteen. So too did 'un particulier Savoyard' mentioned in another document. Boys and girls of this age looked on themselves as grown up. A fourteen-year-old working on the *quais* said that he had known a friend 'since his childhood'. They talked in the same way as adults, making judgments of their own. Gone are the baby words and the childish expressions.[18]

The authorities more or less respected this division. Children under eleven were hardly ever sent to prison and rarely appeared in the courts. Those over about twelve, however, were treated by the police in the same way as adults: arrested, interrogated, imprisoned. They in turn rarely made any attempt to use their youth as an extenuating factor.[19]

With adult status came a change in the parent–child relationship, and it was at this stage that the position of sons and of daughters diverged most sharply. For most working people the last economic obligation of parents towards their sons was to provide them with a means of earning a livelihood. In this, as in providing for younger children, most people relied heavily on neighbours, family, and sometimes colleagues. Thus a master gilder was able to apprentice his son to another gilder whom he also knew as a neighbour: this had the advantage that the boy could work for his father as well. The widow of a glass-polisher had a niece among her apprentices, and a fruiterer found a job for a relative of his wife's with an innkeeper not far away. More often than not people seem to have found work for their sons (and often for daughters too) through neighbourhood contacts alone. A *chirurgien* on the Quai Pelletier apprenticed his son to a painter on the Pont Notre Dame; and the daughter of a journeyman painter was apprenticed, at the age of nine, to a nearby seamstress. It is because arrangements of this kind were so common that journeymen, in particular, rarely had the same occupation as their fathers.[20] People looked less for occupational continuity than for a trade of roughly equivalent status, most commonly in the vicinity.

[18] Y15099, 2 June. Y11468, 13 Dec. 1752. Y12596, 3 Jan. Y14436, 17 July.
[19] The youngest defendant before the Grand Criminel in the years examined by P. Petrovitch was eleven: Abbiateci *et al.*, *Criminalité*, p. 235. See also Farge, *Délinquance*, p. 117. Y13728, Lenoir to *commissaires*, 4 Oct., 15 Dec. 1774. Y15100, 30 July. Y12597, 25 Aug. Y12596, 3 Jan.
[20] Y15350, 25 May. Y13290, 24 Sept. Y13819, 17 Mar. 1788. Y15350, 2 Dec. Y11239, 19 June. Y13290, 7 Jan. Daumard and Furet, *Structures*, p. 67.

For this reason master craftsmen and journeymen paid without hesitation for the apprenticeship of their sons, and often daughters too, which meant keeping them into the mid or late teens. For the unskilled poor however, both the means and often the ambition to do this were absent.[21] Poverty made it imperative that children should go to work early and parents were neither able nor willing to make sacrifices for those who were old enough to fend for themselves. It was not something that anyone expected of them.

Once boys started work, or in artisanal circles when the apprenticeship was finished, parents felt quite justified in objecting if they continued to be a burden. A tripe-seller on the Montagne Ste Geneviève, for example, complained to the police that her son refused to work and that he kept coming to her for money. There was no opprobrium attached to throwing out a son who did not work.[22]

For girls the situation was completely different. At all levels of society they normally stayed at home until they married, unless they were apprenticed and lived with their mistress. They remained part of the economic unit of the family. With marriage and the payment of a dowry the responsibility of the parents was transferred to the husband. But if he died or abandoned his wife her family often came to the rescue, if they could: helping her with her finances; perhaps by looking after a child; or even by taking her back to live with them.[23] Low female wages could make this sort of assistance vital. Some parents considered themselves to have a responsibility to help their daughter and son-in-law even in normal circumstances: an *ébéniste* and his wife stated that until times got too hard they had willingly given their only daughter as much as they could – for sixteen years.[24] There is never any trace of such help to a son.

In affluent circles parents could and did continue to accept varying degrees of economic responsibility. Girls did not work and therefore remained totally dependent on their parents until marriage. Young noblemen also relied on their parents for an income. The sons of wealthy non-noble families usually studied, and according to the career for which they were destined would do some form of apprenticeship: in a commercial or banking house, with a *notaire*, or as secretary to an office-holder. Throughout this time they generally remained dependent on their parents.[25] Among better-off merchants it was generally the father who bought a business for his son, or at least acted as guarantor. If he could not afford to buy one he might arrange for the lease of a shop to be transferred to his son. A good example is that of a provincial innkeeper who through his contacts in Paris established his son as a *marchand de vin* in the rue de Bretagne, paying 300 *livres* deposit and guaranteeing payment of the remaining two and a half thousand.

---

21 O. Hufton, *The Poor of Eighteenth-Century France* (Oxford, O.U.P., 1974) pp. 330, 355–67.
22 Y13290, 26 Oct. See Y15117, 17 Jan. 1788. Y15100, 30 July, 28 Aug. Y10994, 11 Aug.
23 Y15350, 21 July. Y13290, 29 Nov. Y10994, 2 Sept. Y11239, 13 June.
24 Y10994, 13 Sept. See Y11239, 27 Oct.
25 Y15115A, 'Lettres et papiers concernant le Sr Thevenot qui a été clerc chez moi', 1777–1778. Y15100, 13 Nov.

When the son fell sick his mother came to help in the shop, and the father reassured the previous tenant that the debt would be paid.[26]

The degree of economic responsibility assumed by parents therefore, in the case of adult children, depended both on means and on the sex of the child. When the position was reversed and it was the parents who needed help in sickness or old age, means were again a determining factor. For well-off people, of course, the problem of looking after aged parents usually did not arise for they were able to provide for themselves. Folk who were reasonably comfortable, and who had room in their lodgings, might take in a widowed parent: a waggoner in the Faubourg St Antoine looked after his paralytic mother, and the mother of a master joiner had a small room in his apartment.[27] Most working people seem to have considered it the duty of children to provide some help, if possible. A libel posted by journeymen locksmiths on the doors of the *jurés* advised one of them 'that he would do better to help his mother who was at the door of a church with a beggar's bowl'.[28] Assistance given to parents would be spontaneously cited. The wife of a *garçon marchand épicier* complained that she was attacked by a neighbour when going to see her mother, whom she often went to help. Ménétra seemed to consider this role to be especially that of a daughter, for while he apparently did little more than go to see his father from time to time he was indignant when his sister had the old man taken to the Hôtel Dieu and later when she refused to pay for his funeral.[29]

It was quite a common practice for those who could afford it to provide a parent with a small pension, perhaps in return for receiving their inheritance early. After the aged mother of a locksmith died suddenly in 1788, he explained that she had lived with him and that her heirs had provided a small pension. In other cases it seems to have been just a matter of filial duty. In 1780 a woman suggested to her son, a *marchand de vin*, 'that you could ... each put in and give me a pension to provide for me'.[30]

Among the poor, however, expectations do not seem to have been so high. Those who were least able to help their sons and daughters, and of whom only the minimum was expected, were also those who were least likely to claim help in their turn. The very poor worked until they died or were too sick to continue. They could not afford to pay for someone to look after them and nor could their children, who were unable and unwilling to give their own time and did not hesitate to say so. A flower-girl said that her sister-in-law's recovery 'seeming almost impossible, we were going to take her to the Hôtel Dieu', a statement confirmed by the sick woman's daughter, wife of a joiner. A mender of old clothes, whose death, according to the police doctor, 'arose from weakness of all her

[26] Y12596, 8 May.   [27] Y15117, 7 Jan. 1789. Y15100, 29 Nov. See also Y10994, 3 Nov.
[28] Y13751, 17 Nov. See Y13290, 4 June.
[29] Y12597, 6 Oct. B.H.V.P. MS 678, ff. 134–5.
[30] Y14436, 23 Dec. Y16003, 8 May 1788. See also Y10994, 11 Apr.

functions and from acute poverty', had gone to the Hôtel Dieu after a sickness lasting several months, although she had family living in the same quarter.[31] It was people in her position, and those completely alone, who had to turn to neighbours.

Other forms of solidarity, however, were not dependent on means. When family honour was at stake parents and children were inseparable. A master embroiderer complained of the slight 'that the Sieur Gaze and his son had made against him in the persons of his two children'. When a student told the twelve-year-old son of a *marchand de vin* 'that when he was a *marchand de vin* he would be a fine rogue', the mother and then the father came to demand satisfaction.[32] Parents and children were seen as a unit and had an interest in taking each other's part, whether they normally got on or not and without enquiring who was in the right. Even before the *commissaire* a man could justify picking a fight by explaining that his father had been insulted. People assumed that parent and child would side together, 'comme de raison' (as of right), one witness said. Likewise their enemies would attack both indiscriminately: a fight with one was a fight with the other.[33]

In the case of daughters this solidarity extended even to action against her husband. If he mistreated her more than they felt a husband should, parents would rapidly intervene, long before friends and neighbours. They would if necessary complain to the *commissaire*, or they would take her in. This was the behaviour expected of them.[34]

Parents were of course expected, from the beginning, to exercise ultimate control over their children, and to continue in this role even after the economic responsibility ceased. Although no longer directly blamed for the actions of their offspring they could be reproached for failing to intervene. One complaint accused a woman of insulting someone 'without her father rebuking her'; and another claimed that a man had attacked a woman with a pitchfork and that his mother had made no effort to intervene. People might still go the parents in order to get satisfaction from the children, like a quarryman who eventually made a formal complaint of theft against the eighteen-year-old son of a laundryman, but only after first approaching the mother.[35]

Whatever their age, the children in turn owed respect and obedience. An unmarried woman, thirty-eight years old, protested that 'she is very far from abandoning the sentiments of respect which a daughter owes to her mother'. Numerous complaints by parents stress the lack of respect on the part of their children, and this was not just rhetoric, for parents did frequently try to exercise their authority if they considered it necessary. A man who arrived to visit his

[31] Y14436, 2 Apr., 9 June.   [32] Y11239, 26 Jan. Y12596, 26 June.
[33] Y11239, 2 Oct. Y14078, 25 Sept. See Y14078, 14 Oct.
[34] Y11239, 12 July. Y10994, 24 Aug. Y15350, 21 July.
[35] Y10994, 16 July, 25 Aug. Y12597, 25 Dec. See Y14436, 6 Feb. Y15099, 28 Jan.

daughter, wife of a master shoemaker, found her quarrelling with a neighbour and told her to go back to her room. When the widow of an *ébéniste* heard her adult grandson, whom she had brought up after the death of his mother, insulting his sister and even 'murmuring' against her, she went out to 'luy en imposer' (rebuke him), and when he refused to listen tried to slap him.[36]

In cases of grave disobedience parents could and did go to the authorities. Many went first to the parish.[37] Some approached the *commissaire*, asking him to use his personal authority. Others made a formal complaint, no doubt in the hope that this would frighten their errant son or daughter into line, for they could not take any real judicial action against their children merely for disobedience. There are other examples of adult children being arrested by the *garde* at the request of their parents. In 1774 and again in 1776 Lenoir found it necessary to ask the *commissaires* not to be so ready to imprison children, whatever their age, at the simple request of the parents.[38]

The most usual course of action taken by parents of all ranks, if they felt that their children had got completely out of control, was to present a petition to the *lieutenant général* himself, asking to have them imprisoned for varying lengths of time. The wife of a *maître perruquier* requested the detention of her twenty-year-old son 'for indolence and laziness'. A master locksmith wanted his step-daughter, aged twenty-one, imprisoned because of her 'debauchery'. There was then a police enquiry in which witnesses – usually neighbours – were questioned. Until about 1750, the parents had to pay for a police enquiry and for detention, and this action was therefore limited to the better-off. But after that date it cost nothing for the poor.[39]

Parents therefore had considerable power over even adult children, which many were quite prepared to use. Yet in practice their ability to exercise control, and indeed the extent to which they attempted to do so, varied considerably. It was limited by the degree of contact; wealthy parents had greater economic control than poor ones; and people of all ranks tried to keep a closer eye on daughters than on sons. The local community, too, could reinforce parental authority, or could in other cases limit it.

Nowhere is this better illustrated than in the marriage process. In theory parents could choose a marriage partner for their children, or at least had a major say. In Paris law their consent was obligatory for sons and daughters under

36 Y11265A, 10 Jan. 1775. Y12597, 6 Sept. Y10994, 3 May, 5 June.
37 Y15114A, *femme* Lebas to *commissaire* Trudon, 10 Feb. 1772. Y11239, 25 Aug. Y13377, petition to *lieutenant général*, n.d. [Jan. 1752].
38 Y10994, 3 May, 11 Aug., 13 Sept. Y12597, 11 Sept. Y13728, Lenoir to *commissaires*, 3 Aug. 1776. Y15117, 14 Jan. 1788. Y15350, 2 July, 2 Dec. Y13728, Lenoir to *commissaires*, 15 Dec. 1774, 3 Aug. 1776.
39 Y15114A, *femme* Lebas to *commissaire* Trudon, 10 Feb. 1772. Y13377, *placet* Ménage, n.d. [c. June 1752]. *Placet* Teil, May 1752. Orléans MS 1422, ff. 965, 995. Y13728, de Sartine to *commissaires*, 8 Jan. 1766, 22 July 1769. Lenoir to *commissaires*, 3 Aug. 1776. Bast. 10028, ff. 670–8, Lenoir to *inspecteurs*, 4 Oct. 1774. Y11963, Albert to *commissaires*, 23 Sept. 1775.

twenty-five. In practice this affected women more than men because they usually married earlier. It was enforced by the clergy, and there is even one example of a priest who refused to marry a woman who was over twenty-five because she did not have her parents' permission.[40] Immigrants had to send home for the necessary papers. Many parents did not consider promises of marriage made by their children as binding on them, and refusal of consent is sometimes mentioned in *déclarations de grossesse* (declarations of pregnancy) (where it could of course provide a convenient way out for the young man).[41]

Parents could thus veto their children's choice of partner even if they were far away. For the families of immigrants, of course, it was limited to a veto. There was no way of supervising whom their son or daughter saw or frequented and it was virtually impossible to arrange a marriage until they came home. The letters of parents reveal their frustration: one mother reproved her son for not writing and added, 'with regard to your sister who is in Paris we do not know if she is dead or alive, it is more than seven or eight years since she put pen to paper to write to us'.[42]

Wealthy people of course had somewhat more control, even if they were in the provinces, as their children long remained economically dependent. Among the upper classes, too, because the society they moved in was fairly restricted there was little escape from family surveillance, even in the big city. The long imprisonments of Mirabeau and de Sade illustrate the continuing power of noble families over adult sons.[43] The legal code also gave better-off parents greater leverage, although not nearly as much as in the south of France. The customary law of Paris forbade parents to advantage any one of their children over the others. They could effectively disinherit all of them to some extent by willing their possessions to someone else, but this power was limited: four-fifths of the wife's dowry, for example, belonged to the children by law. This was nevertheless a means of control which poor people did not have.[44]

At all levels of society parents had, and tried to exercise, greater influence over daughters than over sons. I have already mentioned their greater control over the marriage of daughters because of the earlier female marriage age. Young men were also less likely to be living at home, for as we shall see many male occupations involved considerable mobility. Among working people economic independence came early for sons, and whatever their social position they were

---

[40] Y15384, 23 Sept. 1775. On marriage age, E. Labrousse *et al.*, *Des Derniers Temps de l'âge seigneurial aux préludes de l'âge industriel (1660–1789)*, in E. Labrousse and F. Braudel (eds.), *Histoire économique et sociale de la France*, vol. 2 (Paris, P.U.F., 1970), p. 29. See M. Garden, *Lyon et les Lyonnais au XVIIIe siècle* (Paris, Université de Lyon, 1970), p. 91.

[41] Y14436, 12 May. Y15350, 29 Dec.

[42] Y16003, 8 May 1788, papers of J. Quatremer. Y15384, 23 Sept. 1775.

[43] Y15115A, dossier Thevenot. Talleyrand, *Mémoires*, vol. 1, chs. 1, 2. Orléans, MS 1422, f. 23. Darrow, pp. 46, 50.

[44] *Nouvelle coutume de Paris*, in *Nouveau coutumier général, ou corps des coutumes générales et particulières de France* (Paris, 1724), arts. CCLV, CCLXXII, CCXCII, CCCIII.

expected to range more widely and to be more boisterous and unruly than daughters. Among people of rank the term 'jeunes gens' ('young people') was applied to unmarried young men of good family who frequently went in for irresponsible behaviour. The Chevalier D'Ossun 'indulged in the usual expenses of *jeunes gens*'.[45] The riotous activities of such individuals were more or less tolerated by the police, who were nevertheless considerably less sympathetic towards those of lower rank who played up in similar ways. Even so, in 1752 two domestic servants and a journeyman cooper were released after arguing that their dispute with two young women and their subsequent resistance to the *garde* was 'a simple error of youth which could be pardoned'.[46] Men belonging to this age-group were permitted, and to some extent expected, to display a disorderliness not encouraged in more sober married men.

Daughters on the other hand, if their parents were in Paris, had much less freedom of movement. Some relied on parents for a dowry, and in most social groups they were subject to much stricter supervision. According to Mercier, 'the daughters of the upper bourgeoisie are also, like those of the nobility, [put] into convents; those of the second floor [well-off but of lower rank] never leave their mother and girls in general have absolutely no freedom or informal contact before they marry'.[47] Mercier makes an exception for 'the daughters of the bourgeois, of the simple artisan and of the [common] people, yet in these groups too there are very few examples of unmarried women living away from their families, except for domestic servants and those who had all their relatives in the provinces. Girls of lower rank undoubtedly enjoyed more freedom of movement and much more contact with men. The very fact that they worked gave most women contact with clients or employers. Nevertheless, parents and neighbours usually kept a watchful eye on them. One has only to read Restif de la Bretonne to get an idea of the barriers surrounding young women, an impression largely confirmed by the papers of the *commissaires*.[48] Even where the girl was confided to a guardian he made the same attempt at control: a journeyman shoemaker and his wife, learning that their ward was at the *guingettes* with a man they had forbidden her to see, went looking for her and had both of them arrested.[49]

The way girls were brought up encouraged close ties between mother and daughter, who usually spent more time together than sons did with either parent. This is visible even after marriage, when women tended to live closer to their parents than did men. Conflict with in-laws was often between the

---

45 B.N. J. de F. 1590, f. 94. Y14484, 25 Jan., wit. 1. See Y13728, *syndics* to *commissaire* Chastelus, 16 July 1756.

46 Y15350, 11 Nov., 7 Aug., 1 Nov. Y15100, 8 Dec., 18 Dec.

47 Mercier, *Tableau*, vol. 3, p. 143.

48 Restif de la Bretonne, *Les Nuits de Paris* (Paris, 1788), 14e Nuit, 'Les Méchantes'; 18e Nuit, 'La Marchande de tabac'.

49 Y15350, 2 July. See also Y15350, 1 Dec. Y10994, 15 May.

husband and the wife's family, who were accused of encouraging her to neglect her home.[50]

Partly because women had less freedom of movement it was generally the man who played the active part in courting. He came to see the girl: 'la fréquenter' ('to frequent her') was the set expression, and the regularity of his visits was taken as a gauge of the seriousness of his intentions. 'He came to their place every day because of his courting,' reported a laundrywoman, 'which they thought to be honourable and serious.'[51] The initiative was his and his family may or may not have been aware of what he was up to. The woman's kinfolk, on the other hand, were often in a position to supervise the courting and could reject him if they did not find him suitable. The words of a *porteuse de pain* (woman who carried bread), in this case not living with her parents but with her sister, betray the concerned presence of the family: 'She [the plaintiff] is being courted by one Martin, a waggoner ... and she and her family have so to speak not discouraged him.'[52]

At all levels of society the family had a say, but ideas on who should finally decide varied considerably in different socio-economic groups. Among the nobility and wealthy people in general, where dynastic or economic considerations were very important, arranged marriages were the rule for both sons and daughters.[53] For the bulk of the working population, the size of the city and of its labour-market facilitated relatively greater independence for children. Even here, however, there were important variations. In better-off artisanal and merchant circles parents spoke as if the decision was entirely theirs. A master butcher and his wife described the marriage of their daughter as though she had had no say in the matter of all. The young man had proposed the alliance to them and they had wanted to consider it further, but their hand had been forced by his having had 'the temerity to enter their daughter's bedroom and to climb into her bed while she was asleep'! There is no mention at all of the girl's preference. In the case of Mercier's 'petite bourgeoise' her parents approve the suitor before he even meets the girl and it is the boy's parents who decide whom he will approach.[54] In practice, of course, it is difficult to tell to what extent the children did have a say, for people were often presenting themselves according to a conventional model. But it is true that in this sort of family daughters had relatively little opportunity to find a match for themselves. Sons had greater freedom, and it may be that in their case the role of the family was in practice restricted to a veto.

In humbler circles still the long courtships indicate concern for the couple to

[50] Y12597, 6 Oct. Y15350, 16 Jan., 9 Aug. Y11239, 12 July. Y10994, 15 May, 14 June. Y13419A, 7 May 1789. Garden, *Lyon*, p. 89. See also Phillips, *Family Breakdown*, pp. 188–91.
[51] Y11706, 13 Aug. See Y11239, 16 June. Mercier whimsically describes a similar approach among 'la petite bourgeoisie', *Tableau*, vol. 1, p. 80.
[52] Y15350, 1 Dec.   [53] Mercier, *Tableau*, vol. 3, p. 143. Garden, *Lyon*, pp. 428–30.
[54] Y12596, 11 July. Mercier, *Tableau*, vol. 1, pp. 81–2. See also Y13290, 1 Dec. and Garden, *Lyon*, p. 425.

get to know each other before marriage, and suggest that the choice was largely theirs. 'The plaintiff has been courted for six months, ... although things have still only reached a certain point', explained a *porteuse de pain*. In general courtship seems to have lasted between six months and two years, the time for mature reflection.[55] It was the woman who was courted, rather than her parents, and the way the latter spoke about marriage arrangements, even before the *commissaire* where they might have been tempted to exaggerate their own rule, suggests that they were content to play a secondary part. A *commissionnaire* at the Gobelins said a young man had told him 'that his intention was to marry his [the *commissionnaire's*] daughter'. There is no question here even of requesting permission. A launderer stated that when his son was courting he and his wife 'ont prêté leur main à son mariage' (encouraged his marriage), a more ambiguous description of their role.[56]

Very often the influence of parents in practice depended also on the degree of everyday contact that work permitted them to have with their children. Where they worked together parental influence was potentially greater. There were virtual dynasties in certain corporations and in some geographically restricted trades: the workers of the *manufacture des glaces* and of the Gobelins; the porters at the central market, the women in the markets; fishermen on the Seine.[57] They had common interests and use of time, common acquaintances and associates, belonged to the same trade community where the hierarchy of seniority often reinforced that of family. If they did not work together, of course, it was that much more difficult for parents to know what their children were doing. 'Being engaged in trade,' wrote one mother on discovering that her daughter was pregnant, 'I am unable to stay at home ... and unknown to me they have maintained their liaison until this very day.'[58]

Working parents therefore relied on neighbours to keep an eye on their children and neighbourly scrutiny, particularly of women, could be far more efficient and continuous than that of parents. In fact neighbours, friends and colleagues played an important part in the marriage process, complementing and even replacing the family. For a start their role in socialization allowed them to help determine what young people looked for in a marriage partner (generally the same things parents looked for). They also helped to determine the timing of marriage. Once a young man reached a certain age and had a trade, hints from

[55] Y15350, 1 Dec. See Y11239, 25 July. Y13290, 1 Dec. Y11706, 13 Aug.

[56] Y11706, 13 Aug. Y10994, 15 May. See Y10994, 3 May.

[57] Daumard and Furet, *Structures*, pp. 60–72. *Almanach Royal*, 1788, p. 11, 'Avis de l'éditeur'. A. Gobert, 'Le District des Enfants trouvés au faubourg St Antoine en 1789', *La Révolution française*, new series 6 (1936), 134–48; 15 (1938), 260–81 (no. 15, p. 270). H. Burstin, 'Le Faubourg St Marcel à l'époque révolutionnaire: structure économique et composition sociale', unpub. doctoral thesis, Université de Paris I, 1977, pp. 280–96. S. Kaplan, 'Réflexions', p. 30. On *marchandes*, Y15100, 11 Nov., Y12596, 20 Jan., 15 Mar., 30 Mar. On fishermen, Y15099, 30 May, Y15100, 10 Sept.

[58] Y15114A, *femme* Lebas to *commissaire* Trudon, 10 Feb. 1772. Y11705, 26 June.

those around him and the example of friends made him think about settling down. Ménétra's memoirs illustrate this:

I invite old Ferand, a journeyman at Vilmont's ... [he] begins to lecture me, saying that he could not understand why a young man like me who knew my trade, who had seen something of life, and who furthermore had a Paris master's ticket, did not seek to settle down ('faire une fin'), that he knew a likeable, well-behaved girl with some property ... I think it was the first time that I seriously thought of stepping into the bonds of Hymen.[59]

For women there was even greater pressure to marry, although of a different kind. A girl's whole life was a preparation for marriage: she learned a trade which, while ensuring her livelihood until she married, would enable her to supplement her husband's income. She learned how to run a household. Those who had no family, who came from the provinces, or whose parents were poor sought to save enough for a dowry and a trousseau. They spent fourteen to sixteen years working towards marriage and placed their hopes for a relatively comfortable existence in finding, if not a wealthy husband, at least a reliable one.[60]

Social pressure increased as the girl got older. It came partly from parents afraid of the economic burden of an unmarried daughter or simply concerned for her well-being if they died.[61] There was also pressure from other people, especially women, on parents and daughter alike. 'If Fanchon the [plaintiff's] eldest daughter was not yet married it was not surprising because she was a slut', screamed a baker-woman amid a storm of other insults against a rival. The neighbours noted the age of the girl and who came to visit. Courting was a very public affair, and a marriage proposal cause for celebration. The widow of an *ébéniste* in the Faubourg St Antoine spoke of 'a meal she gave on the occasion of some marriage proposals made for her grand-daughter'. The proceedings were followed with interest by all. 'She [the witness] saw the said Bouret and the Arnoult girl whom he was then courting take one of the widow Arnoult's dresses to the wife of Copin, a seamstress, to have it altered to fit the said Arnoult girl, for her wedding.'[62] The girl was well aware of this interest and of the envy of other unmarried girls who aspired to her status. A woman whose suitor abandoned her, on the other hand, was open to ridicule and persecution. This might happen even if it was she who had refused him: 'When she passed in front of him when he was accompanied by other journeymen shoemakers he made them all look at her and call her, making her an object of ridicule.'[63]

Neighbours might even play a part in the choice of partner. They could obviously ridicule a choice of which they disapproved. But they would also, as in the case of Ménétra, suggest suitable candidates. The twenty-nine-year-old daughter of a master carriage-maker living in the Faubourg St Germain was

[59] B.H.V.P. MS 678, f. 116.   [60] Y15350, 19 June. Hufton, 'Family Economy', p. 7.
[61] Y14078, 10 Nov., 19 Nov. Y10994, 15 May. Cf. B.H.V.P. MS 678, f. 76.
[62] Y11239, 16 May. Y10994, 3 May, 19 Jan.   [63] Y13819, 22 Sept. 1788. See also 11 Mar. 1788.

invited to dinner by a neighbouring master tailor, together with her father, sister, and a female cousin, 'to arrange an interview for her marriage'.[64]

For most people therefore, marriage was not just a matter for parents and children. The local community, through gossip and direct comment, pushed young people towards marriage and put pressure on their family as well. Neighbours and friends vetted prospective partners, although there was no longer any organized control of the marriage market such as had traditionally been exercised by youth groups. As we shall see, the locals also played an important role in forming the aspirations and expectations of young people by their judgments on married behaviour.

In the choice of marriage partner, therefore, as in the rearing of children, the roles of family and local community varied according to social, familial, and to some extent occupational, situation. People who were poor or without family, or who because of their work were unable to look after dependent relatives, could often count on neighbours for help. All along the line the local community could back up parental authority, particularly over daughters, through the vigilance of neighbours and the social pressure of gossip. For most Parisians, therefore, family and community were in harmony, rather than rivals for the allegiance of the individual.

II. MARRIAGE AND SEX ROLES

The social division between those for whom family and community were complementary, and those in whose lives the neighbourhood had little part, is clearer still if we look at relations within the conjugal unit. An examination of sex roles within marriage – both the idealized stereotypes and the real division of function – enables us further to explore the character and the social limits of the local community. For the respective roles and aspirations of men and women in different social and occupational groups helped to determine the nature and extent of their participation in neighbourhood life.

The elite stereotype of the perfect wife is abundantly represented in eighteenth-century French literature, and recurs in the papers of the *commissaires*. It is the model of the *femme de qualité* (lady of quality), and is admirably defined by Mercier, whose allegiance is never in doubt:

She bears on her brow the imprint of sweetness and of kindness. There is nothing more . ingenuous, more naive and more modest; her eyes fear to encounter the glances that her beauty attracts. When she speaks, a delightful blush is on her cheek; and such timidity is a new charm, for I am convinced that it is born of modesty and not of mediocre wit. The misfortunes of humanity find her receptive, and she could not hear them recounted without feeling almost indisposed. How sweet it is to see her shedding tears over the

[64] Y14078, 10 Nov.

8. The 'quality' ideal: *L'Exemple des mères* by Jeaurat (*Photo. Bibliothèque Nationale*)

misfortunes of others! There was never a soul more sensitive, more sweet, more loving; she will live, she will breathe for me alone.[65]

---

[65] Mercier, *Tableau*, vol. I, pp. 84–5. The earliest examples of the expression *gens de qualité* or *homme de qualité* given by the Littré and Robert dictionaries date from the seventeenth century. See also L. Stone, *The Family, Sex and Marriage in England, 1500–1800* (London, Weidenfeld and Nicolson, 1977), p. 257. The *Encyclopédie* gives *qualité* as a synonym for *talent* (art. 'Qualité'). See Talleyrand, *Mémoires*, ed. Couchoud, vol. I, p. 40, note 4. Audigier, *La Maison réglée* (1692) describes how 'la maison d'un grand seigneur' should be run, then 'la maison d'une Dame de qualité'. Quoted in M. Botlan, 'Domesticité et domestiques à Paris dans la crise (1770–1790)', unpublished thesis, Ecole des Chartes, 1976, p. 83.

This is the model which the widow of a *contrôleur des messageries* (official of the postal service) was appealing to when she described 'the innocence and the purity of heart ... the goodness and the modesty ... the trusting nature and ... the innocence of her daughter'. The *femme de qualité* went only 'dans des endroits décents' (to decent places); she kept a dignified and lady-like posture. She feigned to know nothing of sex and had no sexual appetites; she endorsed only 'sentiments of virtue and decency'.[66] Such a woman was also delicate, easily alarmed by cruelty or violence: 'elle a affecté de ne point sortir de chez elle par la sensibilité et la frayeur extrême qu'elle éprouve en voyant les querelles' (she declined to venture out because of her sensitivity and the extreme fright she suffers in witnessing quarrels). The wife of a *sous-directeur des fermes* (sub-director of the *fermes*) 'saw Master Bonnomet, *notaire*, chasing his dogs on the stairs with a whip, this violence ... caused Madame Conty ... to suffer a revolution which required her *chirurgien* to be summoned; he found her to be in danger for several days'. For women of superior rank, states the *Encyclopédie*, 'insults are just as hurtful as are blows for ordinary people'.[67]

As a wife, as Mercier intimated, such a woman was gentle, patient and thoughtful, trying to foresee her husband's every whim. This is the portrait which women seeking separation often painted of themselves: 'The plaintiff thought that her patience would recall her husband to his duty'; 'she is not only devoted to her household, but also to anticipating everything which might please her husband'. She took care of the household, directed the servants, looked after the children. She was always there when her husband came home: her role was to provide for him a haven from the cares of the world.[68]

Corresponding to this ideal was that of the *honnête homme*, not the egocentric hero of Cornelian tragedy, but the new man of the *Encyclopédie*:

An *honnête homme* has often to say to himself, I renounce that which gives me most pleasure, but which would cause pain to my friend ... *Honnête* ... is the character of men whom one esteems ... and who ... maintain in the nation the spirit of justice, good morality, decency, finally the taste and the tact of good manners.[69]

Such a man was restrained and polite in language and behaviour. He displayed 'great delicacy and extreme kindness', considered the feelings of others and especially of ladies, towards whom he behaved with respect. 'My respects to

[66] Y15402, 16 Apr., 28 June, 5 July.
[67] Y15402, 31 Dec. Y15682, 20 Oct. 1788. *Encyclopédie*, art. 'Séparation'.
[68] Y15099, 16 Mar. Y15350, 25 July. See Y13290, 10 Apr. Mercier, *Tableau*, vol. 1, pp. 169–70.
[69] *Encyclopédie*, art. 'Honnête'. Compare the use of *honnêtes gens* by the Thermidoreans and by the *sans-culotte* militants. Cf. *intendant* of *généralité* of Caen to *contrôleur général*, 7 Apr. 1760: 'a rich man, not an ennobled gentleman, but what is commonly called an *honneste homme* and consorting with the nobility of the region'. Quoted in A. Davis, 'The Origins of the French Peasant Revolution of 1789,' *History*, 49 (1964), 24–41 (p. 26). See also R. Darnton, *The Great Cat Massacre* (London, Allen Lane, 1984), p. 139.

Madame', wrote one *commissaire* to another, even though they used the informal *tu* to each other.[70]

But true *honnêteté*, the *Encyclopédie* insists, went beyond the observance of forms: 'It is based above all on the interior feelings of the soul ... *Politesse* cannot be learned without a natural predisposition, which in truth must be perfected by education and by experience of the world.' The *honnête homme* was therefore naturally sensitive, compassionate, and at the same time rational: qualities which were never in opposition to each other. Like Mercier's philosopher he objected to unnecessary violence or cruelty, was easily moved by benevolence.[71]

As a husband he treated his wife with gentleness, respect and patience. 'He made it a duty to display the consideration and the gentleness which he owed his wife', said one man. His role was to protect her from the crassness of the world, to safeguard her modesty and her innocence. 'We must ensure', says Mercier of obscene graffiti on the walls, 'that the eyes of our wives and daughters ... do not encounter such images.' A good husband should set her an example of good morals and conduct, be faithful to her. If she strayed, he should correct her gently. J-L. Flandrin suggests that 'l'homme galant' would never demand sex – 'la dette conjugale' – when she did not feel like it.[72]

For most of the working population, needless to say, the models were quite different. That of the ideal wife is summed up by a journeyman shoemaker testifying in support of a request for separation: 'She is a very thrifty, virtuous woman who is very devoted to her work, and who enjoys the highest reputation both in the house and in the quarter.' 'He has always found her trying to placate her said husband by working every day and maintaining her household as best she could', added another witness.[73] There is no mention here of timidity or delicacy, of soft-heartedness or modesty. Hard work, however, was essential; and thrift, for she looked after the household. Equally vital was a good reputation as a 'virtuous and steady woman' which as the last example suggests meant sexual fidelity. She was expected to be very restrained in her relations with men other than her husband. Above all the ideal wife should stand by her husband, whatever his failings. Women who complained to the police about their husbands were always careful to point out that they only did so under the most extreme provocation, having waited as long as they could and exhausted every other means to reform them.[74]

The ideal husband whom this model woman would look for was one who like her enjoyed a good reputation. This meant essentially that he was a good worker,

[70] Y15402, 16 Apr. Y11267A, *commissaire* Dorival to *commissaire* Thierry, 2 May 1776.
[71] *Encyclopédie*, art. 'Honnêteté', 'Politesse'. Mercier, *Tableau*, vol. 3, pp. 268, 273.
[72] Y13419A, 7 May 1789. Mercier, *Tableau*, vol. 1, p. 109. Y15117, 3 Oct. 1788. J-L. Flandrin, *Familles, parenté, maison, sexualité dans l'ancienne société* (Paris, Hachette, 1976), p. 212. Cf. Y13377, Maupassant, *greffier des enquêtes*, to *commissaire* Grimperel, 16 June 1752.
[73] Y15100, 11 Dec.
[74] Y15100, 17 Oct. Y15402, 27 Oct. See Y15100, 16 Jan. and Y13816, 4 Feb.

reliable, providing her with money to run the household. A nail-maker, in a complaint against his wife, claimed that 'he brings home his earnings to her regularly to provide for the household', and pointed to 'the steadiness of his conduct'. It meant that he was not violent or spendthrift – above all not 'débauché', a word which in eighteenth-century Paris denoted both having abandoned work and, as in more modern usage, getting drunk, spending money wildly, chasing women.[75]

The extent to which these models appealed and the degree to which people strove to conform to one or the other depended very much upon their way of life and their place in society. The ideal of the *femme de qualité* and its male equivalent originated among a well-off middle section of society in search of an identity, which saw its own worth as lying in its moral qualities, as opposed to birth or inherited rank. Moral superiority, brought out by breeding, made it the equal of any and placed it above the rabble. This assumed a certain level of wealth: the woman did not have to work, and could therefore devote herself entirely to her home and to her husband's pleasure. She had the sort of home from which the outside world could be excluded: a comfortable apartment or *hôtel* designed to be lived in and not simply slept in. And because she did not have to work she could allow herself a delicacy of health and of feeling which those who had to spend much of their lives in the street and in the market-place could simply not afford. She had servants to do the household chores and to cushion her against the outside world. The model of the gentleman also implied the existence of a certain choice: he could largely avoid the things he found distasteful. His form of prudery, like the woman's, required a home in which privacy was possible, and like hers involved a withdrawal from the life of the street.

In its most perfect form, therefore, the model of quality is found among the wealthy middle classes: *négociants* and bankers, 'bourgeois', royal and municipal office-holders, magistrates and lawyers. It is the wife of a 'bourgeois de Paris' who faints with fright when her husband threatens her; a *commissaire au Châtelet* who complains indignantly of the conduct of his cook, whose insults, notably that of *drôlesse* (hussy), had deeply hurt his wife. A complaint about the language of a coachman was made by a *greffier des enquêtes* and it is an 'écuyer, notaire au Châtelet' who says of the vulgar insults of a saddler that 'la qualité ne lui permet pas de les détailler' (his position does not permit him to repeat them).[76] By the late eighteenth century however, these values had been adopted by a range of social groups. Among the nobility they appear to have been well established. A convent education imposed equally on the daughters of nobles and of high-ranking commoners the forms of behaviour considered necessary in young ladies

---

[75] Y10994, 14 Mar. Y13290, 9 July, 17 July. Y10994, 24 Aug., 13 Sept.
[76] Y14436, 18 Dec. Y14994, 3 July 1775. Y13377, letter to *commissaire*, 16 June 1752.

of quality. Extensive contact made for the acceptance of many of the same values by the nobility and by the upper ranks of the middle classes.[77]

For the poor, of course, the middle-class model had little appeal. They had little privacy, and were forced to spend much of their time in the street or at work where feminine delicacy and timidity were a handicap, male gallantry meaningless.

Nevertheless, there were those in between, notably in fairly affluent artisanal and shopkeeping circles, who did belong to and participate in the life of the local community but who because of their social aspirations found the ideal of *qualité* strongly appealing. It was not entirely compatible with their life-style: the woman usually had to work, and their behaviour, as described by witnesses and sometimes even by themselves, did not always conform to it. Before the *commissaire*, however, where people tried to present themselves as they wished to be seen, their pretensions are clear. Thus we find the wife of a master baker, not normally a particularly genteel occupation, who having been insulted and threatened by her former journeyman was 'so greatly affected that it left her senseless'. The same 'sensitivity' occasionally appears at an even humbler level. In 1788 the wife of a journeyman nail-maker, seeing a fight in the street, 'was so greatly frightened by it that she withdrew from the window'. She was apparently not too frightened to have another look, however, as she was able to describe what happened.[78]

An appeal to the 'quality' model is also visible among some domestic servants, particularly those of high-ranking people. The chambermaid of the Baudry girls, for example, had seen their governess take liberties with them that 'modesty does not allow her to recount'. Another female servant, insulted in the street, 'returned home all a-tremble and with great difficulty'.[79]

The two ideals are thus found side by side, and this, too, was a form of social adaptation. As we shall see, many domestic servants and the more affluent artisanal and shopkeeping groups were outside or moving away from the local community.[80] They had frequent contact with people outside it, both socially and geographically, and were therefore less parochial, more open to new influences. Many were relatively well-off, often upwardly mobile, their life-style better adapted to the ideal of quality, for they could afford the necessary education and more comfortable domestic trimmings. They were thus in an ambiguous position and it was in these groups that the model of *qualité* made headway during the second half of the eighteenth century. The evolution was slow and uneven, depending on the strength of the local community and on each person's degree of implantation, individual experience and personality.

---

[77] N. Elias, *The Civilizing Process*, 2 vols. (London, Blackwell, 1978–82), vol. 1, ch. 2, and vol. 2, pp. 300–19.
[78] Y10994, 16 Oct. Y13290, 23 Sept.   [79] Y15402, 5 July. Y15350, 14 Nov.
[80] See below, chapter 3.

I have, in order to contrast the two models, stressed the differences between them. But certain other elements were common in both. The most obvious one is the authority of the husband. It was the message of the moralists and of the church; it was the expectation of the law, which did not allow married women to dispose of their possessions or to bring a court action without their husband's permission. The police backed up the husband's authority by imprisoning his wife at his request, in theory after enquiries of their own.[81] At all levels of society the ideal wife was expected to obey her husband, just as he had the responsibility of correcting her: 'their husbands did not rebuke them', complained the wife of a *chirurgien*, insulted by three bakers' wives. A saddle-maker protested that 'despite his prohibition' his wife continued to frequent the neighbours.[82]

A second element common to both models of marital behaviour and which helped to maintain male dominance, at least in public, was the necessity for conjugal unity. In their relations with each other couples offered the world a united front. Y. Castan mentions a similar attitude in towns in Languedoc: between husband and wife 'on maintient un cérémonial courtois qui distrait la malveillance des voisins' (there existed a ceremonious courtesy which defeated the ill-will of the neighbours). Sometimes it worked: 'he had heard nothing out of the ordinary in their apartment. On the contrary they seemed to live together in perfect unity', said one principal tenant.[83] More often the neighbours were not deceived. Thin walls, narrow streets, and crowded houses made it difficult to keep anything a secret. But it was none the less frowned on to wash one's dirty linen in public.

This was a feeling common to a range of social groups. In Mercier's couple, although the wife spends 'whole weeks at home without speaking to him or seeing him', nevertheless 'in general company she addresses her husband and smiles at him'. Domestic quarrels usually took place in the relative privacy of the room or apartment and few came before the *commissaire*. When they did, mostly in cases of severe mistreatment of the wife, any public insults or beatings were specifically evoked. Going to the *commissaire* meant unwanted publicity and was a last resort. 'In order to avoid scandal', the wife of a master roofer said, she had tried to hide the fact that her husband beat her, even from her family.[84] Complaints of this nature were often made to a *commissaire* in another quarter of the city and the police were sensitive to this, for *enquêtes en séparation* were usually done by a *commissaire* outside the area where the couple lived.[85]

Separation was frowned on unless there was a very good reason. One woman complained that a water-carrier had slapped her as she was walking through the

[81] Flandrin, *Familles*, p. 126. P. Guyot, *Répertoire universel et raisonné de jurisprudence civile, criminelle, canonique et bénéficiale*, 81 vols. (Paris, 1775–86), vol. 24, p. 472. Y13728, Lenoir to *commissaires*, 3 Aug. 1776.

[82] Y10994, 6 Nov., 29 June.   [83] Y. Castan, *Honnêteté*, p. 169. Y15350, 18 Aug.

[84] Mercier, *Tableau*, vol. 1, p. 86. Y14436, 18 Dec. Y15402, 27 Oct. Y15350, 25 July.

[85] Y12596, 11 July. Y15350, 20 July.

Halle: 'Take that you slut, whore, why don't you live with your husband.' Sympathetic witnesses would assure the *commissaire* that the woman 'had left her husband solely on account of his debauchery', and family, friends and neighbours would do all they could to bring about a reconciliation.[86]

In disputes with outsiders – family quarrels were different – solidarity was the rule. Husband and wife invariably made common cause and were expected to do so. When, for example, a woman tried to stop the co-owner of the house from removing a door and was physically attacked, other neighbours told her husband who came to her rescue.[87] Husbands would also intervene in disputes between women. The day after a fight between a fishwife and a *marchande de beurre*, the latter's husband appeared in the market place: 'So it's you who's talking about my wife you slut', and he punched the fishwife several times while his wife shouted triumphant insults from behind. Women would threaten to send their husbands to avenge them, a threat quite often executed. If, A. Farge has shown, quarrels between women were sometimes considered unworthy of male attention, on occasion men would make them their own.[88] Similarly women would intervene in their husbands' disputes and were expected to do so. Husband and wife were seen as a unit: an attack on one was an attack on the other, and if one offended the other was held to blame as well. Their reputations were inseparable, their unity a sign of good morals.[89]

Between man and wife, therefore, there existed a special relationship characterized by solidarity against the outside world. Unlike ordinary social relations it was private and self-contained, not normally open to public scrutiny and judgment. Neighbours usually knew what was going on but would not normally intervene, even in cases where, had those involved not been husband and wife, people would have stepped in quickly. There was a different yardstick for measuring family behaviour. When a *marchand de vin* beat with a cane both his wife and his *garçon* claiming to have caught him kissing her, one of the witnesses stated that 'the said Sieur Garnier is very hot-tempered and brutal, even jealous, and that it is not the first time that he has beaten his *garçon*'. Violence against an employee was condemned where the same attack on a wife was not.[90] It may not have been condoned, but it lay outside the jurisdiction of the local community.

Only if one of the partners seriously departed from the norms of marital behaviour would neighbours intervene. We have seen that community pressure encouraged mutual solidarity; and friends and neighbours would likewise, as R.

[86] Y10994, 2 Sept. Y15402, 28 Feb. Y15350, 10 July.
[87] Y10994, 27 Oct. See also 6 Nov., 31 Oct.
[88] Y11239, 8 Sept., 18 Sept. Y10994, 10 July. Y13819, 14 July 1788. Farge, *Vivre dans la rue*, pp. 138–9.
[89] Y15402, 14 May. Y15100, 10 Nov. Y15402, 23 Oct. Y15350, 18 May. Y10994, 6 Dec., 29 Apr. Y11239, 30 Apr.
[90] Y15350, 28 Sept.

Phillips has shown in Rouen, condemn a woman whose behaviour threatened to bring her husband into disrepute, or a man who abandoned or severely mistreated his wife. They spoke out against one man who beat his wife 'without cause', and 'because she refused to give him money to drink and amuse himself'. On at least one occasion the porter of the house had intercepted her on the way home, knowing that her husband was waiting for her, and had hidden her until he had gone.[91]

The point at which people would intervene and the level of violence they considered acceptable varied. Among people of higher rank where the ideal of the *femme de qualité* was firmly entrenched, almost any violence was strongly condemned by witnesses.[92] Among most of the population however, occasional blows or even beatings, for what was considered a good reason, were generally accepted. After a labourer was informed by a malicious neighbour that his wife had borrowed money and often went out on the town witnesses heard him beating her, but nowhere in their testimony is there a trace of condemnation, either of his having believed the calumny or of his violence.[93]

Even where intervention was considered necessary, however, people still preferred it to be done by another member of the family. For example after a man beat his wife 'to the point of outraging the neighbourhood', three of the neighbours complained to her father. The local community would intervene in conjugal relations only as a last resort.[94]

These universally accepted ideals of male dominance and of conjugal unity did not in practice preclude women from enjoying considerable autonomy in their own domain. In fact men and women fulfilled quite different roles and often led largely separate lives. This in turn gave them different functions within the local community.

At the heart of the female domain lay the home. It was the wife who saw to all the household chores. In the case of Marie Lorlot, wife of André Cautat, *écuyer*, this was even specified in the marriage contract.[95] The same applied to working women, who were expected to do the cleaning and to get the meals. The washing was, even in the case of quite poor people, done by a laundrywoman, the mending by a *ravaudeuse*, because the wife's time was better used for paid work. But she was nevertheless the one who saw that it was done. If a man's wife got sick he relied heavily on female relatives and neighbours. If she died he would usually remarry very quickly, and might in the meantime leave his belongings

---

91 *Family Breakdown*, esp. pp. 180–7, 109–13. Y15100, 11 Dec.
92 Y15402, 18 Dec., 27 Oct., 1 July. Y15099, 16 Mar.
93 Y13290, 9 July, 17 July. Y10994, 21 July.
94 Y10994, 24 Aug. On very similar conventions in East London see E. Ross, '"Fierce Questions and Taunts": Married Life in Working-class London, 1870–1914', *Feminist Studies*, 8 (1982), 575–602 (pp. 591–2).
95 Y12597, 30 Sept. See Y15402, 1 July.

and his children with his mother-in-law and go to live with his own parents. Or he might abandon them altogether.[96]

As O. Hufton has pointed out, for the working woman these chores were far from being a central preoccupation. They nevertheless tied her to the home: she usually returned first to prepare the midday or the evening meal, while her husband could go to the wineshop for a drink.[97] In cases of theft it is almost always the wife who discovers the door unlocked or open, the chest of drawers rifled. Furthermore, while the husband is sometimes not quite sure exactly what has been taken, she always knows down to the last detail: a theft represented an unexpected hole in her carefully husbanded resources.[98]

A great many female occupations were also based on the home: seamstresses and embroiderers, laundresses, those who ironed and spun. Numerous manufacturing industries used female labour on a piece-work basis.[99] There are also many examples of women employed by the day who, when they were not thus occupied, did sewing or embroidery at home for clients of their own.[100]

The home also tended to be more important in a woman's social life than in a man's. Because she spent more time there she chatted with the neighbours, especially with other women. A common practice was to leave the door open, and those coming up or down the stairs, if they knew her, would stop for a talk or at least say *bonjour*. Or she might take her work to a neighbour's room. Her evenings would often be spent either in her room with the neighbours, or with friends at their home, where they would talk, play cards, perhaps work. W. Cobbett, writing in 1829, mentioned the habit of French husbands of spending their evenings in cafés, leaving their wives at home, and this is confirmed both by numerous mentions of men drinking with their friends in wineshops, where the busiest time of day was normally between seven and ten in the evening, and by occasional glimpses of wives waiting for their husbands to return.[101]

A woman of higher rank might spend even more of her time at home. She did not go out to work, as her husband usually did, and her whole existence revolved around the apartment or the *hôtel*. Friends and family would be invited there for meals and *soirées*. When she went out it was to visit relatives or friends at their homes, perhaps for a promenade with them in a private garden, or to church.

96 Hufton, 'Family Economy', pp. 11, 18. Y12597, 19 Sept. Y10994, 18 Mar. Garden, *Lyon*, pp. 92–3.
97 Hufton, 'Family Economy', p. 11. Y15099, 1 May. Y11705, 23 June. Y15100, 29 Sept., 4 Oct.
98 Y14078, 15 June. Y15099, 17 May. Cf. Y13290, 5 Sept. Y15099, 12 Apr.
99 Andrews, 'Political Elites', pp. 313–35. Y12597, 15 Nov. Y12596, 7 Apr. R. Monnier, 'L'Evolution de l'industrie et le travail des femmes à Paris sous l'Empire', *Bulletin d'histoire économique et sociale de la Révolution française*, 1979, 47–60.
100 Y10994, 29 July. Y15350, 22 Nov. Y10994, 20 June. Y11239, 16 Feb. Y13290, 30 Sept. Y12597, 6 Sept. Y14078, 23 Dec.
101 Y12597, 6 Sept. Y14078, 21 Aug. Y13290, 14 Aug. Y14436, 10 May. Y15099, 21 Feb., 29 Mar. Y13819, 22 Sept. 1788. W. Cobbett, *Advice to Young Men* (1829), pp. 145–6, cited in Stone, *Family*, p. 403. Y15117, 6 June 1790. Y10994, 6 Dec. See Garden, *Lyon*, p. 432. Y11239, 18 May.

Occasionally she might participate in a *partie de campagne* (outing to the country) with both male and female friends, but normally her home was the centre of her activities.[102]

Husbands and wives of rank tended to lead separate social lives. In Mercier's somewhat exaggerated portrait of the young married woman he has her, six months after her marriage, frequenting her own circle of friends, sleeping in a separate apartment, and hardly seeing her husband at all. That there may be some truth in this description is suggested by La Rochefoucauld's surprise at the behaviour of couples in English high society:

Husband and wife are always together, they keep the same society . . . they make all their visits together. It would be more ridiculous in England to do otherwise than in Paris to be always accompanied by your wife.[103]

Upper-class women in Paris therefore enjoyed a considerable degree of physical independence, reinforced by the respect due to 'le sexe'. Ladies would have their own room or apartment, which assumed an almost sacrosanct character. 'In the apartment of the lady the plaintiff had not committed the slightest impoliteness.' The wife of a *conseiller au Châtelet*, attacked by her husband while they were out on business, took refuge in their hostess's apartment.[104]

At the other end of the social scale too, among couples who were too poor to own a shop or who for some reason did not work together, there was potentially a high degree of day-to-day independence for both partners. Most often the man was a salaried worker: a journeyman, day-labourer, or employee of a large enterprise. He would therefore go out to work, normally for very long hours. The female occupations open to those of equivalent status were street-selling, perhaps keeping a tiny shop, piece-work at home, semi-skilled artisanal work, or else independent sewing and dress-making. Husband and wife therefore might see very little of each other. Domestic servants and some other workers who were obliged to live with their masters were an extreme case, for they usually could not live with their spouses at all.[105]

Most couples of course did live together, and the cramped living conditions of the poor ensured a degree of close contact. But different work and separate forms of leisure activity tended to keep it to a minimum. A good example is that of a soldier of the *guet* and his wife, who nursed women in childbirth. They lived in the rue du Petit Carreau, and his job took him out both day and night to different parts of the city. When he was not on duty, three days a week, he

---

[102] Y15402, 16 Apr., 24 Apr., 18 Dec. Y14436, 21 July, 1 Aug. Y15099, 26 Jan., 16 July. Y14078, 24 Aug.
[103] Mercier, *Tableau*, vol. 1, pp. 85–6. F. de la Rochefoucauld, *La Vie en Angleterre; ou Mélanges sur l'Angleterre*, 1784, edited by J. Marchand (Paris, 1945), p. 79.
[104] Y14078, 27 Dec. Y15099, 16 Mar.
[105] Botlan, 'Domestiques', pp. 245, 254. Y15099, 1 Jan., 3 Mar. Y15402, 14 June. Y15117, 3 Sept. 1788. Y18580, Chambre civile, 21 Nov. 1782.

worked as a framework-knitter, presumably at home. One day in their life is revealed by an enquiry. He had finished his stint of guard-duty that morning and had spent the day at home. She was out looking after a client and when she returned at 10 p.m. their daughter said that he had gone out. He had been seen at a nearby beer-shop at half past seven. Thinking he would soon return his wife went to bed.[106]

Every combination of jobs involved a different timetable, of course, but this example illustrates a way of life which those concerned found quite normal. Husband and wife pursued their own concerns, their own habits and networks of acquaintances. This division, while not as strict as in Languedoc or in Provence, ensured both husband and wife a large measure of independence.[107]

The function of running the household could also give women in certain occupational groups considerable domestic power, especially where it involved control over finances. In manufacturing trades it was the woman who ran the shop while her husband spent all his time in the workshop, and most master artisans seem to have left the business accounts to their wives. It was usually the wife who appeared to claim money owed when the debts of a deceased estate were being settled. In the shop she was to be found at the cash desk (*comptoir*) and her jurisdiction even extended to paying the employees: when journeymen left they would see her to calculate what they were owed or how much they should give back if they had received a cash advance. Ménétra recounts that his wife quickly took over the accounts and to his annoyance even began giving money to her family. Later she lent money to a neighbour, apparently without asking him at all.[108]

The story was slightly different in merchant trades, where the husband worked in the shop and conducted most of the transactions himself. Thus a spendthrift *marchand de vin* could squander money that was needed to buy merchandise; a *marchand de bois* left his wife in charge of finances only when he was away.[109] Much depended, clearly, on individual personalities, but here the separation of function was less marked and the wife had less room for manoeuvre.

Where husband and wife did not work together she was often even more dependent on him. Although she had her own income, female wages were extremely low. If they were both wage-earners, therefore, the convention seems

---

[106] YI1239, 18 May, 29 May. J. Chagniot, 'Le Guet et la garde de Paris à la fin de l'ancien regime', *Revue d'histoire moderne et contemporaine*, 20 (1973), 58–71.

[107] Y. Castan, *Honnêteté*, pp. 164–78. L. Roubin, *Chambrettes des Provençaux* (Paris, Plon, 1970), pp. 44–6, 157–66. R. Reiter, 'Men and Women in the South of France: Public and Private Domains', in R. Reiter (ed.), *Toward an Anthropology of Women* (New York, Monthly Review Press, 1975), pp. 252–82.

[108] YI5350, 24 Nov., 28 Sept. YI4436, 5 May. YI0994, 1 Feb., 16 Apr. See Y9893, Chambre criminelle, Sept. 1780, dossier Yon. B.H.V.P. MS 678, ff. 123, 125, 128, 141, 149. See Ross, 'Survival Networks', p. 7.

[109] YI1239, 13 June. YI2597, 30 Sept. See YI3290, 1 Dec., wit. 3.

to have been that he should hand over a certain amount to provide for housekeeping expenses. Complaints by working wives against their husbands specifically mention failure to do this and women did their best to ensure that the money was not spent before it got home. On the Port de la Rapée, for example, the wives of the men who unloaded wine from the boats were prominently in attendance on pay nights.[110] On the other hand, if she kept a shop of her own it is possible that she might earn as much as he did: in a voluntary separation between a *perruquier* and his wife, 'not being able to get on together', he agreed to leave her to continue her commerce if she would give him 300 *livres* to set up somewhere else.[111]

In practice, despite the model of the submissive wife, Parisian women acted with considerable autonomy and personal pride. It is clear that the wife was the dominant partner in many marriages, and husbands would openly admit it: 'His wife was the mistress at his place', said a *marchand de vin* in 1782. Early in their marriage Ménétra's wife refused a business proposition without even asking him, and subsequently put their daughter into a boarding school against his will. In another case a wood merchant decided that discretion was the better part of valour when his wife threatened to break a log over his head – and in the presence of witnesses. Women could even boast publicly of their authority: 'her husband had come on her orders', one wife shouted at her adversaries. Community opinion in Paris tended, if not to approve, at least to accept the domineering wife, even in public, a far cry from Y. Castan's Languedoc where strong social pressure forced husband and wife alike to preserve the appearance of male superiority.[112]

The relative independence of Parisian women is reflected in their behaviour before the *commissaires*. In theory they could not initiate any sort of judicial proceedings without their husband's authorization and in practice it was systematically required for enquiries, but women frequently made formal complaints on their own initiative. The *garde* would arrest men at their request and they could occasionally even have their husbands arrested. One woman managed to get her husband imprisoned after she had caught him with his mistress in a wineshop.[113]

The greater independence of the Parisian wife is partly attributable to the customary law of the capital, which allowed women to inherit on equal terms with men and which protected the wife's dowry, at least in theory. In certain social groups it therefore gave women potentially greater economic independence and put male and female siblings on an equal footing.[114] Of course the

---

[110] Y10994, 7 Apr. Y13290, 2 Sept. Y15100, 11 Dec. Y13760, 24 Jan.

[111] Y14692, 18 Jan. 1774.

[112] Y18580, Chambre civile, 21 Nov. 1782. B.H.V.P. MS 678, ff. 125, 146. Y9893, Chambre criminelle, Sept. 1780, dossier Chevenot. Y Castan, *Honnêteté*, pp. 173, 175–6.

[113] Y15117, 31 Jan. 1788. Y11239, 29 Oct., 6 Nov.

[114] Y. Castan, *Honnêteté*, p. 208. *Nouvelle coutume de Paris*, arts. CCCIII–CCCXLI.

legal code reflected social reality, but it also helped to maintain certain rights for women. A further factor contributing to the independence of the Parisian wife was the urban environment itself, in which there was a great deal of contact between men and women outside the family unit. Large buildings containing many households placed totally unrelated people in close physical proximity. A big city made for anonymity outside one's own neighbourhood and this meant that men and women came into frequent contact with strangers of both sexes. Both the size of the city and the nature of female occupations made it impossible for a working woman to be continually under the protection of her family or even, in many cases, of the local community. Rich women would normally take a carriage when they went out, and would in any case be accompanied by their servants, but workers like laundresses and seamstresses frequently had clients in other parts of the city.[115] Street-sellers moved around even more. And virtually everyone had family or contacts of some sort outside their own quarter. Parisian women therefore had to learn to deal with a far larger number of people than anyone in a rural village was ever likely to meet. The division of function between the sexes, while it often separated husband and wife, did not necessarily separate men and women.

This in turn had implications for social relationships. The combination of anonymity, together with the existence of large numbers of young male immigrants; the largely separate leisure activities of men and women, particularly unmarried ones; and late marriage, especially among the poorest groups of the population, favoured the development of a predatory male mentality which had a significant effect on the relationship between the sexes. Propositioning a woman rarely involved any risk, for the man was unlikely to be recognized and there was little fear of retaliation by her menfolk. At worst he might encounter the reprobation of the onlookers, although for them, as for him, it was usually a game, the sort of behaviour expected of young men and which could be tolerated as long as it did not go too far.

The greater freedom of Parisian women had other disadvantages. For, whereas in Languedoc men would not deign to fight with women, in Paris where the separation of the sexes was less rigid, a man could strike a woman without much fear of incurring public condemnation. Although public opinion generally held a husband responsible for his wife's actions, if she insulted another man she would expect retaliation against her. 'The wife Hardy is very quarrelsome', said a pork-seller, 'having already this morning had a dispute with a man who slapped and kicked her.' No holds were barred: punches were quite commonly used against women, and kicks in the groin were almost exclusively reserved for them, especially if they were pregnant. Working women aspired to a high degree of personal autonomy and independence and in so

---

[115] Y14436, 21 July, 22 Aug. B.N. Ms. fr. 6682, p. 168, 2 Feb. 1776.

doing lost some of the privileges which in other places went with lack of responsibility.[116]

It is true that to some extent the lesser responsibility accorded to women, in both models of male–female relations, gave them special status, notably in dealings with the authorities. They could get away with things that men could not. They were less heavily punished by the courts and were in any case less likely to be sent to prison by the *commissaire*. People were aware of this and there are instances of men sending their wives in their place when there was a risk of arrest.[117] We find women very prominent in riots and rebellions against authority, inciting the crowd against *huissiers*, against the officials of the corporations, against the *garde*, often speaking with the voice of the local community. They were quite conscious of their power to rally a crowd.[118]

It was not, however, their lesser responsibility alone which allowed women such power. The division of function between husband and wife and the nature of female occupations and sociability contributed to give women a major regulatory function in the most important areas of community life: the house, the street and the market. They were the ones, more often than not, who intervened to prevent or break up fights. They would separate men who were fighting, fearlessly standing between would-be combatants. And they were able to do this not just because they were women, but because they spoke with the voice of the local community. Theirs was the privilege of commentary and judgment, their jeers and laughter acting as a form of social correction. Ménétra recalled that as a boy he had one day seen his father come to punish him, rope in hand, but instead 'he called me and promised to say nothing because all the good women pelted him with abuse'. The role could on occasion be more serious. A *tripière* (woman who sold tripe), meeting on the stairs a man accused of raping the nine-year-old daughter of a neighbour, 'reproached him but he did not [reply], not even to the punches that [she] directed at him . . .'. 'Ne me frappé pas, je m'en va' (don't hit me, I'm going). In normal circumstances a woman could not thus have attacked a man with impunity, but in this case she had all the force of public opinion behind her.[119]

Sex roles, both within marriage and within the community, thus developed in accordance with Parisian conditions while remaining true to the inherited values of French society. Because of the woman's role in the family and the division of function between husband and wife, but also because of the nature of the urban environment, women were more present in and more in control of key areas of neighbourhood life than were men.

[116] Y. Castan, *Honnêteté*, pp. 175–6. Y11239, 24 June. Y10994, 13 May, 13 Apr. Y13819, 4 Sept. 1788. Y13290, 14 Aug. Y11705, 22 Mar.

[117] Y14078, 4 Nov. Y15117, 9 June 1788. Petrovitch, in Abbiateci *et al.*, *Criminalité*, pp. 231–2. Y9893, Chambre criminelle, Sept. 1780, dossier Chevenot.

[118] Y15350, 5 June. Y13454A, 10 May 1789. Y10994, 17 June. Farge, 'Le Mendiant', p. 322. Some examples are given in chapter 1, above.

[119] B.H.V.P. MS 678, f. 11. Y15100, 1 July.

Naturally the reality of conjugal behaviour and the models people appealed to were often very different: in practice there were not two distinct patterns of marital relations but a whole spectrum. Nevertheless the models reflect the economic and social circumstances of people living in a crowded urban environment, and both reveal much about the relationship between the family and the local community. The 'quality' model appealed to those those who could afford, or at least aspire to, the privacy, the delicacy, the style of life that it required. It involved the erection of behavioural barriers which emphasized the individual's moral qualities and which thus set him or her above the common herd. It therefore implied, in its purest form, a rejection of ordinary neighbourhood sociability. It provided an alternative social identity, one based on the home and the conjugal unit rather than on the street and the neighbourhood, and involved a different sort of relationship between men and women. For those who adopted this model family and local community were to some extent alternative poles.

For people who adopted the second model of marriage, on the contrary, family and community were largely complementary. There were some areas of life which belonged primarily to the family, although in certain circumstances the community might intervene. But the two remained interdependent, roles within the family running in tandem with those in the community. This is particularly marked in the case of women, whose complementary functions of organizing the family economy and of expressing and enforcing community opinion arose from the same physical, economic, and social constraints, and gave them a central role in family and community alike.

III. SIBLINGS AND OTHERS

So far I have omitted one of the most important of all kin relationships: that between siblings. Brothers and sisters were the members of the family whose lives overlapped most. They shared many childhood experiences and were subject to very similar conditions and pressures. During the years before they started work the children of working parents might well see more of each other than of their father and mother – particularly siblings of the same sex – and links formed then often proved long-lasting.

It was common for siblings, especially those of the same sex, to remain in close contact even as adults. We often find them sharing lodgings, particularly if one or both were unmarried. They frequently had the same trade or in the case of sisters married into it, and often worked together.[120] Among migrants siblings tended to be particularly close, perhaps coming to the city together or following older brothers or sisters who would help them to find jobs.

[120] Y13290, 14 Jan., 18 Oct., 8 Sept. Y10994, 10 Dec. Y15402, 2 Oct. Y10994, 21 Jan. Y14436, 27 Mar. Y13290, 9 Nov. Y15402, 7 Jan. Y15350, 7 Oct. Cf. B.N. Ms. fr. 6682, f. 147, 13 Dec. 1775.

Even when as adults they neither lived nor worked together siblings were generally the members of the family who saw each other most in their leisure hours: brothers in wineshops, sisters at home or with mutual friends. A *pantalonnière* (woman who made trousers) said that her sister was 'the only person she frequents during her leisure moments'. Siblings of both sexes tended to keep in touch, going to visit each other more or less regularly, even if they lived in different parts of the city. Among both migrants and Parisians they were the members of the family whom people most consistently turned to for help in sickness, in old age, in daily emergencies.[121] It was frequently through a brother or a sister, too, that people found a marriage partner. Even in humble circles, given the separation of male and female activities and the circumspection imposed on women by social pressure and male aggression, it was usually only through common friends or neighbourhood ties that men and women could get to know each other. It was very often a brother or sister who provided such contact, as they were about the same age.[122]

At all levels of society they displayed the solidarity which was characteristic of other family relationships. We frequently read that 'his brother espoused his quarrel'; 'the brother of the woman took her part'. A letter to the *commissaire* Ninnin in 1778 thanked him for suspending proceedings against the writer's brother: a glimpse of the behind-the-scenes functioning of family connections at the modest level of minor officials. Brought before the *commissaires*, brothers would stand together in interrogations even when they betrayed other accomplices: solidarity between them went beyond that due to a comrade.[123]

The mutual obligations of siblings did vary according to their respective ages, and the frequency of remarriage made big age-differences quite common. Older brothers and sisters were considered to have a duty towards younger ones, in much the same way as parents towards their children, to help them financially and with contacts. A complaint by a young linen-worker reveals that she had apprenticed her fourteen-year-old sister to a *ravaudeuse* not far away, had undertaken to provide bread and clothes, and to pay twenty-four *livres* per year for two years. Finding that the sister was no longer with her mistress she had gone looking for her, found that she had been arrested and put into prison, and managed to bail her out. In another case a *maître perruquier* had, so he said, 'always provided for his brother the services necessitated by his youth'. lending him money, putting him up on several occasions. The limits to this help were similar to those on assistance by parents: the brother was not grateful, 'seeks to do him injury', so further help was refused.[124]

The relationship also varied according to sex. A man was felt to have a special

---

[121] Y15099, 2 Feb. Y14436, 1 Jan. Y12596, 11 Mar. Y15402, 2 Oct. Y15100, 20 Sept. Y15099, 8 June. Y12596, 20 June. Y15350, 20 July.

[122] Y15350, 23 Oct., 27 Oct.

[123] Y15115A, dossier Thevenot. Y15100, 21 Nov. Y14436, 1 Jan. Y15350, 6 Aug. Y11239, 29 Oct.

[124] Y13760, 1 Feb. Y14436, 18 Sept. See also Y15100, 20 Sept.

obligation towards his sister, particularly if she were unmarried, for he would then take the husband's role of defending her against all comers. In disputes with men unmarried women would threaten to send their brothers, who often did avenge them.[125] Sometimes men also took a role more like that of parents, in the same way as with younger brothers. In 1775 when a lace-worker was seduced by a journeyman blacksmith her brother went to see him to find out his intentions. Some brothers even felt themselves to have some sort of say in their sister's future. 'My son who was then in the Paris *garde*, knowing that his sister was pregnant, came one evening and created a scene at the house', said one mother. Ménétra recalled that he was not invited to the marriage of one of his sisters with their father's journeyman for fear that he would try to prevent it.[126]

Yet there were limits to solidarity between siblings. It normally did not prevail against parents. If one of them had a dispute with their father or mother the loyalty of the others was divided. They would first try to pacify the dispute, but if that failed would usually incline towards the parent, to whom all of them owed obedience. 'A little girl who came along ... cried out to one of the men who were fighting "My brother, go away rather than lack respect for my Papa."' A founder's son thrown out of his father's workshop for insolence was restrained by his brothers to prevent him from retaliating.[127]

The second situation in which solidarity broke down was when a brother or sister in some way betrayed or dishonoured the family. One man, called by the *commissaire*, when his brother was arrested, refused to bail him out because he was a 'libertine', and 'reproached him bitterly'. Older siblings reacted in the same way as parents. A *marchand fripier* had his sister imprisoned in the Salpêtrière three times, paying a hundred *livres* per year for her keep, because of her bad behaviour which he feared would dishonour that whole family. Even more striking is the action of a master tailor who, learning that a *lettre de cachet* had been issued against his brother, turned him over to the police, 'fearing some greater dishonour for himself and his family'. This may not have been his only motivation of course, but he could use family loyalty to justify betraying his own brother.[128]

Other factors could affect the nature of the links between siblings, too. Obviously, the degree of contact was once again important both in determining the opportunities for solidarity and in the initial development of the relationship. Hence many of the same things which restricted or increased contact between parents and children were vital here, too: the quarter they lived in and their place in it; occupation and social group. As we have seen, the children of the poor grew up in the street and this, together with limited contact with their parents,

---

125 Y13819, 13 May, 26 Nov. 1788. Y10994, 29 July. Y15350, 12 Sept.
126 Y15384, 23 Sept. 1775. Y15114A, *femme* Lebas to *commissaire* Trudon, 10 Feb. 1772. B.H.V.P. MS 678, f. 126. See also Y10994, 3 May.
127 Y15100, 25 Nov. Y10994, 11 Aug.   128 Y12597, 19 Dec. Y11239, 16 Mar. Y14078, 30 Sept.

favoured the development of strong peer-group loyalties. Among the wealthy on the other hand, brothers and sisters might hardly know each other if they had been sent to different *pensions*. The role of the eldest son would be different if there was a family seat which he would inherit and which would make him the future head of the clan. Among those with property there could be jealousy over their inheritance, although less against the eldest son than in areas of Roman law. At the same time the ties between the younger sons which common jealousy of the eldest could create were likely to be weaker in the north of France, where his privileges were fewer.[129]

Despite differences in the nature of the relationship according to sex and age, and despite the limitations on solidarity and the variations in different social groups, the link between brothers and sisters was still one of the strongest of all family ties. This in turn helped to define certain other relationships. That of brother-in-law was privileged, and particularly with regard to male siblings: common responsibility towards their wife and sisters seems to have brought them closer rather than causing friction (although it is possible that in many cases their relationship preceded the marriage).[130] In the papers of the *commissaires* the relationship is one of the most frequently mentioned, an indication of the degree of contact between them. They were often to be found together: the two brothers-in-law of a journeyman printer, for example, accompanied him to ask the master of his intended bride, a domestic servant, to give her leave. At a more affluent level of society, the bookseller Hardy had two brothers-in-law with shops in the same quarter who are frequently mentioned in his journal, and who were obviously a source for some of his information.[131] Brothers-in-law commonly had the same occupation, especially of course in trades with high endogamy, and often worked together. The relationship is not always obvious because the names were different, but its importance in trade and in many other aspects of Parisian life should not be overlooked. For example, one *marchand limonadier* was able to get premises in the Place Maubert, probably one of the best places in the city for sales of drink, because his wife's brother, also a *limonadier*, was principal tenant of the house.[132]

There are also many examples of the same sort of solidarity between brothers-in-law as existed between real brothers, and people linked them closely. When a servant was badly injured in a fight, a witness came to inform a nearby draper, 'he being the brother-in-law of the said Sieur Leconte', the servant's master. Two master bookbinders, brothers-in-law but with different workshops, complained that two journeymen had insulted and slandered them, 'to destroy their reputation'. A further suggestion of the significance of the

---

129 Y. Castan, *Honnêteté*, pp. 209–15.   130 Y13290, 25 Apr. Y12597, 25 Dec.
131 Y15350, 27 Oct. S. P. Hardy, *Mes Loisirs*, edited by M. Tourneux and M. Vitrac (Paris, Picard, 1912), p. vi. B.N. Ms. fr. 6682, f. 212, 3 May 1776.
132 Y12596, 15 Feb.

relationship is the example of one man who, according to his wife, was so attached to a friend that he passed him off as his brother-in-law.[133]

Between brother-in-law and sister-in-law the link was also in many ways similar to that between siblings. A man would act to defend or help his sister-in-law: one woman was even able to go and spend the night at her husband's brother's place after the husband had turned her out. The sister-in-law, in turn, would take his part and defend his reputation, as when a coachman, his wife, his sister-in-law and his niece all joined in abusing a domestic servant who had quarrelled with him.[134]

On the other hand women hardly ever mention their sisters-in-law. They obviously had contact through the brother yet rarely appear together, and there is even little trace of conflict between them. They did not turn to each other for help as did real sisters. The relationship was in every way a less important one than that of brothers-in-law. Perhaps the reason is that, because of the strong ties between mother and daughter, women remained, very much more than men, part of their blood family rather than of that into which they married.

Solidarity between siblings, as well as influencing relations between in-laws, helped to make uncles and aunts very important. The obligations of parents were to some extent shared by their brothers and sisters. The uncle and aunt were often the god-parents and the uncle was also, if one of the parents died, a common choice for *tuteur* (someone who watched over the child's interests).[135] They took an active interest in the upbringing of the children. In 1779, after the death of his brother, a *perruquier* took the child and refused to return it to its mother until she had remarried. If both parents died it was often their brothers or sisters who took in the children: unmarried men and women quite frequently lived with an uncle or aunt. An uncle also had a moral responsibility for his nephews and nieces: someone could go to him to complain about their behaviour, particularly in the absence of the father, and he might be called by the *commissaire* to collect a nephew who had been arrested or injured. In return the younger generation had a similar obligation towards him as towards their parents, one of respect and obedience.[136]

It was also extremely common for nephews and nieces to live and work with an uncle or an aunt as apprentices or journeymen, and in this case the family obligation was strengthened by that between employer and worker. Journeymen could sometimes find work for nephews through their contacts in the trade, and among unskilled workers too it was common to find them working together.

[133] Y15402, 30 June. Y12597, 22 Sept. Y13819, 4 July 1788.
[134] Y12597, 20 Dec. Y15100, 17 Oct. See Y13290, 9 Nov. Y13819, 26 Nov. 1788.
[135] *Encylopédie*, art. 'Femme'. Y13290, 26 Oct. Y15350, 27 Oct. Y11239, 5 Aug. M. Baulant, 'La Famille en miettes: sur un aspect de la démographie du XVIIe siècle', *Annales: E.S.C.*, 27 (1972), 959–68, p. 967.
[136] Y13819, 22 Nov. 1779. See Y15350, 27 Oct., 1 June. Y13290, 26 Oct. Y12596, 12 Apr., 17 Apr. Y12597, 4 Sept. Y13760, 21 Jan., wit. 4.

They would often spend leisure time in each other's company, as did aunts and nieces.[137]

Outsiders saw uncles, nephews, aunts and nieces as very much part of the same family and knew that an insult against one rebounded on, and was likely to provoke a reaction from, the other. It was also possible to describe someone with reference to an uncle, in the same way as to their father: 'he was told that the said individual was the nephew of a tile-merchant'.[138] The relation was a special one, although naturally with the same limitations of contact and proximity as for other members of the family.

These applied equally, of course, to first cousins, the most distant relatives with whom most people felt any real solidarity. If they lived close by and were of much the same age they might well grow up together and the link between them could be almost as strong as that between siblings. In Ménétra's memoirs his cousins are mentioned frequently: he even went to lend moral support when one of them asked for a woman's hand in marriage. We find in the papers of the *commissaires* a father writing that, as he was so far away, his son should consult a cousin about a proposed marriage.[139] In the same way as brothers, male cousins would often drink and spend leisure time together. It was also common for one to work for another, although unlike brothers they rarely appear as associates. There was obviously a sense of having a duty to take on a young cousin, usually as a shop-assistant, sometimes as an apprentice, even to the extent of dismissing someone to make room for them. Failing this, contacts could be used to find work for them or to get them established.[140] A newcomer to the city could often rely on cousins for accommodation and other initial help, and there is also evidence of solidarity against outsiders.[141]

Beyond first cousins there is little trace of contact, much less of solidarity. They stand at the normal limits of the family as people saw it. Yet even here there are important social variations. Among the most mobile sections of the population – male workers recently arrived in the city, soldiers, certain categories of domestic servant – contact with any relatives was often occasional, even coincidental, and likely to be limited to siblings. The most stable groups, with the greatest implantation in the capital, tended to have more family close by and to have more contact with them. Very occasionally ties would then extend beyond first cousins. In an enquiry into a dispute a witness said that it had started when a *compagnon sculpteur*, drinking in a wineshop, had insulted his master's great-aunt, who was also the grandmother of one of the other journeymen: these two had

[137] Y13290, 21 Aug. Y10994, 1 June. Y12597, 13 Sept. Y15350, 6 Nov.
[138] Y13290, 24 Sept. Y11265A, 12 Feb. 1775. Y13760, 21 Jan.
[139] B.H.V.P. MS 678, ff. 59, 81–2. Y15384, 23 Sept. 1775.
[140] Y15350, 1 Nov. Y11239, 18 Sept. Y12596, 5 Apr. Y12597, 12 Oct. B.H.V.P. MS 678, f. 135. Y15402, 26 May.
[141] Y15100, 29 Nov. See also example in Cobb, *Police*, pp. 224–5. Y15402, 27 Mar. Y15099, 10 Feb. Y13290, 24 Dec. B.H.V.P. MS 678, f. 16.

made a joint complaint.[142] Here second cousins with the same trade were united by loyalty to a common relative whom both felt to be fairly close. But the scarcity of this sort of example suggests that most families had by that stage drifted apart, either through one branch moving away, through their adopting different trades, or simply because their main link, the common ancestor, had disappeared. Only for the elites did kin outside the first-cousin limit consistently remain important, both in noble circles and among high-ranking commoners. Y. Durand has shown how extensive were the family networks by which certain *fermiers généraux* came into office.[143] Among groups such as this, birth, patronage, and inherited wealth were the foundations of individual fortune and position, and therefore an awareness of the wider kin network and a certain reciprocal loyalty were extremely important.

IV. CONCLUSION

For a great many people the family was vital for economic survival, for psychological and moral support, and in giving people a place in society. In all of these functions however, we have seen that among working people family and neighbourhood were frequently inseparable. In finding work, in making friends and useful contacts, in finding a marriage partner, family and local ties frequently overlapped. Roles within the family were important in determining someone's place in the community, and marriage itself was for many people both a family and a community event, drawing its significance and its legitimacy from that dual recognition. I have emphasized the overlapping functions of family and of neighbourhood in preparing the children of working people for their place in society, providing models and communicating the values which would not only give them a particular identity and social skills, but which at the same time were essential for the survival of family and community alike.

Even for these people, however, the functions of family and community were in other respects quite distinct. We have seen that particular relatives, in certain social and economic contexts, had the primary responsibility for looking after young children, the sick and the old. It is true that in the absence of kin and in some other contexts the neighbourhood might carry out these tasks, but the onus was first and foremost on the family. Similarly family ties imposed an obligation of moral solidarity which neighbourhood ones did not: on the contrary, in a dispute the fact of belonging to the local community normally required active neutrality although not necessarily impartiality. There was therefore, returning to the question posed by O. Harris, a difference between the morality and function of the neighbourhood, and those of kin. It was a difference both of

---

[142] Y15350, 23 Oct.
[143] Flandrin, *Familles*, pp. 25–8. Stone, *Family*, p. 323. Y. Durand, *Les Fermiers généraux au XVIIIe siècle* (Paris, Presses universitaires, 1971), pp. 75–6, 326–83.

degree and of kind, depending on the context. In certain cases family and community were interchangeable, although the primary responsibility might belong to one or the other. In other situations the two had quite different roles, as in disputes involving family honour. Here the obligations of family members were qualitatively different from those of neighbours. Sometimes, however, the difference seems to have been at once of degree and of kind, for example in disputes between husband and wife where certain relatives had not only the primary responsibility for intervening but were expected to do so at an earlier stage. The exact division between family and neighbourhood functions varied according to the issue, but also in different social and occupational groups, in different economic situations, between men and women. It also to some extent depended on which relatives were present, because different family members had slightly different obligations.

Another important fact must be borne in mind when contrasting the functions and morality of family and local community. The family was in practice very often absent, because of death or geographic mobility, whereas the neighbours were always there. This meant that for most Parisians the locals played a greater role in everyday life than did kin outside the conjugal group. What R. Phillips observes in Rouen – the very important role of neighbours in all aspects of disputes between husband and wife – was true of Paris as well. But it is inaccurate to infer from this that the ties between neighbours were stronger than those of kin, for such a conclusion fails to recognize the difference between family and neighbourhood obligations. Even if neighbours intervened to prevent wife-beating in ninety-nine per cent of cases, it may merely indicate that no relatives were present. This distinction was in fact recognized in the revolutionary family tribunals, which decided on separations, and to which neighbours could be appointed in the absence of relatives.[144] Family and local community were not, in most people's lives, in conflict, but had distinct and clearly defined functions and degrees of responsibility.

My analysis has also shown, however, that this was not true of everyone. Although I have looked at the social elites only briefly, it is clear that for them the neighbourhood played virtually no role. Where birth and rank were the basis of social position, relatives outside the conjugal family tended to replace neighbours in providing necessary contacts and in controlling the individual's behaviour. For a well-off middle section of society, too, other models and forms of behaviour had great appeal, precisely because they enabled such people to distance themselves from the usual forms of urban sociability. These models provided a means of social differentiation and a sense of moral superiority for groups whose economic situation, education, and social ambitions sent them in search of a new yardstick for measuring social worth.

Even where family and community were both important, however, they were

[144] Phillips, *Family Breakdown*, ch. 4 and conclusion.

not necessarily all-important. Each had its own, admittedly flexible domain, where it had first claim to the allegiance of its members. Was this also true of other social institutions? Were other social bonds similarly dominant in certain groups and particular contexts, and do social, economic, occupational and geographic variations in their nature and extent enable us further to define the limits and functions of the local community? This is what the next three chapters will explore.

3

Work

Much historical writing makes two assumptions about work. The first is that it is a significant factor – and for many writers the most significant one – in determining someone's place in society. The second is that similar work will give people essentially similar interests, values, and places in society, and that they will behave in similar ways. Neither of these assumptions is necessarily accurate. It is conceivable that people's jobs might be of relatively little importance in determining their everyday relationships. They might have more to do with, and stronger ties with, family, *pays*, neighbours, or friends. Different sorts of work could encourage the formation of different bonds: I have emphasized the role of particular trades, such as *marchands de vin*, *perruquiers*, *traiteurs* and bakers, within the local community. Before using occupation to classify people, therefore, we must be aware of how important work-ties were in social organization.

Even supposing that work was a significant factor, it still does not necessarily follow that all those who did the same sort of work, either in relation to the means of production, in the same economic sector, or within the same trades corporation, should be treated as a single group. It is of course very likely that people of the same occupation and status will have shared concerns: two master locksmiths may both be affected by the level of wages and by the regulations of their trade. On the other hand their interests could conflict precisely because of their common occupation: if they are in the same street and therefore directly competing with each other, or if one has a large business and the other a small one. Yet again, if they specialized in different types of work and thus had different markets and a different work-force, they might have little in common beyond their title. It is therefore vital to study the structure and organization of each trade.[1]

I have space to look at only five of the occupational categories which are generally used in describing eighteenth-century Parisian society. The first, corporate trades, had a strong work identity and an institutional structure which could give its members ties outside the local community. The second and third groups – street trades and domestic servants – are often seen as unstable, even outcasts. Soldiers, my fourth group, are often overlooked. The last category is

---

[1] A point stressed by M. Garden, 'Ouvriers et artisans au XVIIIe siècle: l'exemple lyonnais et les problèmes de classification', *Revue d'histoire économique et sociale*, 48 (1970), 28–54 (p. 41).

that of office-holders, at a completely different social level. We will see how the character and structure of each of these types of work helped to make people part of the local community or to exclude them, and what role each one played in the creation and maintenance of the local community.

I. CORPORATE TRADES

By far the most numerous and varied occupational category was that of corporate trades: the official corporations, the *Six Corps*, and a number of other groups with a similar trade structure and work patterns.[2] Nearly all were based on the shop or workshop, both of which were referred to as a *boutique*. Even those without a *boutique*, like gardeners, the Seine fishermen, or the building trades, were set apart from other groups by their centralized structure and their professional unity: their 'corporateness'. Above all they shared particular relationships not found in other trades: that between master and journeymen or *garçons*; between workmen within the one shop, and between those of the same trade in different parts of the city; between the established master or merchant and his clients and suppliers.

This is not to say that the corporate trades were homogeneous. On the contrary there were infinite variations which made some of them much more open to the neighbourhood than others: those which were primarily engaged in production on the whole provided fewer local contacts than those mainly concerned with sales or service. A *marchand de vin*, for example, spent most of his time serving customers and was often at the very heart of the local community. Most food suppliers were in a similar position, as were service trades like hairdressing, and to a lesser extent merchants like *fripiers, merciers, épiciers* and booksellers. Even here, however, there were variations: a *traiteur, rôtisseur,* or *pâtissier* had to prepare and cook the food he sold; a baker would do much of his work at night. The serving in the shop might not be done by him but by a shop assistant or by his wife. The customers would vary too. Whereas a *marchand de vin*, a *traiteur,* or a *perruquier* had most contact with the men of the neighbourhood, butchers or fruiterers saw more of the women. A bookseller, a butcher, or an *épicier* had a somewhat wealthier clientele than a tripe-seller or a baker, and might deal more with servants.

At the other end of the scale were those engaged purely or primarily in production. Joiners and cabinet-makers, wood-carvers and sculptors usually did little in the way of counter-sales, most of their work being done on a contract basis. Much the same applied to printers. These trades therefore gave people little contact with their neighbours. Their workshops were often physically

---

[2] *Coiffeuses, imagers, ferreurs d'aiguillettes*, artisans working in *lieux privilégiés*. See J. Savary des Bruslons, *Dictionnaire universel de commerce*, 2 vols. (Paris, 1723), art. 'Communauté'.

closed as well, for unlike a retail trader a manufacturer had no need of street frontage, which in a commercial thoroughfare was very expensive.[3]

A huge range of trades lay between these extremes. There were many service professions which actually went to people's homes to deliver goods or to do work there: glaziers, carpenters, locksmiths, plasterers and roofers, hairdressers, to name but a few. There were also a great many craftsmen who both produced goods and sold them. They might work in the shop itself, though more often the artisan had his workshop at the back. The typical Parisian house was designed with this in mind, one or two rooms deep on the ground floor, with easy access to the courtyard or entrance passage. If there were two rooms there would normally be a communicating doorway (see figure 12, p. 222). Thus the artisan and his workmen, even if they were not in direct contact with the customer, were nevertheless aware of what was happening in the shop and could participate in the conversation if they so desired. A goldsmith in the rue St Jacques de la Boucherie was able to give a full account of the sale of several pairs of buckles, even though he had been in the workshop, his wife looking after the customers.[4] Here too of course the type of client varied with the trade: a *tapissier* or a saddler, selling luxury items, had a different range of customers from a candle-maker, a tailor, or a cobbler, who served less wealthy people and primarily locals.

Whatever the branch of trade the shop remained open to the street, the focal point of community life. A beer-seller was in his shop in the rue de Lappe when he heard a noise in the street, and from his doorway witnessed a fight between two neighbours. A *cuirassier* (armourer) a couple of doors away emerged from his workshop in time to intervene. Access to the courtyard and passage opened both shop and workshop to the rest of the house as well: two shopkeepers in a house in the rue du Coeur Volant, a joiner and a gilder, heard cries on the stairs and emerged in time to catch the thief.[5] At slack times, of course, and in the evenings, the shopkeepers would stand at their doors to watch the passers-by and chat with the neighbours.

Many artisans also made up for restricted premises by working in the street in fine weather. Ménétra recounts his father's rage and the amusement of the neighbours when a female dog on heat, pursued by a number of males and several young men, ran over and smashed a number of sheets of glass that he had laid out in the street. Police ordinances repeatedly forbade '*marchands épiciers*, *marchands de vin*, *tapissiers*, *fripiers*, *sculpteurs*, cartwrights, marble-masons, joiners, locksmiths, box-makers, fruiterers, hirers of carriages, waggoners and others to work in the streets'. Even workshops tucked away at the backs of the houses would spread into the courtyard, and into the street if more space were

---

[3] F. J. B. Watson, *The Wrightsman Collection*, vol. 1 (New York, Metropolitan Museum of Art, 1970), Introd., p. lviii. F. Boudon, A. Chastel, H. Couzy, F. Hamon, *Système de l'architecture urbaine: le quartier des Halles à Paris*, 2 vols. (Paris, C.N.R.S., 1977), vol. 1, pp. 90, 92. Y15100, 8 Aug. Y14078, 17 Aug.

[4] Y15099, 23 Jan., wit. 3.   [5] Y10994, 29 Apr., wit. 1, 2. Y14078, 28 June, wit. 5, 6.

required.[6] Some trades gave people more contact with the locals than did others, but few cut them off completely.

The second major way in which occupation could affect the degree to which people became part of the local community, this time negatively, was in the ties it gave them in other parts of the city. Some trades had a very strong corporate tradition which set them apart. Foremost among these were the *Six Corps*, largely because of their social position.[7] Savary clearly distinguishes them from the ordinary corporations, listing them at the head of his entry on 'Communauté' (guild). Since the sixteenth century they had had a sort of official position, taking a prominent part in public ceremonies: in 1745 the *Six Corps* as a body stood as godfather to the child of the *lieutenant général*'s secretary![8]

All the corporations, of course, had their Bureau. They had their statutes and their officials, in theory elected by all the masters at an annual general meeting. In most cases the *jurés* visited all shops several times a year, and this could help create a city-wide sense of professional identity. Each trade, too, had its patron saint, its feast-day, and its confraternity – run by the *jurés* – to which every master contributed. There was thus an institutional framework which could create a city-wide 'moral community'.[9]

Corporate identity could also be encouraged by a distinctive appearance. Many artisans had a particular garb by which they could instantly be recognized. An *épicier* recalled that at about seven one evening 'a young man wearing a jacket who looked like a *garçon rôtisseur* came into his shop'. Joiners wore a particular sort of apron, and butchers could always be identified by the blood-stains on their clothes. Certain trades could still be detected even when out of uniform: interrogating a thief in November 1789 the *commissaire* Le Roux asked him 'why his hands were black like a locksmith's'.[10] This sort of physical work-identity helped to give men of the same trade something in common even if they did not know each other.

However a long corporate tradition, an institutional framework, or a distinctive appearance were not the only potential sources of unity. The extent and frequency of contact between members of the same trade were vital, and they were determined by many factors. The first was geographic. Some groups were concentrated in particular areas of the city: printers and booksellers were obliged

---

[6] B.H.V.P. MS 678, f. 119. Ordonnance de police, 26 July 1777, article 12, in Y12830. Ordonnance du Bureau des Finances, 12 Mar. 1748, in Peuchet, *Collection*, vol. 1, p. 388. Ordonnance de police, 8 Nov. 1771, in Peuchet, vol. 8, p. 420. Y14078, 21 June. Y11239, 13 Apr.

[7] The wealthiest, most prestigious merchant guilds: drapers, mercers, goldsmiths/jewellers, spicers, furriers, *bonnetiers*. Reorganized in 1776, and the *marchands de vin* added.

[8] E. Levasseur, introduction to A. Franklin, *Dictionnaire historique des arts, métiers et professions exercés dans Paris depuis le 13e siècle* (Paris, H. Welter, 1906), pp. xiii–xx. E. Coornaert, *Les Corporations en France avant 1789* (Paris, Editions ouvrières, 1941), p. 189.

[9] B.N. J. de F. 1590, f. 35, A.P.P. Lam., vol. 39, f. 145. Sewell, *Work*, pp. 32–7.

[10] Y11239, 21 Apr. Y14078, 14 Oct. Y14436, 29 Feb., wit. 5. Mercier, *Tableau*, vol. 1, p. 125. Y14436, 18 Oct. Y15100, 30 Nov. Y14484, 30 Nov.

by law to live in the university area. Goldsmiths congregated in the rue and Quai de Gesvres, and on the Ile de la Cité around the Palais, the Place Dauphine, and of course the Quai des Orfèvres. Manufacturers of cloth, garments and accessories were established primarily in the north-central districts along the rue St Denis; joiners to the north of St Eustache; *ébénistes* and furniture retailers at the city end of the Faubourg St Antoine. These are only a few examples. For all these groups occupational ties overlapped with and reinforced those of neighbourhood. A good illustration is provided by a letter to the *commissaire* Ninnin from the wife of a butcher in the rue de la Vieille Lanterne near St Jacques de la Boucherie. Her husband had taken their dog out for a walk at six o'clock that morning. As he passed another butcher's door in the rue de la Vieille Place aux Veaux, several journeymen butchers from two shops in the street set their dogs onto his then fell on him with broom-handles, joined by a neighbouring *marchand d'eau-de-vie* 'who is also a journeyman butcher'. The impression is of a whole street dominated by the one trade, even the local liquor-merchant butchering part-time, the ties of occupation and neighbourhood further reinforced in this case by their being the only people up.[11]

Right next to the central market lay another area dominated by one trade. The office of the *marchands fripiers* was in the rue de la Tonnellerie, and their shops lined that street as well as the two adjoining ones, the rue de la Friperie and the rue de la Petite Friperie. The papers of the *commissaire* of the quarter show them participating in disputes in the street and also reveal the existence of numerous family ties.[12] In these areas occupation obviously helped to make people part of the local community, and belonging to the community in turn strengthened corporate ties.

Even where a locality was not so occupationally homogeneous, however, those of the same trade might still get together. Two *marchands de vin*, neighbours just outside the *barrière* of the rue de Charonne, went off together one morning to the market at La Vallée in the centre of Paris, returning home late in the evening. A journeyman locksmith and two workmates went to have breakfast in a wineshop in the rue du Chevalier du Guet, where they found another locksmith and his wife. Two more arrived shortly after, followed some time later by three others from yet another workshop.[13]

The further importance that trade-ties within the quarter could assume is demonstrated by an enquiry of December 1752, following a fire in the house of a *mercier-peaussier* in the rue St Germain l'Auxerrois. Awoken by neighbours, he at once sent for assistance to three *marchands merciers* and a currier a few streets away. Another *mercier* from just round the corner was also quickly on the

---

[11] Y15114B, *femme* Bonnevie to *commissaire* Ninnin, 3 Dec. 1779.
[12] Y11239, 15 Sept., 5 Aug., 16 Mar., 17 Mar. Y15350, 22 Nov., 24 Nov.
[13] Y10994, 3 Dec., 6 Dec. Y13751, 19 Sept., interr. 1.

scene.[14] In this case occupational ties, over a distance of several streets, were at least as important as those with the immediate neighbours.

These examples illustrate different ways in which occupational ties within the one general area could affect someone's place in the local community. Where they overlapped with ordinary neighbourhood bonds they helped to make a person all the more part of the community, although the examples of the butchers around the Vieille Place aux Veaux, or that of the *fripier*, suggest that work-ties could create a kernel, a sort of sub-set within the community. For the locksmiths mentioned, or the *merciers*, corporate bonds to some extent cut them off, giving them stronger ties with each other than with the immediate neighbours. The distinction is a fine one, however, as the case of the *marchands de vin* shows, for although their calling brought them closer together it did not separate them from the other locals: when one of them quarrelled with a neighbouring gardener, the other separated them and escorted the slightly injured gardener home.

Geographic proximity was of course not the only thing which determined the degree of contact between members of the same occupation. The type of work, the structure of the trade, and the materials used were of prime importance. Many artisans and merchants, for instance, had a single supply centre. All grain had to pass through the sixteen Paris markets, so bakers and grain merchants would meet there on market days: Wednesday and Saturday. Other wholesale merchandise had to be sold in the central market: leather, rope, eggs and butter, and each week merchants of many trades would congregate there. There was also the fish-market, later moved further north, and the oyster-market along the rue Montorgueil. In September 1752 we find a *maître traiteur* from the rue Dauphine coming to the Halle to buy his supply of seafood. Many other trades also had common supply centres. There was the Halle aux Draps (cloth) next to the Marché des Innocents, the Halle aux Cuirs (leather) in the rue Mauconseil, the Halle au Vin (wine) on the Quai de la Tournelle. The horse-market was in the Faubourg St Marcel, wood and charcoal could be purchased on various *quais*, straw at the Port St Martin.[15]

In some trades, too, merchants would sell to each other. *Fruitier-orangers* sometimes supplied each other with stock, not necessarily from wholesaler to retailer, and the same happened among booksellers. A jeweller dealing mainly in precious stones might, to satisfy a customer, buy buckles from a colleague who

---

[14] Y15350, 26 Nov.
[15] S. Kaplan, *Bread, Politics and Political Economy in the Reign of Louis XV*, 2 vols. (The Hague, Martinus Nijhoff, 1976), vol. 1, pp. 35, 68. Y11239, 8 May, 22 Mar. Y9532, 12 Dec. 1718. Y12612, 3 Sept. 1763. Savary, *Dictionnaire*, art. 'Cordonnier'. Y11239, 12 Oct., 28 Feb., 14 July, 20 July, 11 Feb., 20 May, 15 Nov., 13 Oct. *Mémoires des intendants sur l'état des généralités*, vol. 1, *Mémoire de la généralité de Paris* (Paris, 1881), pp. 669–70. J. Hillairet, *Dictionnaire historique des rues de Paris*, 2 vols. (Paris, Editions de Minuit, 1963), 'rue Montorgueil'. Y11239, 18 Sept., wit. 2. *Mémoires des intendants*, vol. 1, pp. 671–2. Ordonnance de police, 12 Oct. 1756, in Peuchet, vol. 6, p. 253.

did a bigger trade in those. Many artisans co-operated with colleagues or with masters of other specializations within the same sector. Two sawyers together purchased a lot of walnut wood, presumably more than either wanted. We find a *traiteur* helping another out with plates for an especially large gathering; a mirror-maker and a joiner producing framed mirrors but getting a local wood-carver to do the decoration. Journeymen of one trade might work directly for a master in another, although the corporations generally tried to stamp out such practices. The *jurés* cutlers seized the tools of a journeyman gunsmith whom they caught working for a master cutler on the Pont St Michel. More legitimate was the work done by a *compagnon ébéniste* for a master corset-maker.[16]

There could therefore be a great deal of everyday contact between artisans within the one sector. Where there was co-operation they were normally in the same quarter, often in the same street, and in such cases occupational ties overlapped with and reinforced neighbourhood ones. A common supply centre could equally strengthen any local links that might exist, but it could also help to create city-wide ties between members of the same trade, perhaps in competition with neighbourhood ones. On the other hand a merchant or artisan who was geographically isolated from his colleagues and whose work gave him little occasion to go to a common market or to co-operate with those in the same trade or sector would have little opportunity to develop strong corporate ties. The work of a *savetier*, for example, who dealt only in old shoes, would bring him into contact mainly with clients, mostly neighbours.[17]

Another important factor affecting both work identity and the degree of contact within the trade was workshop size. Individually owned establishments ranged from the family shop, employing sons and daughters, to virtual factories like that of the blanket-maker Nicolas Lepy, who employed over a hundred journeymen and workers.[18] In some sectors large workshops were very common – in printing for example – whereas in others, such as cabinet-making, small ones seem to have been the rule. But in most trades the range was considerable.

Whatever the job, a large workshop provided more contact with others of the same trade than did a small one, and not just at work. Especially in the first half of the century, journeymen employed by one master were lodged together on an upper floor and it was quite natural for them to spend their free hours in each other's company. The documents frequently show us men from the same workshop drinking together in wineshops. There was often a strong sense of unity created both by working together and by the way others saw them: in 1763 five ribbon-makers walked out when their master refused to pay one of their comrades a higher price, both from solidarity with him and because, 'as soon as

---

[16] Y15350, 7 Oct. Y11239, 7 Jan., 8 Nov. Y13290, 10 Dec. Y10994, 28 Apr. Y13750, 8 June 1745. Y10994, 3 Feb. Y15350, 24 May, 7 Oct. Y11239, 17 Oct.
[17] Y11239, 4 Nov.
[18] Some of these were outworkers, but he did have a large manufactory. Y14935, 8 Dec. 1724.

they went into a wineshop, the other workers who were there said to them "There are those *jeanfoutre* from Dubois' shop"'.[19]

The development of strong ties between journeymen in a large workshop could be further encouraged by their relationship with the master. It was likely to be one of authority and subordination, with less personal contact than in a smaller shop. There is a considerable difference between the master locksmith who during the strike of 1746 told his journeymen to stop work to prevent him from being mistreated and another whose reaction was to lock his workmen in an upstairs room. It is partly a matter of personal style, but the latter reaction was more likely from a large employer. In the biggest enterprises there might be virtually no contact at all between the owner and his men. In a factory in the rue de Charenton in 1752 it is a *commis* who makes a complaint against a *compagnon tabletier* for leading a number of other workers astray. A textile manufactory in the Faubourg St Marcel had a foreman to keep the men in line: not unskilled factory workers, but artisans like the engraver arrested by the *garde*.[20]

In trades where large workshops were essential, the cost of setting up meant that journeymen often had little hope of ever becoming masters. In printing, for example, a single press cost two hundred and fifty to three hundred *livres*, even without the necessary tools, and the memoirs of a journeyman, written about 1762, tell us that to be received as a master one had to have at least four presses. The capital investment and contacts required for brewing, or the production of saltpetre, may likewise have excluded most journeymen from possessing their own establishments. There was in such cases a difference in expectations and an awareness of the divergent interests of owner and worker. There were problems of discipline which were much less likely in a shop where master and journeyman worked side by side. There was often a significant gap between their levels of wealth, their way of life, and their values. The master printer portrayed in N. Contat's *Anecdotes typographiques* moves in a completely different world from his employees. He lives royally by comparison with them, he never appears in the workshop, and all are afraid of him or at least deeply respectful.[21]

A large workshop was therefore likely to encourage a strong sense of unity among its members and in so doing could somewhat cut them off from the local community. An establishment as large as the Gobelins factory virtually created its own community, with the workers spending much of their free time together. The clientele of a *marchand limonadier* in the rue de Hurepoix in 1789 was largely composed of employees of the publisher Firmin Didot. Contat describes the isolation of printing workers, those from each workshop having their chosen tavern, spending Sundays and holidays together, and rarely associating with

---

19 Y9529, Chambre de Police, 29 Nov. 1763.
20 Y12596, 7 Aug., wit. 4. Y13751, 19 Sept., interr. 10, 14. Y10994, 31 May. Y11705, 1 Jan.
21 N. Contat, *Anecdotes typographiques* [1762], edited by G. Barber (Oxford, Oxford Bibliographical Society, 1980), p. 75. See also Darnton, *Great Cat Massacre*, ch. 2. On brewing Y10994, 13 Dec. and Burstin, 'Faubourg', pp. 206–14. On saltpetre, Y12596, 28 Feb.

workers in other trades.[22] The workshop, potentially a means of integration into the local community, could also become a quarantine, almost a socially self-sufficient unit.

The strong sense of professional identity encouraged by a large workshop could also distance journeymen from the local community by giving them stronger ties with their fellow-workers in other parts of the city. It was necessary in most trades to do some years with a master after the apprenticeship before becoming eligible for the master's certificate, and the larger the workshops a man was in – and obviously the more he moved around – the more people he would know in the same trade, the more numerous his links outside the one quarter.

There is some evidence to suggest that large workshops were important in labour disputes which saw journeymen combining to defend their interests. Firstly, trades in which large workshops were common are prominent among those involved in such action during the eighteenth century: printing-workers, silk-workers and hatters, building and textile trades.[23] Secondly, in the best-documented strikes the leaders of the journeymen are very often from large work-shops, frequently those of the *jurés*. This is the case in the ribbon-makers' strike of 1763 and seems also to be true of the locksmiths' strike of 1746.[24] Of course these were the men about whom the *jurés*, making their complaints to the police, were most concerned and whom they could best identify, but peer-group pressure was clearly greater in a large workshop, and the workers tended to be less close to their master, better able to resist him in a group.

For the master too, a large shop or workshop and the flourishing trade that this represented usually meant extensive ties outside the quarter. Their exact range varied somewhat according to the nature of his commerce, those selling luxury items like furniture or carriages often catering to a more geographically dispersed market. Food retailers generally had an essentially local clientele. But even here a large business naturally drew customers from further afield.

There was also the supply side. A tailor with a big business got his materials from a variety of sources: he required cloth of different kinds, thread, buttons, ribbons of silk and cotton, perhaps of gold. A less affluent master with a smaller commerce might not need such a range of stock and could often get much of what he required from a neighbouring retailer. Wealthy merchants did not necessarily obtain all their supplies of one kind from the one source, but might buy small quantities from a number of different people. In sectors where a sub-contracting system operated, a large-scale enterprise would farm out work

---

[22] G. Capon, 'La prise de la Bastille. Lettre inédite', *L'Intermédiaire des chercheurs et des curieux*, vol. 86, no. 1582 (10 June 1923), cols. 517–20 (col. 517). Y11706, 26 Aug. Contat, *Anecdotes*, p. 73.

[23] G. Martin, *Les Associations ouvrières au XVIIIe siècle, 1700–1792* (Paris, A. Rousseau, 1900).

[24] Y9529, 20 May 1763. Y13751, 13 Sept., 19 Sept., 17 Oct., 22 Oct., 17 Nov. Y14391, 7 Sept. 1746.

to a number of small masters. A *tapissier*, for example, in addition to his shop staff and possibly other employees, would sign contracts with joiners and wood-carvers, both for work on a regular basis and for specific jobs. The very largest merchants, who often preferred to call themselves *négociants* or simply *marchands*, had dealings not only across the city, but internationally. Many merchants dealt in bills of exchange and speculated on the Bourse (stock exchange), which gave them extensive contacts with merchants in other sectors, as well as with stockbrokers.[25]

A master with a large workshop, often having little in common with his own workers, also tended to have stronger ties with other masters. He was likely to be among the wealthier, longer-established members of his trade and this gave him a prominent place in the corporation: among shoemakers and tailors, according to Coornaert, even in the eighteenth century those with six or eight workers were quite important within the trade.[26] It was from among such people that the *jurés* were normally chosen: but they were the best-known, considered most responsible by the authorities, and could afford the time that the job required. There might be other restrictions working in their favour, too, like the 'gift' of 200 *livres* paid by newly elected *jurés* shoemakers. Those who were active in the trade, either as *jurés* or as *anciens*, had considerable contact both with each other and with a large number of the masters. They met regularly to discuss the business of the corporation. They might supervise supply and distribution of merchandise at the central market and would there-fore see all the masters regularly. In most corporations, the *jurés* and the *anciens* supervised and assessed the *chef d'oeuvre* presented by a candidate for the master's certificate. Part of the *juré*'s job, too, was to inspect the shops and merchandise of masters to ensure that everything conformed to the required standards.[27] Their duties frequently took them away from their shops and could give them a strong sense of identity with other masters, especially those of similar standing within the corporation.

The small master, on the other hand, tended to be closer to his workers and to have less contact with other masters of the same trade. There are many examples of men who employed one or two journeymen going to drink with them. In a small shop master and man would often do the same jobs: the picture Ménétra gives us is of journeymen glaziers doing exactly the same work as their masters, except that the master found the clients and dealt with them. In most small shops the journeyman would serve the customers, open and close the shop, chat with the nearby shopkeepers and with clients. Like a full-time shop-assistant, he was

25 Y14078, 2 Aug. Y14436, 4 July. Y11239, 17 June, 7 Jan., 8 Nov. Y10994, 19 Jan., 6 Oct. Watson, *Wrightsman*, p. lviii. Y14484, 31 Jan. See also Y15100, 25 Sept. Y15350, 12 Oct. Y14436, 4 July. Y15402, 2 May, 19 July.
26 Coornaert, *Corporations*, p. 268.
27 Y11952, 11 July 1764. Savary, *Dictionnaire*, art. 'Jurande'. Y12596, 3 July. Y15363, 29 July 1753. Y11239, 12 Oct., 18 Oct., 30 Oct., 29 Mar.

as much a part of the local community as his master. An eighty-year-old hatter, 'childless and without fortune', wrote to the *lieutenant général* in 1764 to ask for the release from prison of his faithful *garçon*: his only support, the only one who knew all his customers.[28]

If there were only a couple of journeymen, too, they were more likely to be integrated into the master's family life, and might in that way form local ties. They would be housed and fed, were as likely to be ruled by his wife as by him, and might work alongside members of his family. A journeyman joiner recalled one day having gone with his master's seventeen-year-old son to deliver a mantelpiece.[29] Very often, as we have seen, a master would employ a relative as his *garçon*.

Admittedly, the idyllic picture of the journeyman marrying his master's daughter and inheriting the shop seems to have been largely utopian. Ménétra's memoirs do recount a number of offers that he had from various masters, and tell us that his sister married their father's journeyman, but the papers of the *commissaires* provide very few examples, although there are several cases of journeymen marrying the widows of masters. In the sample of marriage contracts analysed by A. Daumard and F. Furet about a third of the journeymen married daughters of *maîtres marchands*, but most of them were sons of masters and therefore in a somewhat different position. There were probably differences from one trade to another, however. In Lyon it was quite common for outsiders to marry into the family of a silk-merchant, but rare in the hatting trade. This applied to provincial masters, not journeymen, but it illustrates the differing degrees of openness of different trades. In the case of the hatters the workshops were large and the proportion of workers to masters high, a fact which M. Garden relates directly to poor relations between them.[30]

A small master might also have relatively few ties with other masters of the same trade. Many trades were dominated by the wealthiest, best-established members, and small masters were increasingly excluded from the life of the corporation. As in Lyon, attendance at meetings appears to have fallen during the century, leaving the *anciens jurés* speaking for all. A deliberation of the potters' guild in September 1750 decided that in future only the *anciens* and twenty representatives of the other masters would be summoned to meetings for the election of new *jurés*. After 1777 general meetings of all trades were formally limited to twenty-five, the others being 'represented' by two deputies.[31] This strengthened the position of the *jurés* and *anciens*, although in many cases they

---

[28] Bast. 12202, f. 107.   [29] Y10994, 3 Feb.
[30] B.H.V.P. MS 678, f. 55. Daumard and Furet, *Structures*, pp. 60–1, 74–5, 78. Garden, *Lyon*, pp. 77–8, 322, 568–9.
[31] Garden, *Lyon*, pp. 555–6. Sentence de police, 13 Jan. 1751, in A.P.P. Lam., vol. 40, f. 1. Coornaert, *Corporations*, p. 218.

were already firmly in control. In lists of officials one frequently encounters the same family names and sometimes there is evidence of ties by marriage.[32]

The large masters were thus often able to run the corporation in their own interests. In 1764, the *jurés* shoemakers were accused of having rigged a meeting called to decide how their inspections should be paid for. They had invited only eight of each of the three categories of masters (*petits jurés*, *modernes*, *jeunes*) instead of twelve, twenty, and twenty respectively. Furthermore, instead of voting by 'column', with each of these groups having an equal voice no matter what their number, the fifty *jurés* and *anciens* had insisted on a straight numbers vote. Therefore, the plaintiffs pointed out, 'the *anciens* always get their way in the clauses which further their despotism and their interests'. Not only that, but they planned their action before the meeting, whereas the other masters 'arrive at the assembly without knowing what is to be discussed ... or ... have been intimidated by no less illicit means'. As a result the original proposition that inspections by the *jurés* be paid for by charging each master according to his work and number of journeymen was defeated, it being decided instead to impose a single, higher charge for all.[33]

A similar case came up in 1775 in the corporation of the master card- and paper-makers. A complaint by five masters accused four *jurés* and another man of taking on apprentices instead of employing masters without shops, or even journeymen. Not only that, but 'through a private meeting of these principal manufacturers' they had received permission for the corporation to take on additional apprentices. The *anciens* and the *jurés*, concludes the complaint, 'who between them control the greatest part of the manufacture, [are] anxious always to maintain their despotism in the corporation ...'[34]

Manoeuvres of this sort naturally antagonized small masters. Ménétra recorded the satisfaction of the masters when in 1776 'all these *jurés* and *syndics* of such great importance were abolished'. The papers of the *commissaires* contain many complaints of abuses in the administration of the corporations, some of which clearly reflect this antagonism. The eighty-year-old hatter mentioned above, who petitioned the *lieutenant général* for the release of his *garçon*, went on to portray the whole affair as a plot against him by the *jurés*: they were keeping his *garçon* in prison in order to ruin him. His letter displays complete alienation from those who supposedly represented his interests.[35]

On occasion there is evidence of disaffected masters getting together in opposition to the *jurés*, in combination, significantly, with their journeymen. Several master dyers, for example, were among the administrators of a confraternity which rivalled the official one. In 1746 a large number of master

---

[32] Y15363, 29 July 1753 (*grainiers*). Y12596, 3 July (*limonadiers*). Y11239, 30 Oct. (*cordiers*). Y15350, 7 Oct., wit. 5 (*selliers*). B.H.V.P. MS 678, f. 184 (*vitriers*).
[33] Y11952, 11 July 1764. [34] Y14560, 13 Sept. 1775.
[35] B.H.V.P. MS 678, ff. 146, 180–6. Bast. 12202, f. 109.

locksmiths supported their journeymen's fight against compulsory registration at the Bureau, which the *jurés* wanted to impose.[36] But what is more difficult to grasp is the extent to which their alienation from the official corporation cut them off from their fellow-masters. This must certainly have happened in trades where their main contact with each other had always been at general meetings, at services of the confraternity, and in the public processions in which all the masters had once paraded, as they apparently still did in Lyon, in the colours and under the banner of their trade. It was inevitable that such activities would decline, or cease to involve everyone, as the city and the number of people engaged in each trade grew. This was the reason given by the potters for restricting the number at what had been general meetings.[37] In many trades it was simply no longer possible for everyone to know everyone else, and corporate unity was the victim.

We can therefore distinguish two extremes among masters in the corporate trades. At one pole we find, particularly in widely distributed trades with many members, a relatively small group of the wealthiest and best-established masters largely in control, sharing a strong sense of corporate identity reinforced by frequent contact, pride in their position, and sometimes by family ties as well. At the other end of the scale were many masters whose wealth or contacts were not sufficient for them to become *jurés*. Depending on the nature of their work, they were less likely to form trade ties right across the city. They were quite probably closer to their workers and to their neighbours than to others of the same trade in other parts of the city.

The work contacts of journeymen within the local community were often similar to those of masters. If the workshop was small and open to the street; if the trade encouraged contact with local clients; if the journeyman worked alongside his master and participated in the latter's family life, then he was clearly likely to become part of the local community. If, on the other hand, the workshop was large and the type of work cut it off from the neighbours, both master and man tended to have stronger links with others of the same occupation in other areas of the city.

For journeymen, however, still other factors were important. Whereas masters had a stake in the quarter by virtue of their establishment, many journeymen moved around a great deal. Workers in some trades, notably those in the construction industry – masons, carpenters, glaziers, some wood-carvers and locksmiths, roofers and pavers – had to move from site to site and therefore might have little chance to form ties in the neighbourhood of their work. But the mobility of the work-force was more often determined by fluctuations in

[36] Y15364, 17 Sept. 1741. Y13751, 19 Sept., interr. 5., 11 Oct.

[37] Coornaert, *Corporations*, pp. 228–30. N. Z. Davis, 'Women in the *Arts mécaniques* in Sixteenth-Century Lyon', in *Lyon et l'Europe. Hommes et sociétés. Mélanges d'histoire offerts à Richard Gascon*, 2 vols. (Lyon, Presses universitaires de Lyon, 1981), vol. 1, p. 144. B.H.V.P. MS 678, f. 67. Sentence de police, 13 Jan. 1751, in A.P.P. Lam. vol. 40, ff. 1–2.

demand, reflected in the conditions of employment. Again the building trades are a good example. Y. Durand had shown that the way building-workers were taken on was well adapted to a job where the type and duration of work and the numbers of men required varied enormously. The master mason would employ a 'maître compagnon' who was responsible for hiring and overseeing the workers, but he might be the only permanent employee. The stone-cutters and labourers were paid on a daily basis and could therefore be put off as soon as the job finished. Durand even found mentions of thirds and sixths of days in the lists of payments.[38]

A similar structure existed in other trades. Many journeymen were paid by the day: carpenters and locksmiths, joiners, saddlers, wheelwrights, tanners, bakers, saltpetre workers, painters and gilders.[39] Some bakers employed a *maître compagnon*, and there is one mention of a 'maître garçon de chantier' working for a butcher. The accounts of a master brewer in 1752 show that he too had a 'maître garçon' paid by the year, and at least three *garçons* paid by the month, which suggests a somewhat less mobile work-force. Other industries coped with fluctuations in demand by paying their journeymen by the job. Framework knitters were paid for each pair of stockings, ribbon-makers for each *aune* (just over a metre) that they wove. A similar system operated for makers of gauze, nails, and for some hatters.[40]

In many trades, therefore, journeymen could be taken on and put off according to the work the master had at that moment. This explains the irregular and frequent changes of master which many journeymen describe in interrogations and enquiries. A journeyman joiner living in the rue St Jacques de la Boucherie stated that he had worked for many masters over the years, and mentioned spending six months with one in the rue Bailleul near St Germain l'Auxerrois, returning there recently for a week, and now working for another master near St Eustache.[41] In a case like this the journeyman might spend little time working in any one neighbourhood and would be likely to contract trade ties right across the city.

This was so not only because he would work in many different places, but also because of the links formed through simply looking for employment. In many trades the normal procedure was simply to go from shop to shop asking whether an extra journeyman was needed. There were sometimes traditional gathering-places for men who were out of work: the Place de Grève for masons and

---

38 Y. Durand, 'Recherches sur les salaires des maçons à Paris au XVIIIe siècle', *Revue d'histoire économique et sociale*, 44 (1966), 468–80. Y9949, 2 May 1785. Y15402, 24 Jan.

39 Andrews, 'Political Elites', p. 343. Martin, *Associations*, p. 138. Y15099, 6 May, wit. 6. Y12596, 28 Feb., opp. 31. Arrêt du Parlement, 24 Mar. 1766, in Bast. 12369, ff. 6–8.

40 Y9532, 12 Dec. 1718, wit. 1. Y15350, 12 July. Y10994, 13 Dec. Martin, *Associations*, pp. 133, 137, 140. Y9525, 20 May 1763. Y15363, 21 June 1751. A.P.P., Lam., vol. 40, ff. 22–4, Sentence de police, 30 Apr. 1751.

41 Y15350, 17 July. See changes of work-place between declarations of 23 Apr. and enquiry of 24 May, Y15099. See also 24 Jan.

building-workers, the rue de la Poterie for *garçons pâtissiers*, the rue des Ecouffes for joiners. Among hatters and silk-workers, early in the century, it was the journeymen themselves who found jobs for their fellows, perhaps on the same lines as many London trades. In 1720 it was the makers and sellers of tools who acted as an employment agency for journeymen *savetiers*. Increasingly that function was taken over by the Bureaux of the corporations, and towards the end of the century some of these also became important meeting places. A journeyman shoemaker in the rue Bordet said that he knew another *garçon* 'indirectly', having seen him at their Bureau.[42]

The nature of the work and the terms of employment were not the only factors which determined geographic mobility. There was some variation according to age and marital status. Unmarried men tended to move around more. In certain trades there was the Tour de France. For many, too, the attraction of the army was strong, and there are innumerable examples of journeymen who at some stage combined their ordinary calling with that of soldier. Young men might also move on in search of a better position. Once again the locksmiths' strike of 1746 is instructive. The work stoppage was opposed by 'about twenty who were the senior journeymen (*anciens*), at which the young ones said ... that it was because they had good workshops that they did not want to stop'.[43]

Yet another factor determining mobility within the trade was birth-place. Men from the provinces tended to go home from time to time. A *garçon marchand de vin* who arrived in Paris in 1744, looking for work, found a position with a *marchand* for one month, then spent eight months working for the Princesse de Conti before returning to his home in Picardy for another month. He then returned to Paris and worked for the same *marchand de vin* for a further three years. Provincial origin could create a certain sense of detachment, particularly for unmarried journeymen: it was pointless, said one locksmith, for him to register at the Bureau, 'because he was returning to his *pays*'. The *jurés* cutlers, making a complaint in 1748 and perhaps exaggerating a little, emphasized the relative rootlessness of many of their journeymen, 'because in general all these journeymen are provincials, not married or domiciled in this city ... where they have no home other than with the masters for whom they are working'.[44]

There was, however, another form of geographic mobility: commuting to work across the city. Not all journeymen lived with their masters. According to the above quote most of the cutlers did, and the same was true of *garçons marchands*

---

[42] Y10994, 30 Oct. Y14484, 30 Nov. Ordonnance de police, 10 May 1719, in Martin, *Associations*, p. 96, note 1. Kaplan, 'Réflexions', pp. 43, 47. Bast. 12369, f. 4. Martin, p. 161, note. C. Dobson, *Masters and Journeymen* (London, Croom Helm, 1980), pp. 38–46. Ordonnance de police, 5 Sept. 1720, in Martin, p. 162, note 1. Y13290, 19 Sept., wit. 1. See Y15402, 10 Feb.

[43] Y13751, 19 Sept., interr. 15; see also interr. 11. On the Tour de France see E. Coornaert, *Les Compagnonnages en France du moyen âge à nos jours* (Paris, Editions ouvrières, 1966).

[44] Y14078, 24 June. Y13751, 19 Sept., interr. 13. Sentence de pol., 4 Mar. 1748, in B.N. Ms. fr. 8090, f. 386.

de vin, perhaps because of the type of work and the hours involved. Masons on the other hand never did, which is understandable given the terms of their employment. In other trades the situation is less clear, with some workers lodged by their masters, others – including most of those who were married – settled in their own lodgings. Even if these settled men went from one master to another, they did not change their residence or lose their contacts in the quarter in which they were living.

The evidence suggests that unmarried journeymen increasingly lived in lodging-houses and rented rooms. 'The custom of lodging ... journeymen properly is disappearing', lamented Restif. His statement is supported by the evidence in the papers of the *commissaires*, and it was certainly the tendency in Lyon during the same period. Restif adds that as a result journeymen of different trades tended to lodge and eat together more than before, but the police records indicate that very often men shared a room with others of the same trade.[45] There were even lodging-houses which were consistently used by certain trades: S. Kaplan has identified some seven for journeymen bakers. In the rue de la Vannerie was a 'lodger of *perruquiers*', and in 1788 a lodging-house keeper in the rue St Denis was described as 'mère ['hostess'] des perruquiers'. Perhaps in the same category was a 'logis de garçons tailleurs' in the rue St Honoré.[46]

These establishments were on the whole unlikely to encourage the formation of local ties. But they could also be long-term residences for men working now for one master, now for another. One *compagnon menuisier* lodging in an inn in the rue Maubué had been there for three years.[47]

Considering the absence of public transport and the size of the city, a surprising number of people lived some distance from their place of work. An increasing number of workers lived in the *faubourgs* and walked to work in the city proper.[48] Where there were large numbers of people commuting together, work and neighbourhood could overlap, but in most such cases work contacts did not reinforce local ties. It was of course possible for an individual to become part of two local communities, but geographic mobility often reduced the chances for journeymen to form close bonds with their neighbours.

A further factor which determined the strength of city-wide ties among journeymen was, as for masters, their corporate identity. It was affected by many

---

45 Restif, quoted in Coornaert, *Corporations*, p. 271, no date given. Garden, *Lyon*, p. 160. In my sample 67 per cent of journeymen lived with their masters in 1752 and 34 per cent in 1788.
46 Kaplan, 'Réflexions', pp. 65–6. Y15117, 29 Dec. Y15099, 26 Mar. Y14484, 26 Mar., wit. 1. Y15363, 9 Mar. 1743. Despite the use of 'mère', *compagnonnages* were not important in eighteenth-century Paris. See M. Sonenscher and D. Garrioch, '*Compagnonnages*, Confraternities and Associations of Journeymen in Eighteenth Century Paris', *European History Quarterly*, 16 (1986), 25–45.
47 Y15350, 26 Aug., wit. 3.
48 Y12596, 27 July. Y13290, 19 Oct., wit. 3. Y15099, 1 May. Rudé, 'Wage-Earning Population', vol. 1, pp. 155–6. Mercier, *Tableau*, vol. 4, p. 149. A. Goeury, 'Grange-Batelière', p. 139. Andrews, 'Political Elites', pp. 333–5.

of the same things: the master–journeyman ratio, the size of workshops, the structure of the trade and the opportunities for contact. The degree of skill required was also very important, for a trade which was easy to enter and which needed little training was less likely to encourage a strong corporate spirit than one which required a long (and expensive) apprenticeship. Weaving, for example, could be learned quickly, needed few tools, and made a good part-time occupation. Highly skilled trades, however, encouraged a strong work identity.

There is evidence of firm, city-wide solidarity among journeymen of many trades, for example in industrial disputes: nail-makers in 1751; *fabricants d'étoffes* (cloth-makers) in 1756; ribbon-makers in 1762 and 1763; coopers in 1766; book-binders in 1776; stone-cutters in 1785. In quite a number of trades there had long existed structures for journeymen, as well as for masters, usually in the form of confraternities. There were at least thirty-one such organizations, which often functioned as mutual-aid societies or employment agencies, and were involved in organizing strikes in a number of trades.[49] They helped to create a city-wide trade community for men whose participation in the corporations was very limited. And they provided ties outside the local community.

It is probable, however, again depending on the structure and dispersion of each trade, that journeymen's associations declined during the eighteenth century. Many corporations took control of employment away from journeymen by forcing them to register at the Bureau and to carry a certificate. The growth of the city also militated against journeymen's associations, just as it worked against the corporations themselves. If it had once been possible for all the journeymen in a given trade to know each other at least by sight, and to participate in corporate activities, by the eighteenth century this was only possible in the very smallest and most close-knit trades. Both small masters and the more settled journeymen, therefore, had fewer city-wide work contacts which might take them outside the neighbourhood. It did not necessarily mean a loss of work identity. After all, an artisan lived and worked under the symbol of his trade and was known in the area as *the* locksmith or *the* wheelwright. But this sort of identity had its source and its significance within the neighbourhood, and strengthened the individual's sense of belonging to the local community.

One further addition to this discussion of corporate trades is necessary. Women in the corporations were usually in quite a different position. As N. Davis has pointed out, work did not play the same role for them as it did for men.[50] I wish to look briefly at three groups: women who ran their own business; those who worked in shops, often with their husbands; and those who were employed in various corporate trades.

[49] Y15363, 12 June 1751. Sentences de police, 20 Mar. 1756, in Lam., vol. 40, ff. 375–80. Y9525, 20 May 1763. Sentence de police, 19 Nov. 1766 and Arrêt du Parlement, 3 Feb. 1767, cited in Kaplan, 'Réflexions', p. 31. Y12826, report of Dupuy to Chambre de police, 18 Oct. 1776. Y9949, 2 May 1785. Sonenscher and Garrioch, '*Compagnonnages*'.
[50] Davis, 'Women', pp. 139–67.

A few trades were exclusively female. Linen-makers, female hairdressers, seamstresses, the makers of flax, hemp and tow, and midwives all had formal statutes and were later joined, apparently, by the *marchandes de modes* (sellers of female clothes). All of these functioned in more or less the same way as the male corporations. Girls were apprenticed to a mistress just as boys were to a master. They were lodged, fed and instructed in the trade for a fixed period of time, in the case of seamstresses for three years, four years for linen-makers. The *maîtresses* enjoyed a position comparable with some of the male corporations. Lenoir, in describing the method of assessing the *capitation* tax paid by tradesmen after 1776, chose as an example one of the *marchandes de modes*, 'whose credit, commerce, warehouses, number of workers gave her a fortune evaluated at more than that of the others'.[51] The degree of corporate pride among the linen-makers is reflected in the handsome doorway of their Bureau, originally in the Place Ste Opportune and now re-erected opposite the Centre Georges Pompidou. *Maîtresses* in these trades could develop a strong work identity in much the same conditions as masters in the other corporations, although they could not aspire to the same status in public life.

The situation of women in the other trades was very different. In many occupations the widows of masters could continue trading on their own, and the grain merchants actually allowed women in their own right. They were all, however, in male-dominated trades. The *jurés* were always men, and often, as in the case of the dyers, widows of masters were excluded from taking apprentices. Women could perfectly well manage the commercial side of a business, which many handled even if their husbands were alive. But the workshop could be a different story. A widow had no formal training in her husband's trade and could have trouble telling the journeymen what to do. Even where widows did successfully run manufacturing businesses, they nevertheless could never develop a work identity based on the skills of their trade, nor participate equally in the life of the corporation.[52] Of course most shopkeepers had their wives and sometimes their daughters working with them, and many employed a female shop-assistant. The wives of merchants (although not of master craftsmen) would even adopt the title and be referred to as, for example, 'marchande mercière' or 'marchande bouchère'. Like their husbands, therefore, they were to some extent defined by their work. They nevertheless did not have the same status or range of contacts, for they could not participate in the life of the corporation. Wives who were in charge of the accounts – and the evidence suggests that this happened more often in craft industries than in purely merchant ones – did deal with suppliers and clients and therefore had the opportunity to develop many of the same ties as their husbands, according to the

51 Savary, *Dictionnaire*, arts. 'Communauté', 'Couturière', 'Lingère'. Orléans MS 1422, f. 456. Y13760, 1 Feb. Y13290, 7 Jan.
52 Savary, *Dictionnaire*, art. 'Teinturier'. Y13290, 10 Apr., 19 Sept. Davis, 'Women', p. 145.

nature of the trade and to their place within it. In most occupations, however, the wives and female employees who worked in the shop had contact above all with the clients. Depending on the nature of the business, this sort of work for women was therefore most likely to provide local contacts and thus reinforced their place in the local community rather than taking them outside it.

The majority of women in the corporate trades worked in the least skilled areas of the textile and luxury industries: as spinners, wood- and metal-polishers, gauze-, lace-, and linen-workers, fan-makers. Some were employed in workshops, but seem to have developed none of the professional pride of journeymen. There is no trace of women organizing as journeymen did, no doubt partly because of the low level of skill normally required of them. But it is also likely, as N. Davis has argued was the case in sixteenth-century Lyon, that women simply did not see the sphere of work as one in which they had rights. The majority in any case had little chance to develop corporate ties because they did piece-work at home, an arrangement which suited employers because it enabled them to pay lower wages and to respond readily to fluc-tuations in demand.[53] For these women, therefore, work contributed to the formation of women's networks in the locality, rather than providing ties outside the neighbourhood as it did for many men.

A couple of preliminary conclusions emerge from this survey of corporate trades. Where there was a strong concentration of the one trade or of closely associated ones in the same area, work identity played a major role in the for-mation of the local community. In such cases it could create a sub-group within the community in the same way as family ties: particularly close-knit but not normally in conflict with other local loyalties. Elsewhere it reinforced the bonds of neighbourhood between individuals, and through a multitude of such *rap-prochements* contributed to the cohesion and unity of the community. On the other hand, strong corporate ties stretching outside the quarter could distance a man from it, although we must not forget that *pays* and family (particularly wife and children) and perhaps other bonds, could work in the opposite direction.

Precisely where corporate spirit was at its strongest, however, it reinforced the community in another very important respect, by contributing to the develop-ment and maintenance of a collective mentality. The group solidarity cultivated in young men by the experience of work in a corporate trade was very similar to that which existed within the neighbourhood. Thus the alienation of small masters and journeymen from the trades corporations during the eighteenth century, and simply the growth of the city and of the trades themselves, may in the short term have strengthened the local community, but they were ultimately

---

[53] A. Groppi, 'Le Travail des femmes à Paris à l'époque de la Révolution française', *Bulletin d'histoire économique et sociale de la Révolution française*, 1979, 27–46. Monnier, 'Travail des femmes', pp. 47–60. Davis, 'Women', pp. 150–1.

to weaken it by destroying the collective values on which both geographic and trade communities rested.

II. STREET, PORT, AND MARKET TRADES

Largely unskilled, lacking the centralized structure and official hierarchy of the corporate trades, the street, port, and market trades involved a different set of relationships, another sort of work identity, and a different rapport with the local community. The master–journeyman relationship was absent, most street tradespeople being self-employed. *Gagne deniers* came closest to the status of employees, but worked for many different people and were therefore not in the same position of financial dependence as journeymen. Nor could they develop comparable ties with their employers. Similarly, the relationship of workmates was different among street trades. They were not linked by common membership of a highly skilled occupation, by a city-wide corporate identity, or by a shared relationship with a master.

Even here, however, we must take into account the different elements among the street trades. Labourers and ballad-singers, fishwives and waggoners, each had different work patterns and a different relationship with their environment. There were also geographic distinctions. A workman on the ports, a *fort de la halle*, and a *gagne denier* in the streets of the city, all unskilled labourers, did different sorts of work and above all found themselves in quite distinct social contexts. They did not necessarily occupy the same place in the local community.

Let us look first at the world of the market-place, in some ways quite different from that of the streets. Its clientele was composed not just of locals but of people from all the surrounding quarters – in some cases from all over the city. It was also peculiar in being a purely commercial space, not one where people lived. This was especially true of the covered markets: the new Halle au Blé (opened in the 1760s), the leather and cloth markets, later the new fish-market.[54] But even the open markets in the Place Maubert, the Cimetière St Jean or the Carreau de la Halle itself, were wide spaces which had the aspect neither of a residential area nor of a public thoroughfare. This does not mean they were cut off from the surrounding area. Quite the contrary, they were inseparable from it. The waggons, the crowds and the noise, the stalls themselves overflowed into the nearby streets. The whole area was dominated by the market. This made for a peculiar occupational homogeneity, for the neighbourhood belonged to the market trades and not to the diverse groups which were to be found in most streets of the city.

As in areas where a single corporate trade was dominant, work ties were vital in the formation of the local community. The best example is the central market

[54] Lettres patentes du Roi, 25 Nov. 1762, in Peuchet, *Collection*, vol. 7, p. 185. Verniquet, *Plan*, 1791.

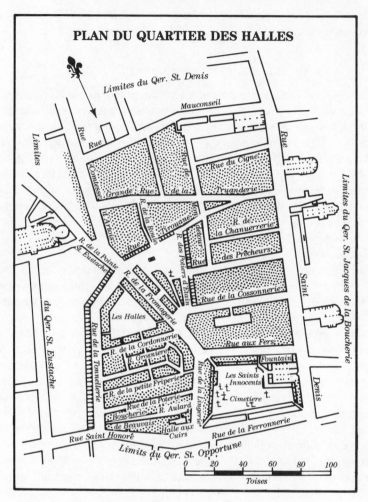

9. The Halles quarter, 1773 (from the map by Jaillot)

area. At the heart of the community were the Parisian stall-keepers, primarily women: sellers of fruit, baker-women, and the *poissardes* (fishwives) of literary fame (although the term is never used in our documents). Those selling each sort of produce were concentrated in one area, in some cases only on certain days. Every day except Wednesday and Saturday, when the grain-market was held, salted butter, cheese and fruit were sold in the old Halle au Blé. Eggs and fresh butter were sold on the Carreau, near the Pillory, as was bread and salt-water fish.[55]

[55] *Mémoires des intendants*, vol. 1, pp. 669–70.

The disputes brought to the *commissaires* indicate the degree of contact and familiarity within each sector, most occurring between people selling the same product. They all knew what the others' husbands did, how many children they had, and whether they were married. There was also co-operation: the loan by one baker-woman to another of a cloth used for covering the bread; or, this time among fishwives, keeping an eye on a stall when some urgent matter called its owner away.[56]

Of course work ties were very often doubled by others. Many stall-keepers knew each other as neighbours, mostly near the market but sometimes further away: two baker-women with neighbouring stalls both lived in the rue du Faubourg Montmartre, and their long-running dispute was considerably sharpened by its having two excellent venues. It was also very common to find family ties in the market-place, especially between mother and daughter. There were also less tangible ties. When two women quarrelled over a measure in the Halle au Blé it emerged that one of them lived in the same house as the other's uncle.[57]

Multiple bonds created a very strong work identity, reinforced by and reflected in the official recognition extended to the 'Dames de la Halle' (ladies of the Halle). They had the privilege, on certain occasions such as the birth of a royal child, of complimenting the king personally. During the Revolution the Dames de la Halle as a group were portrayed in many pamphlets as the core of the patriotic *sans-culotte* movement.[58]

A second important group in the central market were the *marchands forains*, producers or merchants who brought foodstuffs into Paris from the surrounding provinces. They were a less permanent group, not living in Paris and not coming every day. Those selling fruit and Brie cheese, and the pork merchants from Nanterre, came early on Wednesdays and Saturdays and left at eight or nine in the morning to make way for the grain. On the other days of the week there were fruit and vegetable sellers, including a sizeable contingent from near St Denis.[59]

Some of these *forains*, particularly those from the same village or who regularly came together, formed close-knit groups. The same family names recur, and they displayed considerable solidarity in the fights that occasionally erupted with other market groups: one in February 1776 involved the *forts*, the *fruitier-orangers*, and the egg merchants, the latter wanting to charge very high prices because of the extreme cold.[60] At the same time the *marchands forains* were very much a part of the market community. One man, who brought a load of fruit from near Pontoise, said that he and his father had been coming to Paris for over

---

[56] Y11239, 20 Dec., 16 May, annulled complaint on the back of another dated 8 Sept., 18 Sept.
[57] Y11239, 16 May. Y14484, 3 Apr., 12 May. Y11239, 18 Mar.
[58] Mercier, *Tableau*, vol. 4, p. 37. See, for example, the *Liste des clubs aristocratiques et anti-constitutionnels qui ont été fouettés hier au soir à tour de bras par les Dames de la Halle et du faubourg St Antoine* (1791), in B.N. 8° Lb³⁹ 5505.
[59] Y11239, 18 Sept., 15 Nov., 19 Sept., 20 May, 10 July. *Mémoires des intendants*, vol. 1, p. 670.
[60] Y11239, 15 Nov., 20 May, 10 July. B.N. Ms. fr. 6682, f. 174, 16 Feb. 1776.

Table 4. *Disputes in Halles quarter, 1752: relationships and locations*

		Neighbours			Same workplace (different trade)	Seller–client		Strangers	?	TOTAL	%
	Family	Master–man Apprentice only	and same occupation	Same occupation		only	and neighbour				
Workplace of both parties (interior)		2		2						4	6.2
Apartment or shop of one or both (interior)	5								1	6	9.2
Courtyard or stair (house of one or both)			5							5	7.7
Street: near house or workplace of one or both	2	1	4	1		1	2			11	16.9
street elsewhere						1		1	1	3	4.6
Wineshop	1	2	3	2		2	1	3	1	15	23.1
Market	1		5	9	4	2				21	32.3
Total	9	5	17	14	4	6	3	4	3	65	100.0

twenty years, always staying at the same 'Hôtellerie du Paon' at the Pointe St Eustache. Those who came regularly might have the same clients, and had frequent contact with other market trades. One man said that having received only six *livres* for a bag of peas worth six *livres* five *sols*, he had allowed the woman to take them because one of the *forts* vouched for her.[61]

The market porters themselves formed the third major group in the central Halle, and they had almost corporate status. According to S. Kaplan those in the grain-market were personally recruited by one of the *inspecteurs de police* and contained virtual family dynasties. Hardy mentions their having a *syndic*, and a complaint by one of the 'bande des petits forts' in 1752 indicates that they had a common purse into which all their takings went. They took it in turns, two by two, to act as treasurer.[62] It is not clear whether the *forts* on the Carreau, next to the grain-market, had the same degree of organization, but they too displayed considerable solidarity in disputes.

There were, then, a number of identifiable groups within the market-place, each bound by occupational and often family and neighbourhood ties as well. Yet all formed part of a larger market community, or series of communities, based on proximity and regular contact. The Halle was the social context in which disputes took place: 'the plaintiff is always in the Halle, where she is known', points out one complaint. A third of all the disputes in the papers of the senior *commissaire* of the quarter for 1752 took place in the market, most between people of the same or related occupations (see table 4).[63]

At the same time, of course, the market and its trades were inseparable from the surrounding area and the rest of the city. One *fort* living in the rue des Prêcheurs had a sister who sold vegetables in front of St Eustache, just outside the market area, and who lived in the house of a *fruitier-oranger* overlooking the Carreau. Most of the fishwives and *fruitières* were married to men working in unskilled or the humbler ranks of the skilled trades. A German visitor to Paris in 1789 observed that the *poissardes* 'are linked by blood or clientage relationships to all the respectable men of Paris who shine shoes, carry coals, clean out sewers, build or tear down walls'.[64]

There were also certain corporate trades which were supplied from the central market and which had close ties with the market trades. We find the 'garçon de place' of a *factrice aux farines* going for a drink with a baker from the Faubourg St Antoine. The *fruitier-orangers* not only purchased their stock from the *marchands forains*, but in many cases lived close by, some of them even retailing on the Carreau. A number of them frequented a wineshop in the rue Mondetour, just

[61] Y11239, 10 July.
[62] Kaplan, 'Réflexions', p. 30. B.N. Ms. fr. 6680, f. 51, 23 Sept. 1767. Y11239, 28 Oct.
[63] Y11239, 22 June. See table 4, p. 118.
[64] Y15402, 2 Oct. Y11239, 8 Sept. Schulz and Krauz, *Beschreibung und Abbildung der Poissarden in Paris* (Weimar and Berlin, 1789), quoted in Kaplow, *Names*, pp. 46–7.

round the corner.[65] Despite their corporate ties they were very much a part of the local market community.

The other markets are less well documented, but there are traces of similar bonds and patterns of solidarity. The fishwives of the Place Maubert, the main market on the Left Bank, not only had their stalls together but would go in a group to buy stock at the central market, hiring a waggon to take it all back with them. In August 1789 the market women went in procession to Ste Geneviève to thank the saint for delivering them from despotism. Many of the stall-keepers in the Place Maubert lived in the surrounding streets, had contacts with the local shopkeepers, and in some cases traded alongside others of the same family.[66]

One document gives us a glimpse of the society of La Vallée, the poultry- and game-market on the Quai de la Mégisserie. The daughter of a *maître rôtisseur* made a formal complaint against a domestic servant with whom she had been living for some five years, to try to get him to marry her. Recently he had been slandering her, 'which daily causes her arguments and altercations with all the women on the Carreau de la Vallée'. She produced a list of witnesses, including four *maîtres rôtisseurs* and their wives, and a *gagne denier* from La Vallée. This was clearly a market community dominated by the *rôtisseurs*, a corporate trade, but it was a community in which the women on the stalls had an important role of social commentary, and where a *gagne denier* was as much part of the local scene as those working in the shops.[67]

Similar to the market communities were those of the ports, for they too were based on a collection of geographically concentrated trades. It is true that the busy *quais* attracted a floating population of unskilled workers, for there was a great deal of carrying and other casual work. But there was also a permanent work-force of *déchargeurs*, very jealous of their monopoly on loading and unloading the boats. The Prévôt des Marchands fixed the number of each specialized group: the *garçons de la pelle* who unloaded coal and charcoal; the *débardeurs* who specialized in wood and were therefore concentrated at the Grève and near Bercy where the timber-trains and boats arrived. Ten *débardeurs* from Bercy were prominent, as a body, in the sacking of Réveillon's house in April 1789. Further upstream, at La Rapée, could be found the *remplisseurs de vin* who unloaded wine and who, like the *forts de la halle*, had a *syndic* and a common purse from which all were paid. The *officiers forts du port St Paul* likewise had a semi-corporate status, with their own statutes.[68]

The laundry boats, moored near the river-bank and accessible by planks, were also centres where women – mostly professional laundrywomen but sometimes others as well – met daily, chatted, and inevitably quarrelled. They had regular

[65] Y11239, 5 Aug., 7 Jan., 29 Oct., 13 Oct., 19 Sept., 14 July.
[66] Y11239, 18 Sept., wit. 4, 5, 6. Y12596, 20 Jan. Burstin, 'Faubourg', p. 391.
[67] Y15350, 1 May.
[68] Roche, *Peuple*, p. 125. Kaplow, *Names*, pp. 15, 42. Y13454A, 10 May 1789. Y10994, 7 Apr. H747², f. 77, Statutes of 'officiers forts du port St Paul'.

contact with the boatmen: we find a laundrywoman married to one, and another river-man and a laundrywoman were godparents to the same child. The two corporations of fishermen also had constant contact with those on the ports, and most lived along the river. The water-carriers and the laundrywomen were particularly closely associated. Every year, after the thaw and often coinciding with Mardi Gras, a queen was elected on the laundry boats and, at least at the start of the nineteenth century, a king from among the water-carriers (although this may have been confined to the city centre). Similar customs existed elsewhere in the Ile de France, a sort of corporate celebration among the river trades.[69]

There were certainly some links right along the river, yet the evidence suggests that most river people belonged, or saw themselves as belonging, to one port in particular: one man, for example, gave his occupation as '*fort* on the *port au bled*'. Most people in the river trades lived in the streets adjoining the quais and the communities along the river were therefore intimately linked with those in the neighbouring quarters. A complaint by a fisherman, as if spelling out the overlapping social worlds to which he felt himself to belong, spoke of the potential damage of calumnies 'dans le Public, dans les cabarets du quartier et sur la rivière' (amongst the public, in the wineshops of the quarter and on the river).[70]

As in the markets, therefore, the community of the ports was based above all on bonds created in the course of people's work and unlike other local communities did not depend primarily on residential neighbourhood. Yet it remained a local community, because everyone worked in the same place and was conscious of belonging to the quarter. Within it, as in certain other areas of the city, the ties binding those of the same occupation created patterns of solidarity whose contours become apparent in cases of internal division and conflict.

The street trades proper were exercised in a residential and rather more socially varied environment. Their number and variety were enormous, but several main groups can be picked out. There were the semi-permanent stall-keepers stationed primarily along the main thoroughfares, on street corners, on the bridges and at the old city gates, all strategic centres of sociability (a fact reflected in the choice of the same sorts of places for the *corps de garde* [guardhouses]). We have seen the central role that these people, mostly women, had in the neighbourhood. They had particularly close ties with other stall-keepers and with the local shopkeepers. Indeed, many shopkeepers themselves occupied the stalls in front of their establishments. All were neighbours, and

[69] Y15350, 23 Oct. H. Robert, *Démolition des maisons du Pont Notre Dame*, Musée Carnavalet (1786). Y12597, 8 Dec. Y15350, 23 Oct., wit. 5. A. Faure, *Paris Carême-prenant* (Paris, Hachette, 1978), p. 136. See Farge, 'Mendiant', pp. 323–4.

[70] Y15100, 3 July. Y14484, 14 July. Y15350, 23 Oct. Y12597, 8 Dec. (three complaints). Y15350, 13 Nov. Y10994, 7 Apr.

fruitières and *revendeuses* participated on equal terms in quarrels between shopkeepers and with others in the street. Unlike the 'Dames de la halle', they were not normally distinguishable as a group, separate from other people in the area.

There are, however, a few exceptions, cases where stall-keepers had a greater sense of unity and work identity. This would happen where they sold the same thing in close proximity or were dependent on a common source of supply. After a sale in the rue de Baffroi, for example, four *revendeuses* living in the Faubourg St Antoine attacked several local *tapissiers*, claiming that the merchandise purchased should be shared out. The background to this dispute is not clear, but it was only one incident in a longer-running conflict. In the Faubourg St Marcel there was a certain degree of unity among fruiterers who gathered at the Barrière des Gobelins on summer nights between midnight and one in the morning to wait for the cherry-merchants from whom they purchased their stock. When one of them, an old man, was attacked by thieves on his way there, several of the women escorted him home.[71] Even stronger ties, possibly reinforced by *pays*, linked the crowd of *mercandiers* (meat sellers) who set up their stalls in the rue de la Grande Friperie.[72] When in December 1788 the *garde* tried to get them to move so that a waggon could pass they resisted vigorously. There had long been conflict between them and the shopkeepers, yet they were not entirely divorced from the locals, for at least two witnesses, a lodging-house keeper and his wife, testified in their favour. They were also massively supported by what a master purse-maker termed 'the people assembled in great numbers', although this may to some extent reflect the enormous unpopularity of the *garde* after its severe repression of the riots at the end of 1788.

These three examples illustrate different effects of work ties between stall-keepers. In the first case, as in similar examples from other trade groups, they overlapped with neighbourhood ties to create a close-knit group within the local community. For the fruiterers of the Faubourg St Marcel they provided bonds outside the neighbourhood, a *faubourg*-wide sense of identity, although there is nothing to suggest that this weakened their local affiliations. The *mercandiers*, on the other hand, formed a distinct group, perhaps based partly on *pays* as well. They did not live in the neighbourhood and were at loggerheads with a certain section of the locals, although backed up by others. The testimony of the few witnesses who supported them suggests that their regular presence made them part of the neighbourhood, and that the situation was something like that in the rue de Lappe, where there was perennial conflict between the Auvergnat tinkers and the butchers in the next street.[73] Work (and sometimes

[71] Y13290, 21 June, 8 July.
[72] The *mercandiers* acted as middle-men between the animal breeders and the butchers. See Burstin, 'Faubourg', p. 197. M. Reinhard, *Nouvelle Histoire de Paris. La Révolution, 1789–1799* (Paris, Hachette, 1971), p. 58.
[73] Y10994, 6 June.

pays) created a division within the local community, all the more acute in the case of the *mercandiers* because it was not bridged by bonds of common residence. In none of these three cases, however, did their work give stall-keepers stronger ties outside the neighbourhood than within it.

The dividing line between stall-keepers and what were officially itinerant street-traders was often a very fine one. Although forbidden to stop in the street, many had places fixed by custom: sellers of snacks and drinks, of fruit, hats, hardware, or other goods which they displayed on portable trays called *éventaires*.[74] The same was true of street labourers, known by a bewildering variety of labels: *gagne deniers, commissionnaires, crocheteurs, portefaix*, Savoyards, *décrotteurs*. Most had fixed places where they waited for work, and people would in fact often employ the same man. When the *lieutenant général de police* wanted to check on one of the *inspecteurs* whom he suspected of corruption he sought information from a *commissionnaire* who normally stood on the corner nearest the *inspecteur*'s house.[75]

Street labourers also participated actively in local affairs. A good example is a 'rebellion' in the rue Montmartre against a *huissier* who was trying to arrest a man for debt. A *crocheteur* named Dauphiné came to the rescue, while a *fruitière* called for further help and cried encouragement: 'Courage Dauphiné ... we must kill those scoundrels.' Within minutes an angry crowd had gathered, throwing stones and sticks until the *huissier* and his party retreated in confusion.[76] Here we see a street labourer acting very much as part of the local community.

Many hawkers and labourers, however, had places where they gathered regularly, often in defiance of the authorities, and thus were able to form stronger work ties. On 23 June 1751 the *commissaire* Chenon found over 200 sellers of old hats gathered in the Faubourg St Honoré. The sellers of old hardware who mostly assembled on the Quai de la Mégisserie were accorded a semi-corporate status. Their numbers were limited to eighty, and they had the right to confiscate the wares of unauthorized traders and to name successors to vacancies which occurred in their ranks. *Commissionnaires*, too, waited for work in groups rather than on their own. The *commissaire* Chenon had a list of seven stationed on the corner of the rue de la Monnaie and the rue des Prêtres St Germain l'Auxerrois, all of them Auvergnats. Another group waited in the rue de la Tisseranderie opposite the rue de Coq.[77]

Plying their trade in close proximity gave these people a strong sense of identity, suggested in the police condemnation of their gatherings as

---

74 Y15100, 11 Aug., wit. 2. Y14484, 8 Oct. See Kaplow, *Names*, p. 44. Sentence de police, 22 July 1751, A.P.P. Lam., vol. 40, f. 48. Y15117, 13 June 1788.
75 Bast. 12436, letter to *commissaire* Belle, 12 Aug. 1773.   76 Y15350, 5 June.
77 B.N. J. de F. 1103, f. 117. Y15350, 12 June, wit. 1. Y14078, 14 Oct. Bast. 12436, letter to *commissaire* Belle, 12 Aug. 1773. Kaplow, *Names*, pp. 44–5. Y9508, Register of non-corporate trades, 1767. Y11440, 'Noms des commissionnaires qui se tiennent au coin des rues des Prêtres et de la Monnaye', 17 July 1783. Y15115A, letter of 19 May 1780.

'attroupements': not just a crowd, but an assembly with a degree of unity and cohesion. Indeed they sometimes displayed significant trade solidarity. A police ordinance of 1739 condemned

a company of *gagne deniers*, who have accorded themselves the right to load, unload, pack and transport goods at the *foire* St Germain and at that of St Denis ... [they] force people to pay ... whatever price they see fit to impose.[78]

Similar co-operation characterized the 'Savoyards' in the rue de la Tisseranderie, against whom an *avocat au Parlement* complained in a letter to the *commissaire* of the quarter in May 1780: 'You will agree that they combine to form an insolent little Republic.' Wanting to send a message he had called one of them, but found him unsuitable. He had then sent for the man he usually employed but who refused

because the one who had been sent had not been employed ... [he said] that none of them would go and I could carry my own messages. I will not conceal from you, Monsieur, that I gave him a kick in the backside ... he told me he supported his comrades.[79]

In both of these examples the street trades involved displayed considerable solidarity, aware that they controlled the market. But in both cases it was a local market. The ties between them were based primarily on occupation but also on the neighbourhood in which they worked.

The only trace of a wider network of solidarity is the 1786 action by *commissionnaires* against the new *régie* (authority) set up to carry parcels and letters within the city, and especially the march of seven or eight hundred of them to Versailles to petition the king. Although undoubtedly based on work, their solidarity was strongly reinforced by the bonds of *pays*. All those arrested after an attack on the agents of the *régie*, in the rue St Jacques on 2 January 1786, were Auvergnats from near St Flour, one of them not a *commissionnaire* but a *fort de la halle*. One of the witnesses spoke of the number of other *forts* in the crowd, distinguished by their grey hats and red belts, adding 'that he understood nothing of their Auvergnat language except many threats and vulgar swearing'.[80] The movement was not just of a beleaguered trade group, but of the Auvergnat population of Paris. Even here, however, the quarter had a role to play, for all but one of those arrested in this incident lived within a few streets. The rebellion was the work of a large number of Auvergnats working and probably mostly living in the quarter: the ties of locality, work and *pays* were all present.

Those street trades which were attached to a particular place could therefore, especially if they had other ties as well, form a strong group within the local community even if they did not all live in the neighbourhood. But as with the

[78] Ordonnance de police, 22 Dec. 1739, in Peuchet, vol. 5, p. 59.
[79] Y15115A, letter of 19 May 1780.
[80] M. Rouff, 'Une Grève de gagne-deniers en 1786 à Paris', *Revue historique*, 105 (1910), 332–47. Y12816, 2 Jan., 4 Jan. 1786, wit. 14.

corporate trades, close ties between individuals of the same occupation could work both ways. They could place people at the very heart of the community or they could, as in the example of the *mercandiers*, divide it. And from this there was only a step to cutting people off from it altogether, if the trade group was a small minority within the neighbourhood and its members had stronger ties with each other than with the rest of the local community.

It was different, however, for the numerous street folk who had no fixed places. Some had to wander because of the commodity or service they offered: knife-grinders and menders of pots and pans, street-musicians, hawkers of books and lottery tickets. Yet even many of these exercised their trade within a limited, habitual area, like the man whom an innkeeper recognized because he had seen him 'habitually in the quarter selling rabbit skins . . . he knew him by the name of Ture'. A woman testified that she had seen opposite her shop a '*décrotteur* of the quarter' whom she habitually saw wandering along the rue de la Grande Friperie.[81] People who moved around in this fashion were less rooted in a single neighbourhood but had regular contacts. They were part of the local scene.

The same was true of water-carriers, to a degree representative of delivery trades. They were unusual in having a fairly restricted clientele: Mercier estimated that they could do about thirty trips a day, two buckets of water at a time. In addition they were assigned to a particular well or fountain by the police, and both of these factors kept them within the one quarter. When a man fell from the stairs of a house in the rue de la Tisseranderie the wife of a hatter who lived in the house recognized him as 'her water carrier and the one who supplied the whole house'.[82] Water-carriers too were well-known figures in the neighbourhood.

Whereas street stall-keepers generally had more in common with their neighbours than with others of the same trade, the links between itinerant traders were often closer, partly because of their relative rootlessness. As indicated in the various 'Cris de Paris' collections, many had distinctive costumes and cries.[83] The metal badges and numbers that all were supposed to wear, while less important in denoting their identity to passers-by than their calls and general appearance, gave them a sort of official status. There is little evidence of strong ties between different sorts of street trades, but those hawking the same products very often displayed a degree of unity. Within the one area of the city they would all know each other and could often be counted upon to stand together. In June 1752 the *jurés* glovers–pursers–perfumers stopped a parasol-seller whom they suspected of infringing the privileges of their corporation. The

---

[81] Y12596, 22 July, wit. 2. Y15402, 29 Feb., 7 Mar., wit. 3.

[82] Mercier, *Tableau*, vol. i, p. 154. Y13377, Berryer to *commissaire* Grimperel, 19 Apr. 1752. Y12830, de Sartine to Roland, Apr. 1774. Y15099, 10 June.

[83] For example E. Bouchardon, *Etudes prises dans le bas peuple ou les Cris de Paris* (Paris, 1737–46).

man called out for help and immediately another hawker of parasols from the same *pays*, depositing his wares with a nearby *revendeuse*, came to the rescue.[84]

In many other street trades, too, solidarity was reinforced both by proximity and by common provincial origin. In eighteenth-century Paris, as in most places, many of the humbler, more menial jobs were taken by immigrants. Sellers of rabbit skins who gathered on the Quai de l'Ecole were mostly Auvergnats. So too were wandering tinkers. On at least one occasion the *jurés* coppersmiths, who accused the tinkers of illegal selling, were forced to take refuge in a wineshop to avoid being beaten up.[85]

A great many water-carriers were also Auvergnats. Because of the nature of their migration there were often family ties between them as well, and they frequently rented a room together or shared one in a lodging-house. However, even those water-carriers who were not from the Auvergne would know all the others within the neighbourhood, if only because of their dependence on the same fountain. Among those who queued at a fountain in the rue de Baffröid were two with the very un-Auvergnat names of Hardy and Picard.[86]

The position of itinerant street traders with regard to the local community was often ambiguous. They moved around too much to become fully part of it. Where those of the same trade had close ties with each other, and particularly where they came from the same province, they could be marked off from the local community. Yet their ties with others of the same trade were often within a general area of the city, based on frequent contact in the streets. Many had regular rounds and were known in the quarter. We find them participating in local rebellions, like two *porteurs d'eau* arrested in the 1775 riots.[87] And like the hawker of parasols going to the aid of his comrade, street traders might benefit from the sympathy of other people in the vicinity: in this instance he was able to entrust his wares to a nearby *fruitière*.

It is thus possible to make a general distinction between street traders who had fixed places, such as stall-keepers, *commissionnaires* and *gagne deniers*, as well as many officially itinerant trades which in practice had regular places, and on the other hand those who really did move around. The latter were perhaps known in the neighbourhood but did not really belong unless they lived there too. Of course, in their ranks must be placed the true travelling folk, those just passing through, like a charlatan offering wonderful cures whom the *garde* arrested in the Place de Grève. There were also men and women whom poverty drove into the streets, both unskilled provincials looking for work and Parisians whose normal resources had failed them. 'He has been in Paris for about five weeks, he came to practise the trade of weaver but being unable to find work he became a *décrotteur*.' The itinerant street trades were the most

[84] Cobb, *Police*, pp. 24–5. Y13290, 9 June. See Y15100, 7 Sept.
[85] Mercier, *Tableau*, vol. 6, p. 80; vol. 5, p. 10. Y15099, 23 Apr. Y15364, 27 Dec. 1749.
[86] Y10994, 26 June.   [87] Y11705, 4 May, 5 May.

vulnerable to the influx of the hopeless and the poor during periods of dearth.[88]

People with fixed places, however, were at the very heart of the local community, despite the apparent instability of their work. They occupied the street – the community space *par excellence*. They knew everyone and had a vital role in the communication of news and gossip. The dominance of women in many of the street trades gave them considerable importance as the voice of the community, and nowhere more than in the markets. In street, market-place, and on the ports, ties formed through work – not within the same trade but across a wide spectrum of Parisian society – were central in the development and maintenance of local communities.

III. SERVANTS

The third major occupational group I will consider is domestic servants. Could they become part of the local community or did their dependence and menial work separate them from other sections of the population? What was their relationship with their employer: are they, for example, to be considered part of the family? If so, then they had a good chance of becoming part of the community in the same circumstances as their employer. To answer these questions we must look closely at the various types of servants and at attitudes towards them.

Even defining servants is not easy. Someone working for a master artisan did a different job from the employee of a noble house. Some servants were jacks of all trades, while others specialized in certain tasks: valets, cooks, *portiers* (gate-keepers), stable-boys and coachmen. There was a hierarchy among them, and considerable differences of wealth and life-style.[89]

There were also people who might or might not be included as servants: *intendants* (stewards), secretaries, private tutors, governesses. There is the question of whether shop-assistants, journeymen and apprentices are to be considered as domestics. *Filles de boutique* (female shop-assistants) in particular were in a very ambiguous position, and the job often seems to have involved some household tasks. We find the sister of a *marchand épicier* referring to their shop-assistant as 'sa servante', and another woman described herself as the 'domestique fille de boutique' of a master goldsmith.[90] Male shop-assistants, on the other hand, enjoyed very similar status to journeymen, who were not usually thought of as servants. In 1746 a master locksmith exclaimed indignantly 'that his journeymen were neither servants nor lackeys, but workers'. Apprenticeship contracts in Lyon often specified that no domestic tasks would be required, and a tax law of 1790 declared that journeymen should not be put down as domestic

---

[88] Y15350, 26 June. Y15099, 2 June. M. Sévegrand, 'La Section de Popincourt pendant la Révolution française', in Reinhard, *Contributions*, 3rd series, pp. 9–91 (pp. 60, 62).

[89] Garden, *Lyon*, p. 249. Daumard and Furet, *Structures*, pp. 33, 76. Botlan, 'Domestiques', pp. 72, 80–90.

[90] Y11239, 28 Nov., wit. 4. Y15350, 24 July. See Y15100, 29 Sept., 7 Oct.

servants. It is true that masters normally paid the *capitation* tax for servants, journeymen, and apprentices, and that all were legally subordinate to their employers, but normally a clear distinction was made.[91]

Another problem in defining servants is the possibility that they were related to their employer. A complaint by a manservant in February 1752 accused his master of beating him and revealed that the master was in fact a well-to-do cousin. The latter in turn complained against the servant for infidelity but made no mention at all of their kinship. Those of the servant's witnesses who knew him well mention the relationship, yet without particularly stressing it. If these attitudes were typical, the economic relationship was in such cases the principal one, while kinship might be expected to ensure respect for the normal obligations of master towards man.[92] But such examples are very rare: either servants were not normally related to their masters, or else we are not told of the relationship, which in turn suggests that the employer–employee link was more important.

Given these problems of definition we can do little more than treat as servants those who are described as such: *domestiques, laquais, valets, cuisinières, portiers* in an *hôtel particulier* (and *Suisses* when used in this context), *palfreniers, cochers* when an employer is specified, and so on. *Intendants* and secretaries are excluded, together with teachers, journeymen and apprentices, and any other employees whose status is not clear.

Most historians have argued that domestics were separated from the rest of the population by their different way of life and their lack of independence, which made people look down on them, and by their imitation of their masters and the airs they adopted. They are seen as being isolated in the city, uprooted, even *déclassés*.[93] Yet such generalizations ignore the diversity of servants, and are in any case based on evidence which is somewhat shaky. The most common sources for attitudes towards servants are eighteenth-century social critics like Mercier, who disliked the ostentation and privilege that liveried servants represented and who condemned lackeys putting on airs.[94] But these middle-class judgments were not necessarily representative of the opinions of the bulk of the Parisian population.

The same applies to a second major source for 'public' opinion: police

---

[91] Y13751, 19 Oct., wit. 3. Garden, *Lyon*, pp. 187–8, 248. Botlan, 'Domestiques', p. 16. See J-P. Gutton, *Domestiques et serviteurs dans la France de l'ancien régime* (Paris, Aubier Montaigne, 1981) pp. 14–15. Y16003, quittance de capitation, 1774, with doc. of 8 May 1788. Y13728, Albert to *commissaires*, 5 May 1775. Y10994, 16 Oct. Y13377, petition to *lieutenant général*, Jan. 1752.

[92] P. Laslett, introd. to P. Laslett and R. Wall (eds.), *Household and Family in Past Time* (Cambridge, C.U.P., 1972), pp. 57–8. M. Chaytor, 'Household and Kinship: Ryton in the Late Sixteenth and Early Seventeenth Centuries', *History Workshop Journal*, 10 (Autumn 1980), pp. 25–60 (p. 56). Y12596, 15 Feb., 7 Mar., 8 Mar.

[93] Kaplow, *Names*, pp. 47–50. Daumard and Furet, *Structures*, p. 662. Roche, *Peuple*, pp. 67–8, 94, 108, 111. Gutton, *Domestiques*, pp. 212–13.

[94] Mercier, *Tableau*, vol. 2, pp. 208–12; vol. 1, p. 171.

ordinances and reports. A servant who left his master had to obtain a certificate and could be imprisoned for not possessing one. He could stay in the city no more than a week if he were unemployed, and there were heavy penalties for people who lodged him after that length of time. There were also severe punishments prescribed for theft by domestics, and for insubordination. The police attitude was one of deep suspicion: 'Check whether the accused is in the class of servants or vagabonds', reads Alletz' *Traité de police*.[95] There is thus a certain similarity between the police attitude and Mercier's view that servants are corrupt, dangerous, and uprooted. Yet here too caution is necessary, for domestic crime directly affected the elites and they were preoccupied with it.

It is certainly true that servants' lack of independence gave them an inferior social position. A skilled trade, independence, and a certain level of wealth were the principal components of social respectability among the urban populace.[96] The examples given above of the distinction between journeymen and servants imply that the latter were generally considered of lower status. The term 'lackey' was in general a derogatory one, although curiously it figures hardly at all among the insults used in disputes. Yet there was a certain ambivalence in this attitude, typified by the remark of a woman who came to the *commissaire* Regnaudet to try to get her *de facto* husband to marry her. 'They are more than matched in rank, the plaintiff being the daughter of a *maître rôtisseur*, whereas the said Usé is only a simple servant.' A servant was of inferior rank, but this should not stand in the way of their alliance. It seems that quite a number of master artisans and shopkeepers felt the same way, for just on one-fifth of the three hundred-odd domestics in Daumard and Furet's sample of marriage contracts in 1749 married the daughters of *maîtres marchands*.[97] There was certainly no reason that the formal inferiority of servants, any more than that of *gagne deniers*, should separate them from the rest of the population.

Better founded is the suggestion that a servant's way of life cut him or her off from other Parisians. It was difficult for servants to have a real home, and husband and wife often had to live apart. Many could not marry at all. A large proportion of servants moved around a lot. At the same time, it is argued, they picked up habits and values from their employers which cut them off from their peers.[98]

For some servants this may have been true, yet there is much evidence that many had strong ties with other groups in the city and that domestic service did not necessarily isolate people. Many servants probably did not marry, yet they remain the third-largest group in Daumard and Furet's sample. Of these,

[95] Kaplow, *Names*, pp. 50–1. Botlan, 'Domestiques', pp. 2–10. Gutton, *Domestiques*, pp. 133–47. Alletz, quoted in Cobb, *Police*, p. 15. See police report, 1709, quoted in Kaplow, *Names*, p. 29. Roche, *Peuple*, pp. 67–8.

[96] Garden, *Lyon*, pp. 231–2.   [97] Y15350, 1 May. Daumard and Furet, *Structures*, pp. 74–5.

[98] Botlan, 'Domestiques', pp. 212, 242–58. Kaplow, *Names*, pp. 50–1. Gutton, *Domestiques*, pp. 169–86, 212–13.

two-fifths married daughters of artisans or shopkeepers. There were also 10.8 per cent of the journeymen, 9.7 per cent of the *façonniers* (humblest artisans) and 12.1 per cent of the *gagne deniers* in the sample who married female servants or daughters of servants, in the former two cases much the same proportion as chose women in their own socio-professional category. In Lyon, too, many female servants married market gardeners, artisans, and unskilled workers.[99] There were therefore quite a number of domestics whose contacts with other occupational groups were close enough to win them a spouse there.

There is also evidence that some servants, like many migrants, moved along family networks. A young woman from Dijon, coming to Paris to seek work as a domestic servant, immediately went to stay with her brother-in-law and returned there during the following four years wherever she was out of work. Inventories of deceased estates indicate that most of the more prosperous servants had family in the city, although M. Botlan, working from *scellés*, concludes that few did. My analysis reveals a sprinkling of relatives, rarely other domestic servants. One pattern does seem to emerge. Wherever a servant has a relative who is a *maître* or *marchand* the relationship is usually by marriage, and the domestic is normally in the upper ranks of his profession: a *maître d'hôtel*, a *chef de cuisine* (in charge of the kitchen) an *officier de maison* ('house officer'). If this is a general rule, it would seem that the more prestigious forms of domestic service allowed some assimilation into the best-established and most Parisian part of the population.[100]

Other evidence, too, suggests that servants could be very much part of the local community, for we find them participating in everyday neighbourhood sociability. The cook of a *marchand mercier* in the Cimetière St Jean discussed the state of her employer's marriage with a number of neighbours in the shop next door. A number of servants from nearby noble houses regularly went to play bowls in the Vieux Marché d'Aguesseau, Faubourg St Honoré, where most of them were known to the other locals. There are even cases of crowds mobilizing in defence of servants: J. Kaplow gives two examples from the 1720s in which the public took action against employers who had had their domestics sentenced for some offence.[101]

In fact it was quite possible for domestic servants to become part of the local community, in some cases precisely because of their occupation. But no generalization is possible, because servants did not form a single, uniform group. In practice we can distinguish two main sorts of servants, as far as membership of the local community is concerned: those employed in large houses, and those

99 Daumard and Furet, *Structure*, pp. 74–5. Garden, *Lyon*, p. 250. See Roche, *Peuple*, pp. 67–71.
100 Anderson, *Approaches*, pp. 79–80. Y15350, 19 June. Y14484, 30 Nov. Roche, *Peuple*, p. 70. Y11239, 19 June. Y15350, 1 Nov. Y12596, 11 Mar. Botlan, 'Domestiques', p. 169. Y15350, marriage-contract of 1723 in *compte*, May 1752; 16 May, 11 Aug. Y14078, 14 Oct.
101 Y13290, 14 Aug. Y15350, 21 July. See Y11239, 8 Mar. Y15402, 6 June. Kaplow, *Names*, pp. 137–8.

who worked for much humbler people, most often as the sole domestic employee. By large houses I mean those of wealthy people who had their own *hôtels*, but also the slightly humbler ones who may not have had a house to themselves but who employed a relatively large number of servants. This is precisely the distinction made by N. Castan in studying thefts in Languedoc: on the one hand there were servants who were close to their employers, whose lives they shared; on the other, those of rich houses and *châteaux*, where servants were kept at a distance. It also corresponds roughly, although not entirely, to the division between male and female servants, which M. Garden sees as most significant in Lyon. In the figures given by Expilly, drawn from the capitation rolls, male servants are very much more numerous than female ones in the quarters where large houses were most common: the Place Royale (Place des Vosges) and the Marais; the Palais Royal; St Germain and St Eustache. Women are far more numerous in the more popular quarters of St Denis, St Marcel, Hôtel de Ville, the Sts Innocents, and the Cité.[102] Where there was only one servant it was usually a woman.

The conditions of life and employment were very different in these two cases. Those working in a large house were, like their employers, physically cut off from the neighbourhood. They did not normally meet the neighbours on the stairs or in the courtyard, and did not share the quarrels and joys of other tenants, either indirectly through paper-thin walls or directly in daily intercourse with them. Such servants were unlikely to form close ties with their employers, but on the other hand were very likely to develop strong links with their fellow employees. The bonds between them were sometimes further reinforced by common national or provincial origin. A great many Swiss were employed as doorkeepers, for example. There were large numbers of Germans employed as servants, often as coachmen. Some rich families recruited domestics on their estates, preferring to be served by people from the same province.[103]

Male employees of large houses tended to stick together in their leisure time as well. They were often to be found in groups in wineshops and in the streets. 'La Bastille du Père Eternel', a wineshop near Les Porcherons, was a gathering place for German and Swiss domestics. Groups of lackeys wandered around the city in their free time, frequently arrogantly dressed and looking for trouble.[104]

These were the servants who so aroused Mercier's ire. Like the emerging *bourgeoisie* of rural Languedoc, whose need to assert themselves made them very

---

[102] N. Castan, *Criminels*, p. 223. Garden, *Lyon*, p. 250. Roche, *Peuple*, p. 69. J-J. Expilly, *Dictionnaire géographique, historique et politique des Gaules et de la France*, 6 vols., vol. 5 (Amsterdam, 1768), p. 402. See Roche, *Peuple*, p. 69.

[103] Cobb, *Police*, p. 228. Y15350, 22 May. Goeury, 'Faubourg St Germain', pp. 49–50, note 49.

[104] Y15350, 22 May. Y13751, 29 Dec. Y15350, 3 May, 2 Jan.

sensitive to any slight, people like him intensely resented the superior air adopted by many domestics. But the tendency of these young men to go around in groups, and their reputation for violence, made many other Parisians wary of them. After a sword-battle between a young man and a number of servants at the entrance to the Hôtel de Tours, near St André des Arts, a passer-by testified that the spectators were outraged by the behaviour of the servants but 'nevertheless did not want to get involved ... with servants who might have been ... in great number'.[105] And indeed the papers of the *commissaires* confirm that male employees of large houses were among the most violent occupational groups in the city.

The relative social isolation of domestics working in large houses was reinforced by their considerable mobility. Wages bore no relation to period of employment, and therefore provided no incentive to stay put. Many of course had no choice, for they could be dismissed without notice and without explanation. As with journeymen, extensive mobility made it difficult for this sort of servant to form local ties, while increasing the number of other servants he came into contact with in different parts of the city.[106]

Strong occupational ties, relative isolation from the rest of the population, considerable geographic mobility, lack of security and attachments, violence and arrogance: these were common traits of male servants in large houses. Where they were found with other trade groups it was usually with people who were also largely outside the local community, and generally on a casual, passing basis. A good example is that of a postillion and a kitchen-hand who went together to a wineshop on the Boulevard du Temple, where they met up with three soldiers and a journeyman marble mason, complete strangers. All six then moved on to another establishment where one of them danced with a prostitute. All appear to have been similarly unattached, prepared to drink with anyone who came along, and quite ready for a fight if the occasion arose. These were also the sorts of people whom servants met in the lodging-houses where most went when out of work.[107]

This general picture, nevertheless, was not without exceptions. Some servants working in large *hôtels* spent many years with the one employer. Some married and led a very settled existence, perhaps even living with wife and children under the employer's roof or nearby. As in the case of the servants mentioned above, who played bowls in the Marché d'Aguesseau, those who regularly went to the one wineshop or frequented the same area could become part of the neighbourhood. In this particular example, too, it is noteworthy that a fair number of the local women were wives or widows of servants in nearby *hôtels*, reflecting the importance of domestic service in the Faubourg St Honoré. The local commu-

---

[105] Y15350, 28 Nov., wit. 6. See also Y11705, 13 June. Gutton, *Domestiques*, p. 20.
[106] Botlan, 'Domestiques', pp. 78, 212. Y12596, 13 June. Y14484, 30 Nov., wit. 5.
[107] Y15350, 2 Jan. Botlan, 'Domestiques', p. 204. Y14436, 12 Jan.

nity in that part of Paris was strongly linked, socially and economically, with the great noble houses.[108]

It is also important to distinguish variations within this general category of servants according to their particular specialization. Those concerned with supplying the house would have more contact with the locals. Gatekeepers (*portiers*) could often have their families living with them and this could help to bring them into the local community. Furthermore, many *portiers* ran a business on the side, especially selling liquor illegally.[109]

There were also the women who worked for large houses, primarily as cooks or chambermaids. They rarely appear before the *commissaires*, partly because they were relatively few in number, but perhaps also because their way of life cut them off from the life of the streets which provides the stuff of so many documents. They were subject to many of the same conditions as their male counterparts, but were less likely to go out in their free time, given the nature of female sociability. The evidence suggests that they married other domestics.[110]

As a general rule therefore, domestic service in a large house was not a good means of integration into the city. Those who worked for humbler employers, however, were less cut off. They generally had fewer contacts with other domestics, having at most one or two others working for the same employer, and were therefore less likely to be found in groups or to develop strong occupational ties. They were not physically cut off, but would meet the neighbours on the stairs and in the courtyard. Above all, they were potentially able to form closer ties with their employer, and this could directly affect their integration into the local community.

They can in turn be divided into two main groups, according to type of employer. Potentially best-off were those employed by affluent people who nevertheless did not have a house to themselves: minor office-holders, wealthy merchants, army officers, reasonably well-off clergymen and the like. There might be more than one servant in the household, so the duties required were sometimes, as in large houses, semi-specialized. A cook might be employed, and a personal servant. There was a possibility of perks, especially clothes. The food was likely to be reasonable, and the servants might have a room to themselves.[111]

The more humble and the less well-off the employer, in general, the fewer and the more exclusively female the servants, the more general their work, the worse their conditions. Artisans and occasionally even unskilled workers employed female servants whose main function was to free the woman of the house so that she could work. They would do all the household chores, and might also be required to help their mistress in her trade, often doubling as

---

[108] Y15350, 21 July. Y13760, 21 July.
[109] Botlan, 'Domestiques', pp. 66, 254. Y15350, 'procès-verbaux cartes à jouer', Apr. 1752, *procès-verbaux* of 23 June, 13 Dec. Y15350, 26 June, wit. 1.
[110] Daumard and Furet, *Structures*, p. 76.
[111] Y15350, 26 Oct. Y15100, 20 Oct. Y13290, 14 Aug. Y15099, 25 Mar.

shop-assistants. For them domestic service was often a temporary state, a means of earning enough to form a dowry, and they therefore did not develop a strong work identity.[112]

Roughly corresponding to these two groups were two distinct models of domestic service. Once again, the first is well defined by Mercier:

Servants were in those days part of the family; they were treated less politely, but with greater affection; they perceived this, and were grateful. The employer was better served, and could count on a loyalty which today is quite rare. They were protected both from poverty and vice; and in return for obedience they received benevolence and protection ... Once their lives were laborious, hard and frugal; but they counted for something, and the servant died of old age alongside his master.[113]

This ideal of necessary affection between master and servant appealed to many of the more affluent employers, the same sort of people who were attracted by the 'quality' model. A former *procureur au Parlement* made a declaration against a servant whose mistress, an old friend of his wife's, had fallen ill. She was not looking after her mistress properly, but was entertaining her friends in the apartment. This conduct, he concluded, 'is not only contrary to humanity, but [also] to the loyalty and affection that a servant owes to his master'. Servants owed their employers both affection and fidelity, and in return were protected and treated fairly.[114]

The model was to some extent followed. Examples of close relationships between employer and employee are common enough among affluent people, especially between female servants and their mistresses, partly because of the nature of female sociability. The wife of an *écuyer*, fearing the violence of her husband, left her apartment to seek refuge with a woman who had been her chambermaid for ten years, and who lived some blocks away in the Faubourg St Martin. Not only had a close bond been formed between them during those ten years, but the two women had clearly kept in touch. Female servants could also be companions.[115]

Set against such cases are others where relations were clearly very bad: servants who fell sick were dismissed; others were never paid.[116] Conformed to or not, however, the model is significant. Those who appealed to it were seeking a relationship that was not just a temporary economic one, but which involved a lasting commitment on both sides. For this reason some people preferred employing servants through family connections, to ensure greater loyalty. This was certainly the idea of a doctor and his wife who sent the sister of their own

---

[112] Y15350, 23 May. Expilly, vol. 5, p. 402. Hufton, 'Family Economy', pp. 3, 11. Garden, *Lyon*, p. 250.
[113] Mercier, *Tableau*, vol. 1, pp. 171–2.
[114] Y13290, 27 Feb. See Botlan, 'Domestiques', p. 148.
[115] Y15402, 1 July. See Y13760, 2 Sept., wit. 10, and Y15402, 6 June.
[116] Y15350, 1 Nov., 26 Oct.

domestic to serve an older woman whom they had befriended. The same quest for permanence is reflected in promises of inheritance and of pensions, designed to lay the economic foundations for a long-term relationship. 'They would live like two brothers, eating and drinking together', promised a *clerc tonsuré*: 'He would pay him a salary and would leave him a pension of two hundred *livres* a year.'[117] The aim was to ensure good service, but it was much more than that. The desire for a stable relationship similar to that within the family (the use of 'brothers' in the above quote is significant) reflects a social need. It corresponded to the world view of people whose worth, in their own eyes, lay in their moral qualities of humanity and sensitivity, and who therefore idealized the sentimental basis of relationships. Such a view could also only be relevant to people who enjoyed a degree of affluence, for it implied an economic commitment on the part of the employer to look after the servant who fell ill or who became too old to work.

The significance of this model of domestic service, as far as the local community is concerned, resides in the attempt to make the servant part of an intimate, inward-looking household, rather than one which emphasized collective values and which participated in the life of the neighbourhood. To some extent a servant shared the employer's way of life and where this tended to exclude the local community he or she was less likely to become part of it. If, on the other hand, the master or mistress to some extent participated in neighbourhood life then so too would the servants, although in either case they would certainly have much more contact with the locals, through their work, than did their employers.

The 'loyalty–affection' model of the servant–employer relationship was not relevant to the material conditions of most working people. For them a domestic was less a luxury than an economic necessity. Female servants were taken on both because of the type of work and because they were cheaper.[118] Affection, therefore, was not part of the model, nor was any long-term commitment. It could be vital for the employer's own survival to be able to dispense with a servant who got sick or pregnant, or who became superfluous after the children were old enough to fend for themselves or to help with the chores. This was accepted by the servant, who in any case was usually a young woman working to build up a dowry, intending to return to her village to marry, or ready to accept the first reasonable offer she received. Most female servants gave up work when they married.[119]

Neither side, therefore, expected any great commitment. The employer did, however, expect loyalty. It was perfectly legitimate to dismiss a servant on the merest suspicion of theft, and whatever the personal conflict which might underlie the sacking this was usually the explanation furnished.[120]

---

[117] Y13290, 5 Sept. Y12596, 8 Mar., 7 Mar., wit. 5. Y13290, 27 Feb.
[118] Hufton, 'Family Economy', pp. 11–12. Botlan, 'Domestiques', p. 71.
[119] Hufton, 'Family Economy', pp. 3–9. Garden, *Lyon*, p. 250. Botlan, 'Domestiques', p. 253.
[120] Y15350, 18 Sept., wit. 1. Y13290, 14 Aug. Y13816, 26 May. Y12596, 7 Aug., wit. 4.

In return for fidelity, however, the employer was expected to treat the servant properly. Witnesses, and domestics themselves, specifically condemn physical mistreatment, failure to pay wages on termination of employment, and unfair dismissal: 'without cause', or on a false accusation of theft. The former mistress of a servant arrested for theft said that the girl's new employer

was a wretch who, when his servants left, 'was in the habit of accusing them of having robbed him so that he would not have to pay their wages, adding that he also uses the capitation tax as a pretext for keeping their belongings, so that if he comes in the course of a year to change his servant five or six times, he makes all of them pay the capitation.[121]

Complaints touch little on living conditions, but we might perhaps add that the model employer was one who fed and lodged his employees decently: this was certainly among the requirements of journeymen, but they were in a better position to do something about it.[122] It is also possible that there was some evolution in ideas on the obligations of employers. J. Depauw, studying declarations of pregnancy in Nantes, suggests that during the century masters were less and less held responsible for the welfare of their servants, who were increasingly pushed outside the family.[123]

Ideally, master and servant were seen as a unit. The best expression of this comes in complaints by neighbours against both the servant who had insulted them, and the master or mistress who had failed to rebuke her ('lui en imposer'). Because the domestic was expected to obey, the employer was held responsible. There are also examples of people attacking a servant because of their quarrel with her employer.[124] It was in the interests of servants to stand by their masters and mistresses, and the documents provide many examples where they did. Instances of solidarity the other way are rarer, reflecting the direction of dependence: the servant knew that if she were lukewarm in defending her master's interests she might find herself on the street. The master, however, was under no such pressure to defend his servant. If she quarrelled with the neighbours or threatened to dishonour him by her behaviour, he could simply sack her.[125] These were not necessarily conscious motives: the servant's obligation to defend her employer was built into the code of behaviour governing the relationship.

In practice relations between servant and employer were very varied. The model I have elaborated does not include affection or friendship, but nor does it preclude it. A female domestic and her mistress did after all spend much time together. The wife and domestic servant/shop-assistant of a *marchand tabletier* in the rue St Barthélemy, after a day spent working in the shop, went off an hour

[121] Y10994, 30 Mar. Y13290, 14 Aug. Y15350, 18 Sept., wit. 2.   [122] Y9533, Nov. 1748.
[123] J. Depauw, 'Amour illégitime et société à Nantes au XVIIIe siècle', *Annales: E.S.C.*, 27 (1972), 1155–82 (1168–9, 1181).
[124] Y15350, 12 Sept. Y15099, 19 June. Y15350, 3 Aug.   [125] Y13290, 14 Aug. Y13816, 26 May.

before closing-time to get the supper ready.[126] The separation of male and female sociability brought the servant closer to her mistress at the same time as it distanced her from her master. A good example is provided by an enquiry into a burglary in the rue du Petit Lion, near the Luxembourg. The widow of a *marchand épicier* was in bed one night, her servant, Marie Hauttefeuille, sleeping in the same room. Hearing a strange noise, she woke the servant who went to the door: '"Ha Mon Dieu Madame everything is open" ... the said Hauttefeuille went back to her bed where she felt quite sick; the witness told her to get into bed with her and the two of them resolved to open the window and shout "fire".' There is in this example evidence of real sympathy and a fairly close relationship between the two women, yet the subordination of the servant was never forgotten. It was she who got up, and even in her fright she did not omit to address her employer as 'Madame'.[127]

On the other hand there was often a strong element of fear in the relationship. It was very easy for an unscrupulous employer to exploit the servant, who was in an extremely vulnerable position, could be dismissed without notice, would receive scant sympathy from the authorities, and who was often from the provinces, perhaps with no one to turn to in the city. In a hard-pressed family, struggling to keep itself afloat and with its first duty to its own members, there was a strong temptation to use a servant to the maximum. Many domestics were no doubt overworked: there are never any complaints of this, but given the nature of domestic service and the attitude of the authorities we would hardly expect to find any. There are, however, numerous cases of wages not being paid. The usual arrangement was to settle up only at the departure of the servant, giving her advances on her wages if she needed money. It was also very common, and not just in poorer households, for servants to be obliged to meet many of the household expenses out of their own pockets, in theory to be reimbursed later. A woman who had worked for five months for a merchant dealing in oilcloth on the Pont au Change, at the very low salary of 75 *livres* per year, estimated that she was owed not only her wages but also 239 *livres* that she had lent 'for the household', and thirty-two *livres* sixteen *sols* that she had paid out for food for herself and her master. On presenting these claims, with two receipts, her employer had threatened and kicked her, and had torn up the receipts. Usually it was the master or mistress who kept a written tally of what was due, and disagreements were common. There was also the very real danger of bankruptcy, or that an employer might simply not have the necessary cash when the time came.[128]

There was also a risk of sexual exploitation by master, journeyman, or apprentice. The servant was usually far from home, often starved of affection, and ill-fitted to cope with her leisure hours. She was desperately seeking

126 Y15100, 29 Sept.   127 Y14078, 9 Aug., wit. 1.
128 Y15350, 18 Sept. Y10994, 30 Mar. Botlan 'Domestiques', p. 93. Y14484, 6 Apr., opp. 9. Y13760, 10 Apr., wit. 7.

economic security and was therefore very vulnerable to promises of marriage or of assistance. Such promises were by far the most common excuse given by young women in declarations of pregnancy, where servants figure most prominently.[129] If they got pregnant they were usually sacked. It was hard to prove who the father was, and would involve publicity which, given the sexual basis of female reputation, would be more damaging to the woman than to the man.

If the employer was easily able to exploit his or her servants, the latter were for their part tempted to get as much out of the job as they possibly could. They were struggling to save, and particularly if they did not have close ties with their master or mistress were strongly exposed to the temptation of theft. M. Botlan points to the very high proportion of women among servants accused of stealing.[130] Exploitation and domestic theft were probably far from being the rule, but fear of them was endemic.

In this form of domestic service, too, the relationship between employer and servant could be important in determining to what extent the latter became part of the local community. If the employer belonged to it, as was probable, then the servant too would be likely to join in the life of the house and of the street. The solidarity expected of the servant brought her into her employer's quarrels, and to the extent that she shared the way of life of the family she would make many of the same contacts. If her relationship with her master or mistress was close, she was likely to be well integrated into the neighbourhood.

But there were also independent means for her to become part of the local community, through her everyday work and her inevitable contact with the neighbours. There is no sign of contempt for servants, either in behaviour towards them or in insults used against others. Insults used by a servant could be as damaging as those by anyone else. Their status was clearly lower than that of an independent worker, but it did not stop them from participating in the life of the neighbourhood. The only limitation was the solidarity that they were obliged to show towards their employer, which denied them the freedom of action that others enjoyed and without the compensation of family solidarity.

There is therefore no simple answer to the question of the place of domestic servants in Parisian society. They were an infinitely diverse group, and the enormous variations in their work, conditions, and relationships with their employers must all be taken into consideration. The position of the predominantly male servants of large houses was quite different from that of those employed by people of humbler rank living in shared houses. But even within these general categories there were important variations. In large houses there was a whole hierarchy of domestics, with different functions, incomes, and conditions of work. At every level there were differences according to the rank,

---

[129] Hufton, 'Family Economy', p. 8. See Depauw, 'Amour illégitime', pp. 1163–6.
[130] Botlan, 'Domestiques', p. 289.

occupation, and way of life of the employer, and according to whether the servant was a luxury or an economic necessity.

Analysis of the models of employer–servant relations illustrates the way that ideas on domestic service fitted in with family attitudes. It is already well documented that among the elites the increasing desire for privacy led to servants being more and more pushed out of sight, less and less sharing the lives of their employers.[131] Here, as also in the middling ranks of society, servants formed part of the buffer for the new-found intimacy of family life against the intrusions of the outside world. They were therefore half-way between the local community and the family.

It is quite clear that at no level were servants automatically excluded from neighbourhood life. Some forms of service did militate against the formation of strong local ties. But for those who entered a household which was firmly anchored in the neighbourhood, domestic service provided a very rapid and easy means of integration.

IV. SOLDIERS

Soldiers are often overlooked by historians. They do not fit easily into any clear economic category, and in socio-professional classifications tend to be slotted into some general left-overs group. Their presence is of course disguised by the fact that they managed to escape many official documents. They were not usually affluent enough to draw up a marriage contract, or else took up another trade when they came to marry, for soldiering was primarily for the young and unattached. Soldiers often had another job anyway, and might therefore escape identification. They were subject to military discipline and are thus under-represented in criminal records.[132] During the revolutionary period, when the first real censuses took place, most soldiers were away at the front – and, if they were not, might wish to conceal their identity.

Yet the number of soldiers in eighteenth-century Paris was quite large. Some eight thousand were stationed there, if we include the *garde*, to which must be added those on leave from elsewhere, officially about three thousand a year.[133] But the importance of the army went far beyond this. A great many young men succumbed to the devices of recruiters at some stage in their career, some joining up in search of adventure, as Ménétra apparently did, others because

---

131 Botlan, 'Domestiques', pp. 36, 97–125. Ariès, *L'Enfant et la vie familiale sous l'ancien régime* (Paris, Plon, 1960), p. 451. F. Hamon, 'Le grand parcellaire et l'architecture aristocratique', in Boudon *et al.*, *Système*, vol. 1, pp. 181–246 (p. 191).

132 J. Chagniot, 'La Criminalité militaire à Paris au XVIIIe siècle', in *Criminalité et répression (XIVe–XIXe siècles)*, in *Annales de Bretagne et des Pays de l'Ouest*, 88 (1981), 327–45 (328–30).

133 Chassaigne, *Lieutenance générale*, pp. 215, 253, 261. Chagniot, 'Criminalité militaire', p. 330. J. P. Bois, 'Les Soldats invalides au XVIIIe siècle: perspectives nouvelles', *Histoire, économie, et société*, 2 (1982), 237–58.

they could not find work in their usual trade. 'Having no more money', said a locksmith, he 'signed up with the Burgundy regiment.' It is common in interrogations to find some mention of time spent in the army and for men, when asked if they had ever been in prison, to say no, 'except for military discipline'.[134] The influence of the army went far beyond its numerical representation at any one time.

The place of soldiers in the local community is ambiguous, and once again it is essential to take into account the organization of the 'trade' and to distinguish between different types of soldiers. There were four main groups in eighteenth-century Paris: the Swiss guards; the French guards (*gardes françaises*); regular soldiers of various provincial regiments; and the men of the Paris *garde*.

The largest group was the French guards, who numbered about 3,600. Most lived in barracks in the Faubourg St Marcel, although they were permitted to work in the city part-time and some had rooms there. Many worked on the ports, specializing in unloading timber for building and thus infringing the official monopoly of the *déchargeurs*. Others worked as casual labourers and some at skilled artisan trades, no doubt at piece-work which could be done part-time: we find tailors, shoemakers, *ébénistes* and joiners, even a bookbinder. This leads J. Godechot to argue that they had close ties with the Paris population. Some French guards undoubtedly did, particularly those who were married (presumably a small number, since most lived in barracks). Their wives generally worked in the humblest female trades: *ouvrière pour les blanchisseuses* (working for the laundrywomen), *crocheteuse* (street labourer), *porteuse de hotte* (porter). The widow of a sergeant sold vegetables in the Place Maubert.[135]

Integration into the neighbourhood is also suggested by their prominence in street disturbances and 'rebellions', where their presence was specifically noted by witnesses. When, for example, the *garde* was summoned in August 1752 to protect a bailiff threatened by a hostile crowd, the sergeant noted that there were 'five to six hundred people among whom were several soldiers of the [French] guards'. The taking of the Bastille was largely the affair of small tradesmen and artisans, but the list of the 'takers' includes many French guards among the seventy-six soldiers, nearly an eighth of the total.[136]

The guards did therefore have links with the rest of the population. In the papers of the *commissaires*, however, we generally find them in the company of the most mobile, least established sorts of people. A typical case is that of a French guard arrested on the Pont Royal for the alleged theft of a tobacco-box. He and a river boatman from St Cloud, who was also arrested, claimed that the

---

[134] Y12597, 19 Dec. B.H.V.P. MS 678, f. 25. Y15099, 23 Apr., 6 June. Y13419A, 1 May 1789.

[135] Godechot, *Prise*, pp. 112–13. Y13290, 12 Jan. Y11705, 1 Jan. Y14078, 7 Feb. Chagniot, 'Criminalité militaire', p. 331. Kaplow, *Names*, p. 44. Y14078, 9 Mar. Y12596, 28 Mar. Y15350, 24 July, wit. 1. Y12596, 9 July, wit. 1. Y12597, 1 Nov. Y12596, 20 Jan., wit. 3. Y12597, 19 Sept., wit. 1.

[136] Y15350, 11 Aug. Farge, 'Le Mendiant', pp. 326–7. Rudé, *Crowd*, p. 57.

woman from whom they had taken the box was a prostitute who had robbed them. The only witnesses called were soldiers of the *garde*, and not, as one would expect, other *marchandes* on the bridge. None of those involved in this incident seem to have been integrated into the society of the quarter.[137]

Another incident, this time from the St André des Arts quarter, introduces a *garçon marchand de vin* recently arrived from Rouen and lodging in a *garni* in the rue de l'Hirondelle. He had moved from one job to another, and his account of how he had come by different belongings did not satisfy the police. A purse had been given to him by the mistress of a French guard, and he had exchanged a pair of silk stockings for a coat with another French guard whose name he did not know. He had spent the previous day drinking with two more *gardes françaises*.[138] Examples such as these occur time and again in the papers of the *commissaires*.

Indeed, the French guards had a bad press, and not just among middle-class observers. For working people their name was a by-word for violence and semi-criminal activity. To say that a man frequented 'soldats aux gardes' implied that he was a thoroughly unsavoury character capable of anything; and to say it of a woman suggested vile debauchery and prostitution.[139] This reputation was largely justified. The French guards were one of the most violent groups in the city. They could readily be employed to beat up an opponent, were often armed, and were involved in a large proportion of the nevertheless relatively rare homicides in the city. J. Flammermont showed that their later reputation as pimps was partly due to Taine's efforts to discredit the Revolution, but in fact they were frequently associated with prostitutes. They also crop up regularly in investigations of all sorts of shady activity, whether it be the sale of stolen goods or the manufacture of illegal playing cards.[140]

The French guards had a very strong sense of identity, reinforced by living in barracks and by their distinctive appearance: bearskin hats and red-and-blue uniforms. They were often to be found in groups in wineshops and stuck together in disputes. They were also separated from the rest of the population by their functions. Although after the late 1770s they manned posts in several parts of the city, they were really riot police. In 1750 they and the Swiss guards took firm action against the insurgent populace, and again in 1788 and April 1789 when they fired into the crowd, according to Hardy also beating up even those who asked for mercy.[141] Their willingness to fire reflects their alienation from the people and was hardly calculated to endear them to Parisians, although they

---

[137] Y15350, 26 June. [138] Y12596, 1 Aug.

[139] Y11239, 14 Aug., 29 May. Y15350, 10 Jan., 20 July. Y14078, 23 Dec., wit. 1, 6.

[140] Y12596, 15 May. Y10994, 21 Jan. Y12597, 4 Sept. Chagniot, 'Criminalité militaire', pp. 334, 340–2. Y14078, 3 July. Y11239, 29 May. Y13377, petition to *lieutenant général*, Feb. 1752. Y15350, 26 April, 'procès-verbaux pour les cartes à jouer'.

[141] Chassaigne, *Lieutenance générale*, p. 254. B.N. Ms. fr. 6687, ff. 85, 97, 100 (17, 25, 28 Sept. 1788). Godechot, *Prise*, pp. 144–5, 219–20, 230–1.

did become extremely popular when in June and July 1789 they refused to obey orders.

Other regular soldiers in Paris were in a similarly ambiguous position. The Swiss guards also lived in barracks, had distinctive uniforms, and many were also isolated by their language and religion. They too could have part-time jobs in the city, but seem to have kept largely to themselves: there was at least one Swiss German wineshop in the rue Montmartre. While they did not have the bad reputation of the French guards, they too were notable for their solidarity in disputes. There is little evidence of participation in the local community, and in general they too, when found with other groups, frequented the least-established sections of the population.[142] Much the same was true of the third type of soldiers to be found in Paris: regular troops, either on leave from one of the provincial regiments, or members of the Paris regiment. They almost invariably had another trade, presumably that which they had practised before joining up, yet this did not necessarily bring them into the local community. Most commonly they worked as journeymen: tailors, joiners, shoemakers, glaziers, locksmiths, sometimes as unskilled labourers, notably on the ports. Quite a lot of waggoners were also soldiers.[143] In all of these trades they formed the most mobile, least-established proportion of the work-force. A good example is a twenty-one-year-old journeyman tailor who shared a room with a number of others in a lodging-house in the rue de la Vannerie and who was also a soldier in the Paris provincial regiment. He moved frequently from one job to another and seemed to spend most of his time in gambling houses or in wineshops in different parts of the city. Arrested for theft at the request of his room-mates, he said that the previous day he had spent at La Courtille, the day before that drinking at Vaugirard with another tailor, also a soldier on leave in Paris. He apparently had a mistress living in the rue Jean de l'Epine, in the same quarter, but otherwise his account reveals little trace of local ties at all.[144]

The army in general drew on the most aggressive and rootless elements of the population, and its ethic encouraged these traits. It obliged them to leave their homes and to move around. It gave them the right to carry swords and taught them how to use weapons: not surprisingly it was among soldiers that duels were most prevalent, often resulting in death or serious injury.[145] The conditions of life on service, as in modern armies, encouraged an aggressively masculine *camaraderie*, exalting violence, bravado, and drunkenness. They created a strong professional identity, an ethic, and a high degree of mobility which put most soldiers outside the local community.

The last group, the soldiers of the Paris *garde*, was in a completely different

---

[142] Y10994, 10 July. Y15350, 22 May. Y11239, 8 Mar.

[143] Y15350, 23 July, 3 Dec., 1 Jan. Y12596, 28 Mar. Y10994, 22 Nov. Y15117, 1 Feb. 1788.

[144] Y15099, 24 Jan., 19 Feb.

[145] Y10994, 21 Jan. Y12597, 4 Sept. Y15100, 23 Aug., 6 Sept. Y12596, 16 May. Chagniot, 'Criminalité militaire', pp. 323–3.

position. These men were very much part of the neighbourhood community, although not always directly through their job. Unlike other soldiers they did not live in barracks, and as they worked only every second day and were very poorly paid they had to have another trade. Normally they kept a small shop or a lodging-house, something that their wife could run while they were on duty, or else they went into relatively unskilled work such as framework knitting.[146]

There is very little trace of strong professional identity. Soldiers of the *garde* rarely appear in groups in wineshops. On the contrary, they were normally to be found with neighbours, usually in the quarter where they lived. They were generally older men, many of them soldiers who had served their eight years in the army. The average age of an apparently random sample of 135 soldiers, corporals, sergeants, and *appointés* who testified before the *commissaires* in 1752 and 1788 was 42. The non-commissioned officers were on average slightly older than the men, although the range was greater among the sergeants, several being in their late 50s or early 60s. Most soldiers of the *garde* were married and established in their quarter. In fact, officially they had to have a recommendation from a merchant domiciled in the city in order to be accepted.[147] Furthermore, men tended not to stay in the *garde* very long, probably because the pay was so bad, and this also prevented them from developing a strong *esprit de corps*.

Their work, unlike that of the French guards, integrated them into the city, and in everyday situations they acted as an extension of the local community. It was rare for them to arrest a malefactor themselves, usually taking into custody people already seized by the crowd. They were therefore very sensitive to public opinion, and would cite the judgment of the onlookers to justify their action.[148] This, and the small size of the patrols, made them unreliable for use against a rebellious crowd, and one of the aims of the reforms carried out by the *lieutenants généraux* de Sartine and Lenoir was to make the *garde* more responsible to its superiors. A gauge of their success is the fact that, whereas in 1750 and even in 1775 the *garde* simply evaporated in the face of angry crowds, in 1787, 1788 and April 1789 they faced up to the people and even fired on them.[149]

The corollary to this development, however, was that they became increasingly divorced from the population. As they became more disciplined, and as the police tightened their hold on every aspect of life in the city, their unpopularity grew, especially as a result of their efforts to enforce the regulations on street

---

[146] Y11239, 29 May. Y12596, 1 Aug. Y15114B, petition to *procureur du roi* from soldier, Chagniot, 'Guet', pp. 67–9.

[147] Chassaigne, *Lieutenance générale*, p. 218. Chagniot, 'Guet', pp. 65, 68.

[148] Y11705, 21 May. Y15100, 11 Aug., wit. 1. Y15350, 20 June. Y15117, 9 June 1788.

[149] Y13728, de Sartine to *syndics*, 7 Sept. [1765], 12 May 1770. Y12830, Lenoir to *syndics*, 28 Aug. 1779. *Commissaire* Belle to *commissaire* Fontaine, 28 Jan., 1783. Chagniot, 'Guet', p. 71.

stalls. It was only in the 1780s that insults against the *garde* became widespread, and that derogatory nicknames such as 'tristes à pattes' began to appear.[150]

Until the 1780s, therefore, the *garde* remained quite close to the people, their role in disputes, in particular, making them an extension of the local community. In this they were quite different from other soldiers, whose functions, recruitment and way of life largely divorced them from the populace. As a group, soldiers therefore provide a good example of the difficulty of defining the local community socially, for their presence in the crowd during rebellions and riots, while to some extent a reflection of their love of strife, is also an indication that they found themselves aligned with the locals over some issues. The community was not rigid, and the contours of solidarity appear at different levels according to the question at stake, the people most directly involved, and in this instance according to the source and direction of the attack upon it.

V. OFFICE-HOLDERS

There is one last group of professions I will look at briefly, which are different from any examined so far: office-holders. It is a very hybrid category, including those who had a professional practice, like *notaires*, *huissiers*, members of the Parlement, *agents de change*, *receveurs* and *payeurs de rentes* attached to various institutions, and the *commissaires au Châtelet* themselves.

Most of these groups were organized along the corporate lines typical of the *ancien régime*, usually with a limited number of offices each purchased by the holder. They involved a considerable investment, and most defined their incumbent socially, with some accuracy. In many cases the office-holders formed a company which had considerable control over its own affairs. The forty-eight *commissaires* are a good example. They had a *bourse commune* (common purse). They had their own chamber in the Châtelet, with a library, and held regular meetings, electing *syndics* to look after their business and finances. They could determine who bought any office which fell vacant, and had a flourishing corporate social life, with regular meetings, masses, and dinners on particular feast-days and special occasions.[151] The one hundred and thirteen *notaires*, the sixty *agents de change*, the two hundred and thirty-seven *procureurs au Châtelet* (in 1789) and many other legal and commercial groups had a similar structure.[152]

---

[150] Chagniot, 'Guet', p. 70. *Arrêté des soldats de la garde de Paris dits tristes à pattes* (1789), B.H.V.P. 605, 708, Y15117, 29 Dec. 1788.

[151] Y15115B, MS *mémoire*: 'Marche à tenir tant par le vendeur que par l'acquéreur d'une charge de commissaire'. Y12159, 10 Oct. 1756. Y15114B, letter from *lieutenant civil* to *commissaire* Guyot, 18 Oct. 1786. Y11037, extract from accounts of the Company, 1780. Y11735, accounts of the Company for 1713. The collection of edicts concerning the *commissaires*, Y16023–Y17623, comes from their library.

[152] C. Desmaze, *Le Châtelet de Paris* (Paris, 1863), p. 149. Savary, art. 'Agens de change'. *Encyclopédie*, art. 'Notaire au Châtelet'.

Not all these professions worked in exactly the same way, or necessarily formed as close-knit a group as the *commissaires*, but nearly all had some centre which gave them considerable contact with each other and often with related professions: the Châtelet and the Palais de Justice for lawyers; the stock exchange for those involved in finance. The Hôtel de Ville was a centre for municipal officials and for some financiers. Nearly all such office-holders had a steady stream of people in and out of their studies, many of them regular visitors: one needs only to skim through the notebooks in which people left messages for the *commissaires* while they were out in order to see how often they had dealings with particular *notaires, procureurs, huissiers*, and of course *inspecteurs*.[153] *Receveurs, avocats, commissaires*, and naturally *notaires* also functioned as agents in all kinds of business affairs, occasionally lent money themselves, and often acted as go-betweens for people seeking credit or investments. *Huissiers* and *procureurs* sometimes fulfilled similar functions, generally for a somewhat humbler clientele.[154]

The work done by these people therefore involved many contacts right across the city, and the evidence is that although these were often purely professional, it was with colleagues and certain clients, rather than neighbours, that they had the closest ties. The *commissaires* Dorival and Thierry were close friends and actually said *tu* to each other. The *commissaire* Ninnin had friends in both legal and financial circles, having been clerk to a *notaire* before becoming a *contrôleur de rentes* and later a *commissaire*. We find him invited to the wedding of a *procureur au Parlement*, and on another occasion dining with 'his friend' the *commissaire* Duchesne.[155] Such ties may have dated back to a common apprenticeship, for a great many of these office-holders were trained in law at the University, a three-year course. Some 1,431 men qualified as *avocats au Parlement* in the thirty years between 1760 and 1790.[156] An apprenticeship as a clerk was for many the next step, and could provide lasting ties. A number of the contacts made by one young man while principal clerk to a *notaire* – with another clerk who later became a *négociant*, with a *commissaire au Châtelet*, and with a *directeur des domaines* – later proved invaluable when he became an agent for a stock-broker. One gets the impression of a series of overlapping circles based primarily on professional contacts but reinforced by social ones, and perhaps occasionally by family ones. Again the *commissaires au Châtelet* are a good example. The *commissaire* Dubois was son of a *négociant*; the uncle of another *commissaire* was an

---

153 Y15100, 31 July, 27 Aug., wit. 3, 12. Y13163, Y15118.
154 Y10994, 9 Oct. Y12596, 16 June. Compare J. P. Poisson, 'Les Déplacements professionnels d'un notaire parisien à la fin de la Restauration. Essai de sociologie historique', *Revue d'histoire moderne et contemporaine*, 29 (1982), 125–40.
155 Y11267A, Dorival to Thierry, 2 May 1776. Y15115A. Y15114B. Y14483, 28 Feb. 1788.
156 A. Poirot, 'Le Milieu socio-professionnel des avocats au Parlement de Paris à la veille de la Révolution (1760–1790)', in *Positions de thèses de l'Ecole des Chartes*, 1977, pp. 113–22 (pp. 114–15).

'intéressé dans les affaires du Roi' (a business man with investments in government bonds). Yet another was son and grandson of *commissaires* (although this was exceptional); and others were related to people in the top levels of commerce in Paris.[157] Not all the *commissaires* moved in these circles, but all seem to have had closer ties across the city than in the neighbourhood.

Their work, like that of *notaires, procureurs* and *huissiers* but more than that of most other office-holders, did bring them in touch with the locals, although their functions hardly encouraged the development of ordinary neighbourly ties. Most office-holders, even *huissiers*, generally tried to maintain a certain distance, feeling themselves above 'the people'. A *notaire* in the rue des Tournelles treated with contempt the insults directed at him by a journeyman saddler, 'despite the annoyance caused by such vulgarity, especially for a public official'.[158] Such people are rarely found gossiping on the stairs or in the courtyard. They had servants to do the shopping and the household chores, and this too enabled them to remain aloof. They spoke a different language, which comes out in the documents. Like the increasingly numerous minor office-holders of eighteenth-century Languedoc, those of Paris were anxious to claim the esteem and respect they felt to be due to them, and like the members of the sovereign courts two centuries earlier were refusing the open urban sociability, cutting themselves off as far as possible from the crowds around them.[159] The community they belonged to was a city-wide professional one, not a local one.

VI. CONCLUSION

I have by no means looked at all the trades or at all the possible work structures in eighteenth-century Paris. Some groups lie outside the general categories I have used, and others bridge them: midwives, for example, belonged to a corporation but had no workshop. The members of some corporations, like the *fruitier-orangers* around the Halle, formed part of the market community.

It is clear, however, that certain trades and work structures facilitated the formation of local ties, whereas others hindered the process. On the other hand, no trade automatically made someone part of the neighbourhood community or excluded them from it. It was clearly important whether they worked in artisanal production or in domestic service, in a food or a construction industry; whether they were masters or journeymen, skilled or unskilled, dependent or independent, with a shop or with only a barrow. But a multitude of other factors were just as important. It is vital to understand the structure of the trade: whether it was

---

[157] Y14483, 28 Feb. 1788. Y14483, invitation to funeral, undated. Y15100, invitation to funeral, dossier for Sept. Y13103, 3 June 1752. Y15114A, extract from parish register of St Roch, 1698. Y15100, invitation to funeral, 20 Nov. 1788, with unrelated *scellé* of 16 Dec.

[158] Y10994, 9 Oct.

[159] N. Castan, *Criminels*, p. 52. C. Kaiser, 'Les Cours souveraines au XVIe siècle: morale et Contre-Réforme', *Annales: E.S.C.*, 37 (1982), 15–31. See Mercier, *Tableau*, vol. 3, pp. 6–7.

corporate or unorganized; concentrated in certain areas or spread over the whole city; where it got its raw materials and its work-force; whether the work-place was open to the neighbourhood or cut off from it. The nature of the work is equally important: was it manufacturing for a restricted range of clients or did it involve direct sale to the locals? Did it require much or little training? Did it involve movement around the city? People's place within their trade could of course be significant, not just whether they were a master or a mistress, or a journeyman or worker, but also how long they had been practising it, and where; whether they had family ties or other contacts within it; how many people they employed, and what volume of trade they handled. Age and sex might make a difference, for similar jobs done by men and women did not necessarily create the same opportunities for contact. Age, and particularly marital status, were other potentially important factors, for different forms of behaviour were expected from married and unmarried. Geographic and occupational mobility, often sex- and age-related, varying according to provincial and social origin or according to the economic state of the industry and of the individual, also had a major impact on a person's chances of becoming part of the local community.

It must also be emphasized that nearly all of the structures and factors I have discussed have only potential importance in the maintenance of the community or in making someone part of it. The contacts that were facilitated by certain work patterns were not necessarily made.

If work was extremely important in creating and maintaining the local community, however, we have also seen that its importance varied greatly in different parts of the city. In some streets and areas it appears to have been based largely on the bonds between colleagues, between related trades, or between trades and clients. In the markets and on the ports, proximity at work was just as significant as residence.

Some other general conclusions also emerge. We again find a tendency, as in family attitudes and behaviour, for certain social and in this case occupational groups increasingly to move outside the local community. Minor office-holders, the wealthier, best-established employers, and those in the most socially prestigious trades often formed extensive ties outside the quarter, and were thus able, if they wished, to distance themselves from their neighbours. This phenomenon, as we shall see, was an important factor in the transformation of the local community.

The examination of trades in which there was a very high proportion of migrants, notably domestic service and certain street trades, leads to a somewhat unexpected conclusion. It was not necessarily difficult for a new arrival, even for a temporary migrant, very quickly to become part of the community, perhaps through contacts with family or *pays* already in the city, but frequently with the help of the very jobs which might be supposed to cut him off. Migration was not always a cause of dislocation, either for those who moved or for the society which received them. This is another point I shall return to, but it is clear that the local community was able to adapt to dramatic social change.

On the other hand, analysis of work ties has revealed a group which did not really appear in my study of the family. There were many young men in a range of trades whose way of life and whose geographic or sometimes occupational mobility reduced their participation in the local community. They belonged largely to the age-group of unmarried men who were expected to move around, although this did not automatically exclude them from the community or prevent them from becoming part of it later when they settled down.

We are left, therefore, with a picture of an extremely varied local community in terms of social bonds, or of trades and levels of wealth, but one which was primarily composed of relatively settled people with local commitments rather than city-wide ones.

4

Religion

Alongside family and work, community studies have attributed great importance to the parish church, and in a more general sense to popular religious
culture. The church provided a regular meeting place for all the inhabitants of
a village. Their collective life often centred on it, with dances and markets,
feasts and celebrations all taking place in or in front of the church or the cemetery. Meetings of the village administration were held there. The church
linked the living and the dead, many activities taking place in the churchyard
where people's ancestors were at rest. In many ways the parish defined the
members of the village community in opposition to those from surrounding
parishes.[1]

Church and parish could thus be a major factor, perhaps the single most
important element, in the creation of a collective identity. They were at the
same time a source of individual identity with the community. The order in
which people received sacraments, their place in processions and their seats in
church, and many other honorific privileges all reflected and reaffirmed their
place within the village.[2]

On a deeper level lay the unity provided by a common religious culture: the
local patron saint; shared moral values on a religious foundation; the observance of holy days; the faith in miracles and a belief in the direct intervention of
God in the daily affairs of man. The year was broadly divided up by the major
feast-days. There was a whole shared system of religious cultural references,
some peculiar to the one place, some Europe-wide. All this has led a number
of writers to see popular religion and the parish church as the primary sources
of collective identity in rural France.[3]

The place of church and parish in the cities, however, is much less well
known. The role of confraternities in urban religious life has recently received
some attention, and the last few years have seen some important work on the

---

[1] G. Bouchard, *Le Village immobile: Sennely-en-Sologne au XVIIIe siècle* (Paris, Plon, 1971), esp.
pp. 283–340. P. M. Jones, 'Parish, Seigneurie, and the Community of Inhabitants in Southern
Central France during the Eighteenth and Nineteenth Centuries', *Past and Present*, 91 (May
1981), 74–108. Y-M. Bercé, *Fête et révolte* (Paris, Hachette, 1976), pp. 127–9. J-P. Gutton, *La
Sociabilité villageoise dans l'ancienne France* (Paris, Hachette, 1979), pp. 75–7, 185, 224–45.
[2] Bouchard, pp. 329–34. N. Castan, *Criminels*, pp. 131–3.
[3] Bercé, pp. 127–36 and ch. 4. Bouchard, p. 340. Jones, p. 104.

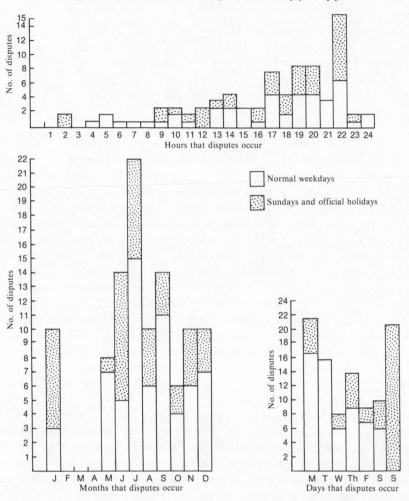

Graph 1. Disputes in Grève quarter, 1752: calendar and timetable (96 disputes)

social functions of religious practices.[4] Popular religion has been increasingly studied, and the growing disaffection of sections of society, particularly in the towns, is well documented. Very few studies, however, shed much light on the place of the parish or of the church in urban social organization and there is next to nothing on this subject for eighteenth-century Paris. Yet in studying the local community it is vital to know whether the parish itself constituted a social unit;

[4] C. Trinkaus and H. A. Oberman (eds.), *The Pursuit of Holiness in Late Medieval and Renaissance Religion* (Leiden, 1974), papers from the University of Michigan Conference. Vol. 10 of *Studies in Medieval and Reformation Thought*, edited by H. A. Oberman.

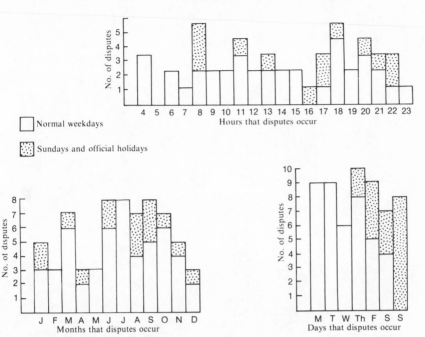

Normal weekdays

Sundays and official holidays

Graph 2. Disputes in Halles quarter, 1752: calendar and timetable (68 disputes)

and if it did whether it overlapped with, complemented, or was in conflict with the neighbourhood community. Even if it was not a real social unit we need to investigate the impact of the church on the community: did it create additional bonds or did it take people outside? What role did religious celebrations and beliefs play in the creation and maintenance of a sense of community?

It is obvious right from the start that the church played a major role in everyday life. The sheer number of religious establishments in the city – fifty-two parish churches, some fifty male and fifty-three female orders – is already some indication. These institutions owned much property in the city and many had tax rights over large areas. From a purely physical point of view the churches and monasteries occupied a prominent place in the topography of the city and as a result in people's minds. They were among the largest and certainly the most imposing edifices, and their prominence is reflected in the way people used church buildings in descriptions and in finding their way around. The parish was the normal way of defining any area of the city, even for the *commissaires* who might have been expected to use the police administrative divisions. Almost everyone, even newcomers to the city, knew what parish they lived in.

To what extent this was due to actual attendance at services is impossible to estimate. Mercier suggests a waning of enthusiasm in Paris when he says that

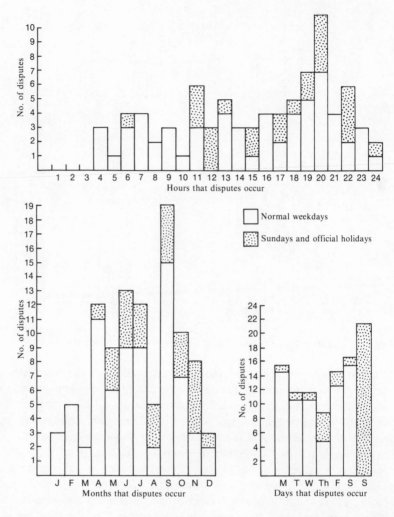

Graph 3. Disputes in Faubourg St Antoine, 1752: calendar and timetable (102 disputes)

ordinary people no longer went regularly to vespers, but he asserts confidently that 'the people still go to high mass'.[5] It is interesting that in some quarters there is a noticeable gap in the calendar of disputes recorded by the *commissaires* at around twelve on Sundays, just the time when the main church service was held.

There is also evidence of considerable religious fervour among the Parisian population. J. Kaplow stresses their devotion to the Virgin and their fidelity to

[5] Mercier, *Tableau*, vol. 4, p. 160.

religious ritual. He cites two examples given by Hardy of conflict between the clergy and the onlookers; one in 1783 when the priest wanted to postpone or cut short the Corpus Christi procession because of rain and the crowd forced it to go on: another in 1786 when the parishioners protested against the decision by the clergy of St Nicolas des Champs to change the service.[6]

On the other hand, the dechristianization programme in Paris during the Revolution seems to have met with relatively little opposition. Kaplow suggests that the patterns of belief among the population were so deeply ingrained that they remained even when the institutions had disappeared, but it is surprising that people apparently so attached to forms should accept their abolition with relative composure.[7] It certainly seems to indicate that the institutional church was of considerably less importance to many Parisians than was the case in the west or in the south of France where dechristianization met with great resistance.

Be this as it may, the parish had a direct impact on virtually every inhabitant of eighteenth-century Paris. It was for a start one of the largest employers and consumers in any area. A glance at the deliberations of the administrators of Ste Marguerite, certainly not the wealthiest parish church in the city, suggests the role of the church in providing work for local artisans. In 1759 they had six new bells made, 'at great expense'. The following year a new chapel was decided upon, for which they were prepared to spend up to 12,000 *livres*. In 1779 a new building for the charity school was authorized and five years after that a new clock costing 3,000 *livres*. Minor expenses included the purchase of wax, oil, and candles, a new costume for the doorman, as well as the salaries of the various employees. There were also vestments to be laundered and eventually replaced.[8]

Religious functions provided income for a great many people. For Corpus Christi and other processions there were tapestries and flowers. *Epiciers* sold tapers for use in church; there were all kinds of religious artifacts in the shops and hawked through the streets. There was the impetus to trade provided by the different *foires* and feast-days. At the doors of the churches and even inside were stalls selling both religious and non-religious items: one old woman made a precarious living by selling candles in the monastery church of the Filles Dieu. One or more people in each parish hired out chairs in the church, quite a lucrative occupation.[9]

There were also those directly employed by the parishes. The larger ones had a whole legion of priests: some eighty at St Eustache, fifty at St Paul and St Sulpice, sixty at St Nicolas des Champs and at St Roch. Even the tiny parish of Ste Opportune, with three hundred communicants, had nine. There was in addition a host of lay employees: *bedeaux* (vergers), doorkeepers, bellringers,

[6] Kaplow, *Names*, p. 117.   [7] Kaplow, *Names*, p. 116.
[8] LL836, Deliberations of *fabrique* of Ste Marguerite, ff. 1, 9, 30, 68, 99, 118.
[9] B.N. Ms. fr. 6682, f. 147, 13 Dec. 1775. LL836, f. 24. See Y12596, 20 Jan. Y13290, 27 Feb.

clerks, organists, gardeners, gravediggers, servants. Ste Marguerite, and no doubt other parishes too, had a full-time librarian. Even the lay confraternities, perhaps a dozen or so in each church, often had a *bedeau* of their own.[10] Then there were the lay people who did most of the administration of the parish churches – the *marguilliers* – and those in charge of the various confraternities. At every level of society there were people involved with the administration and maintenance of the parish.

The significance of this was social as well as economic. Almost anyone who lived in Paris for any time would come into contact with the parish church, directly or indirectly. Everyone knew someone employed by the church: Ménétra, recalling scattered incidents from his boyhood, mentions a woman who had fallen or thrown herself out of the window, the wife of the man who laid out the dead in their parish. The widow of a *bedeau* of St Yves sold herbs in the rue des Noyers and the wife of a bellringer at St Eustache was a fish-seller in the central market.[11] The church was strongly present in the community through its employees.

It also influenced the lives of local people through its role in administration, in poor relief, and in education. The observance of Sundays, of the principal feast-days and of Lent was inscribed in the law and enforced by the police (particularly when the clergy complained!). Jews, Protestants, and religious groups of whom the church disapproved were pursued by the civil authorities or at least were kept as quiet as possible. Marriage was a legal as well as a religious requirement and it too was enforced by the police if it became publicly known that people were living together out of wedlock. In return the church functioned as an arm of the administration, royal edicts being read out from the pulpits. It was also seen as an important means of influencing public opinion. After the disaster of 1770, when a large number of people were killed during the celebrations for the marriage of the Dauphin, de Sartine requested all the *curés* to reassure their congregations and to minimize estimates of the number of dead in order to combat the rumours that were flying. It was also to the *curés* that he went to try to estimate the total numbers of injured and to provide relief for the victims and their families.[12]

The role of the parishes in poor relief has claimed somewhat more attention than their other functions, and all the evidence suggests that their efforts made little impact on the mass of the poor. Most churches had an elected official, the *commissaire des pauvres*, charged with administering the funds set aside or donated for the poor, and it is possible that some of these men were very

---

[10] Expilly, *Dictionnaire*, vol. 5, pp. 479–80. LL836, ff. 5, 15, 39. LL837, Deliberations of administrators of Confraternity of St Sacrement at Ste Marguerite. LL838. In 1789 the figures were much higher: 120 at St Sulpice, 80 at St Roch. Reinhard, *Nouvelle Histoire*, p. 22.

[11] B.H.V.P. MS 678, f. 8. Y12816, 2 Jan. 1786, wit. 16. Y11239, 30 Sept.

[12] Orléans MS 1421, ff. 94, 139. Y13728, Albert to Gillet, 10 June 1775. Y15707, dossier on the accident of 1770.

conscientious. But there was only a little money available, mainly drawn from bequests, private charity, and the low poor tax in theory paid by every inhabitant. At Ste Marguerite it was possible to donate money to the poor of the parish in return for a life-long pension and several thousand *livres* were invested in this way.[13] However, the money went only to the 'honest poor' known to the priest or to the *commissaire des pauvres*, and these were apparently not over-abundant in the Faubourg St Antoine: in 1763 we read in the deliberations of the administrators that there were one thousand *livres* in the poor-relief fund and that 'not having been able to find a use for it', this money was to be lent to the church, which was in need of extra funds! Some years later one of the former *marguilliers* 'being in his closing years in a state meriting the assembly's compassion', having apparently gone bankrupt, was given an annual pension of 500 *livres* from the poor-relief funds.[14] In fact the police tended to take over poor relief more and more. During the winter they provided work clearing the streets and the quais. I have mentioned the disaster relief in 1770. In October 1768, a time of very high bread prices, the *lieutenant général* de Sartine obtained funds primarily to help bakers, but he also asked the *commissaires* to inform him of any worthy poor families who merited assistance. 'He meant', it was explained to the *commissaires*, 'families of bourgeois, merchants or artisans who were in straitened circum-stances and in difficulties, that he would find them aid in the form of bread'. When word of this spread, such crowds flocked to the *commissaires* that the scheme was deemed impracticable.[15] Nevertheless, it was a sign of the times that the secular authority was taking over a role which had for so long been that of the church.

Another area in which the church had traditionally played a major part was education. Each parish had a certain number of choir-boys, who were taught to read and write. Much more important were the *écoles de charité* (charity schools) run by nuns or brothers in each parish: by 1765 there were forty-five for boys and twenty-nine for girls. In theory the children stayed for two years learning to read, write and count, and to recite the catechism. Although there is little evidence on who actually went to these schools or on what proportion of the population benefited from them, it does seem that at any one time there could be a couple of hundred children at the schools in a large parish.[16]

Equally poorly documented is the pastoral role of the clergy. There are scattered mentions of people going to the parish priests for this or that: mainly wives protesting about the conduct of their husbands, parents about that of their children, or people complaining about prostitutes or about the sexual morality of

[13] C. Bloch, *L'Assistance et l'état en France à la veille de la Révolution* (Paris, Picard, 1908), pp. 129–30. Hufton, *The Poor*, pp. 122, 160–76. LL836, ff. 21–2, 122.

[14] LL836, ff. 23, 121. See P. A. Alletz, *Tableau de l'humanité et de la bienfaisance* (Paris, 1769).

[15] Y12830, de Sartine to *syndics*, 26 Sept. 1768. Mouricault to *commissaires*, 5 Oct. 1768. Y13728. Chénon to Coquelin, 10 Oct. 1768.

[16] LL836, ff. 5, 60. Fossoyeux, 'Ecoles', pp. 277, 292.

their neighbours.[17] Here, as we have seen, the police also usurped what had been the place of the church and more and more people petitioned the *lieutenant général*. In 1752 we even find the *curé* of St Laurent advising the parents of a nineteen-year-old girl, who had come to complain about her conduct, to present a petition to the *lieutenant général*. An innkeeper retorted to a priest who had come at the request of the neighbours to admonish him for letting rooms to prostitutes 'that if it were true that he had whores in his house, it concerned only the Police and not priests'.[18] These examples point to the declining importance of the church in the enforcement of morality.

Little is known about the other pastoral activities of the parish clergy. They presumably spent some time visiting the sick, a function they shared with the various charitable companies like the Soeurs de la Charité. The regular clergy were certainly busy taking the sacraments to the sick and dying. Whenever there was a serious accident or someone fell suddenly ill, the first thought of passers-by and neighbours was to send – not for a doctor – but for the sacraments. Death was very much present and as long as it remained so a priest bearing the host was a common sight in the streets of the city.[19]

Nor must the visual and aural impact of the church be underestimated. I have already mentioned the physical presence of religious buildings. Perhaps less obvious is the impact of the bells, whose ringing could not fail to reach the highest garret or the most sombre courtyard. They provided warning in emergencies, were a rallying-call, as they were to remain during the Revolution, as well as tolling the advent of religious festivals. But for impact, nothing surpassed the Corpus Christi processions with their crowds, the displays of flowers and tapestries, the decorated *reposoirs*, and of course the clergy in all their robes, the civil authorities who joined the processions, the magnificent church treasures which accompanied the host. All the senses were assailed at once: the eyes; the ears by music and singing, by the firing of the guns and the murmur of the crowd; the nose by the perfume of the flowers and the incense.[20] Days of intense preparation preceded the ceremonies as the city was cleaned and the way laid clear. The Fête Dieu brought the whole city into physical and symbolic unity: those who did not participate watched from the street or from the window. The processions penetrated every part of the city, and no one could remain unaware of the celebration.

Corpus Christi was the principal festival of this kind but not the only one. At Easter the sacraments were carried with great pomp to all the sick of the parish, again drawing crowds to the windows and into the streets. The Feast of the

---

[17] Y10994, 29 Aug., 2 Sept., 13 Dec. Y12596, 14 June. Y15350, 20 Dec. Y13290, 29 Nov., wit. 1. Y15114A, *femme* Lebas to Trudon, 10 Feb. 1772. Y13760, 19 Jan., 13 Dec.

[18] Y13377, petition Billant [early 1752]. Y15350, 20 Dec., wit. 3.

[19] Y10994, 21 Jan., 12 Oct., wit. 4. Y15402, 15 May. Y14436, 9 June. Y15099, 10 June, 17 July. Y14484, 19 Feb., wit. 2. Restif, Nuit 140e, 'Le Saint Viatique'.

[20] Mercier, *Tableau*, vol. 3, pp. 78–80.

Assumption was marked by a grand procession, not just of the clergy but also of the officials of the municipality, the members of the Parlement and of the sovereign courts. It too drew large crowds.[21] Alongside the regular festivals of the liturgical calendar were other, occasional ones: the processions of the relics of Ste Geneviève in times of severe crisis; the semi-religious ones associated with a royal birth, death, or marriage, or with the entry of a new archbishop. The funeral procession of the *curé* of St Sulpice, who died in August 1788, included all the confraternities and congregations in the parish, one hundred children from the hospital of La Pitié, one hundred chosen poor people, and some 200 lower clergy followed by thirty-three *curés* and two bishops. A huge number of people gathered along the route.[22]

All of these ceremonies invaded the city, going out from the sacred places, usually the parish churches, into the everyday world of the street, following the routes which were those of daily movement around the city. They penetrated the workaday world and helped to fashion its rhythms. No inhabitant of eighteenth-century Paris could remain unaffected by the calendar, the practice, and the celebrations of the parish.

But all this tells us little about its role in helping to create or maintain the local community. We need to look at the extent to which church attendance reinforced the ties of neighbourhood and affirmed local hierarchies; at whether the parish with its various auxiliary organizations created a sense of unity and of community among its adherents; at the role of 'popular' religious culture in affirming the collective identity of the neighbourhood. Ideally we should consider what sections of the population used the church and participated in parish life, but also in what ways they did so and with whom.

Not all of these aims are attainable. There is little evidence on the proportion of the population who went to church or on frequency of attendance, much less on who the faithful were. The church records themselves are confused and many have disappeared, but even where they survive they tell us little about the bulk of the population. Such evidence as exists, however, suggests that most parishes were no longer social units, and nor were they in most cases major centres of local community sociability.

It is clear, first of all, that the parishes were much wider and more populous units than the neighbourhood communities we have been examining. Some were absolutely enormous. St Eustache stretched from the rue St Honoré to Les Porcherons, and in the south from the rue St Denis to the rue de Richelieu. St Sulpice included most of the Faubourg St Germain, and Ste Marguerite had the Faubourg St Antoine. St Paul embraced most of the Marais, from the river to the Boulevard. Some of the parishes, furthermore, had little geographic or topogra-

---

21 B.N. Ms. fr. 6686, f. 397, 28 Mar. 1788 Ms. fr. 6687, f. 46, 15 Aug. 1788 Ms. fr. 6682, f. 106, 15 Aug. 1775.
22 B.N. Ms. fr. 6687, f. 47, 18 Aug. 1788.

phic unity. St Jean-en-Grève took in a few houses on the Quai de la Grève and a few small blocks around the Place de Grève, then stretched north in a corridor leading as far as the rue d'Anjou in the Marais. The block immediately to the rear of the church itself was in another parish. St Gervais was among the most divided of all: the bulk of the parish lay along the rue du Temple between the Boulevard and the rue du Roi de Sicile, all but cut off from the area around the church. Only the smallest parishes were compact geographic units: St Hilaire, Ste Opportune, and those on the Ile de la Cité.

In terms of population the story was similar. In 1766, according to Expilly, the population of the parish of Ste Marguerite was forty-two thousand. The *curé* of St Médard wrote in 1743 that his church had fifteen to eighteen thousand communicants, and the *curé* of St Gervais estimated in mid-century that there were over thirteen thousand poor people in his parish: it is clear that the recommendations from the *curés* which were sometimes sought by the police were not always based on intimate personal knowledge![23]

Obviously, except in the very smallest parishes, it was impossible for all those who technically belonged to the parish even to fit into the church at the same time. There was therefore a profusion of services, particularly on Sundays and feast-days, so that even if the high mass (at eleven on Sunday morning in most parishes) continued to be the most frequented, other people could go to vespers, to an early morning service, or to one of the numerous services paid for by the confraternities which might even be going on in one of the chapels at the same time as other ceremonies were taking place in the nave or the chancel.

In the large parishes the churches of the religious orders also catered to a section of the population. That of Ste Geneviève, for example, attracted many people from the surrounding area, especially on the saint's feast-day, of course. The Cordeliers was another very popular monastery, and with quite a range of people. We find at different times the wife of the portier at the Comédie Française (what is now the Odéon), the receiver general of the estates and forests of Languedoc, the *chirurgien* of the Duc d'Orléans, and the Comte de Fontenoy among the congregation. In mid-century it was a rendez-vous for journeymen locksmiths. In the parish of Ste Marguerite, too, we find people going to the church of the Enfants Trouvés and to that of the Madeleine de Trenelles convent. In one case a *gagne denier* sent his eight-year-old son to the parish church of Ste Marguerite while he and his wife went to the Enfants Trouvés.[24]

The parish churches therefore did not assemble, either at one time or even in the whole day's services put together, anywhere near all the inhabitants of the quarters for which they were technically the religious centre. Not only this, but

[23] Expilly, *Dictionnaire*, vol. 5, pp. 481–2. S7493, dossier on St Gervais, petition of *curé* [c. 1766]. *Curé* of St Médard to Cardinal Fleury, 1743, cited in M. Brongniart, *La Paroisse St Médard au faubourg St Marceau* (Paris, A. et J. Picard, 1951), p. 106.

[24] Y12596, 20 Jan., 13 Apr., wit. 2, 3 Apr., 7 Feb. Y14078, 20 Jan., 8 Feb., 23 May. Y14391, 7 Aug. 1746. Y10994, 11 June, 17 June, 14 Nov.

they might well cater to people from other areas completely: the witnesses of an incident at a service at St Etienne des Grés (next to the Collège Louis-le-Grand) in late 1775 came from all the surrounding parishes and even from the other side of the river.[25] This was particularly common in the churches which had a large number of trades confraternities. In 1760 St Sépulcre contained no fewer than fourteen such organizations. There were at least four at St Hypolite, and at one stage Ste Marguerite housed five. Very little is known about most of these confraternities and it may be that some catered primarily to members of the trade who lived locally. This was certainly the case with that of the *petits forts de la Halle* (the porters of the central market) at St Sépulcre, or the Confrérie Ste Clair at Ste Marguerite, for the employees of the Manufacture des Glaces. But many did attract men from all over the city. In 1752 on the feast-day of St Eloi, patron of the *fondeurs en terre et sable* (metal founders), a gathering in a neighbourhood wineshop after the service at the Chapelle St Bon (admittedly not a parish church) included inhabitants of the parishes of St Barthélemy, St Jacques de la Boucherie, la Madeleine, and St Etienne du Mont. All the *jurés* and *anciens* of the grain-merchants' corporation were obliged to attend the service held on the last Sunday of each month in the parish church of Ste Croix de la Cité.[26] The parish churches were not just for the locals.

In French villages and small towns the churches played a vital role in collective activities, but in Paris this function was less apparent. Popular recreation, as we shall see, belonged to the street and to the boulevards, not to the churches and their environs. The markets were not located in front of the parish churches, and non-religious public celebrations, organized by the police or the municipal authorities, were held in the Place de Grève and on the quais, later in the Place Louis XV, and along the boulevards. Only on specifically religious occasions, the national and local feast-days, did the churches become the focus of collective activity.

On those holy days, the parish did bring the locals together in a common celebration. A larger number of worshippers than usual would attend mass and there is evidence of local participation in the organization of processions. In 1752 the inhabitants of the rue de la Roquette built a *reposoir* in their street. In the same year, on the Sunday following the Fête Dieu, a *marchand de vin* and the wife of a *maître charcutier* in the rue de la Montagne Ste Geneviève stretched a tapestry, lent by a *marchand fripier*, across the street for the procession from St Etienne du Mont.[27]

There was also neighbourhood participation on a more informal level. The locals lined the streets to watch the procession: in 1788 we find a prostitute from

[25] Y11092, 14 Dec., 17 Dec. 1776.
[26] B.N. J. de F. 1590, ff. 27, 28. J. Gaston, *Images des confréries parisiennes avant la Révolution* (Paris, A. Marty, 1910). Y15350, 25 June. Y15363, 29 July 1753.
[27] Y12596, 4 June.

a lodging-house near the port going to visit a friend in the rue de la Coutellerie in order to watch the parade on the octave of Corpus Christi. The faithful gathered especially around the *reposoirs* where the procession stopped: people like the wife of a shoemaker in the parish of St Merri who passed her crippled son under the *arche* of the St Sacrement in the hope of a miracle.[28]

The feasts of the patron saints of the parishes were in some cases true local festivals. That of Ste Marguerite seems to have been widely celebrated in the Faubourg St Antoine, and in 1750 the *curé* aroused considerable opposition from his parishioners when he decided to postpone the services for a week. There were often, particularly in the first half of the century, dances and other celebrations, attested by repeated police ordinances forbidding them. Frequently the local saint's day was also marked by a fair (*foire*) in the quarter, although by the mid eighteenth century most of these had become largely commercial events, providing entertainment but not inviting popular participation. The *foires* of St Germain, St Laurent, and St Ovide were massive festivals which certainly drew many locals, but were not local events.[29]

Other celebrations of feast-days tended to be private and small-scale. Unlike southern French towns and villages, Paris had no races or competitions, no open-air feasting. Instead people celebrated in small groups at home or in wineshops, like the 'associés à la Vierge' ('associates of the Virgin') who organized sumptuous repasts for the Fête Dieu and the octave; like the beer-seller and ten or twelve friends and neighbours who celebrated the feast of St Martin in his shop on the Port au Blé. Many trade groups organized feasts on the main holy days as well as on that of their patron saint. The people in general, according to Mercier, celebrated the St Martin and the Feast of Kings (Twelfth Night): 'the wineshops start to fill up from the morning on'.[30]

In all of these ways, therefore, religious festivals brought the locals together, reinforced the ties between them, and in this sense strengthened the local community. Some of the celebrations were of course those of every non-working day, and had little to do with the church. Others were both religious and local, but even these were physically centred less on the church building than on the street, the *reposoir*, or the wineshop. They did not make the whole parish into a single social unit.

This conclusion is further reinforced by the curious absence of the parish churches from complaints and enquiries. Whereas in eighteenth-century Languedoc churches provided the best and most public location for altercations, at

28 Y15099, 29 May. Y10994, 14 June.
29 LL838, 19 July 1750. Ordonnances de police, 19 Jan. 1742, 29 Oct. 1760, in Peuchet, vol. 5, p. 187; vol. 6, p. 466. Y14078, 30 Nov. Y12596, 3 Jan., 9 Jan., 25 July, 3 Nov. Y14078, 21 Mar. Y15114A, papers concerning *foire* St Ovide, 1771.
30 M. Vovelle, *Les Métamorphoses de la fête en Provence de 1750 à 1820* (Paris, Aubier/Flammarion, 1976), pp. 59–62. Seine D5 B6 472, account book of *marchand de vin-traiteur*, 6 June, 13 June 1776. Y15350, 12 Nov. Mercier, *Tableau*, vol. 4, pp. 164–5.

least among a section of the community, in Paris very few disputes took place there – although they may have been more common earlier in the century.[31] The evidence suggests that, even if people met their adversaries at church, it was not a suitable venue for developing their quarrel openly. This is illustrated in a complaint made by a *marchand fripier* in the Faubourg St Antoine, against a *revendeuse* and her family. He and his wife had received a libellous letter and there had been scenes outside their house. Finally, at church on the feast day of St Martin one of the daughters had several times pushed her chair back into the legs of the plaintiff's wife. Here the church takes its place among the other venues of neighbourhood sociability. Yet it was not the scene of a full-scale quarrel or publicity exercise: these occurred later, in the main street.[32] A Paris church, it seems, did not usually provide a local audience which knew the disputants and their quarrel and which could fulfil the necessary role. It was physically and socially too far removed from the neighbourhood.

This does not necessarily mean, however, that churches, either parish or monastic, did not act as important centres of community life for part of the population, for example for those who lived close by. They may have attracted and united certain social groups; or even strengthened the ties between small groups of parishioners already linked by neighbourhood, family, occupation, or place of origin. The use of particular churches by individual trade groups, some of them locally based, has already been mentioned. There is also evidence in certain areas of the city of a very local population using the church as a meeting place. An enquiry of 1752, following an attack on a *garçon jardinier* while he was on his way to mass one Sunday morning, introduces a number of locals who had seen the two accused waiting for their victim in the Cours Montparnasse, the route all of them took to the Capuchin monastery church in the rue d'Enfer. The two men had chosen a place and time guaranteed to provide a wide audience. The church provided a regular meeting place for those in this particular area (although not for them alone), and played a part in the life of the local community. It is worth noting, however, that the attack did not take place right outside the door.[33]

The parish church played a more direct role in community life through weddings, baptisms, and funerals, bringing together small groups very often united by both neighbourhood and occupation. Such events are poorly represented in the police archives, although the celebrations after weddings are well documented, and it is virtually impossible to know exactly who was invited and actually present in the church. It is likely that for people who belonged to the local community the participation of neighbours was important: certainly the neighbours of Marie Baremont from the rue Dauphine, some of whom she also knew from the market of La Vallée, were able to testify that her consort had been

---

[31] N. Castan, *Criminels*, p. 131. See, for example, Y15747, 13 June 1700.   [32] Y10994, 14 Nov.
[33] Y12596, 30 July, 6 Aug. See also Y10994, 3 May.

present at the baptism of their first two children and had there declared himself to be the father. There are other mentions of godparents among neighbours, very often people who worked with the parents as well as living nearby.[34]

Attendance at funerals is even more difficult to gauge. In the case of office-holders and prosperous merchants invitations were sent out, and their distribution reflects the wider family and business ties that such people maintained. Among the papers of Doublon, *commissaire* of the St André des Arts quarter in 1752, we find invitations to a number of funerals: of relatives of other *commissaires*; of the wife of a distiller and *bourgeois de Paris* in the parish of St Séverin; of a master locksmith, one of the *jurés* of his corporation and former administrator of the Confraternity of the Sait Sacrement at St Benoît; of the wife of a merchant jeweller and *bourgeois de Paris* at St Jacques de la Boucherie; and of an *avocat au Parlement* in the parish of St Etienne du Mont.[35]

In all social groups, the funerals of men were likely to be organized and attended by others of their trade. This was one of the functions of the trades confraternities, which existed both for masters and journeymen.[36] It was probably also true of non-corporate occupations: the principal mourners at a funeral in St Sulpice in March 1788 all seem to have been rivermen living along the nearby bank of the Seine.[37] The parish confraternities also arranged funerals for their members, although as we shall see these organizations were not necessarily confined to the one parish, much less the one neighbourhood.

Women's funerals are very poorly documented. Invitations found in the archives of the *commissaires* describe the deceased only by their husband's 'quality' and the person involved most often had professional links with him.[38] Humbler women were presumably laid to rest in the presence of the female friends and neighbours who had been their daily associates in life, but it is impossible to know how well attended such funerals were.

Attendance at a funeral, therefore, even more so an invitation to witness a marriage or become a child's godparent, clearly cemented existing bonds and gave them a more permanent, religious dimension. Such events reinforced the sense of common identity, but only for people who were already part of the local community.

There were other aspects of church life which were potentially very important in social organization in the city. For example, were the *fabriques* – the lay administrations of the parishes – or alternatively the various parish confraternities, potential centres of collective life, perhaps in competition with the local community? They could conceivably have provided committees for organizing neighbourhood life, based on the church but really much more localized.

---

34 Y15350, 1 May, 23 Oct., wit. 5. Y13816, reports of the *garde*, 1 April 1788.
35 Y11468. Invitations re-used to bind *scellés*.
36 See Sonenscher and Garrioch, '*Compagnonnages*'.
37 Y13816, reports of the *garde*, 1 April 1788.
38 Y11468. Y15100, 30 Aug., 16 Dec. Y13728, 15 Dec. 1786.

The exact structure and functions of the *fabrique* varied in each parish but those who composed it – the present and former *marguilliers* (administrators) – were consistently chosen from the local elite. Their professions reflected the social composition of the parish but most were office-holders, lawyers, or *marchands*, with a few nobles and very occasionally, in the humbler areas, a master artisan. At St Jean-en-Grève, 'les gens mécaniques' (those who worked with their hands) were explicitly excluded. Even at Ste Marguerite a high proportion were members of the *Six Corps*: of thirty-one *marguilliers* elected between 1760 and 1788 there were nine *marchands merciers*, six *marchands épiciers* and one *marchand bonnetier* who was also a *juré* of his corporation. Two were to become *dixainiers* (representatives of *dixaines*, subdivisions of the quarters used by the Hôtel de Ville), and one was a former *juge consul*.[39] The way they were elected was guaranteed to maintain this situation. At Ste Marguerite it was the former *marguilliers* who named the new one each year. At St Séverin the tradition had long been that twelve parishioners (summoned by the *curé*?) chose two men from a list of four drawn up by the *marguilliers* in office. At St André des Arts they were elected by notables of the parish.[40] It is therefore not surprising to find that at Ste Marguerite, even over the short thirty years which the records span, a number of the same family names appear.

What relation, then, did the *fabrique* bear to the local community? The *marguilliers* did not come from any one neighbourhood: those at Ste Marguerite came from every part of the parish, the largest number from the most densely populated areas. This was a deliberate policy at St Séverin, at least in the seventeenth century, when one *marguillier* was chosen from each *dixaine*.[41] The bonds between them were therefore not those of neighbourhood. There were some occupational ties and some of family, and it is likely that they belonged to an elite community outside the local community. It is true of course that they owed their election at least partly to their local pre-eminence, which in turn the position of *marguillier* undoubtedly reinforced. It was a place of honour and a title to be cited with pride. It conferred privileges within the parish, such as a prominent seat close to the altar and a place of honour in public processions. It bestowed a measure of power, 'the authority that the *marguillier comptable* [in charge] should naturally have', as a *marchand mercier* expressed it in 1771.[42] It is also possible that there were networks of patronage. In 1785 an old woman living just near Ste Marguerite in the same house as one of the former *marguilliers* was

[39] Brongniart, *Paroisse*, p. 96. s7493, dossier St Germain le Vieil. LL836, *marguilliers*. De St Jean, elected 1775, former *juge consul*; Boudin, elected 1767, *dixainier* 1767 (H2 1951, Ordonnance du prévôt des marchands, 26 Sept. 1775); Hericourt, elected 1776, *dixainier* 1777 (H1956¹, Ordonnance du prévôt des marchands, 25 Sept. 1785).

[40] 'Les Paroisses de Paris', D. Richet's seminar at Ecole Pratique des Hautes Etudes, 28 Mar., 10 Jan. 1979, 24 Mar. 1981.

[41] 'Le Paroisses de Paris', 28 Mar. 1979.

[42] Y15101, 3 Apr. 1789, wit. 1. LL836, f. 69, 21 Apr. 1771.

accorded a life pension in return for 1,000 *livres* given to the poor of the parish. After her death the pension was to pass to another woman living in the same house and after that to yet a third woman, apparently a relative of the second, living just around the corner in a house occupied by another former *marguillier*. Neighbourhood, family, and church ties are here inextricably linked, and perhaps occupation too, for the two *marguilliers* concerned were both *marchands merciers*.[43] Did the first persuade the woman to invest her money thus, or was he doing her a favour? What was the exact link between her and the other two women, and was it significant that all three were living in houses owned or occupied by former *marguilliers*, whose combined support at the meeting of the *fabrique* might well have won the consent of the assembly? It is impossible to know, but this example suggests that the former *marguilliers*, while they had ties beyond the local community, might continue to provide a link between the neighbourhood and the larger unit of the parish where they might on its behalf exercise a measure of power and wider influence.

What then of the confraternities? Little work has been done on eighteenth-century urban confraternities, which are seen as being in decline, especially in the north of France. It is true that few new ones had been created since the missionary explosion of the late seventeenth century and that their number steadily decreased during the eighteenth century, yet many survived until the Revolution. At St Germain l'Auxerrois in 1753 there were at least four still in existence. Four of those at Ste Marguerite were suppressed in 1760, but the remaining three lasted until the 1790s. Virtually every parish had a Confraternity of the Saint Sacrement, and a list of 1760 includes quite a number of others which were not restricted to a single trade.[44]

It is impossible to know who the members of most parish confraternities were. In a few cases the cost clearly excluded many people: the confraternity of St Prix at St Etienne des Grés had a joining fee of twelve *livres* twelve *sols*, with a monthly payment of twelve *sols*, and twenty *sols* for the feast-day of its patron.[45] But most seem to have been cheaper, and it is likely that a wide range of people could have joined some sort of confraternity. In each parish there was a pecking order which presumably reflected the social composition of each one. Not all of them restricted membership to the parish in which they were located: that of Ste Anne at St Jacques du Haut Pas was for 'women from all the quarters'. A rare list of over 280 members of the Confraternity of La Sainte Famille at St André des Arts, unfortunately not giving occupations, includes a good number who lived in neighbouring or even more distant parishes. So too does an enquiry of 1776

---

[43] LL836, f. 122, 23 Dec. 1785.
[44] N. Z. Davis, 'Some Tasks and Themes in the Study of Popular Religion', in C. Trinkaus and H. O. Oberman (eds.), *Pursuit of Holiness* (Leiden, Brill, 1974), pp. 307–36 (p. 316). 'Les Paroisses de Paris', 24 Mar. 1981. LL836, ff. 8, 98. B.N. J. de F., 1590.
[45] B.N. J. de F. 1590, f. 123.

which introduces twenty or so members of the Confraternity of Notre Dame de Bonne Délivrance at St Etienne des Grés.[46] These were not local organizations.

A partial picture of the sorts of people whom the confraternities served, and of the ties between them, may be gained from looking at the administrators. Admittedly they were not necessarily representative of the ordinary membership, for like the *marguilliers* they were normally elected by the former administrators who, if Ménétra is right, could even choose men who were not members. This would not however disguise their geographic recruitment, and it seems from the lists which survive that the confraternities were on the whole parish-wide rather than neighbourhood institutions.[47]

In social terms the administrators, like the *marguilliers*, reflected the social composition of the area and varied according to the prestige of the confraternity. That of the Sait Sacrement in the rich church of St Nicolas des Champs enjoyed an income of 1,200 *livres* per year and had administrators 'of good birth, and always chosen from among the upper magistrates' (of the Parlement and sovereign courts). At St Séverin the Confraternity of La Conception de la Sainte Vierge was apparently very prestigious and counted among its administrators many merchants of the *Six Corps* and of the corporation of the booksellers and printers. Other confraternities drew their administrators from the less prominent but always well-established citizens of the parish. In 1760 the confraternity of the Saint Sacrement at St Etienne du Mont was run by a master carpenter and a master mason. The former administrators included three more master masons, two more master carpenters, and six master butchers. Six more were *marchands* of other descriptions: a *tapissier*, a *limonadier*, a perfumer, a *fripier*, a paper-merchant and a horse-merchant. The remaining two were a locksmith and a *charcutier*, both masters. One lived in the Faubourg St Germain but the others came from all parts of the parish of St Etienne.[48]

At Ste Marguerite, a much humbler parish, fairly complete lists exist for two confraternities from about 1740 to 1790. That of the Saint Sacrement had among its administrators ten master gardeners, four master bakers, and three *maîtres sculpteurs-marbriers*. The *Six Corps* were represented by a *mercier* and two *marchands bonnetiers*. Nearly all of the others, of very varied trades, were *maîtres marchands*, and this in the Faubourg St Antoine where a great many independent artisans did not have the *maîtrise*. In the Confraternity of Ste Marguerite the picture was similar, with seven master bakers, six master gardeners, four *marchands de vin*, three husbandmen and three master joiners. The most

46 LL836, ff. 4, 98. B.N. J. de F. 1590, ff. 27, 234–42. See YI1092, 14 Dec., 17 Dec. 1776.
47 B.H.V.P. MS. 678, f. 128. LL837 (St Sacrement, Ste Marguerite). LL838 (Ste Marguerite, at Ste Marguerite). Minutier Central, LXXVIII, 622, 12 Nov. 1751 (St Laurent, at Ste Marie du Temple), and CV, 1236, 29 June 1751 (Ste Vierge, at St Paul). YI1585A, 13 Mar. 1786 (St Sépulcre de Jérusalem, Cordeliers). B.N. J. de F. 1590, f. 152 (St Sacrement, St Etienne du Mont, 1766).
48 B.N. J. de F. 1590, ff. 260, 316–17, 152.

prestigious corporations were represented by three *merciers* and a *marchand bonnetier*, and most of the others were other master craftsmen or *marchands*. The range of trades is fairly representative of those in the area, without any one or any particular sector standing out. In both confraternities, furthermore, the administrators were drawn from all over the parish. A number of family names recur, most often father and son. All were fairly well off, as the occupations suggest and as the evidence of the deliberations shows, for both confraternities got into financial difficulties during the century and had to be bailed out by the administrators. In the case of that of Ste Marguerite all of them put in twenty-four *livres* in 1751 and another ten *livres* in 1771. All could sign their names, some very elegantly, although a few wrote clumsily.[49]

The administrators of the parish confraternities, even the humbler ones, were among the best-established citizens and drawn from all parts of the parish. The recruitment was not based on neighbourhood, at least in those for which records remain. Nor was it by economic sector or occupation, although there were clearly minimum requirements: unskilled workers and artisans below the level of *maître marchand* were in most cases automatically excluded. The administrators were chosen on the basis of a more subtle assessment of who was acceptable, one in which wealth and family ties clearly played a part, perhaps in some cases place of origin, and probably business contacts of a less obvious sort. Some were undoubtedly neighbours but this was not a primary bond. Both they and the *marguilliers* formed a local elite with parish-wide contacts which, while boosting their local standing, might also take them outside the community.

This was possibly not true of the ordinary members of the confraternity. Among them neighbourhood ties may well have been more important. Yet by the eighteenth century these groups had lost much of their former organizational role and appear to have played no part in neighbourhood life beyond arranging parish-wide processions and collections on particular days. In some cases they functioned as mutual-aid societies but others seem to have been purely devotional.[50] Their main social function lay in giving their members, mostly men, a place in the church and in the parish, in certain processions and religious services. There were special masses said for each confraternity. In some there may even have been a uniform: one document mentions 'an epaulette of a confraternity' found in a trunk.[51] Membership provided a sense of identity within the parish and perhaps even within the neighbourhood, a measure of distinction for ordinary members in the same way as for the administrators. In this sense the confraternities did have a local role and function, although they were being replaced by other forms of sociability more suited to a large city and to the more secular spirit of the eighteenth century.

We have to look beyond formal religious organizations to find a stronger sense

[49] LL836, f. 3, 2 Feb. 1740. LL837 and LL838.   [50] B.N. J. de F. 1590, ff. 123, 140, 267.
[51] Y14436, 8 Feb.

in which religion contributed to the cohesion of the local community. Among the most frequently mentioned landmarks which people used to describe places were the numerous statues, most often of the Virgin, placed in niches at street corners or above doorways. Delou, *marchand mercier*, lived 'on the Petit Pont opposite the Virgin of the Hôtel Dieu'. Another man lived opposite the Black Virgin of the rue du Four. One statue, on the corner of the rue Ste Marguerite and the Grande Rue du Faubourg St Antoine, achieved city-wide renown in 1752 when the head reportedly turned from one side to the other and people flocked from all over Paris to pray in front of it. Overlooking the locations of neighbourhood sociability, such statues belonged to the community and were in fact maintained by the locals, perhaps by women. That was certainly the case for the one situated on the corner of the rue Neuve d'Orléans and the rue Vieille Notre Dame, just behind St Médard, which was looked after by a domestic servant living in the house. It is however possible that the all-male 'associés à la Sainte Vierge' of the rue aux Ours maintained the tiny chapel located on the corner of that street.[52]

Did people pray and burn candles in front of these statues? It seems likely that they did and that, as still happens today in Italian cities, flowers were placed in front of the images, at least on the feast-days dedicated to the Virgin. Certainly the statues were noticed, and played a prominent part in at least one of the few remaining unofficial local celebrations: the burning of the Swiss of the rue aux Ours. According to tradition a Swiss soldier had on this spot struck a statue of the Virgin which had started to bleed, and every year on 3 July he was burned in effigy at the corner of the rue aux Ours and the rue Quincampoix. The bonfire was preceded by a rowdy procession, in the course of which the mannequin was made to bow before all the statues of the Virgin in the neighbourhood.[53]

This was the people's religion, unconnected with the parish and not consecrated by any clerical presence. Such celebrations were dying or being stamped out: the police only allowed the burning of the Swiss to continue because the *lieutenant général* was informed of 'an irreligious spirit among the young men of the quarter'.[54] But the corner statues remained and continued to be venerated, providing a spiritual focus of a purely local nature.

Religion and religious institutions did therefore have a role to play in the creation and maintenance of the local community, but a fairly diffuse one. Despite the undoubted influence of the church in people's everyday lives, all but the smallest parishes, and those on the semi-rural fringes of the city, were too vast and too populous to constitute real social units. People's sense of belonging to the parish went beyond the neighbourhood, was more like their awareness of being part of a *faubourg*, or of the whole city. Neighbours did meet at mass, if they

---

52 Y15350, 26 Nov., wit. 12. Y15099, 24 May, wit. 9. Y10994, 12 and 13 June. Y12597, 2 Nov., 13 Nov. B.H.V.P. MS 678, f. 9. Ménétra gets the street wrong! Seine D5 B6 472.
53 Orléans MS 1421, f. 95. Mercier, *Tableau*, vol. 4, p. 97.   54 Orléans MS 1421, f. 137.

attended the same service at the same church. But their quarrels had to wait until they got back to the streets and houses which were the real centres of community life. The *marguilliers* and the administrators of the parish confraternities were drawn from the elite of the whole area and such organizations seem above all to have helped to create ties and aspirations outside the neighbourhood; ties which, if they did not necessarily conflict directly with local ones, might provide people with a means of moving out of the local community.

The importance of organized religious practice and belief, for the local community, lay in neighbourhood co-operation in erecting *reposoirs* and decorating the streets, in the unifying force of participation, even as spectators, in processions along local streets. Baptisms, weddings and funerals brought groups of neighbours, colleagues, and friends together, strengthening and consecrating existing bonds. And, above all, the remaining local foci of religious belief – statues, the very occasional tiny chapel, local traditions – reinforced the sense of belonging and gave an added spiritual dimension to membership of the community.

5

Recreation and leisure sociability

Work, family, and parish have long been recognized as social bonds of the utmost importance. Interest in leisure sociability, as a vital if somewhat elusive element in social organization, has been much more recent, and such work has stressed the long-term evolution of patterns of sociability. The early modern period is seen as one in which dramatic changes were taking place, especially among the social elites who were withdrawing from popular festivities. The process was a long-term one and occurred at differing speeds in different places, but the eighteenth century saw its fair share of changes. There was the development of freemasonry, of clubs, of literary circles and academies. Coffee houses appeared in France at the end of the seventeenth or at the beginning of the eighteenth century. There was an important although very gradual change in religious sensibility which led to the decline of confraternities and of religious sociability in general.[1]

Recreational forms may be studied in several ways. One can look at what people actually did, where and when they did it and at exactly who was involved. One can ask what participation meant to the people involved and to outsiders; and what was the function of recreational activity in expressing or transmitting values? Finally, there is the question of what patterns of leisure sociability can tell us about the way society worked and about its evolution? All of these questions are clearly crucial to the study of the local community. Whether people sought recreation within the neighbourhood or outside it, and whether they participated in collective sports or festivities, helped to determine the quality of community life. Examining just who did or did not join in, and why, is crucial to defining the social limits of the local community. None of these factors, furthermore, is static. We must also consider how changes in patterns of recreation affected the local community.

In eighteenth-century Paris it is of course next to impossible to separate

---

[1] Agulhon, *Sociabilité*. Gutton, *Sociabilité*. D. Roche, *Le Siècle des lumières en province: académies et académiciens provinciaux, 1680–1789*, 2 vols. (Paris, Mouton/De Gruyter, 1978). N. Z. Davis, 'Tasks and Themes'. M. Vovelle, *Piété baroque et déchristianisation en Provence au XVIIIe siècle* (Paris, Plon, 1973). M. Vovelle, *Les Métamorphoses de la fête en Provence de 1750 à 1820* (Paris, Aubier/Flammarion). E. Le Roy Ladurie, *Carnival. A People's Uprising at Romans, 1579–1580* (London, Scolar Press, 1980). Bercé, *Fête*. M. Ozouf, *La Fête révolutionnaire* (Paris, Gallimard, 1976).

'recreation' from other day-to-day activities. Working people had little leisure and did much of their socializing at work and during working hours. Many trades had slack periods which alternated with very busy ones, and these allowed time for a drink and a chat either in the workshop or nearby. An excursion to deliver some item, to do work outside the shop, or to draw up a contract, provided many opportunities for social contact. As we have seen, many business deals were struck in wineshops. Street traders might sell their wares there. And of course the weary walk home after work could become a *promenade*. Even among the rich, 'leisured' population, *soirées* and dinners were occasions for making contacts, discussing investments, planning marriages. Any division between work and leisure is therefore arbitrary, and I have already mentioned many forms of 'recreation' in the preceding chapters. Here I will concentrate on voluntary sociability, as opposed to that required by daily contact at work or in the neighbourhood. I will look first at forms which were favoured for the most part, although not entirely, by better-off people: dinner invitations, leisure migration, clubs and societies. I will then turn to more 'popular' types of recreation: wineshops and *guinguettes*, *la promenade*, outdoor and indoor games and, finally, popular celebrations.

I. HOME SOCIABILITY: DINNER INVITATIONS

It is at once obvious that there are important differences between popular recreation and the forms of leisure chosen by the elites of the capital. Better-off people had more living space and could therefore do more things at home. We have already seen, in looking at the family, that noble and non-noble elites alike were able physically to insulate themselves from the neighbourhood, and that entertaining at home played an important part in their social life.

Nevertheless, such entertaining was not confined to the rich, and differences in form and style reflect people's place in the local community. Private dinner parties, for example, were common among a range of social groups, but a general distinction can be made between their use by people like office-holders, wealthy merchants, even reasonably well-off master artisans, on the one hand, and by humbler folk on the other. For the former they were often business occasions. We find in the papers of the *commissaire* Ninnin a note inviting him to 'give us the pleasure of coming to sup with us tomorrow and discuss our business for a few moments'. More often still dinner parties were purely a family affair, as when a former clerk of the Parlement entertained his mother, brother, and brother-in-law, or when a former merchant, now calling himself 'bourgeois de Paris', invited an elderly cousin. Somewhere in between was a meal put on by a master tailor and his wife for the family of a master carriage-maker living several streets away, at which they discussed a marriage for the carriage-maker's eldest daughter.[2]

---

[2] Y15114B, correspondence, 7 Aug. [1780]. Y15402, 23 Oct., 27 Mar. Y14078, 10 Nov.

Intimate dinners were also favoured by women for whom the model of the 'lady of quality' held some appeal, particularly those who did not work. Thus the wife of a *négociant* invited a young 'bourgeoise de Paris' to dinner in her apartment one March evening. On the night of Mardi Gras 1788 the wife of a *chirurgien* living in the Place Ste Geneviève came to dine with a close friend, whose husband was an instrument-maker in the rue des Saints Pères.[3]

For these people therefore, the informal dinner was for business, or else a domestic, family form of sociability, and if those involved lived anywhere near each other it was largely coincidental. Among humbler people, however, neighbours were generally present, both on special occasions and on less formal ones. The widow of an *ébéniste* invited selected neighbours to a meal to celebrate a wedding proposal made to her grand-daughter; a *garçon marchand de vin* invited his family and selected neighbours to supper. A seamstress in the rue Jean Pain Mollet, having got to know a domestic servant and his wife who lived on the same floor, was invited to eat with them five or six times in the four months she had been living there.[4]

Much the same division is observable in other forms of home-based recreation, such as card and games evenings, or even informal social visits. A female beer-seller, for example, complained that she had been grievously insulted by the woman next door while playing cards with several neighbours. Another complaint recounts an evening spent playing various card games with neighbours of both sexes. One game included penances, one of which, falling on a male participant, involved kissing all the women present; a task he tried to fulfil with a little too much ardour.[5] For humble folk, therefore, home sociability reinforced neighbourhood ties, and particularly for women, who were excluded from the wineshops where working men spent much of their leisure time. Among the more affluent social groups, however, the weight of the neighbourhood dwindled, with guests far more likely to come from all over the city and to be relatives, friends, or business associates.

The division, however, was not simply between elites and common people, but also varied according to whether individuals were 'established' or not, a factor closely related to age and occupation. Thus a married couple were far more likely to issue a dinner invitation, whatever their rank and position, than a single person of either sex. The use of the home was limited both by the space available and by the sexual division of labour.

II. A HOUSE IN THE COUNTRY

One of the most common of all recreations today, one which we treat almost as a natural human activity, is leisure migration: going away for a holiday. The

[3] Y13760, 10 Apr. wit. 1. Y15402, 18 Dec., wit. 3.
[4] Y10994, 3 May. Y14078, 25 Sept. Y15350, 17 Aug., wit. 2.
[5] Y13760, 1 Dec. Y13819, 22 Sept. 1788. Y11705, 3 Feb.

practice is nevertheless a relatively recent one whose popularity increased greatly during the eighteenth century, partly thanks to improved transport and roads, and partly because of the contemporary taste for landscape and countryside. Wealthy nobles, many magistrates, *fermiers généraux* and high-ranking commoners had country estates where they would go in summer. This was certainly not new, but the buying of 'maisons de campagne' (country houses) by people of humbler rank was. 'The affluent bourgeoisie leave on the eve [of holidays and Sundays] for their little country house, situated near the *barrière*', wrote Mercier in the early 1780s. His archetypal 'affluent bourgeois' is a shopkeeper with two sons in boarding school and an older daughter whose hand is worth ten or twelve thousand francs in dowry.[6]

This was certainly one sort of person who purchased houses in the country. We find a *marchand épicier* from the Faubourg St Antoine who had one at St Maur; a master clockmaker with a house at Conflans; a butcher in the Faubourg St Germain who owned a property at Arcueil. Any of these could be Mercier's shopkeeper. But there were other people who bought houses in the country, too. A *factrice aux grains* at the central market owned a place at Bagneux, and a retired *mesureur de grains* had one at Vincennes. The principal clerk (*premier commis*) of the Comte d'Argenson had a country house at La Folie Regnault, on the fringe of the Faubourg St Antoine. A variation was a shared house, such as that at Bercy occupied by the wife of a *négociant* and by a *huissier*.[7]

A range of occupational groups, therefore, went in for what we would today call holiday houses: affluent shopkeepers, merchants and prosperous master craftsmen, minor office-holders, the better-off employees of the largest noble houses. They were the sorts of people to whom the new ideas of domesticity appealed, and the way that the house in the country fitted into their lives illustrates the point. For Mercier's *bourgeois* the weekend away was a family affair, with the couple perhaps taking their shop-assistant as a special treat. And indeed we find a *bourgeois de Paris*, his wife and his brother, and a friend, sitting down together in the privacy of his house at Clignancourt.[8] The house in the country was a retreat from the noise and bustle of the city, from the confined space of an urban apartment.

It was at the same time a retreat from the local community, a family domain removed from the surveillance and the curiosity of neighbours, and of course a sign of prosperity and social advancement. Withdrawal from the community was not necessarily complete, of course. Occasionally there is evidence that the fugitive from the city to some degree became part of the village society to which he or she retreated. When the *marchand épicier* who occupied the first floor of a

---

6 Mercier, *Tableau*, vol. 4, pp. 163–4.
7 Y12596, 1 June. Y14436, 17 July. Y14078, 23 Dec. Y15402, 5 Aug., 30 Apr. Y10994, 9 Oct. Y14436, 21 July.
8 Y14436, 19 May.

house at St Maur found his parents invaded by three men claiming to be his creditors, he called for help from the neighbours, who rushed in to repel the unwelcome visitors in the same way as would the locals in his weekday residence in the rue de Lappe.[9]

Another possibility is that people from the same part of Paris went to the same place, and that part of the Parisian local community was thus transplanted. However, a look at the tax rolls for villages near Paris makes this appear unlikely, even though people did tend to go to villages on the side of the city where they lived. The roll for Argenteuil, for example, brings to light a sprinkling of Parisians: a *marchand épicier*, a *marchand éventailliste* (fan-maker), a police *inspecteur*, two *bourgeois de Paris*. But their Paris addesses are so scattered that if they knew each other before buying country houses it was certainly not as neighbours.[10] There is of course no guarantee that in Argenteuil they had any contact with each other, but if they did it served only to create ties outside the Paris neighbourhood, and at a similar socio-economic level. Either way, the house in the country provided certain elements of the population with a means of withdrawal from the local community, and helped to make such withdrawal socially prestigious.

III. CLUBS AND SOCIETIES

The increasingly popular clubs which eighteenth-century Parisians called *sociétés* ranged in seriousness from literary academies to groups that were little more than an excuse for social or gallant encounters. Best known are the *salons*, presided over by women and posing as patrons of the arts. More restricted in membership were the literary clubs which blossomed during the eighteenth century: the more serious ones forbidding gambling, feasts, and drinking, but others meeting at table under the patronage of a generous host.[11] There were various musical and theatrical societies. Maurepas, the Marquis de Montalembert, the *fermier général* de la Popelinière, and many others, organized dramatic societies which wrote and acted their own plays. Numerous dining clubs also flourished, like the 'Société des Mercredis', a group of seventeen individuals who met in a restaurant in the rue Croix des Petits Champs. Another was the 'Société des Gobe-Mouches', founded some time during the reign of Louis XVI by a former army officer. There were also many 'sociétés d'amitié' ('friendship societies') such as the 'Ordre de la Félicité', which lasted from 1740 to 1745 and which met for formal meals, conversation, and song. It was open to both men and women. So too was the 'Loge de la Candeur', a semi-masonic group restricted to

[9] Y12596, 1 June.　[10] Z¹g 463^A, *capitation* and *taille* registers for Argenteuil, 1761.
[11] Roche, *Académies*, vol. 1, pp. 15, 64. A. Dinaux, *Les Sociétés badines, bachiques, littéraires et chantantes, leur histoire et leurs travaux*, 2 vols. (Paris, 1867), vol. 2, pp. 351, 121.

10. Physical separation from the street: *hôtel particulier*, 10 rue de Seine

nobles, which existed between 1775 and 1785.[12] Yet another form of *société* characteristic of elite sociability towards the end of the Ancien Régime was charitable groups. They began to appear in Paris from about 1770 on: the 'Ordre de la Persévérance' of 1771, the 'Société Philanthropique' of 1780, whose list of members for 1789 reads like a Who's Who in Paris.[13]

Most of these societies, whatever their particular activities, were very much for the elite. Some were specifically restricted to people of rank. All were by invitation, and membership could be quite expensive. Serious literary groups met in libraries, studies, or private gardens and were very concerned to mark their separation from the noisy, ignorant mass. Salons and theatrical groups, too, met in private town houses or quite often in the country house of one of the members, thus adding physical separation from the city to their isolation from the crowd.[14]

There are a few indications, however, that not all the societies were so high-class. A draft complaint by a *chirurgien* against his *garçon* mentions, as evidence of the latter's dissolute behaviour, 'that he has recently joined a *société*

---

[12] Dinaux, *Sociétés*, vol. 2, pp. 13, 60, 152, 33. Mercier *Tableau*, vol. 12, p. 303.

[13] *Calendrier philanthropique*, 1789 (in B.N. 8° Le Senne 13 617). Dinaux, *Sociétés*, vol. 2, pp. 128–33.

[14] Roche, *Académies*, vol. 1, pp. 48–9. J. Quéniart, *Culture et société urbaine dans la France de l'Ouest au XVIIIe siècle* (Paris, Klincksieck, 1978), pp. 432–3.

of young men of modest means in order to perform plays'. Enclosed is the young man's membership card, a playing card bearing on the back the words 'Société Bourgeoise faubourg St Martin, Bon pour une personne' (admit one), accompanied by a seal of red wax.[15] Perhaps even more humble were the 'associés à la Sainte Vierge, rue aux Ours', mentioned in the 1775 account-book of Clemandot, *marchand de vin*. The name seems to come from that of the leader's wine-shop, although this in turn is clearly taken from the chapel dedicated to the Virgin which stood on the corner of the rue aux Ours and the rue Quincampoix. The eighteen members are referred to as 'confrères', but in other respects it was quite unlike a religious confraternity. The leader was titled 'Roy' (King), perhaps an echo of the youth abbeys of provincial villages, and the major entry concerns the wine, food, and flowers which were provided for a feast on the day of the octave of Corpus Christi. Even if some religious activity was combined with these festivities, the group clearly functioned as a sort of club. Except for the *marchand de vin* himself, who was well enough off to own two shops in Paris, the occupations and rank of the members are unfortunately not given. There is, however, a mention on the back of the book of a 'Mr Lebrun, ancien camarade du Collège, architecte juré du Roy rue Fontaine au Roy seconde Barrière du Temple', who may be the Lebrun mentioned among the 'associés'. The addresses of two others are given: both lived in the same part of the city but still some distance apart, and – an important fact if the group did have a religious purpose – in different parishes.[16]

It would clearly be misleading to group all these societies together without emphasizing the differences between them. D. Roche has stressed the clear separation between, on the one hand, the *académies* and the associated literary circles and reading groups, and on the other the salons which retained an older code of gallantry and frivolity.[17] There was obviously a world of difference between a club run by a *marchand de vin* and a society organized by a peer of France. Yet all of these formed part of the same general development of eighteenth-century sociability.

So, too, did freemasonry, whose membership is far better documented and which is therefore more useful for our purposes. The lodges were in some respects very different from the societies I have mentioned. They had an extended, centralized organization, and shared a more or less consistent set of symbols and practices. But we should not be misled into looking on eighteenth-century freemasonry as the highly monolithic organization it later became. Some lodges, for example, admitted women: what was obviously a very high society one, the Loge St Charles, included forty-eight 'maçonnes', and had a Grand Mistress as well as a Grand Master. Many of its members, both male and female,

---

[15] Y15115A, draft complaint [Jan. 1788] in dossier marked 'projets de plaintes'.
[16] Seine, D5 B6 472. Mercier, *Tableau*, vol. 4, p. 97.
[17] Roche, *Académies*, vol. 1, pp. 46–8.

were of high rank and its composition was more like that of a salon than of what we have come to regard as a typical lodge. But it was affiliated with the Grand Orient, and its papers lie among those of the Orient.[18]

There was plenty of room for variation within freemasonry, therefore, and in practice the lodges had much in common with other clubs. Their meetings were primarily social gatherings and dining was a central activity. The early lodges in fact met in wineshops and eating places. As late as 1785, Lenoir was regularly informed of meetings in advance, 'that there would be dancing, music and a meal, and subsequently a collection to aid prisoners'.[19] Like many other societies, lodges mostly had between twenty and thirty members, about as many as could fit comfortably around a large table. Mercier's comment, also in the 1780s, indicates an overlap not only with the dining and musical clubs but also with literary societies: 'the freemasons eat and drink together, play music, read verse or prose'. He puts them firmly in the same category as 'all these new assemblies' concluding that 'men who need and desire sociable gatherings worry little what sign they assemble under'.[20] Lenoir's reference to a collection for prisoners after meetings of lodges also illustrates the similarity between freemasonry and the various charitable societies.

Chronological and historical links between freemasonry and other societies are obvious. Lodges appeared and grew alongside clubs of other sorts, and their boom period, after 1770, is also that of literary societies. They flourished pariculary in the south of France where there was already a marked taste for this sort of association. Even the more distinctively masonic forms share many features with both older and contemporary societies. M. Agulhon has shown that confraternities of penitents and lodges of freemasons in Provence were strikingly similar in many of their practices and in their recruitment.[21] The penitents were absent from Paris but the vocabulary of freemasonry and of other social clubs was often similar, as is illustrated by the names of many societies. Fraternal terminology was widespread, and the use of different grades – and in some cases even the names for them – was shared by a number of groups. For example the Chevalerie de la Coignée had, like the lodge, a *Grand Maître* (Grand Master) and an *Orateur*, and its officers were arranged in a hierarchy like that of the masons, being called 'Très Auguste', 'Très Respectable', or 'le Vénérable', according to their rank. The Ordre de la Félicité explicitly pointed out, in its statutes of 1746, its similarity to the masons and other groups: 'What the Masons call a Lodge, the Frères des Quatre Vents a cavern (*caverne*), ... the Ordre de la Félicité calls a squadron (*escadre*)'.[22]

Sometimes there is evidence that such groups actually borrowed from the

18 B.N. FM³ 162.   19 Bast. 11556. Y13750, 8 June 1745. Orléans MS 1422, f. 103.
20 Mercier, *Tableau*, vol. 7, pp. 226–8.
21 Roche, *Académies*, vol. 1, pp. 28–47, 55–61. Agulhon, *Sociabilité*, esp. pp. 327–9.
22 B.H.V.P. MS 5207. Dinaux, *Sociétés*, vol. 1, pp. 210–14, 301–10; vol. 2, pp. 93–4.

lodges. The 'Ordre des Fendeurs' with its grades, its use of the term *compagnon*, and of *chantier* (literally 'building site') instead of 'lodge', was founded by Beauchaine, himself a mason and already a founder of another masonic fringe-group. But it is also clear that the masons did not themselves invent all their terminology or rites and may have borrowed from older societies: the term 'Grand Maître', for example, was used in 1696 by a group called the Chevaliers de la Joye (and of course long before that by the Templars).[23]

The societies and lodges were therefore very similar. Both were primarily for the upper classes, although there were some humbler examples, and it is likely that they had similar social limits. The police pursued the early lodges vigorously and their membership is thus well documented. One such, of humbler membership than most, was the Loge de la Cité, which the police watched from September 1743 to March 1744.[24] The Master was Chauvin, a former *marchand de vin* in the rue de la Harpe. The secretary was Midy, a former *huissier-priseur*, the treasurer Mornay, *marchand lapidaire* (lapidary) in the Cour de Lamoignon, himself recruited by Midy and Chauvin. Chauvin also seems to have helped to enlist Potel, *employé à la volaille* (an official in the poultry market), who lived in the rue des Mauvais Garçons, Faubourg St Germain, and Alet, market-gardener, rue de Loursine. Other officials included a building entrepreneur, and a man whose name is not given but who lived in the Cour du Palais.

Among the ordinary members traces of a network can be distinguished. It seems that the core of the lodge was formed from the friends and acquaintances of Chauvin and Midy: both a *marchand de vin* and a *huissier* were likely to have a wide range of contacts. We can pick out a legal, or rather a Châtelet group: a second *huissier-priseur*, two of the clerks employed by Bechu, *procureur au Châtelet*, as well as Bechu's son; the clerks of another *procureur*, of a *commissaire au Châtelet*, and of a notary. Most of these would have occasion to visit the law courts from time to time, and this may have provided the connection with a second, geographically based group. I have already mentioned one official of the lodge who lived in the Cour du Palais next to the central law courts. The treasurer, Mornay, lapidary, lived in the nearby Cour de Lamoignon, as did another member, a *metteur en oeuvre* (mounter of precious stones). Other men in the jewellery industry were also involved: two more *metteurs en oeuvre*, one living in the Place Dauphine and the other near St Gervais, along with a master goldsmith on the Quai Pelletier. A second *employé à la volaille* was presumably recruited by Potel. The links between the other members are not obvious: there was an architect, a *bourgeois de Paris*, a *marchand tapissier*, a *marchand de vin*, a Capuchin priest, and the son of a master perfume-maker. Most of the members were in some way connected with small commerce, including the *huissiers* and

23 Dinaux, *Sociétés*, vol. I, pp. 331–3, 422. A. Le Bihan, *Francs-maçons et ateliers parisiens de la Grande Loge de France au XVIIIe siècle (1760–1795)* (Paris, B.N., 1973), ch. 2.
24 Bast. 11556, dossier Potel.

legal clerks, and with trade rather than purely artisanal production. All of them had links across the city, which were not only commercial but also social: their common membership of the lodge shows that. None of them were in unskilled trades. Only the *metteurs en oeuvre*, among the tradesmen, were not masters or *marchands*, but they belonged to one of the most highly skilled trades in the city. Perhaps the most interesting aspect of the network of contacts in this lodge is the way it crosses all sorts of barriers: occupational ones, not only between different socio-professional groups, but also between people in completely different economic sectors; geographic ones, for the ties extend outside the one quarter, and across the river. There is only one mention of family ties, and if *pays* had any role to play it is certainly not evoked. The Loge de la Cité illustrates the complex nature of social contacts at this level of society. Nevertheless, both occupational and neighbourhood links were clearly present, and the members formed a group which was socially very homogeneous.

A similar picture emerges if we glance at the membership of another lodge: that of St Jean de la Parfaite Union. In 1775 it includes two *hommes de loi* ('men of law'), three *employés*, a *rentier*, another man described as *propriétaire* (property-owner), a musician, a *militaire*, a plumber, a master tailor, *a limonadier*, a confectioner, and a metal polisher. Like the Loge de la Cité, therefore, it was based largely on small commerce and the humbler liberal professions. The presence of three *employés* reflects the growth in public administration. The addresses are mostly around St Germain des Prés, St Honoré, and the north-central area – the main business districts – and reflect the existence of numerous ties across the river. Neighbourhood was perhaps important in the case of four men living in the rue St Dominique, two at number 970, one at 967, and another at 1041.[25]

Such examples could be multiplied. But a number of conclusions already emerge. The first is that, although different lodges catered to a very wide social range, each one had a socially homogeneous core. Secondly, it seems that while family ties were occasionally present they were not of any great importance (unless relatives by marriage greatly outnumbered those with the same name). Neighbourhood ties were sometimes present, more often in the humbler lodges than in the high-class ones. But above all the lodges were based on professional and business connections which extended right across the city. The personal networks visible in individual lodges indicate that those who joined were principally people with active links outside their own quarter. As our study of work ties has shown, these were men who were at the top of their trade, or who belonged to a profession which necessitated or encouraged the formation of such outside connections. Indeed, many lodges welcomed masons from other places, and thus provided merchants and *négociants* with contacts across the country.[26] It is interesting to note, in A. Le Bihan's list by occupation of the masters of the

[25] B.N. FM² 93, f. 6.   [26] Quéniart, *Culture*, pp. 449–53.

Paris lodges of the Grande Loge from 1760 to 1799, the weight of what might be called the *objets d'art* sector: jewellery, decorative arts, luxury furniture.[27] Craftsmen in these trades, as we have seen, often had to co-operate in their work. Many had a socially restricted range of clients, and sold extensively to each other and to wholesale merchants both in France and abroad. They had a strong sense of corporate unity, and their forming societies was a natural reflection of this. However the police frowned on what they saw as unofficial trade organizations: in 1767 we find an ordinance banning a 'société' of jewellers, goldsmiths, lapidaries, mercers and *metteurs en oeuvre* which met for banquets.[28] Freemasonry, by the 1770s and 1780s, was a safer form of association.

It was not one favoured, however, by other trade sectors. In the lists preserved in the Bibliothèque Nationale there are very few freemasons from the food trades, and the same is true of Le Bihan's list of lodge masters: these were trades much more closely linked, as we have seen, with the local community. A glance at the areas of the city represented, even in the humblest lodges, reinforces this general conclusion. The northern and eastern *faubourgs* very rarely appear. Most prominent of all, on the other hand, is the Faubourg St Honoré, not only an increasingly exclusive area but also the centre of finance and big business. The humblest of the Paris freemasons were people already, or potentially, outside the local community.

The little information we have on the social composition of eighteenth-century societies in general points in the same direction. The *garçon chirurgien* of the 'Société Bourgeoise' would not, his apprenticeship completed, have appeared out of place in a list of freemasons. I have already mentioned semi-masonic societies, as well as the jewellers' 'société' banned in 1767. The host of the 'associés à la Vierge' was himself a freemason: there is a list of the members of his lodge at the back of his account-book (although none of the others appear among the 'associés') and he is also mentioned in a document of the Grande Loge.[29]

Perhaps most important of all the common characteristics of the lodges and other societies was their shared taste for exclusivity. Membership of a literary group obviously required education, time, and privacy for reading. That of a dining club or of a lodge necessitated sufficient leisure to attend meetings and the ability to meet the cost of feasts and perhaps of costumes. This automatically cut out the poorest elements of the population. But most groups were also actively exclusive. Many placed restrictions on membership, and the lodges and similar groups cultivated secrecy and mystery by the use of symbols, titles and special ceremonies. The Chevalerie de la Coignée decided in 1748

---

[27] Le Bihan, *Grande Loge*, pp. 481–5.
[28] Ordonnance de police, 12 Sept. 1767, in Peuchet, vol. 7, pp. 84–5.
[29] Seine D5 B6 472. Le Bihan, *Grande Loge*, p. 339.

that to protect ourselves from the Curiosity of the Profane and in order to prevent any knowledge or suspicion of the days and locations of our meetings, the *frères chevaliers* will henceforth be free to arrive in their ordinary clothes on those days . . .[30]

There is some evidence to suggest that freemasonry was becoming increasingly exclusive. In Paris the Grand Orient gradually extended its control over the lodges. Whereas in the 1740s police reports suggest that lodges admitted whoever they liked, without reference to the Grande Loge, by the 1770s all certificates and masonic grades were issued by the Grand Orient to which most of the lodges were by then affiliated. On 27 December 1773 the Orient decided that artisans, domestics, and actors would henceforth be admitted only as *frères servants* ('serving brothers'), and that all artisans other than masters would be totally excluded. This was followed in 1774 by an order that no lodges would be allowed to meet in wineshops or restaurants: they could therefore not continue unless they had some member with premises suitable for meetings.[31]

The eighteenth-century societies, including freemasonry, represented a general move away from the locations and forms of local-community sociability. Their development, and particularly that of literary circles, reflects a new concern with individual 'improvement' and a means of marking one's distance from the unenlightened, uneducated masses.[32] The sorts of people to whom the eighteenth-century societies – and Enlightenment philosophy – appealed were those who valued the sense of being among the initiated, the select few, set aside from 'the profane' and from the crowd. Their membership is a measure of the spread of new values and accompanied their rejection, albeit partial, of the open and predominantly neighbourhood sociability vital to the continued existence of a broadly based local community.

IV. WINESHOPS

Wineshops (*cabarets*) and drinking establishments in general are the recreational institutions which best embody the spirit of popular sociability and of the local community. We saw in chapter 1 that some wineshops played a very important role in the life of the quarter. This does not mean, however, that they were used exclusively by locals, or by all the locals. It does not necessarily follow, either, that locality alone determined where someone went. Exactly who, therefore, used wineshops, and which ones? Just as importantly, who did they go with, and were there differences in the things they did there? Answering these questions will bring us closer to defining the social limits of the local community.

There was a wide range of drinking establishments in Paris, referred to by a variety of terms. There were shops run by *marchands de vin*, by *marchands de bière*,

---

[30] B.H.V.P. MS 5207, ff. 14–15.
[31] Le Bihan, *Grande Loge*. Examples can be found in B.N. FM series.
[32] Roche, *Académies*, vol. 1, p. 15.

and by *limonadiers*. A look at the way eighteenth-century Parisians spoke of the various drinking places, however, suggests that they were seen in very much the same way, whether they sold wine, beer, or spirits. The one real distinction sometimes made by contemporaries was between *café* and *cabaret*.[33] Lenoir cites Berryer, writing in the 1760s, as saying that for fifty or sixty years the wineshops had no longer attracted

the bourgeois, or even people above the bourgeoisie; the wineshops of Paris were generally frequented only by soldiers, workers, coachmen, lackeys, and by prostitutes. A few petit bourgeois or *marchands* still went to the *guinguettes* on Sundays and feast-days; but many more of them frequented the cafés, the clubs, even houses of ill repute.[34]

Most sources of the time, however, do not permit any clear distinction at all. Mercier describes the *tabagies* and *tavernes* or 'cabarets borgnes', frequented by 'the scum of the people'. The common people spent their last *sou*, he tells us, on 'the bad wine of the *cabarets*'. Elsewhere he writes of 'six or seven hundred cafés: the habitual refuge of idlers and an asylum for the indigent ... It is no longer respectable to dally in cafés.'[35] In other documents, too, we find the term 'café' used interchangeably with *cabaret*, and gradually supplanting it. A police patrol of January 1752 went round a number of 'cafés et cabarets', turning out late drinkers. In examples from 1788, a *garçon marchand de vin* and a *limonadier* both refer to their shops as 'cafés'; and a peddler mentions buying second-hand clothes 'in a café while drinking beer'.[36]

The term 'café' seems quite simply to have followed the diffusion of the beverage. Coffee first appeared in exclusive, expensive places like Le Procope, but during the century became cheaper and increasingly popular. It came to be sold in a range of drinking establishments which, perhaps by pretension, began to call themselves 'cafés' instead of *cabarets*. Thus the distinction which existed early in the century gradually disappeared. With it went the upper-class clientele which the first cafés attracted: some literary cafés remained, but they were few in number.[37]

In my analysis therefore, I will – with one exception – treat all the drinking establishments together, following the most general late eighteenth-century usage. The exception is the *guinguettes*, the taverns beyond the *barrières*, which because of their prices and location attracted people from all over the capital. Being outside the city proper they could not function in the same way as neighbourhood cafés, and I will therefore deal with them separately.

33 T. Brennan, 'Cabarets and Labouring Class Communities in Eighteenth-Century Paris', unpub. Ph.D. thesis, Johns Hopkins University, 1981, pp. 27–9.
34 Orléans MS 1421, f. 275, Cf. Ariès, 'Family and the City', p. 231.
35 Mercier, *Tableau*, vol. 2, pp. 19–21; vol. 7, p. 237; vol. 10, p. 198; vol. 1, pp. 227–30.
36 Y15350, 1 Jan. Y15100, 24 July. Y14436, 19 Jan. Y15100, 5 Aug.
37 Cf. R. Darnton, 'The High Enlightenment and the Low Life of Literature in Pre-Revolutionary France', *Past and Present*, 51 (1971), 81–115 (100–1). See the illustration in Darnton, *Great Cat Massacre*, p. 180.

How can we know exactly who used wineshops? Literary material gives a general impression, but for more detailed information we must again turn to judicial sources. The evidence is of two sorts. On the one hand there are the comments people made about behaviour, condemning violations of norms or else referring to things in such a way as to suggest their banality. Secondly, it is possible to count the examples of a given type of behaviour and see what sorts of people engaged in it. Wineshops are mentioned in a variety of documents: in reports of the *garde*, which was generally called to break up fights; in declarations of theft; and in occasional enquiries where a range of those who had been present would testify. Then there are frequent references to time spent in wineshops and mentions of people seen there, evoked as part of the background to a complaint, declaration, or testimony. Given this variety of documents and situations, any major group which used wineshops frequently will sooner or later appear.

The literary evidence indicates consistently that the urban elites did not frequent wineshops, or did so no longer. Mercier and Berryer's observations have already been quoted, and are confirmed by statements made to the *commissaires*. Affluent merchants and masters, at least when moralizing in *enquêtes en séparation*, cited frequenting wineshops as evidence of lack of thrift and dedication to business, a sure sign of moral decline. Affluent people drank their wine at home and would have it delivered. Many kept their own cellars, as *scellés après décès* show. The existence of a well-furnished cellar is in itself an indication of physical isolation from the local community.

A second observation based on similar evidence is that relatively few women used wineshops. I have already mentioned the insulting accusation that a woman 'courait les cafés' (ran round the cafés). On one occasion we even find a *marchand de vin* accused by his wife of having said that 'there should be no women working in wineshops because they embarrassed the women who came to eat and drink with the men'. The *commissaires* showed little mercy to women who were arrested in wineshops, seeing the very fact of their presence in such places as circumstantial evidence of suspect morals.[38]

If we now look at the people whose presence in wineshops is mentioned, and first at the women, we find this judgment partially confirmed. A fair proportion of the women, and nearly all who went alone to wineshops, were prostitutes. But there were others, mainly in the humblest and roughest trades whose work forced them to rub shoulders with all comers: itinerant street-sellers and porters, stall-keepers and *revendeuses*, including the infamous *poissardes*. In the papers of the senior *commissaire* of the Halles quarter in 1752 there are only eighteen women mentioned as being in wineshops. Four were sellers of fruit or fish in the

---

[38] Y18580, Chambre civile, 21 Nov. 1782. Y10994, 17 Mar., 19 Apr., 22 Nov. Brennan, 'Cabarets', pp. 49–52. Cf. A. Farge, who claims that women went to wineshops 'sans contrainte': *Vivre*, pp. 75–6.

Table 5. *Occupations of women in wineshops, 1752 and 1788 (five quarters)*[a]

Occupation (or that of husband or parent)	Number of women
Market vendor or stall-keeper	12
Textile worker	10
Prostitute[b]	9
Master artisan or *marchand*	8
Journeyman artisan	7
Servant[c]	6
Itinerant street-traders	5
Manufacturing trades other than textiles[d]	4
Tripe-worker	3
Laundrywoman	3
Sick-nurse	2
Female porter	1
Charwoman	1
Other[e]	12
Unknown	12
Total	95

[a] Grève, Halles, Faubourg St Antoine, Place Maubert, Luxembourg (1752 only), St Germain des Prés (1788 only).
[b] Described as such by themselves or by witnesses. It is clear from context that a number of those here included as textile workers were also prostitutes.
[c] Includes one group of five servants.
[d] Button-making, bookbinding, metal-polishing, mattress-making.
[e] Wives of water-carrier, waggoner, pawnbroker, innkeeper, horse-merchant, billposters, labourers, *agent de commerce*, gardener, *officier du grenier à sel*.

market or in the streets, and three of these were accompanied by their grown-up daughters. Two more worked in the nearby fish-market, one was the wife of a water-carrier, and four were described as 'seamstresses' or 'linen-workers', at least one of whom was a part-time prostitute. The remaining four on whom some information is given were wives of masters or *marchands*. If we look at the papers of one of the *commissaires* for the Grève in the same year, the pattern reflects the different social composition of the riverside quarters but without changing the general picture. Of twenty women mentioned, for whom occupation or husband's occupation is given, three were definitely prostitutes. Three more were wives or daughters of artisans (one a master). Another, accompanied by her mother and grandmother, was a tripe-worker, one was a sick-nurse, one a pawnbroker. There were also five serving girls from the Salpetrière, a domestic servant, a laundrywoman, a beer-seller, and the wife of a billposter. The police records from other quarters and other years tell much the same story: few women, and almost always in the humblest occupations, their husbands usually in unskilled or semi-skilled trades.

But even these women were not free from constraints. Closer examination of

Table 6. *Family ties of women in wineshops, 1752 and 1788 (five quarters)*[a]

Nature of group	Number of women
Husband (legal or *de facto*)	22
Father	3
Brother	1
Son	1
Female family member(s) only	8
Total number with family member	35
Women alone	10
With unrelated man/men (and sometimes other women)	24
With unrelated woman/women	19
Relationships unknown	7
Total	95

[a] As for table 5.

the circumstances in which they appear in wineshops reveals that many went with another member of their family, usually male, and most often their husband. Almost without exception the wives of masters, *marchands* and indeed of artisans in general were with their husbands. It was also permissible in some cases to go with a female member of the family, most often mother or daughter, or with a number of other women. The five serving-girls from the Salpetrière, mentioned above, were together in a wineshop near the hospital when a *commissionnaire* accused one of them of being a prostitute. Three of the witnesses took their part, pointing out that they had been drinking quietly, 'saying nothing to anybody', a comment which reveals the behavioural constraints upon women if they did enter a wineshop, even in a group. If they behaved in any other way they were asking to be treated as prostitutes.[39]

There were two other sets of circumstances in which women could go to wineshops more freely and behave in a somewhat more outgoing fashion. One I have already looked at in chapter 1, a local dance, although even there they were usually accompanied by a male relative. Secondly, they could go to a wineshop where they were well known to both proprietor and customers, usually in the same house or very close by. In cases where the addresses are given it is striking how often women lived in the same street or the same house. Others were within a stone's throw of their place of work.

These are the main circumstances in which women did use wineshops. There is no trace of older women enjoying more freedom of movement than younger ones, or of a noticeable difference between the behaviour of married and unmarried women in this respect. As in other parts of France the wineshop was

[39] Y15350, 3 Aug.

Table 7. *Occupations of men in wineshops, 1752 and 1788 (five quarters)*[a]

Occupation	1752 No.	1752 %	1788 No.	1788 %	Total No.	Total %
Master artisans and *marchands*	74	21.1	25	10.1	99	16.5
Journeymen (*garçons/compagnons*) excluding those also soldiers	70	19.9	81	32.7	151	25.2
Artisans/shopkeepers of unspecified status	45	12.8	24	9.6	69	11.5
Soldiers (excluding those with other professions)	50		10		60	
Journeymen (*garçons/compagnons*) also soldiers	6	21.1	3	5.2	9	14.5
Artisans of unspecified status also soldiers	13		0		13	
Domestic servants also soldiers	1		0		1	
Unskilled workers also soldiers	4		0		4	
Domestic servants (excluding those also soldiers)	15	4.3	14	5.6	29	4.8
Unskilled workers (excluding soldiers)	16	4.6	32[b]	12.9	48[b]	8.0
Street-sellers	5		7		12	
Employés	2		5		7	
Misc. military (officers)	2		2		4	
Agents	0		3		3	
Clerks (*commis, clercs*)	0		2		2	
Chirurgiens	4		3		7	
Public letter-writers (*écrivains*)	1		2		3	
Workers in factories (*manufactures*)	8		1		9	
Innkeepers, lodging-house keepers	0		4		4	
Rural trades (*terrassiers, vignerons, marchands de bestiaux, jardiniers* other than masters)	4		12		16	
Bourgeois de Paris	9		2		11	
Avocats	1		2		3	
Manufacturers (*fabricants*)	1		2		3	
Cab-owners, coachmen, waggoners	3		4		7	
Huissiers	1		1		2	
Boatmen (*compagnons de rivière*)	2		0		2	
Musicians, acrobats	1		1		2	
Framework knitters	2		0		2	
Travelling merchants (*marchands forains*)	1		2		3	
Gardes	1		1		2	
Others: architect, 2 *receveurs*, building entrepreneur, *pensionnaire, boursier*, optician, *ancien marchand, commandant, facteur*, doorkeeper, bill-poster.	9		3		12	
Total	351		248		599	

[a] Halles, Grève, Faubourg St Antoine, Place Maubert, Luxembourg (1752), St Germain des Prés (1788).
[b] Includes one large group of twenty men. There are no other groups larger than seven.

male territory, and the female who ventured in risked her reputation unless she was well known and respected or unless she was clearly chaperoned. Even then the social range using wineshops was very restricted.

Turning to the male customers mentioned in our sample, a total of some six hundred, we find that the range of trades represented reads like a combined list of the trades corporations and the *Cris de Paris*. We usually know little about the wealth or standing of these men, but the few indications that are given do reveal a general pattern. The most numerous groups are *maîtres marchands*, journeymen (*garçons, compagnons*), artisans of unspecified status, and soldiers. Next come unskilled workers and domestic servants, followed by a whole range of other trades which are difficult to fit into such categories. This overall pattern more or less reflects the relative numerical importance of these groups in the city, if we go by the *cartes de sûreté* (identity cards) issued during the Revolution. Only in two cases do the figures change considerably between 1752 and 1788. The proportion of masters and *marchands* falls dramatically: they appear, as Berryer claimed, to have been deserting the wineshops. This is confirmed by T. Brennan's study, which shows that the number of masters and *marchands* going to wineshops was already declining in the first half of the eighteenth century.[40] The even greater fall in the number of soldiers, over-represented in 1752, probably results from their being moved increasingly into barracks and from the general tightening of discipline.

More prestigious social groups are very poorly represented in the sample. The liberal professions provide only three *avocats*, an optician, one architect, three public letter-writers (if this can be counted as a liberal profession), a couple of *receveurs à la Ville*, and a handful of *employés*. There are no *négociants* and only one building entrepreneur. The most prestigious corporate trades are also scarcely represented, there being only five merchants from the Six Corps. A rough upper limit to the use of wineshops can therefore be distinguished. Many master artisans did not hesitate to frequent them, but those occupations conferring higher prestige are absent.

Turning to the addresses of male customers and looking at their choice of wineshop, we find little variation from one quarter to another. In the Halles area and in the Faubourgs St Antoine and St Marcel about half of those whose addresses are given lived in the immediate vicinity, and nearly three-quarters lived within a few blocks. In the city centre, around the Place de Grève, almost half lived in the surrounding streets. The consistency of this pattern confirms the local importance of the wineshop, but also indicates that a significant portion of the drinking population did not always go to an establishment near their home. This was not merely a reflection of the ordinary mobility of eighteenth-century Parisians around their city, however, and nor is there a simple division between those who went locally and others who went further afield.

For if we look at how and why men used wineshops, and at who they went with, it is possible to pick out not two, but three main groups. There is, first of all, a *maître marchand* group whose behaviour fairly consistently conforms to a double pattern. When they appear in drinking establishments in their own

---

[40] Brennan, 'Cabarets', pp. 45–6.

quarter they are found with quite a variety of people: members of their own family; their journeymen or workers; and most commonly of all with neighbours in a wide range of occupations. Where masters and *marchands* appear in wineshops outside their own quarter, however, they are most often in the company of other masters of the same trade. Occasional meetings of the corporation or of a confraternity were followed by withdrawal to a nearby tavern.[41] Alternatively they went for business. Three master saddlers, for example, went off to the 'Croix Rouge' in the Faubourg St Germain to discuss the sale of a carriage. Business arrangements also account for the presence of most of those few individuals who belonged to more prestigious professions, such as a *receveur à la Ville*, an *employé* at the Hotel des Fermes, and two *bourgeois de Paris*.[42] For these sorts of people a visit to a wineshop outside their quarter was not normally just for pleasure, and they tended to be found with others of similar trade or status. It is thus possible to make a distinction between their use of local wineshops and their presence in more distant ones.

No such pattern is visible among the second main group, comprising most journeymen, most artisans of unspecified status, and most unskilled workers. They went to wineshops purely for pleasure, and their choice of drinking partners was much the same whether they went locally or further afield. They were often to be found with men of the same or of a related trade, particularly if they belonged to one with a strong corporate identity. Or else they drank with others from their *pays*, relatives, or with people described simply as 'friends', without further elaboration.

The sorts of behaviour that both this group and the *maître marchand* one indulged in were fairly consistent. They would laugh and joke over their drinks, gossip, and if the establishment offered suitable facilities they would play bowls. Games of chance were also popular, the stakes usually confined to a bottle of wine or a small sum of money: serious gambling was normally done not in wineshops but in billiard-rooms and *académies de jeu*. The time spent drinking varied considerably: if they were busy they would stop only briefly, but otherwise might stay for hours.

This behaviour contrasts somewhat with that of the third category, in which the most conspicuous groups are soldiers and domestic servants but also quite a number of journeymen and unskilled workers. They used wineshops exclusively for recreation, and were most often to be found drinking outside the neighbourhood in which they lived. Soldiers and male domestic servants tended to stick together, and because of their conditions of work were often very geographically mobile. Many journeymen and unskilled workers were also among the most mobile groups in the city, again largely because of their conditions of employ-

[41] Y15350, 31 July, 18 July, 25 June. Y15364, 17 Sept. 1741. These large groups are not included in table 7.
[42] Y15350, 7 Oct., wit. 2. Y14484, 2 Dec. Y15350, 1 Mar. Y14078, 1 Mar.

ment and because of their age. This mobility is reflected in their drinking habits. Always restless, they would go from one wineshop to another, although the amount of alcohol consumed was rarely great. A good example is that of Jean Menant, a journeyman joiner, who was working in his master's shop when another journeyman joiner, accompanied by a man who turned out to be a journeyman paver and a former soldier in the *gardes françaises*, arrived and suggested going for a drink. They accordingly retired to a wineshop in the rue St Sauveur, where they ordered four glasses of *eau-de-vie*, then moved on to another place a couple of streets away where they drank two bottles of wine. In a third establishment they consumed three more bottles before a quarrel ended their day's drinking.[43]

An even more impressive performance was achieved by a German journeyman tailor and an out-of-work domestic servant early in January 1752. Piecing together their stories, their movements can be traced from about eight o'clock in the evening when they met near the Louvre, one emerging from a wineshop called 'La Porte Dorée' just as the other was passing, until eight in the morning when the servant not surprisingly fell asleep in 'La Pantoufle' in the Cimetière St Jean. They had been first to a wineshop in the rue Croix des Petits Champs, then at various stages during the night had drunk in the shop of a *limonadier* next to the Halle, in another wineshop near the Barrière des Sergents at the far end of the Faubourg St Honoré, and 'in various other wineshops'.[44]

In both of these cases the drinkers knew each other vaguely, but many men were not too fussy about who they sat with. Soldiers in particular, when looking for a drinking partner, would accost any likely looking individual. A soldier in the *milice* (militia), in Paris working as a domestic servant but just then unemployed, collected two strangers whom he encountered on the Pont Neuf, inviting them to 'spend the day together and to go for a drink'. One was the son of a shoemaker, the other a soldier on his way home to Provence.[45] This is a form of sociability which A. Farge comments on in her study of food thieves in eighteenth-century Paris. Many of the accused spent hours walking around the city; many accomplices met by chance in wineshops and often did not know each others' names or even the exact place of their encounter. Over half of those in her sample lived in lodging-houses and many changed their address frequently.[46] Inside the wineshop such men were often joined by prostitutes, who knew the sort of groups they could approach and who frequented the main-street drinking establishments in the areas most often crossed by these itinerant pleasure-seekers.

The behaviour of these men was often aggressive and argumentative, especially as they got drunker. Their 'cabaret-crawls' sometimes take on the

---

[43] Y15350, 3 July. Brennan, 'Cabarets', pp. 210–15, observes how little people drank.
[44] Y15350, 6 Jan., 18 Jan., wit. 3.
[45] Y15350, 23 July.   [46] Farge, *Délinquance*, pp. 123–6, 172–87.

appearance of a test of stamina. Many groups ended up before the *commissaire* because of some bet or joke which led to a dispute, either within the group or with others in the wineshop or the street. Such fights differed from the equally frequent quarrels between neighbours by the degree of violence and by the very fact that those involved, more often than not, were strangers. This sort of behaviour is of course in line with the renowned violence of soldiers and domestic servants, but they were simply the most easily identifiable groups among those who roamed the city, perhaps not looking for trouble but at any rate not seeking to avoid it.

If we abandon socio-professional distinctions and look at wineshop users in relation to the local community, the divisions make more sense. At one extreme are people firmly established in their quarter, although not the most affluent or the most prestigious elements of society. Those well established in the neighbourhood are best represented by master artisans and shopkeepers, who had a permanent stake there. Because of their work and physical location on the street many of them were at the heart of the local community. But there were others, many journeymen, street-sellers, unskilled workers of all sorts, even some domestic servants, who were also firmly entrenched in the community and who may rarely have ventured into a wineshop elsewhere.

At the other extreme were the most mobile sections of the population, often with few local ties. They were predominantly single men, still in the irresponsible years of youth. From this group came many of those brought before the courts, for the men who were most mobile were also frequently out of work, often emboldened by alcohol, encouraged by bets and dares, and at the same time little constrained by the ties of neighbourhood or by the certainty of being recognized. The locals did not hesitate to arrest or accuse outsiders, and there was no one to speak for them when they came before the *commissaire*. The court records show many living in lodging-houses, most of them under twenty-five, highly mobile, and often in the least stable occupations.[47] This should not be taken to imply that the wandering clientele of the wineshops made up the 'criminal classes' of eighteenth-century Paris. It is simply that their conditions of work and way of life made them somewhat more likely to commit certain types of offences, and extremely likely to be arrested.

It must be added, of course, that an individual could well be established in his quarter, form part of the local community, and still move around the city with a variety of drinking partners. This is the picture we get of the young Ménétra, who wandered the city, very often in the company of other young men of his neighbourhood, going from wineshop to wineshop, fighting and playing pranks, on several occasions finding himself under arrest. There existed more than one code of behaviour to which one and the same person could conform to a greater or lesser degree, or at different times.

[47] Farge, *Délinquance*, p. 121. Petrovitch, in Abbiateci *et al.*, *Criminalité*, pp. 235–45.

Returning to my original question, it is clear that drinking establishments, while playing a very important part in the life of the local community, were not exclusively for the locals. There are indications that certain wineshops were used more by neighbours, others more by strangers. There were certainly places that were frequented by particular groups, like the 'Café Militaire' in the rue St Honoré where musketeers and *gendarmes* could be found; or 'Le Gros Raisin' and 'La Ville de Rome' where journeymen locksmiths went in large numbers. In 1778 Jewish cloth merchants congregated in the 'Caffé du prophète Elie' in the rue St André des Arts. There may also have been some sort of social hierarchy, as in Toulouse where one café served nobles and notables, a second catered for merchants, a third for *commis*, and yet a fourth for journeymen.[48] If such a hierarchy did exist in Paris it was not so clear-cut, but there were certainly specializations: business cafés; main-street ones that served all sorts of people; and local ones tucked away in side streets, just as there are today.

It is also clear that wineshops did not cater for all the locals. The more affluent and the more socially ambitious people, amongst them increasing numbers of master artisans and *marchands*, did not use wineshops at all. Nor did most women drink in public: the local community contained a number of subdivisions of which the male/female one was among the most prominent. However, for men who did form part of the community, wineshops reinforced the sense of belonging, and time spent there was largely enjoyed in the company of locals, talking of men's affairs, escaping for a while from the cares of family and workaday world.

V. GUINGUETTES

There remain the *guinguettes*, which, because of their geographic situation and their lower prices, served a different function from other drinking establishments. Situated outside the city's customs barriers, they combined the appeal of duty-free drinks with that of a country environment. They are poorly represented in the papers of the *commissaires*, but it is clear that in general terms their clientele was similar to that of ordinary wineshops. They were not frequented by 'respectable' people. Women went in much the same circumstances as to wineshops of any kind, usually with a male relative. At weekends, in fact, there was probably a higher proportion of women in the *guinguettes* than was normal in other wineshops, because that was one of the few occasions when many husbands and wives were able to spend time together.

It seems to have been very rare for women to go to the *guinguettes* other than in the company of a male relative. Fairly typical of the few who did was Anne Clément, seamstress of no fixed abode, who was arrested for stealing three silver

---

[48] B.N. Ms. fr. 6682, f. 194, 21 Mar. 1776. Y14391, 7 Aug. 1746. Y15099, 6 May. Y9535, Chambre de police, 26 Nov. 1778. N. Castan, *Criminels*, p. 265.

watches from a lodging-house near the Place de Grève. She had subsequently stayed with a sawyer and his wife in the Faubourg St Laurent, and it was with them and a soldier on leave in Paris that she went to a *guinguette* in La Nouvelle France. Before this she had lived in lodging-houses in different parts of the city, never more than a month or two in the one place. Prior to these moves she had lived with a porter from the central market in a lodging-house in the rue Mouffetard, and had often been to the southern *guinguettes* with him and with a female wool-spinner. At one stage the two women had hired a room with the intention of becoming prostitutes. Visits to the *guinguettes* fitted in well with Anne Clément's extreme mobility, and with her disregard for all the rules normally governing female behaviour.[49]

The men who went were mainly of the most mobile occupations: soldiers, quarry-workers, journeymen (who were often soldiers as well). They very often lived in lodging-houses. Most commonly they were accompanied by workmates, very occasionally by members of their family or by neighbours, sometimes by strangers whom they had met in a *garni*, in a wineshop, or in the street. The *guinguettes* held a strong attraction for such people, fitting in with their restlessness. A good example is that of an employee in the wash-house at Bicêtre who, drinking with a woman in the shop of a *limonadier* near St Germain l'Auxerrois, got into conversation with three journeymen bakers who were at the same table. He then went with them to a wineshop opposite, and after that to La Courtille, where after a number of drinks he fell asleep. He woke some time later to find his money and most of his clothes gone.[50] Another eloquent example of the use of *guinguettes* is furnished by the locksmiths' strike of 1746. The natural place for the journeymen to hold meetings was a *guingette*, partly because there were few places large enough to accommodate the numbers, but also because everyone knew the way and would be tempted to attend. The four meetings were held in four different places, partly because of a real concern for secrecy, also perhaps through love of mystery, but the arrangement certainly corresponded well with the footloose character of many of the journeymen. As it was, at each meeting they wandered in and out. 'Many had a drink or two and went off to other wineshops', said a witness.[51]

The available evidence therefore suggests that unlike ordinary wineshops the *guinguettes* (except perhaps at Carnival time) were favoured by those people who were least established in their neighbourhood. They certainly had no role to play in the development of a local sense of community.

[49] Y15099, 24 Jan., 19 Feb. [50] Y15099, 6 May.
[51] Y13751, 19 Sept. For a more detailed description of the way *guinguettes* were used see T. Brennan, 'Beyond the Barriers: Popular Culture and Parisian *Guinguettes*', *Eighteenth-Century Studies*, 18 (1984–5), 153–69.

VI. *LA PROMENADE* (GOING FOR A STROLL)

La promenade was an integral part of Parisian life in the eighteenth century, just as it is today. It was sufficiently firmly established as an institution for a correspondent of the *commissaire* Ninnin to write that he had not called in, 'for fear of not catching you, it being the hour of *la promenade*'. Hardy noted in his journal in February 1788, hardly a time of year when one would expect outside recreations to be popular, that the Carnival figures called *chienlits* had appeared all along the rue St Honoré, interrupting 'la promenade et les plaisirs' (entertainments).[52] But *la promenade* was also popular amongst working people and is frequently mentioned in the papers of the *commissaires*. It was the universal leisure occupation.

As was the case with work or with certain other forms of recreation, *la promenade* could help to make people more a part of the local community but could also, in different circumstances, help them to move outside it. At one end of the scale were those least integrated into the community, who tended to wander far afield, often combining their promenade with a visit to the *guinguettes*, usually in small groups and normally with workmates. Thus we find three journeymen shoemakers living in the rue Pavée who, after spending the day in the country near Les Porcherons and La Nouvelle France, returned along the rue Montorgueil and dropped into a wineshop for supper.[53]

At the other end of the social range, the rich tended to take the air in private gardens. The wealthiest people had their own town houses, but others shared gardens; like the widow of a *contrôleur des messageries* (administrator in the postal service) living in the rue St Martin who used the one behind her house. Still others profited from an open area owned by an acquaintance. The wife and daughter of a *négociant* made a complaint against the principal tenant of their house, who had locked the gate leading into the garden next door 'to force them to go via the street in order to enjoy the promenade which Monsieur Baudin allows them in his garden'. Private gardens like this were most often enjoyed by women of quality, but men would use them too. An engineer ('ingénieur machiniste privilégié') and a *bourgeois de Paris*, both living near the Sorbonne, spent a pleasant afternoon strolling around the Gobelins and in the garden belonging to de Jullienne, the director.[54]

Those without access to a private garden could go to the Tuileries, the Luxembourg, the Palais Royal, or to other semi-private gardens away from the crowded streets. In the early 1780s the Tuileries, and especially the Champs Elysées, delighted Mercier with their beauty, but even more because of the rows of well-dressed, pretty young women who could be seen there. This applied only to working days, however, for on Sundays and holidays 'people of good taste do

---

[52] Y15114B. B.N. Ms. fr. 6686, f. 364, 3 Feb. 1788.   [53] Y15350, 24 July.
[54] Y14436, 21 July. Y12596, 8 June.

not go out ... they flee the promenades and the theatre, abandoning them to the people'.[55]

In between the most mobile elements of the population and the more refined clients of private and semi-private gardens were the ordinary, settled people whom we have seen to be at the centre of the local community, and whom we find taking their *promenade* in the streets with family, neighbours, and friends. A *gagne denier* and his wife, for example, having had dinner in their room in the rue St Germain l'Auxerrois, took their dog out for a walk along the Quai de l'Ecole. A master tailor went for a stroll in the company of his sister and brother-in-law, living a few blocks away from him across the Pont Notre-Dame.[56] In these examples *la promenade* was both a family and a neighbourhood activity, for it took place in the vicinity of people's homes and involved contact with the locals.

By the second half of the eighteenth century, however, the pattern of *promenades* was changing. The gradual disappearance of open spaces in the central quarters made the wide, tree-lined boulevards increasingly attractive, and the amusements, cafés, and street-theatre which sprang up there drew further crowds.[57] Equally important was the change in aesthetic values: the taste was for open spaces rather than enclosed ones, for idealized 'natural' landscapes rather than urban décors. 'One can admire the elegant proportions and the design of the Tuileries', wroter Mercier,

> but people of all ages and of every estate gather in the Champs Elysées: the rural setting, the houses with their terraces, the cafés, a wider and less symmetrical space, everything invites one to go there.[58]

The increasing popularity of the boulevards did little to reinforce the local community. Even for the areas nearby they were not a centre of community life, if the Grange Batelière Section is representative, for few people actually lived on the boulevards and they were not primary axes of communication: these ran towards the city centre.[59] In so far as the boulevards drew people who might otherwise have spent their leisure hours in the neighbourhood where they lived, they were of course destructive of community life.

La promenade, like other activities, could take place within a local context and thus reinforce the sense of community; but it could also take people away, potentially weakening their ties with neighbours. Increasingly, however, as shown by the growing popularity of the boulevards, there was a tendency to separate outdoor leisure, particularly organized leisure, from the working and

[55] Mercier, *Tableau*, vol. 1, pp. 165–7; vol. 4, p. 162.
[56] Y15350, 23 May. Y15117, 1 May 1788.
[57] Mercier, *Tableau*, vol. 3, pp. 41–2. M. Fouquier, *Paris au XVIIIe siècle*, 2 vols. (Paris, 1912), vol. 1, pp. 1–8.
[58] *Apollo*, vol. 101, no. 158 (Apr. 1975), 'Musée Carnavalet, Paris of the Ancien Régime'. M. Ozouf, 'Le Cortège et la ville: les itinéraires parisiens des cortèges révolutionnaires', *Annales: E.S.C.*, 26 (1971), 889–916. Mercier, *Tableau*, vol. 1, p. 161.
[59] A. Goeury, 'La Section Grange-Batelière', p. 97.

living environment. This is clearest in the two forms of recreation we will consider next: games and sports, and public celebrations.

VII. GAMES AND SPORTS

Compared with London, Paris in the eighteenth century was very poor in games and sports. A description of London in 1720 stated that 'the more common sort divert themselves at Foot ball, Wrestling, Cudgels, Nine-pins, Shovel-board, Cricket, Stow-ball, Ringing of Bells, Quoits, pitching the Bar, Bull and Bear baiting, throwing at Cocks, and lying at Alehouses'.[60] Some of these recreations, like cricket or football, required a degree of organization and were likely to flourish where there was a strong sense of community, particularly among young men. A sport like bull-running, which used the common space of the street or market-place, was dependent on the co-operation and tolerance of the locals.

In Paris, however, there is no mention of team games like football and cricket. Dog fighting apparently existed, turning up for example in a court conviction of 1757 which imposed a fine on a number of carters at the central market. During Easter, according to an English visitor to Paris in 1784, the police tolerated bear-pits where dogs, bulls, bears, lions, tigers, and other animals were set against each other, apparently a very popular entertainment. Expilly mentions similar displays held near the *barrière* on the road to Sèvres.[61] In 1781 a first series of bull-runs and fights was held near Belleville, despite the opposition of Amelot, Minister for the King's Household, who expressed his reservations in a letter to Lenoir:

Apart from the fact that it is a new spectacle, and that they are already too numerous, it seems to me disadvantageous to authorize something which is not among our customs and whose effect would be to accustom the people to the sight of blood.[62]

Bull-fighting was un-French therefore, and certainly unheard of in Paris. It nevertheless did catch on, it seems, and despite being suppressed by both Ancien Régime and revolutionary authorities did not finally disappear until about 1833.[63] Like animal fights, however, it was hardly a community sport, for it was organized by entrepreneurs: a 'spectacle', as Amelot put it. Staged for the people, it was not something they did or participated in actively.

People did, however, play bowls and skittles, the equipment frequently being

---

60 J. Stow, *A Survey of the Cities of London and Westminster* (London, 1720), vol. 1, p. 257, quoted in R. W. Malcolmson, *Popular Recreations in English Society, 1700–1850* (Cambridge, C.U.P., 1973), p. 34.
61 Sentence de police, 25 Jan. 1757, in Peuchet, *Collection*, vol. 6, p. 259. John Andrews, cited in G. Bertin, 'Les Combats de taureaux à Paris (1781–1833)', *Revue de la Révolution*, 9 (1887), 160–8 (p. 163). Expilly, *Dictionnaire*, vol. 5, p. 403.
62 A.N. O¹ 491, f. 218, quoted in 'Les Courses de taureaux en France sous l'ancien régime', *Archives historiques, artistiques, et littéraires*, 1 (1889–90), 29–30.
63 Bertin, 'Combats', pp. 163–4.

provided by a *marchand de vin*. I have already mentioned the group of domestic servants who played at skittles in the Vieux Marché d'Aguesseau, watched by a number of the neighbours. Such games were so popular that in the first half of the century alone a police ordinance forbidding them to be played in the street was renewed at least thirteen times.[64]

Also enormously popular were board games like dominoes, chess, and draughts, most often played in wineshops. More widespread still were card games, played by an enormous variety of people whenever and wherever they got together. We find a mistress dyer and her son playing in her workshop in the rue des Arcis; journeymen tailors playing in their room in a lodging-house; a soldier and a *gagne denier* on the Pont Royal; domestic servants in the porter's lodge at the Cordeliers convent.[65] It was a favourite evening occupation for groups of neighbours. Playing cards was a recreation common to all social groups and to both sexes, but like all indoor games tended to reinforce existing ties rather than to create new ones. When played in the street or the local wineshop these games were of real importance in the local community.

This was not the case, however, for billiard-rooms (*billards*) and gambling halls (*académies de jeu*), names normally used interchangeably to describe the establishments run by *maîtres paumiers*. According to Lenoir, there were during his time as *lieutenant général* and that of his predecessor de Sartine only six authorized *académies*, although many more probably remained unknown to or ignored by the police. The evidence of complaints and enquiries suggests that they were not respectable places. A *marchande lingère*, making a complaint against one of her tenants, gave an identikit portrait of the disreputable merchant who went off for two or three days at a time, frequenting billiard-rooms and wineshops. The same stereotype crops up in *enquêtes en séparation* brought against merchants.[66]

It is possible to gain a better idea of the clientele of billiard-rooms from police inspections. In one establishment in the rue St Germain l'Auxerrois the *inspecteur* arrested fifteen unemployed *garçons perruquiers*, all between eighteen and twenty-nine. In January 1774 in a billiard-room in the rue Comtesse d'Artois he picked up a domestic servant living in the rue Montmorency, a lapidary jeweller living on the Montagne Ste Geneviève, an Auvergnat tinker from the Faubourg St Antoine, and an out-of-work 'garçon d'office'. Only the Auvergnat was over thirty.[67] This sample is typical: exclusively male, generally mobile and unattached, often unemployed. Of course it was largely for these

---

[64] Y15350, 21 July. Ordonnances de police, 3 Sept. 1754, 8 Nov. 1771, in Peuchet, vol. 6, p. 192, and vol. 8, p. 420.

[65] Y15117, 6 June 1790. Y15099, 19 Feb., wit. 5. Y15350, 26 June, wit. 1, and 'procès-verbaux cartes à jouer', 13 Dec.

[66] Chardin, *La Partie de billard* (*c.* 1725), Musée Carnavalet, reproduced in *Apollo*, vol. 101, no. 158 (Apr. 1975), p. 311. Y15350, 16 Jan. Y14078, 28 June.

[67] Y11585A, 30 Jan. 1768. Y12469, 8 Jan. 1774.

reasons that they were arrested, but they were obviously among the regular clientele of the gaming houses and billiard-rooms, for several of those we have mentioned had been caught before for the same 'offence'.

Gambling-hall frequenters mentioned in other documents are usually similar. A writing-master from Alsace, living in a hotel in the rue Notre Dame des Victoires and arrested for trying to sell a stolen watch, explained that he spent a couple of hours every day in a *billard* in the Palais Royal and that he also went to other gaming houses. A journeyman tailor and soldier, suspected of theft and asked for an account of his activities, had on the day concerned been to two *académies* along the quais.[68] These establishments were primarily frequented by young men of varying social origins but often with few ties within the city. There may have been other, more respectable clients, but it is noteworthy that most of the gambling places mentioned in the documents were on the main north–south or east–west axes of Paris. Two were on the Quai de la Ferraille where these axes crossed, and another well-known one was on the Place de Grève itself. They were not neighbourhood institutions.

Unlike London, eighteenth-century Paris had relatively few sports or games to bring the locals in any one areas together, with bowls, skittles and the like being virtually the only collective outdoor sports. It appears to be an inherited characteristic of Parisian sociability that organized sport did not flourish. Only indoor games were really widespread, the ones provided in wineshops for the men and those enjoyed at home by women playing a significant role in the local community.

VIII. PUBLIC CELEBRATIONS

It is perhaps in the area of public celebrations, such as feasts and fairs, processions, carnivals, the rites of May Day and of the St Jean (midsummer), that one would expect to find the best evidence of community life. The role of such festivities in social organization has been greatly emphasized, and the concept of the local community is a key one in the work of Y-M Bercé, M. Vovelle, and E. Le Roy Ladurie. Little of this concerns Paris, however, and, whereas the nineteenth-century folklorist Van Gennep recorded popular customs in many other parts of France, he found that by his day Paris had virtually none of its own. There is certainly no trace of youth abbeys, either in different quarters or in different social or occupational groups, even the Roi de la Basoche having disappeared by the second half of the eighteenth century.[69] But there did remain religious feast-days and fairs, Carnival did not die until the twentieth century, and there were still what Vovelle calls 'fêtes occasionnelles':

---

[68] Y14484, 27 Dec. Y15099, 24 Jan.
[69] A. Van Gennep, *Manuel du folklore français contemporain*, 4 vols. (Paris, A. Picard, 1937–58). Mercier, *Tableau*, vol. 3, p. 10.

civil processions, *entrées*, spontaneous popular celebrations.[70] To what extent can we see traces of neighbourhood participation in these?

I have already suggested that religious festivals, while involving some local participation, were on the whole organized from above, additional popular celebrations being actively discouraged by the authorities. People observed feast-days primarily in small groups, at home or in wineshops, or else had corporate banquets. Festive life in the capital, as in urban Provence, centred on ordinary recreational institutions and habits: family, *société*, trade group, and wineshop. People did much the same things on feast-days as on Sundays. On Mardi Gras 1788, for example, a domestic servant and his wife went for a *promenade*, then had supper at the Barrière Blanche together with one of her friends and an out-of-work servant of his acquaintance. Mercier has a chapter on 'Sundays and feast-days' in which he describes the different recreational activities without distinguishing between Sundays and special holy days. Of course some people ignored such days altogether, as numerous police ordinances demonstrate, something that was not possible in a less secular or less crowded environment.[71]

A few very special days were distinguished by particular public festivities. The midsummer feast of St Jean, 23 June, was for most of the century marked by fireworks and a bonfire in the Place de Grève, although this was no longer held by the time Mercier was writing in the early 1780s.[72] The major popular festival was of course Carnival, a vernal explosion of joy which broke down inhibitions and took people onto the streets in costumes and masks. The Faubourg St Antoine and La Courtille were centres of popular rejoicing, but there were numerous local celebrations too. In 1840 the *Gazette des Tribunaux* assured its readers that

good Parisians of mature years can still remember the dances in the public square around the straw man dressed in a harlequin suit, who represented Mardi Gras; in several crossroads, notably at those in the rue du Bouloy and the rue Croix des Petits Champs, it was customary to burn straw men dressed up in this way.[73]

A local as well as trade celebration in the city centre was the election of a queen of the laundry-boats and of a water-carrier as king, followed – at least in the nineteenth century – by a procession through the streets of the quarter and in the evening by a dance. There may have been something similar in the markets, for these were the areas – the Halle, the Temple, Saint Germain, and the Latin quarter – in which the Carnival floats and the processions of the late nineteenth

---

[70] Faure, *Paris Carême-prenant*. Vovelle, *Métamorphoses*, pp. 72–7.
[71] Vovelle, *Métamorphoses*, pp. 86–7. Y13816, 6 Mar. Mercier, *Tableau*, vol. 4, p. 159.
[72] Ordonnance de police de la Ville de Paris, 20 June 1769 in Peuchet, vol. 8, p. 214. Restif, *Nuits*, 72e nuit. Mercier, *Tableau*, vol. 3, p. 65.
[73] 23 July 1840, quoted in Faure, p. 106. Nemeitz, *Séjour de Paris* (Leiden, 1727), quoted in Faure, pp. 61–2.

century originated. Yet another procession, first recorded in 1739, also accompanied a corporate festival which coincided with Carnival: that of the butchers and of the *boeuf gras*. Like the celebrations on the laundry-boats, it was no doubt as much a local festival as a corporate one, given the concentration of butchers around the Grande Boucherie at the end of the rue St Denis.[74]

But Carnival was changing. The police did their best to suppress or harness its most tumultuous activities. In 1768 de Sartine gave orders to prevent 'the liberties taken by the people and even by young men of good family during the Carnival period'. In 1790 the Commune banned masks and dances in order 'to restrain popular licentiousness and prevent passers-by from being insulted'. Both Mercier and Hardy claim that the police paid for the costumed and masked figures popularly referred to as *chienlits*, in order to keep the people happy.[75] A deeper and more ominous change, as far as the popular festival was concerned, was the increasingly private nature of the celebrations. There were still public dances in the squares, but the more affluent inhabitants held masked balls of their own. 'Dances are infinitely multiplied', wrote Hardy in 1786, 'and go by a variety of names like the *Procureurs'* Ball to the extent that some affluent bourgeois have even established their own subscriptions'. In this as in other recreations the elites withdrew from the over-public arena of the street: 'The rabble laugh in the crossroads and people of taste on the velvet-covered benches of the concert-hall and theatre.'[76] This trend was to continue into the nineteenth century, when even those who would in the eighteenth century have danced in the street got together to hire a private room. In the rue de Ménilmontant in 1834 some sixty inhabitants of the quarter, mostly small shopowners and their families, booked a large room above a shop for their Carnival festivities.[77] It was still a local celebration, joined by people who remained at the heart of the local community, but it was no longer a public one.

Parallel with this development was another, already mentioned briefly in connection with religious processions. This was the separation between participants and spectators, between the official celebration and the unofficial spontaneous one which was frowned on by the authorities. It is visible in Carnival and in the many civic processions which took place annually. It is even more marked in the special celebrations held to mark particular events: the illuminations which followed French victories in the Seven Years' War; the big army display when Boulainvilliers was installed as *prévôt de Paris* in 1776. The investiture of the Duc de Brissac as governor of Paris was marked by a procession, ending in the Place de Grève where he threw money to the crowd. Later the same day free wine was distributed in the Place de Grève. Royal births and marriages were

---

[74] Faure, pp. 128, 136–8.
[75] Y13728, 3 Feb. 1768. Faure, p. 93. Mercier, *Tableau*, vol. 4, p. 165. B.N. Ms. fr. 6686, ff. 364–5, 3–5 Feb. 1788.
[76] B.N. Ms. fr. 6685, f. 301, 28 Feb. 1786. Mercier, *Tableau*, vol. 5, p. 243.
[77] Faure, pp. 14–15.

marked by compulsory illuminations and often fireworks. Most spectacular of all were the public rejoicings at the marriage of the Dauphin to Marie Antoinette in 1770. A public holiday was proclaimed, a fair opened on the northern boulevards, and there was a huge fireworks display in the Place Louis XV, although it ended in disaster.[78]

These celebrations were above all spectacles. They were carefully co-ordinated by the authorities: even the illuminations of the houses were enforced by the *commissaires*.[79] When Louis XV came to Ste Geneviève in September 1764, Hardy recorded that all the workers had been ordered to wear their best clothes: breeches and white stockings, and a white cap with a cockade. In return they were given a new apron, a day's pay and unlimited wine. Nothing was left to the public to organize, unlike, in another time and place, the celebrations for the coronation of Elizabeth II, when local committees in London's East End participated in the preparations.[80] The authorities of eighteenth-century Paris had taken over many of the traditions of popular celebration: the lighting of candles, with its religious associations; the use of fireworks, the *boîtes* and *fusées* that people let off in the streets now banned and replaced by displays before an audience. There was no community participation, only a spectator role. Occa-sionally there were supplementary popular festivities: the rue de la Ferronnerie was a gathering place, there were celebrations in the central market after the birth of the Dauphin in 1782, and in the Halle au Blé in 1783 to celebrate the treaty of Versailles. Of course the Halle was known for its all-night dances and its cafés, which attracted people from all over the city, so it is not surprising to find festivities there.[81]

Even where people were no more than spectators, it is true that neighbour-hood interdependence and cohesion could be reinforced. Processions brought people into the street and to their windows, uniting them on the corners and along the main thoroughfares. The processions of the Ancien Régime, both civic and religious, penetrated the heart of the city, and even if they betrayed a preference for the wider, less encumbered streets they nevertheless entered the

---

[78] YII243B, Berryer to Thierry, 24 July 1756 and [June] 1757. B.N. Ms. fr. 6680, f. 101, 22 July 1766. Hardy, *Mes Loisirs*, pp. 309–10, 30 Dec. 1771. B.N. Ms. fr. 6682, f. 122, 30 Sept. 1775, entry of Comtesse d'Artois, and f. 43, 7 Mar. 1775, entry of Comte d'Artois. YII243B, Berryer to Thierry, 10 Oct. 1757, same to same, 20 Oct. 1757. YI5114A, de Sartine to Trudon, 11 May 1771. YI3728, de Sartine to Monnot, 23 Nov. 1773. B.N. Ms. fr. 6682, ff. 109–10, 24–25 Aug. 1775. Hardy, *Mes Loisirs*, pp. 196–201: 16, 19, 30 May 1770. Ordonnance de police, 5 May 1770, in Peuchet, vol. 8, p. 290.

[79] YII265bisB, Albert to Thierry, 27 June 1775. YI5114A, de Sartine to Trudon, 11 May 1771. B.N. Ms. fr. 6682, f. 110 25 Aug. 1775. Ordonnance de police, 5 May 1770, in Peuchet, vol. 8, p. 290.

[80] B.N. Ms. fr. 6680, f. 51, 6 Sept. 1764. Young and Willmott, *Family and Kinship*, p. 109.

[81] Ordonnance de police, 27 May 1757, in Peuchet, vol. 6, p. 275. Boudon *et al.*, *Système*, vol. 1, pp. 328, 350. L. Debucourt, 'Popular Revels around the Halles at the Birth of the Dauphin, 21 January 1782' (1782), Musée Carnavalet, reproduced in *Apollo*, vol. 101, no. 158 (Apr. 1975). B.H.V.P. MS 678, ff. 92, 94, 101.

environment of people's daily lives. This was to come to an end with the Revolution, whose great parades and ceremonies took place on the fringes of the city in the open space of the boulevards, the Place de la Bastille, the Place de la Révolution, and the Champ de Mars.[82]

Despite the efforts of the police, however, spontaneous popular celebrations did erupt from time to time. On 3 February 1775, when some of the magistrates who had returned from exile assembled in the Hôtel Dieu, the people celebrated on the Parvis Notre Dame by letting off crackers and playing musicial instruments.[83] In late August 1788, after the dismissal of Brienne and the appointment of Necker, similar celebrations occurred in the Place Dauphine. The *garde* had tactfully withdrawn, allowing fireworks and the burning in effigy of Brienne. On the following two nights, however, the soldiers moved in and a number of people were killed and injured. Two weeks later when Lamoignon resigned, fireworks were again let off and all the houses in the Place Dauphine were lit up. On Tuesday 16 September the crowd on the Pont Neuf forced passers-by to salute the statue of Henri IV and to shout 'Vive Henri IV, au Diable Lamoignon' (long live Henri IV, to the devil with Lamoignon). Effigies of Lamoignon were paraded round the streets and one was burned in the Place de Grève. Guard posts were sacked in retaliation for repression by the soldiers, and the town houses of Lamoignon and of Dubois, commander of the *guet*, were attacked.[84]

These spontaneous popular celebrations demonstrate yet again the proximity of *fête* and revolt. At first sight the neighbourhood was not important. Things happened mostly in the central area and on the major crossroads of Paris. Yet the locals in these parts of the city were inevitably involved. Hardy wrote of the actions of 'the young men (*la jeunesse*) of the Place Dauphine and of the Palais quarter'. Among those arrested and wounded in 1788 were a number of locals: some claimed to have been seized or attacked by the *garde* while at their doors, while others said they had heard the fireworks and the shouting of the crowd and had gone out to see what was happening.[85] For these individuals the festivities were a local event, and like everyone else they went to their windows and doors, many joining the crowd. It is not surprising that the *garde* was unable to distinguish participants from spectators. Most of those arrested were able to say that they were just watching, or at most accompanying the people carrying the torches and mannequins. For in the older style of *fête*, held in the streets of the city, all were participating. The individuals who fed the bonfires had nothing to distinguish them from the crowd who watched, and the authorities were just as concerned about both.

In other ways, however, these were unlike older community celebrations. In

[82] Ozouf, 'Le Cortège'.   [83] B.N. Ms. fr. 6682, f. 27, 3 Feb. 1775.
[84] B.N. Ms. fr. 6687, ff. 58–63, 26–9 Aug. 1788, ff. 66–105, Sept.–Oct. 1788.
[85] B.N. J. de F. 1103, ff. 83, 86, 114, 116.

the 1788 events, which are well documented, women are virtually absent both from accounts of the festivities and from the lists of arrested and wounded. Nor was there a great social range: no sons of notables or large merchants, not even any students or clerks. According to G. Rudé, nearly half of the fifty or so arrested or wounded whose occupations are recorded were journeymen, apprentices, or other wage-earners; ten were master artisans; and sixteen were small shop-keepers.[86] Nor were they all locals: although most came from the principal areas of disturbance, those living even within several blocks of their place of arrest or injury account for only about a third of the total. The others came from all over the city: from the rue Mouffetard, from the Faubourg St Jacques, one from Vaugi-rard. A number lived in lodging-houses, and the vast majority were in their twen-ties. Those who rioted and celebrated on this occasion therefore, while drawn partly from the local community, came largely from the ranks of the turbulent youth of the city who were such an important element in the clientele of the wineshops and of the *guinguettes*. It is they who seem to have taken the lead in lighting bonfires, exploding fireworks, and in the processions.

The popular celebrations of 1788 prefigure changes in the local community in two ways. Firstly, the places in which people chose to gather were in the city centre, not in places of neighbourhood sociability, and as a result the festivities were not really neighbourhood ones but involved people from all over the city, especially young men. Secondly, the participants were relatively homogeneous in social terms. The elites and even the better-established tradesmen and mer-chants were totally absent. 'Prudent people', wrote Hardy on 27 August, even before the violence broke out, 'took care to keep their distance from these scenes, which were as tumultuous as they were out of place.' This was despite the fact that he wholeheartedly shared the feelings of the crowd towards Brienne and Lamoignon. In exactly the same way, he condemned the *chienlits* of Carnival, 'these celebrations which have no appeal for reasonable people'. Such celebra-tions, like other forms of community behaviour, increasingly became the domain of the humbler social groups, and as 'reasonable people' abandoned and came to condemn them the authorities were able and encouraged to suppress such 'disorders'.[87] What really sounded the death-knell of the popular festival was not the railing of the post-tridentine clergy, but its rejection by people like Hardy.

IX. CONCLUSION

Having briefly examined the main forms of recreation in eighteenth-century Paris, it is possible to draw some conclusions about their role in the formation and maintenance of the local community. Some, like wineshops, private dinners,

---

[86] Rudé, *Crowd*, pp. 32–3.
[87] B.N. Ms. fr. 6687, f. 60, 27 Aug. 1788; Ms. fr. 6686, f. 364, 3 Feb. 1788. Darnton describes the same phenomenon in eighteenth-century Montpellier: *Great Cat Massacre*, p. 133.

or card and game evenings, clearly played a vital part in bringing neighbours together and in creating additional ties between them. These activities were not purely neighbourhood ones, however, and nor were all of them open to the whole community. Wineshops were primarily a male domain, whereas the more domestic card evenings belonged first and foremost to women. There was a further selection, within the neighbourhood, along the lines of family, *pays*, occupation, and of course friendship. The local community was not without its internal divisions and lines of solidarity.

As I emphasized in looking at the family and at work, however, it is vital to consider not just those activities which potentially made people part of the community, but equally the ones that potentially put them outside it. Free-masonry and other societies were socially restricted, creating or reinforcing city-wide contacts which could develop at the expense of local ones. In certain social groups recreations centred on the family and shut out the neighbourhood with its collective activities and values. Like family or work ties, leisure sociability could serve to make people part of the local community, but in other cases could distance them from the neighbourhood, physically and socially.

Furthermore a certain evolution is visible. Occasions when all or most of the community were found together were rare and becoming increasingly so. There were still balls and dances which might bring everyone into the street and help to create an 'urban village' identity, and there were outbursts of spontaneous rejoicing and anger which starkly illuminate the contours of local solidarity. But there was a tendency for organized celebrations to become more private. There was no one to co-ordinate local festivals: the Roi de la Basoche and his peers were dead, the succession vacant. This did not automatically lead to the demise of the local community – the death of the king did not occasion the dis-appearance of his kingdom – but it did help to bring about profound trans-formations.

The aim in this chapter, however, as in the preceding three, is to go beyond an assessment of the role of particular institutions, relationships, and forms of sociability in the development and maintenance of the local community. The study of these relationships sheds further light on the social limits of the community, on who belonged and in what circumstances. The overall impression is one of fluidity and flexibility, yet with certain clear tendencies. Through family, work, parish and recreation alike, the urban and national elites were quite clearly outside the neighbourhood, often physically removed from it, their lives dominated by a multitude of city-wide and nation-wide contacts. I have devoted little space to these people, who have been extensively studied in the past. More central to the study of the Parisian local community are those who belonged to the humbler societies and lodges and those who were withdrawing from the wineshops and the recreations of the streets. They were the same sorts of people who provided the administrators of the parish confraternities and sometimes of the churches. We can recognize them from chapter 2 as those for whom the model of *qualité* held considerable appeal, and whose means, work, education or contacts allowed them a degree of social ambition. The analysis of family relationships and work ties enables us to define them occupationally: they were drawn largely from the ranks of the wealthier masters and merchants, especially those whose work gave them city-wide contacts, and from among the minor office-holders and growing bureaucracy of the capital. Still tied to the neighbourhood by residence in houses shared by people in a range of trades, as well as by certain aspects of their work, they were nevertheless able to escape it to some extent through their wider ties. Remaining vulnerable to local gossip and sanctions, they at the same time belonged to one or more non-geographic communities which provided a partial escape-route and a different set of values: more genteel, more domestic, often more concerned with individual advancement.

But we can also distinguish those at the heart of the local community: many shopkeepers and artisans, whether masters, journeymen, or of unspecified status; stall-keepers and street-sellers of many sorts; some unskilled workers and domestic servants. In particular, working women of all sorts were at the very centre of the local community, thanks to the type of work they did, to the division between male and female sociability, to their inferior social and economic position. All of these people found a place in the neighbourhood through their daily contacts, based perhaps on commerce, on similar work, on blood or marriage ties, on their frequenting the same shops or *cabaret*, on *pays*, on shared childhood experiences within the quarter or elsewhere, or simply on living in the same house; and more often than not on a combination of these.

But there was also a fourth group whose importance emerges strongly from the study of work ties and of leisure activity. Largely masculine, it included most of those whose work required a high degree of mobility. There were journeymen in search of work experience or of a good workshop, or who as the least skilled were the first to be laid off when the employer's work dropped off. There were also a large number of domestic servants and unskilled workers who were similarly obliged to keep on moving in search of work, and who might also be new arrivals from the provinces: into this category come most of the women whose mobility made it difficult for them to become part of the local community. The city's lodging-houses were home to many of them, both men and women. Lacking the mutual solidarity born of belonging, they furnished a sizeable contingent of the unfortunates who appeared before the courts, notably for theft. But equally in this fourth group were young men who, whatever their occupation, status, and origins, were conforming to a widely accepted model of unmarried male behaviour. They could be soldiers, unskilled workers, provincial artisans, sons of Paris masters, but they had in common both youth and an errant life-style which frequently took them outside the local community. They nevertheless shared its values and many would later adopt a more settled, community way of life. For others, condemned by their means of subsistence to stay on the move, rootlessness was a permanent state.

The physiognomy of eighteenth-century Parisian society, looked at through patterns of sociability and solidarity, is in some ways very different from the outline of graphs depicting fortune levels and economic possibilities, or from that perceptible through the spectacles of nineteenth-century social assumptions.

It was, however, a changing physiognomy. I have emphasized the spread of new values and of new forms of sociability, changes in the trades corporations, the growth of bureaucracy. There was in the family and leisure relationships, and to some extent in the work ties of Parisians, the same general movement towards social segregation that is observable in the physical structure of the city, with the formation of wealthy *faubourgs* to the west; the same movement as in eighteenth-century Languedoc where the growing middle classes sought to distance themselves from the rabble.[88] All of this had formidable consequences for the local community and for social organization, which we must now look at in more detail.

[88] N. Castan, *Criminels*, pp. 130–1.

6

The evolution of the local community

I have so far treated the local community as if it were largely static, and this is indeed the impression one gets from the documents. There is little perceptible change in the forms of neighbourhood sociability in the second half of the eighteenth century, or indeed into the nineteenth century. The papers of the *commissaires* reflect a society which unlike our own was more conscious of its stability than of its transformation. Yet evolution there was. I have already mentioned a number of developments during the period, some of which profoundly affected the local community. This chapter attempts to put such changes into a long-term perspective and to see how the local community was evolving.

The varying approaches to the history of local communities all depict their demise under the wheels of advancing modernity, although they differ on the time-scale involved and in their evaluation of the causes. One approach attributes the death of the community primarily to urbanization, and particularly to industrial urban growth, portrayed as a process which corroded social bonds just as the polluted air eroded the fabric of the city and the health of its inhabitants. Traditional values, the family, the community, all fell victim to its inexorable progress.[1] This view found widespread acceptance among eighteenth-century philosophers and physicians, who saw the city as an un-natural and pathological environment, a view shared by many nineteenth- and twentieth-century writers and social commentators. But it is now clear that such a picture is quite inaccurate, and that in many cases established values, family relationships, and even old-style community ties survived and were strengthened in the new environment. Greater mobility may have weakened the rural community from which people came, but it often forced them to rely on their neighbours in the new urban world they moved into.[2]

Nevertheless, urbanization is still perceived by some to be a central factor in the destruction of the local community. P. Ariès, in a rather pessimistic article, traces the disappearance of traditional forms of social intercourse to the arrival in

---

[1] On this view, see Stone, *Family*, pp. 658–60. M. Anderson, *Family Structure in Nineteenth-Century Lancashire* (Cambridge, C.U.P., 1971), introduction.

[2] Roche, *Peuple*, pp. 49–51. L. Chevalier, *Classes laborieuses et classes dangereuses à Paris pendant la première moitié du dix-neuvième siècle* (Paris, Plon, 1958). Wrigley, 'Reflections', p. 81. Stone, *Family*, p. 146.

the eighteenth century of a transient population and to the nineteenth- and twentieth-century expansion of the state into every area of life. This cut down the opportunities for individual initiative. The further expansion of the city, in separating work and home, left no space for social life outside the family.[3]

Elsewhere the *Gemeinschaft/Gesellschaft* model remains persuasive, stimulated by structuralist anthropology and its binary models. It portrays a general change from small, intimate, immobile social units to a large, impersonal, individualistic society. The local community is seen as incompatible with the large city, and on a wider level with the centralized nation-state.[4]

Other accounts of the decline of the local community envisage a longer time-scale. Y-M. Bercé traces it to the development of the state and of a generally greater sense of security in the early modern period. Local solidarity and cultural unanimity had been maintained by common insecurity, by the economic self-sufficiency of the village, and by a united Christian faith, but this pattern was broken by modernization. When life in the town or village became more secure there was greater scope for individuality, and the rigid local norms were no longer necessary for the survival of the society. The elites, drawn by the prestige of the centralized state, better-educated, open to the more intellectual religion and more secular culture of the industrial age, deserted traditional patterns of behaviour. If local communities survived here and there, Bercé explains, it was in backwaters, isolated societies left behind by modernization, and among marginal groups, even as a sort of sub-culture. It was a process spread over three hundred years, and of which urbanization was itself a manifestation.[5]

L. Stone, writing on England, agrees with Bercé that the local community declined during the late sixteenth and seventeenth centuries, but sees the development of the state and of the family not as a cause of this decline but as a result: in other words they developed to fill the gap. The decline of the community was caused by the reduced role of the reformed church (in England) and by the enormous demographic growth of the period. Although the accompanying geographic mobility in the short term strengthened the community, in the long term it loosened collective controls.[6]

There are thus a number of approaches to the history of local communities, all of which agree that they were declining. According to any of the explanations given, therefore, it is strange that late eighteenth-century Paris should offer evidence of extensive local community life. It was a city of over half-a-million people, with a huge immigrant population: some two-thirds of the inhabitants

---

[3] Ariès, 'The Family and the City'.
[4] Stone, *Family*, p. 660; F. Bédarida, 'La Vie de quartier en Angleterre: enquêtes empiriques et approches théoriques', *Le Mouvement social*, 118 (Jan.–March 1982), pp. 9–21 (p. 19). Gutton, *Sociabilité*, pp. 255–60.
[5] Bercé, *Fête*, pp. 53, 189–90.   [6] Stone, *Family*, pp. 92–3, 139–46, 216–17.

were born elsewhere.[7] Both the population and the area of the city were growing rapidly, a severe case of pre-industrial urbanization. Paris was also at the centre of the developing state, the effective seat of government if not the official one. It had since the late seventeenth century been endowed with a police force whose size and efficiency made it the envy of much of the rest of Europe. Furthermore the elites had long distanced themselves from popular recreations and festivities. How then could local communities have survived at all, since all the factors suggested for their destruction appear to have been present? Or is it simply that what we have observed were their last years, and that they were slowly dying, stricken by the withdrawal of the elites, by the development of the state and of the police, and by dramatic urban growth? Let us examine each of these factors in more detail.

The impact of the withdrawal of the elites was considerable, but it was a very long-term process. As Bercé suggests, it seems to have begun as early as the sixteenth century and to have been associated with the Reformation and the rise of the state. C. Kaiser has given us a picture of its beginnings among one group in late sixteenth- and early seventeenth-century Paris: the magistrates of the sovereign courts.[8] The struggle of the state against the traditional authorities made the situation of these men extremely difficult. As prominent citizens of Paris, yet at the same time servants of the state, their loyalties were divided between the city and the king, and their position was still further complicated by the religious conflicts within Paris. They were also expected to deal, on behalf of the monarchy, with nobles who were socially superior to them. Their way of coping with this difficult situation was by developing the ideal of the 'perfect Catholic magistrate', a being of high moral and religious integrity whose qualities were embodied not just in his reputation but in his very appearance and daily behaviour, in private as well as in public. The ideal involved a positive rejection of ordinary urban sociability, of the mixing of social groups and conditions: one writer condemned 'the company that [certain magistrates] continually keep with all sorts of people'.[9] The new model, on the other hand, emphasized their difference, their moral and social superiority. It enhanced their cohesion as a group and by detaching them from their bourgeois origins enabled them to deal on equal terms even with nobles. The similarity between this model and the eighteenth-century ideal of 'quality' is clear. It is possible that, for those in law and administration who were also servants of a monarchy trying to establish its supremacy over nobles and other local authorities, the model of the perfect Catholic magistrate was extremely attractive, although as religious tension decreased in France the Catholic element became less important.

[7] Roche, *Peuple*, pp. 23–4.
[8] C. Kaiser, 'Les Cours souveraines au XVIe siècle: morale et contre-réforme', *Annales: E.S.C.*, 37 (1982), 15–31.
[9] La Guesle, 1577, quoted in Kaiser, p. 22.

Furthermore, the perfect magistrate model must certainly have taken on the prestige of the powerful and influential men who had already adopted it.

By the eighteenth century, the ideal of 'quality', stressing not only moral integrity, manners and breeding but also sensitivity and feeling, was appealing to minor office-holders and affluent *maîtres marchands*. It was not the same model as that of the 'perfect Catholic magistrate', but a related one adapted to the particular possibilities and requirements of other social and professional groups. Its function was much the same: it provided a new sense of identity and gave legitimacy to social aspirations in a society whose values, while changing, continued to stress birth and lineage as prerequisites for rank. Those who adopted it gradually withdrew from the local community, as had the sixteenth-century magistrates, adopting a family- and home-centred way of life, seeking their pleasure with others of similar status and disapproving of the vulgar and disorderly festivities of the street.

The process of withdrawal by a succession of the wealthier, more prestigious groups therefore took a very long time, and was still going on at the end of the eighteenth century. Its effects were correspondingly gradual. It naturally affected collective celebrations very early, because it was traditionally the elites, through the municipality, confraternities, or *la jeunesse*, who had done the organization and provided the funds. It was equally they who controlled the means of repression, and, although popular festivities could survive without their participation, doing so in the face of their growing opposition was much more difficult. Other aspects of community life, such as the rowdy sociability of the street, wineshop, and market-place were both easier to retreat from and more difficult to do anything about. Nevertheless there can be no doubt that the gradual withdrawal of different elements from the local community seriously weakened it, at the same time changing its character. Because a part of the population no longer participated in a whole range of activities, these ceased to reinforce the local bonds which work and proximity might create. The new ties and the new social values developed by those who were moving outside the community undermined its control over them and its regulatory monopoly, for they could appeal to another audience and another set of rules. In turn, the more people who were thus able to escape its sanctions the less effective those sanctions became. Ultimately, of course, the desertion of the higher status groups and their rejection of community values permitted and fuelled the repression of the more spontaneous and 'disorderly' forms of popular behaviour. But it was not just a struggle between new values and habits, on the one hand, and unchanged traditional ones on the others. With each successive withdrawal, with the spread of what were becoming mainstream values, and through other changes that were taking place simultaneously, the community itself was changing. It became more socially homogeneous and more narrowly based, its culture therefore less representative of the whole society. It became more defensive, the contempt and the distance of the elites creating greater social antagonisms and a consciousness of belonging to a section of society which was defined by its separate culture, rather than by its function within an organic whole. The spread of literacy and the growing secularization of urban society, partly a result of the new types of social organization engendered by economic, demographic and technological change, likewise profoundly affected the mentality of working people.

The evolution of the local community, as I have already suggested, was also affected by the development of the state, and in particular of the police force, which in Paris was growing extremely rapidly both in size and in its range of functions.[10] This encouraged changes in the physical environment, in patterns of movement around the city, and ultimately in habits and ways of thinking.

Paris underwent much the same process as most other French cities during the seventeenth and eighteenth centuries, with the royal government displacing local authorities, eroding the power of town councils and seigneurial and ecclesiastical courts. The disappearance of the city walls and the introduction of the *octrois* – the urban import tariff – symbolized the control of the royal government over the city. But by far the most important change lay in the dramatic extension of the powers and jurisdiction of the Châtelet and of the *lieutenance générale de police*, formally established in 1674. In that year nineteen seigneurial jurisdictions were abolished, although several were subsequently re-established with greatly diminished powers. At the same time, the power of the Hôtel de Ville and of the local notables was undermined. The policing of the city had previously been done by men elected in each of the sixteen quarters by all the prominent citizens. The co-ordination was in principle assured by a central body, the *assemblée générale de police*, which included both members of the royal courts and of rival authorities: the *prévot des marchands*, sixteen notables of the quarters, the *échevins* (municipal councillors), the administrators of the Hôtel Dieu, the *jurés* of the corporations, and two prominent citizens from each quarter. Street cleaning and the levying of taxes were the responsibility of the principal inhabitants. Public order and if necessary the defence of the city were assured by the citizen militia, some thirty to fifty thousand men, in theory one individual from every household. The officers of the militia were also prominent citizens, very often the same ones who represented their quarter at the Hôtel de Ville.[11]

By the mid eighteenth century all this had changed. The Châtelet had the real responsibility for local government, including precautions against fire and flood; street cleaning and lighting; the trades corporations; and a host of other attributions. The militia had disappeared, replaced by the *guet* and primarily by

10 Williams, *Police*.
11 Chassaigne, *Lieutenance générale*, pp. 26–7, 42–5. R. De Scimon, 'Contrôle de l'espace parisien', series of papers presented to D. Richet's seminar, Nov.–Dec. 1978.

the *garde*, whose number increased dramatically during the century.[12] The Hôtel de Ville retained control only over the ramparts and over the river and its banks, including the Place de Grève, which did assure it an important role in organizing public festivities. The power of the local notables was admittedly not wholly destroyed. The position of *échevin* remained extremely prestigious, and in certain parts of the city the notables continued to play a local organizing role. For example every year a *syndic* was elected by the owners or principal tenants of the houses on the Quai de Gesvres, to be responsible for the closing and maintenance of the gates at each end of the *quai*, for the lighting, and for collecting a tax from every house and stall.[13] In 1775 to 1776 an attempt was made to revive aspects of the old system. The city was to be divided into *arrondissements*, and each of these into two or three *cantons* whose inhabitants would each year choose electors who would in turn name a *syndic* and two *adjoints* for each *arrondissement*.[14] The similarity to the system established in 1789 is striking: it is clear that the former role of the notables and the old form of administration had not been forgotten.

Nevertheless the changes had deeply affected the habits and the mentality of Parisians. The centralization of administration, in reducing local autonomy and the responsibility of the local elites, had significantly reduced the importance of the quarter as a social and psychological entity. A personal power-base within the quarter was no longer a prerequisite for political or honorific office and the local networks of influence and patronage which the former notables had cultivated began to disintegrate. The quarters could no longer claim the allegiance which during the seventeenth century could bring an officer of the militia to refuse to intervene in a riot in the next quarter, or which during the Fronde led to instances of physical conflict between different quarters. The barriers between different parts of the city were not as great, a fact symbolized by the gradual disappearance from the streets of the chains which had once been used to restrict movement around the streets in times of emergency, and perhaps at night.[15] By the second half of the eighteenth century the emphasis was on easy access for the *garde* and for the police officers who patrolled all areas of the city. The change in political structure affected the elites most immediately, but the reduced importance of the quarter as an administrative and political unit had an influence on all Parisians.

The new authorities, however, were not content simply to take over the functions formerly carried out by the municipal government, but extended them enormously during the century. Successive *lieutenants généraux* were given new powers and the police began to take an interest in every aspect of daily life. Control was strengthened over food supplies and over the labour-force. Soldiers

---

[12] Chassaigne, esp. pp. 36–77. Chagniot, 'Le Guet'.
[13] Y11963, 6 July; Ordonnance de police, 9 June 1769, in A.N. AD I 26.
[14] Y13728, Albert to Gillet, 16 April, 30 Apr. 1776.   [15] De Scimon, 'Contrôle'.

and wet-nurses, hawkers and street-sellers, coachmen and link-boys, the nightmen and the porters in the central market were all (in theory) registered, numbered, or even recruited by the police. Ordinances on a host of matters were codified and rationalized and the apparatus for the enforcement was enlarged and improved. The post of *inspecteur de police* was created, *commis* (aides) and observers were added. The *lieutenant général* supervised the *commissaires* and *inspecteurs* closely; the *garde* was expanded and reorganized; the French and Swiss Guards were placed at his disposal. Brothels and gambling-houses were regulated, and potential political dissent received close attention. Street lighting was improved and extended, the police took over responsibility for collecting rubbish, for maintaining the roads, and for ensuring the safety of buildings. Hardly any aspect of life in the capital remained outside their interest and influence.[16] Alongside the police a number of other institutions and authorities were established or developed. There was the *ferme générale* whose power reached its peak in the last few years of the regime after the building of the famous wall. What is less well documented is the growing presence of its officials. By 1788 we find 'commis ambulants' who patrolled the city, as well as those at the *barrières*, men whose attitude towards their work was very much that of civil servants. On occasion they also acted as an arm of the police, for example in arresting thieves, or at Lenoir's request in searching for Jansenist publications which were being smuggled into the city.[17] As well as the *ferme* there were *régies* (autonomous authorities) like the *grande poste*, carrying letters and packets nation-wide, and later the *petite poste* operating within Paris. There was the Mont-de-Piété, an institutionalized pawnbroker which often proved of considerable assistance to the police in hunting down thieves and in finding stolen goods, as well as in pursuing its original aim of defeating usury.[18]

The reasons for the extension of police power were partly political. The Paris population – notables and people alike – had in the past seriously threatened the monarch. By the mid eighteenth century fears of a new Fronde had receded, but the very process of centralization and of breaking down barriers both within the capital and between Paris and its provinces, combined with the demographic explosion and the growing gap between prices and real wages, made the maintenance of order an ever-present preoccupation. The measures taken to assure the supply of bread, the police concern with rumour, and the action against beggars and the ubiquitous *gens sans aveu* (vagabonds) all testify to the near-paranoid state of the official mind.[19]

But important as political motives were, they should not be over-emphasized. A growing concern with efficiency and immediate utility, associated with

[16] For more detail see Kaplan, 'Réflexions', and Williams, *Police.*

[17] Orléans MS 1421, f. 90. Y13290, 10 Feb., 17 Feb., 21 Oct., 29 Oct., 1 Nov. Y15402, 19 Apr.

[18] Y15100, 27 Aug., wit. 4. Y15099, 6 May, wit. 4.

[19] Roche, *Peuple*, ch. 3. Kaplan, *Bread*. C. Romon, 'Mendiants et policiers à Paris au XVIIIe siècle', *Histoire, économie, société*, 2 (2e trimestre 1982), pp. 259–95. Farge, *Vivre*, part 3.

changing attitudes towards trade and with the increasing importance of an affluent merchant and financier class, also underlay many of the measures taken. Men like Berryer, de Sartine, Albert and Lenoir had a conception of the well-policed state in which everything ran smoothly and rapidly. They streamlined and rationalized police procedure, encouraging in their subordinates a commitment to what they saw as the service of the public. Their concern with speed – being informed of things immediately, receiving details of imprisonments within twenty-four hours and other documents within two days, getting enquiries done within a week of the request – must be seen in the context of a wider change in ideas of time. A greater awareness of and preoccupation with the hours and with speed is reflected in and was encouraged by the spread of watches among even quite humble elements of the population.[20]

The *lieutenants généraux* and their fellow-administrators were men of the Enlightenment, convinced of the progress of their own century and of the perfectibility of mankind, however little their day-to-day work justified such views. They were humanitarians, and sincerely tried to improve public health, morality and conditions of life: it was Albert who had first-aid boxes put in all the guard posts for use in case of asphyxiation by coal-gas or smoke, and Lenoir who later added stretchers. Certain doctors were paid by the police to give free first-aid. In 1765 it was one of the *commissaires*, Thiot, who suggested a reward for anyone who saved someone from drowning, because the practice of paying fishermen who dragged bodies out of the river sometimes prevented them from going to the assistance of those who fell in. De Sartine applauded the idea, obtained money to implement it, and instructed the *commissaires* to publicize the reward as much as possible. Some years later when one of them refused to go to the river to interrogate someone who had been rescued, saying the person should be brought to him, Lenoir rebuked him on the grounds that such a refusal was 'contrary to duty and even to humanity'.[21]

The concern with order was also aesthetic. For the eighteenth century symmetry and uniformity, as in classical architecture, were the essence of beauty. An ordinance of 1761 which required shop-signs to be fixed against the houses instead of projecting over the street was partly inspired by the frequency of accidents, but also evoked their ugliness: 'they offend the eye of the citizen by their enormity'. Mercier, writing some twenty years later, applauded this wise ordinance, for now 'the city, which is no longer studded with these vulgar

---

[20] Y13728, printed instruction to *commissaires*, [*c.* 1760], Moreau [*procureur du Roi au Châtelet*] to *syndics*, 14 July 1762, Grimperel to Coquelin, [n.d.] [Aug. 1764], de Sartine to *syndics*, 8 Feb. 1768. Y11963, Albert to *syndics*, 12 July 1775. Y13728 Moreau to *syndics*, 12 Jan. 1778. Y12830, Lenoir to *syndics*, 11 Mar. 1779. Y12596, 1 Aug. Y12597, 31 Dec. Y14436, 10 May, 31 May, 2 July, 8 Nov., 12 Nov. Roche, *Peuple*, p. 82.

[21] Y13728, Albert to *syndics*, 30 Sept. 1775. Orléans MS 1421, f. 368. Y13728, de Sartine to *syndics*, 7 Sept. 1765, Lenoir to *syndics*, 8 Oct. 1779.

appendages, presents a polished, well-kept appearance'.[22] The urban development of the end of the eighteenth century was concerned with enlarging and straightening, as the removal of the houses from the bridges, the laying-out of the Place Louis XV, of the Panthéon and its semi-circular *place*, of the rue Soufflot and of the boulevards all testify. Openness, order, and accessibility were beautiful.[23]

Many of the measures dictated by the often combined motives of keeping order, of humanitarianism, of the beautification of the city, and of efficiency and utility as ends in themselves, had a significant impact on the local community. Most of them in one way or another served further to diminish the differences between the quarters and to encourage greater movement around the city. With the reduction of local responsibility there had to be more and more communication and movement to and from the new centres of authority. There were now the *hôtels* of the *lieutenant général*, the *procureur du Roi au Châtelet*, the commanders of the *garde* and the newly established fire brigade. There was the Hôtel des Fermes and the Hôtel des Postes. The internal post was a response to the need for more efficient communication, but also created a new demand. Centralization obliged people to deal with authorities outside their quarter and better communication made it easier.[24]

Perhaps most important of all, however, were the measures which removed physical barriers to movement. M. Ozouf has shown the readiness of urban planners of the eighteenth century to use *fêtes* or the erection of statues and monuments as excuses for opening up the city.[25] The Porte St Antoine was demolished about 1780, getting rid of the bottleneck at the end of the rue St Antoine. The Petit Châtelet came down, opening up the end of the rue St Jacques. The *quais* and bridges were cleared. In 1788 the jurisdiction of the Arsenal was abolished, the walls and ditches levelled and new streets put through to facilitate access to the Faubourg St Antoine. From the late seventeenth century many corner houses were demolished in order to ease traffic congestion, and those built in the eighteenth century often had a corner shorn off so as to widen the intersection. As a 'disinterested citizen' wrote in 1767, 'la circulation est le bonheur des Etats' (the free flow of traffic makes for the welfare of nations).[26]

---

22 J. Thibaut-Payen, 'Pot de fleur et jambe de bois: la voirie parisienne à la fin du XVIIe siècle (d'après les registres du bureau des finances)', *Dix-septième siècle*, 126 (Jan.–Mar. 1980), pp. 59–76. Ordonnance de police, 17 Dec. 1761, in Peuchet, *Collection*, vol. 7, p. 123. Mercier, *Tableau*, vol. 1, p. 216.

23 Ozouf, 'Le Cortège', pp. 892–4.

24 Williams, *Police*, pp. 125–9. Mercier, *Tableau*, vol. 3, pp. 339–44.

25 Ozouf, 'Le Cortège', pp. 892–3.

26 Monin, pp. 12–13; Mercier, vol. 6, p. 67; H. Robert, *Démolition de maisons du pont Notre Dame*, Musée Carnavalet. Edict of April 1788, mentioned in B.N. Ms. fr. 6687, f. 414, 25 Apr. 1788. Boudon *et al.*, *Système*, pp. 89–90. Dussausoy, *Le Citoyen désintéressé*, quoted in Ozouf, 'Le Cortège', p. 893.

This was certainly the philosophy of the police and of the Bureau des Finances, who both issued innumerable ordinances aimed at clearing the streets of all encumbrances: against workmen who left wood, stone, or tools in the street; against unauthorized stalls; against letting animals roam free. Fines were levied on vehicles left in the streets and a ban placed on certain games which hindered passers-by and risked injuring them.[27] The very frequency of the ordinances reflects their inefficacy, though, and traffic congestion remained a very serious problem. The expansion of the city and the consequent need for more supplies aggravated it, especially in the main streets and around the markets. Traffic jams were frequent, as the reports of the *garde* amply demonstrate, and the *commissaires* spent a great deal of time sorting out disputes over broken shop windows, overturned stalls, and damaged vehicles.[28]

The letters of the *lieutenants généraux* display a growing preoccupation with the problem. They put increasing pressure on the *commissaires* to carry out regular inspections and to take tough action against those who contravened the regulations. In some cases the *garde* was instructed to move against unauthorized street-sellers.[29] The biggest campaign was launched by Lenoir in 1779 and 1780, when he instructed the senior *commissaires* of each quarter to send him a list of all the street-stalls in their area, indicating the exact location, the name and occupation of the occupier, and an assessment of which ones could safely be left. They should take into consideration the width of the street and the amount of traffic using it, the nature of the terrain, and the needs of the poor, with preference given to needy master artisans. But at the same time, he added, the stalls 'must not hinder public passage and safety, nor spoil the appearance of the city'. In the lists which survive, the abolition of just under half of the stalls was recommended.[30] An assembly of the *commissaires* decided to issue written permission to the owners of stalls which could stay, and to order the confiscation of unauthorized stalls. The *garde* was to make special patrols to enforce this ruling. Measures were also taken to make the remaining stalls smaller, less permanent, and more uniform. The size permitted was indicated on the permit: that issued to a cobbler in 1785, for example, specified that his stall should be no more than three and a half feet wide.[31]

But the measures taken were not purely repressive. Considerable attention was devoted to providing alternative places for street stalls. Special locations were established for selling hay: in the rue d'Enfer outside the Chartreux

---

27 For a selection see Peuchet, *Collection*, and Thibaut-Payen, 'Pot de fleur'.

28 Y15117, reports of the *garde*, 1778–90. Y13816, reports of the *garde*, 1788–9.

29 Y13728, de Sartine to *syndics*, 18 Sept. 1762, printed instructions to *commissaires* on street cleaning [n.d. *c.* 1766], Leblanc to Coquelin, 24 Aug. 1765, Mouricault to Coquelin, 28 Nov. 1766, de Sartine to Coquelin, 22 June 1771.

30 Y12830, Lenoir to [Gillet], 9 Oct. 1780. Y13728, quartier St Jacques, 16 July 1779. Y12481, la Cité [n.d.]. Y13163, St Eustache, 20 Mar. 1779. Y11037, quartier Montmartre, 16 June 1779.

31 Y12830, *Mémoire* sent to *commissaires* for discussion, [1780], Dubois to Gillet, 9 Oct. 1780, Lenoir to [Gillet], 9 Oct. 1780. Y13728, Lenoir to Gillet, 17 Jan. 1785.

monastery; in the Grande rue du Faubourg St Antoine; and in the Faubourg St Laurent, all spots where the street was very wide. In April 1767 a new market was opened in the Priory of St Martin des Champs and stall-keepers in the rue St Martin were instructed to move there. In the same year another new market was set up for the city's market-gardeners, and in 1777 approval was given for yet another in what had been the grounds of the convent of Ste Catherine.[32] The Halles area saw the biggest changes. The new grain-market was built in 1762 on the site of the Hôtel de Soissons, enabling the stalls which cluttered the surrounding streets to be moved into the Carreau. The old Halle aux Cuirs (leather) next to the Innocents cemetery was in 1786 installed in new buildings in the rue Mauconseil, further to the north, and a new Halle aux Draps (cloth) built, at the same time enabling the network of streets surrounding it to be simplified. The closing of the Innocents cemetery provided the market with even more space. Formerly jammed into a tiny area around the old Carreau and the pillory, the central market now exploded in all directions, parts of it moving to completely new locations. At the same time the enlargement of the rue Comtesse d'Artois and of the Pointe St Eustache eliminated a bottleneck where the rues Montmartre and Montorgueil met. The creation of a completely new street, the rue de Calonne, between the rue des Prouvaires and the rue de la Tonnellerie, broke up the block which had divided the Halle from the streets to the west and further opened up the quarter (see figure 9).[33]

All these steps facilitated and speeded up movement between quarters, helping to reduce their isolation and parochialism. At the same time the clearing of the streets began to break up the local community. The stall-keepers, who were so important in local gossip and in the life of the street, were now pushed into the markets away from the places where people lived and worked. A very high proportion of them, furthermore, were women, whose role in the neighbourhood and as the voice of the community was generally greater than that of men. But the official campaign was not just against stalls, although they were its first target. The ordinances forbade artisans to spread their work out in the street, banned the playing of games, all the overflow of the life of the inhabitants into what was for many the only open area they had. Just as street theatre was moved to the boulevards where there was plenty of space, so the real-life theatre of the street was cleared, pushed inside or into specially designated areas. For the authorities the street was not a place for living: it was for access and movement. It did not belong to those who lived there but to the whole city and its traffic.

Eventually the thoroughfare, instead of being a space which united people, was to come to divide them. Without the straggling stalls and the workshops

---

[32] Ordonnances de police, 12 Oct. 1756, 1 Dec. 1758, in Peuchet, *Collection*, vol. 6, pp. 253, 350. Ordonnances de police, 22 April 1767, Peuchet, vol. 8, p. 56; 8 Sept. 1767, Peuchet, vol. 8, p. 90; Lettres patentes, 18 Oct. 1777, A.N. K1028, no. 38.

[33] Boudon *et al.*, *Système*, vol. 1, pp. 25–6.

spilling out from the houses, the street was wider. Without the stones and piles of wood or produce lying around, slowing down the pace of life and causing daily accidents, each one provoking disputes which brought the inhabitants to their doors and windows and the traffic to a complete halt for hours on end, the vehicles moved through faster. There was less time to stop and chat; more risk of being run over by a cart or a carriage which expected to find the way clear; no regular communion of disputes in which the onlookers could participate and which they could gossip about later. The major thoroughfares became barriers in a way they had not been before. This is reflected in the mentality of the planners: the new divisions of the city followed the line of the streets, unlike the mediaeval ones which went down the middle of the blocks.[34]

Of course this development was a very slow, long-term one. The traffic flow did not speed up overnight. It affected the main through-roads long before the minor ones, where the process was not really complete until after the arrival of the motor car.[35] But major progress was made in the second half of the eighteenth century.

In some cases these changes could actually strengthen the community. That in the market-place, always strong, was now more concentrated than ever before, and there were more markets. People who had perhaps previously been spread along one or more streets were now all together, their daily contacts now only with clients and with each other. Action by the ever-expanding police did not necessarily destroy the local community but did ultimately change its character.

The same was true, in the long run, of those organs of police and of central government which took over certain social functions of the community. One example of this is the attempt to make the placing of journeymen with masters a monopoly of the corporation, supervised by the police. Before this workers very much relied on contacts within their families, within the trade, or the neighbourhood: an employer would naturally prefer to take on a journeyman, as did one master brewer in the Faubourg St Antoine, 'at the request and on the recommendation of several people'. A stranger to the city, or to that area of the city, would ask the locals if they knew of anyone who was looking for workers. This was just what a 'garçon jardinier pour la taille des arbres' (journeyman gardener specializing in pruning trees) did when he went looking for work towards La Villette, far from his home in the Faubourg St Marcel.[36] A central employment bureau, while it did not necessarily totally replace more informal systems of finding employment, nevertheless reduced the dependence of workers and masters alike on the grape-vine and on local contacts.

A second institution which likewise made people less reliant on the neigh-

---

[34] Boudon *et al.*, vol. 2, plates 3 and 4. Junié, *Plan des paroisses de Paris, 1786*, A.N. N I Seine 56.
[35] Traffic congestion remained a severe problem throughout the nineteenth century as the amount of traffic grew steadily. See A. Sutcliffe, *The Autumn of Central Paris* (London, Edward Arnold, 1970), esp. p. 28.
[36] Y11239, 23 Mar. Y14484, 30 Nov.

bourhood was the Mont-de-Piété, the officially sanctioned pawnbroker. Earlier in the century those in need of money would borrow from family, colleagues or neighbours, or else from moneylenders recommended by someone else.[37] The establishment of the Mont-de-Piété in 1777 changed all this, providing a more anonymous means of borrowing money.

However the greatest impact was made by the police themselves. As we saw in chapter 1, the community adapted to the presence of the *commissaire* and of the *garde*, with people using them as weapons in disputes. The police conciliation mechanism was integrated into the system of community self-regulation. But at the same time it changed the system. The *garde* was increasingly present in the streets, ready to intervene in fights and thus assuming a function normally performed by neighbours. The *commissaire* often took over the job of bringing the parties in a dispute together and getting them to come to an agreement. This was a new element which, while it did not prevent the community from functioning, altered the forms and to some extent the rules of the game. For the values enforced by the *commissaire* and the solutions he proposed were not necessarily those of the local community. He was the representative of an outside authority whose concerns were different, and himself belonged to a local elite which had long since withdrawn from the community. His neutrality came from his rank and his status as an outsider, whereas the neutrality of neighbours was the reflex action of peers who had a personal knowledge of the parties and of the quarrel. His preoccupation was with keeping order, with maintaining his own authority, and with dispensing an apparently objective justice: theirs was the interest of people who had to live with the disputants.

Increasing reliance on the police modified the models to which people tried to conform. For example, being out of work or having no occupation became minor offences, or at best aggravating circumstances, an attitude quite unlike the older, charitable one towards beggars and wanderers. This was partly the result of wider social changes, but it was hastened by the necessity to conform to the stereotype of the 'honest poor' which recourse to the *commissaire* imposed.

There were other areas where the attitudes and values of the police and of the community were irreconcilably opposed. The unpopularity of the *garde* towards the end of the Ancien Régime was a symptom of this, for in moving on street-sellers and clearing the streets of stalls and workshops it increasingly imposed a law which was not that of the neighbourhood. A second battle-ground was the area of collective sanctions against those who did not conform to the norms of the community. Just as the police actively discouraged the rowdiness and 'licentiousness' of popular celebrations, with the support of the local elites, so too they intervened to prevent the 'disorders' of community self-regulation. The fate of the most spectacular form of sanction, the *charivari*, amply illustrates this point. As early as 1735 an irate brush-maker had the *garde* arrest a goldsmith

37 Roche, *Peuple*, p. 85. Y11239, 8 May, 27 Oct. Y10994, 4 July. Y15350, 25 April. Y14078, 14 June.

who pleaded before the *commissaire* that he had been in Paris for only six months and

did not know that *charivaris* were forbidden at marriages and having learned of the marriage today of a widow and a widower who live in the rue de la Barille near the Palais where he eats at the house of Monsieur Dumont, master goldsmith, he had taken up a saucepan . . .[38]

More truly Parisian were the 1739 disturbances surrounding the 'Cruchon Affair', described as

riotous assemblies in the Faubourg St Antoine made up of an infinite number of workers, of *gagne deniers* and individuals without any occupation or trade, who publicly insult merchants of the Faubourg by singing in front of their doors and shops songs in which the said merchants are referred to and even named.[39]

The papers of the *commissaire* Remy give details of a funeral procession for 'Le Cruchon', consisting of a bier carried by four men with blackened faces and preceded by another man with a bucket full of dirty water which he sprinkled liberally over the passers-by with an old wig. The procession, on the heels of a police ordinance forbidding any further mention of 'Le Cruchon' was obviously aimed at the *commissaire* and paraded past his *hôtel*.[40]

My 1752 sample provides two examples of *charivaris*. In July the *garde* arrested one of 'several young workers of the quarter' who for two or three nights in a row had gathered in the rue de Loursine where they had called out insults and sung 'the most dissolute songs attacking several members of the fair sex and notably the three sisters of the wife of Lenoble, [*charcutier*]'. The *commissaire* sent the young man to prison, although he denied the charge.[41]

A similar event took place only a few days later, this time against a gardener-florist accused by the neighbours of attempting to rape his sixteen-year-old cousin, who worked as his domestic servant. For several evenings in a row they stationed themselves outside his door from nine or ten until midnight, singing 'songs full of dirty language and prejudicial to the plaintiff's honour'.[42]

These examples fit in perfectly with the general pattern of urban *charivaris* which is outlined by N. Davis. In sixteenth-century cities it was not used much against second marriages, as was normal in the country, but more against domineering women and in a general way against anyone suspected of an unjust action. Participation became more socially restricted and it was sometimes politically satirical, although generally in a destroy-and-renew attack on some

---

[38] Y14950, 27 April 1735.
[39] E. de la Poix de Fréminville, *Dictionnaire ou traité de la police-générale des villes, bourgs, paroisses et seigneuries de la campagne*, new ed. (Paris, 1771), p. 305. I have been unable to find out what this affair was about.
[40] Y10986, 30 July, 1 Aug. 1739. I am indebted to M. Sonenscher for this reference.
[41] Y12596, 24 July.
[42] Y10994, 19 July.

form of misrule rather than as part of a continuing campaign.[43] This is very much apparent in the Cruchon Affair where the theatrical funeral suggests a purification: the one man arrested, and the sympathetic witnesses, all speak of burying the affair. One said that he thought they were interring 'la Sainte Anne', and another makes a parallel with the 'carême-prenant' which was buried annually on Ash Wednesday.

Beyond the 1750s I have found no further examples which can be clearly identified with the traditional *charivari*, and by the early nineteenth century it seems to have totally disappeared from the collective memory. In 1827 when an Auvergnat tinker beaten by his wife was mounted on a donkey by his compatriots and led around the Marché St Germain one of the participants published a brochure explaining that this was a ceremony 'de chez nous' (from our province).[44] The *charivari* did survive in other forms though. On the one hand there was the *bacchanale* or *tapage*, a sort of individual *charivari* working on much the same principle, which remained quite common in the 1780s. On the other hand there was the 'political *charivari*', really a satire based on religious or official ceremonies, of which the Cruchon Affair provides a rare early example and which in France reached the peak of its popularity during the July Monarchy.[45]

The disappearance of the traditional *charivari*, or rather its evolution into the *bacchanale* or into a particular kind of political satire, is comprehensible only in the context of the changes in the local community. The *charivari* was a form of social sanction which could be effective only in an enclosed, strongly cohesive community where local opinion was all-important, from which there was no escape, and where there was a very strong sense of corporate identity. It was effective only if the victim was sufficiently part of the community to suffer from it and if it was supported by a large enough section of the group.[46] Once part of the population had withdrawn and rejected the collective values which the *charivari* was designed to reinforce, it obviously lost much of its power. The existence of another audience and set of values which the victim could appeal to provided an escape-route, especially when these values were supported by the police: the Cruchon Affair was vigorously pursued by the *commissaire*. In the other cases I have cited the victim was able to appeal to the authorities and in two of them the *garde* took action. The increasing presence of the police made collective sanctions of this nature difficult at a time when they were in any case proving less and less effective. This may largely explain the continued success of the

---

[43] N. Z. Davis, 'The Reasons of Misrule: Youth Groups and Charivaris in Sixteenth-Century France', *Past and Present*, 50 (Feb. 1971), 63–9.

[44] Faure, *Paris Carême-prenant*, p. 81.

[45] Faure, pp. 95–7. Bercé, *Fête*, p. 44. C. Tilly, 'Charivaris, repertoires and urban politics', in J. Merriman (ed.), *French Cities in the Nineteenth Century* (New York, Holmes and Meier, 1981), pp. 73–91. E. P. Thompson, '"Rough Music": le charivari anglais', *Annales: E.S.C.*, 27 (1972), pp. 285–312 (p. 289).

[46] Thompson, '"Rough Music"', p. 291.

bacchanale, which could in no way be represented as 'attroupement' (riotous assembly). Because it was used almost exclusively against neighbours and very often in the house or the courtyard, the *garde* was not very effective against it and indeed does not generally seem to have intervened.

The spread of the 'political *charivari*' also accompanies the evolution of the local community. The police provided an alternative to community action against individual members but little recourse for those with grievances against the authorities themselves, or against the powerful. A complaint could be effective against a particular abuse, but not when there was no consensus on what constituted an abuse. This was the case (and remains so today) in labour disputes, where the two sides appealed to different systems of values to justify their actions: the employers to the profit-centred ethic of the market-place and the workers to concepts of fair employment. In this situation, where recourse to the authorities was not possible or was ineffective, the only action available to workers was some sort of collective sanction. A strike required organization and money and was difficult to maintain in the face of repression. A satirical *charivari*, on the other hand, involved less risk and was open to people for whom no concerted long-term action was possible.

The shift away from *charivaris* with a sexual pretext towards those aimed to remedy abuses or social injustices was also partly a result of urbanization. In towns a larger marriage-market reduced the need to discourage second marriages and those with outsiders. A larger population permitted the formation of youth-groups based on occupation, alongside those in the neighbourhood, and this could narrow the social range of the participants and perhaps the type of infringements which were punished. More importantly, the withdrawal of the elites from the local community and from the more boisterous forms of collective behaviour left the *charivari* the property of the lower classes, and this inevitably led to a transformation in the way the institution was used. It permitted an element of political satire which was not normally possible when those likely to be criticized were the organizers or prominent participants. Of course, once the *charivari* began to be extensively used for political ends its forms – the masks and disguises, the mock-religious or official procession – became politically charged and could no longer be used in any other way.[47]

The disappearance or transformation of collective sanctions like the *charivari* deprived the community of important mechanisms of self-regulation. Equally important was the loss of a means of socialization. The *charivari* and the youth-groups which in most places organized them played, as N. Davis has shown, a vital role in socializing young men by making them the voice of the community conscience.[48] Likewise the intervention of neighbours in disputes and their role in conciliation helped to create a sense of belonging to a close-knit

---

[47] Bercé, *Fête*, ch. 2.   [48] Davis, 'Reasons of Misrule', p. 55.

group. This was eroded by the ever-greater influence of the state on people's lives.

In Paris, nevertheless, we must bear in mind that the precocious development of the police was encouraged by urbanization on a scale unknown elsewhere in Europe, except in London. The growing role of the *commissaires* and of the *lieutenance générale*, while in itself a major factor in the transformation of the community, was also in part a response to physical and social changes wrought by urbanization. The decline of the mechanisms of self-regulation, so important for the maintenance of a sense of community, may also be attributed to a certain type of urban development.

The dramatic physical and population growth of Paris during the eighteenth century and particularly over the decades leading up to the Revolution have been described in any number of works, from the anxious treatises of contemporary medics and demographers to recent publications on urbanization.[49] Not only did the city expand outwards, but increased population also led to the progressive disappearance of many of the gardens and open spaces in the crowded city centre, a process already well under way at the end of the seventeenth century. The open spaces were lost not only for new houses but also for administrative and commercial buildings. In 1750 the Hôtel de Soissons was demolished and its extensive garden, the only remaining public one in the central districts, disappeared with it.[50] Later in the century the gardens of the Temple and of the convent of Sainte Catherine were invaded by markets, and the 1780s saw the incorporation of the large Innocents cemetery into the central market complex.

Not only did the large gardens go, but equally the small ones hidden behind the houses. The Parisian house, as it developed during the Middle Ages, was built right on the street and was about two rooms deep. Behind it was an open space or a garden, accessible from the street through a corridor or in a larger block perhaps a carriage entrance, leading directly back from the front door and usually placed to one side. The stairway was generally in a corner of the courtyard. On the ground floor there were normally two rooms, the front one often converted into a shop. On each of the upper floors there would be two rooms and a *cabinet* (very small room). Behind the courtyard, if the block were deep enough, there was often a low building which served as a stable, a granary, a kitchen, or a place for animals.

The basic floor-plan remained essentially the same until the eighteenth century. In the central areas, however, pressure of population and the accompanying rise in land prices led to the erection of new buildings on the gardens, and to the conversion of outbuildings into dwellings. On large blocks there might

[49] J-J. Expilly, *Tableau de la population de la France* (1780). see Kaplow, *Names*, ch. 1. Roche, *Peuple*, pp. 11–19, 33–6. P. Lavedan, *Histoire de l'urbanisme. Epoque contemporaine* (Paris, C.L.T. Lanore, 1952). M. Bertrand, *Architecture de l'habitat urbain. La maison, le quartier, la ville* (Paris, Dunod, 1980).
[50] Boudon *et al.*, *Système*, vol. 1, p. 25.

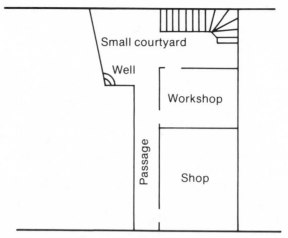

11. Plan of a typical Parisian house: 18 rue Contrescarpe, Faubourg St Antoine (*B.N. Estampes Va 294 fol., vol. 4*)

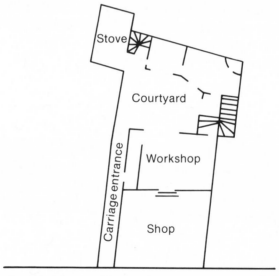

12. Plan of a typical house with a carriage entrance: 15 rue de la Coutellerie (*B.N. Estampes Va 247d fol.*)

be a succession of courtyards and corridors, sometimes very complex. This happened in some places as early as the fifteenth century, a period of rapid population growth, but in most of the central quarters on the Right Bank the process took place in the second half of the seventeenth and throughout the eighteenth century. Its progress can be traced on the Plan Turgot (1739), whose

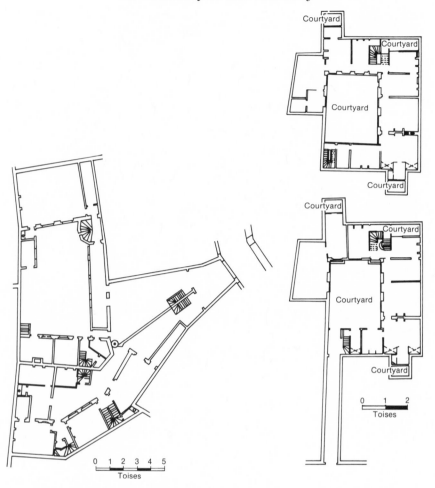

13. Plans of large houses, showing courtyard system (based on plan in Boudon *et al.*, vol. 1, p. 84)

remarkably accurate detail reveals the network of courtyards in the densely built city centre, and the sparser constructions of the periphery.[51]

At the same time the houses and the secondary constructions at their rear got higher and higher. This became sufficiently prevalent to make the authorities issue an edict in 1783 fixing the maximum height of the street facade at seventy feet for the very widest thoroughfares. This did not include the roof, however, and there were sometimes one or even two floors squeezed in under a very steep,

[51] Bertrand, *Architecture*, pp. 28–9. Boudon *et al.*, vol. 1, pp. 77, 86.

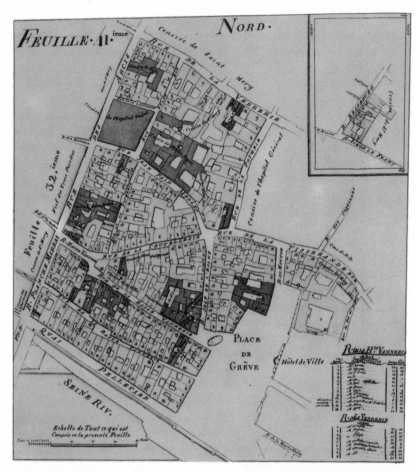

14. Map of part of the Place de Grève quarter, showing courtyards and densely packed houses (Rittmann and Junié, *Atlas des plans de la censive de l'archevêché dans Paris*, 1786. *Photo. Bodleian Library*)

high gable.[52] The main through-streets generally had taller houses: according to the Plan Turgot, in 1739 half of the houses on the eastern side of the rue St Denis were four-storey, and another tenth were five-storey, with only a couple reaching six storeys. In what was later to become the Section des Lombards most of the houses were in 1739 four or five storeys high. None of these figures include *mansardes* or attic rooms, so in most cases another floor can be added to each. The buildings at the rear were generally one or two storeys lower. By the

[52] Bertrand, p. 29. Roche, *Peuple*, pp. 114–16. Kaplow, *Names*, p. 17, Mercier, *Tableau*, vol. 11, p. 4.

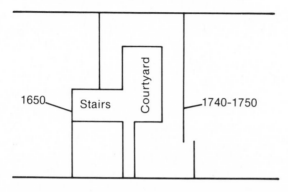

15. Plan showing an eighteenth-century addition to a seventeenth-century house (based on plan in Boudon *et al.*, vol. 1, p. 80)

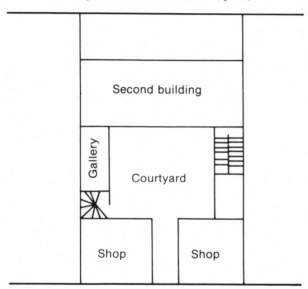

16. Plan of an eighteenth-century double-fronted house (based on plan in Boudon *et al.*, vol. 1, p. 80)

end of the century, as engravings illustrate, the major streets and the prime building sites often had houses of six or even seven storeys, although interspersed with smaller ones.[53]

During the seventeenth century, but even more in the eighteenth, variations of

[53] G. Perrin, 'L'Entassement de la population dans le Paris de la Révolution. La Section des Lombards' in Reinhard (ed.), *Contributions*, 2nd series, pp. 61–76 (pp. 69,71). B.N. Est. Va 247d. fol., extract from bird's-eye view map (n.d. mid eighteenth century?) showing quarter of the Grève; 'La Rue aux fers', Musée Carnavalet, reproduced in Boudon *et al.*, vol. 1, p. 70.

the traditional design made for larger houses. An obvious way of saving space, when building a new house alongside an older one, was to make use of the existing courtyard or stairway. If two houses were built together they could share a courtyard, and in the eighteenth century it became popular to construct mirror-image houses so as to create a single central space. It was only a step from this to building a single, larger house with a double front and a single entrance, often a carriage-entrance. Towards the end of the eighteenth century there appeared a tendency to buy up several small blocks and build one large house on them, rather than a number of small ones. This was cheaper and saved space.[54]

These developments, less conspicuous than the subdivisions and the new constructions in the western *faubourgs*, none the less resulted from the same boom in building speculation. Here, however, the new houses were not built for sale but for rent, a long-term commitment. It indicates the availability of capital for large-scale construction-work, perhaps a switch in investment from rural estates to urban property, and certainly a new confidence in buildings, as opposed to the land itself.

These physical changes are fairly well documented, but their effects on the Parisian population have been much less successfully dealt with. First of all they made it more difficult to know everyone in the area. In the most highly urbanized quarters the population density was very high: N. Karéiev estimated it at anything up to 1,300 people per hectare, with a minimum of 500 to 800 for all the central parishes on both banks of the river during the Revolution.[55] G. Perrin's study of the Section des Lombards shows that the average number of permanent residents per house was about seventeen in the Year V, somewhat more in the Year III, although these figures hide enormous variations. The smallest houses were occupied by only a handful of people: ten per cent of them had fewer than six inhabitants. The four largest had sixty, sixty-eight, seventy, and eighty-six occupants, no doubt in more than one building. But most had between five and twenty-five people living in them.[56] It was therefore in most cases quite possible to get to know everyone in the same house. Beyond the one house, however, it was quite another story. Only the culs-de-sac and the streets containing churches or monasteries had manageable numbers: seventy in the rue du Crucifix next to St Jacques de la Boucherie; between fifty and sixty in the rues St Magloire and de Venise; a dozen or so in the rue Trognon, the cul-de-sac St Fiacre, and the cul-de-sac du Chat Blanc. But in the other streets of the Section even the best-placed person could not hope to know more than a fraction of the inhabitants. The two small blocks of the rue Troussevache sheltered a population of five hundred odd, as did the rue de Marivaux, about 250 yards long.

[54] Boudon *et al.*, vol. 1, pp. 48, 79–81. Bertrand, pp. 28–9.
[55] N. Karéiev, *La Densité de la population des différentes sections de Paris pendant la Révolution* (Paris, 1912), cited in Kaplow, *Names*, p. 21.
[56] Perrin, 'Entassement', p. 75.

The rue Aubry le Boucher, a major through-street although quite short, had over a thousand inhabitants.[57] This crowding was of course not new: already in 1739 the Section des Lombards had tall houses and few open spaces. Even on the level of the street, therefore, in the most densely built-up areas it was not possible to know more than a fraction of the locals.

The effects of high population density – not just within one street, it must be remembered, but over a whole city – are reflected in the sociability and the mentality of Parisians. Unlike in a village or small town, where strangers were rare, it was relatively easy to become a Parisian and to become part of the local community. Work, family, or *pays* could all act as a means of integration. The simple fact of living next door was enough to create ties between people. Parisian sociability was very open, accepting newcomers and strangers easily. There was little of the unconcealed peasant distrust of strangers, but a readiness to talk to people and find out about them. Precisely because one could not be quite sure who an outsider or immigrant was, even though clothes, accent and bearing would reveal something, people developed a formal politeness which enabled them to deal with strangers without alienating or offending them, yet without necessarily conveying real warmth, at least at first. As Y. Castan puts it, in the city there was a formal *honnêteté* which acted as a sort of currency for social transactions.[58]

Underlying the open sociability was a fundamental instability, an uncertainty about people which is reflected even in the behaviour of those who may have known each other for some time. In a sense immigrants had no past. The way they were treated, initially, was less determined by their history, by their known wealth and status or even by the family they belonged to, than by their external appearance, their occupation, and their personality. To some extent this remained true however long they lived there. Their past became a fantasy world where everything was possible, as the insults exchanged and the testimony of witnesses, often nourished on hearsay and supposition, amply demonstrate. 'Le pays' could become a mythical place of past evil: 'She had been whipped and branded in her *pays*.' Or one of mythical possibilities: many a young man told his girlfriend that he had wealth or possessions in his *pays*. Any other place could of course fulfil the same function: I have already mentioned the journeyman baker who accused his former employer of having written false promissory notes in Bavaria.[59] One of the reasons why such calumnies were so successful and so frequent was precisely because they just might be true, however stereotyped and however unlikely they were. The past was rich with possibilities. Even outside the shared, well-known activities of the quarter there remained a mysterious domain where someone might act in a completely different way. A witness remembered, for example, having heard one woman shout at another that she was 'a whore who could be had for twelve *sols* on the boulevards' and that she had

<hr>

[57] *Ibid.* [58] Y. Castan, *Honnêteté*, pp. 26–7. [59] Y12596, 2 July, 11 July. Y10994, 16 Oct.

been arrested there in possession of stolen clothes.[60] The urban environment created a margin where other people could not enter and where only too often they invented what they did not know. There was in the popular mentality an immediate assumption that what was hidden must of necessity be sinister. (This trait was of course not confined to the popular mentality, nor to the eighteenth-century one.) Hence, in part, the overwhelming importance of reputation and the need to be constantly on the alert. Hence too some of the instability of the financial world of eighteenth-century Paris.

Having an unknown past could of course be an advantage. The city provided an escape for people who for one reason or another had to leave their place of birth. There might really be some shameful secret, or they might simply have left a series of personal disappointments behind them. Migration could be an admission of failure but also provided a new start, for the big city provided possibilities which might be absent in a village where people were known, their chances circumscribed by economic and social barriers. Because there were always newcomers arriving or passing through, relationships changed more quickly than in a village. Because the city was so physically crowded, too, others were constantly impinging on the individual's domain, in a sense constantly testing its limits. It was for this reason a relatively aggressive environment which made necessary the open but defensive sociability I have tried to describe. It likewise made the conventions and forms of community self-regulation vitally important.

The community was thus able to adapt to the transformations in the physical and social structure of the city, but in so doing changed its character. By the eighteenth century it was very open, newcomers were tolerated and rapidly integrated, and its norms of behaviour were readily comprehensible to people from a variety of regional and social backgrounds. A sense of belonging and of community did not depend on long residence or on life-long familiarity with every aspect of the lives of friends and neighbours.

It did depend, however, on a degree of stability. The arrival of large numbers of immigrants was not a problem, but that of a more transient population did have serious consequences for the local community. Seasonal workers, for example, were unlikely to become part of it, and the same was true of many others whose work or misfortune obliged them to keep moving. Mobility within the city itself was high. In the Popincourt Section in 1793 nearly a third of the male population was born in another part of Paris, and only a tenth in the Section, an indication that most men were uprooted at least once in their lives, even if many came from neighbouring areas. Furthermore forty per cent of the male inhabitants had been there for less than a year.[61]

The impression of instability that these figures create must be modified somewhat. We must bear in mind that men probably moved around more than

[60] Y13290, 6 Sept., wit. 5.   [61] Sévegrand, 'Popincourt', p. 63.

women, and also that the revolutionary period saw both greater immigration and greater mobility than the preceding years. Nor do these statistics indicate the turnover of population in the Section, and we have seen that certain trades and age-groups were more mobile than others. M. Sévegrand's study of the Popincourt Section reveals that the gardeners, who made up just on eleven per cent of the male population, were extremely stable. Day-labourers and unskilled workers, on the other hand, many of whom were recent arrivals in the city and who married late, were the least so.[62] It is likely, therefore, that certain groups accounted for much of the residential mobility during the Revolution, and that a substantial portion of the population was far more stable. Nevertheless, residential mobility was high and this did create problems for the community, whose functioning depended on a certain level of familiarity and on the efficacy of collective sanctions whose bite was considerably less painful for someone who had no roots in the area and who did not intend to stay.

It must be borne in mind, too, that residential mobility had its greatest effect on the level of the individual house. If it reached, for example, a figure of forty per cent a year in a particular quarter, this was not spread equally over the whole area. There tended to be certain streets and houses which catered to temporary residents: lodging-houses, of course, but also premises hired by large employers for their workers; or houses with concentrations of workers from the same province who would succeed each other. Much depended on the principal tenant or the owner, who might prefer to let rooms to people who were going to stay for some time, or alternatively hire out furnished rooms – at a rather higher rent – to a less stable population. It would also vary according to the nature of the premises: a large house was likely to experience more movement than a small one.

The amount of mobility within the house affected relations between neighbours. Where there was a very stable population everyone knew everyone else, which helped to create a sense of community within the building itself. This became clear when there was conflict with outsiders: examples of neighbours taking action against people not living in the house were given in chapter 1. There was often a very firm distinction between 'les voisins' and those from outside. Marie Michelle Bernier, seamstress, fifty-eight years old and living for the past seventeen years in the same house in the rue du Faubourg St Jacques, testified when the body of a newly born baby was found in the cess-pit that she knew and could vouch for everyone in the house, 'de fort honnêtes gens très anciens ... Ce ne peut avoir été fait que par des Etrangers' (all extremely respectable people of long residence. It could only have been done by Outsiders.)[63] Numerous are the examples of people challenging strangers whom they met in the passage or on the stairs of their house. Their suspicion was partly a result of the prevalence of strangers in the street and reflects their concern to

[62] Sévegrand, 'Popincourt', pp. 21–4, 32, 63, 69.   [63] Y13290, 24 Feb., wit. 6.

defend the more private space of the house. But in a building where there was a high turnover of tenants this was no longer possible. The inhabitants could never be sure whether someone they did not recognize lived there or not, and they therefore adopted the same caution as in the street. A laundrywoman living in the house of an innkeeper in the rue de la Tacherie, testifying after a theft, said that she had seen the culprit on the stairs but that 'as a great many people live in this house, whom she does not know at all, she felt obliged to pass on her way and say nothing for fear of being mistaken'. Another neighbour said the same.[64] In this sort of house there was not the same relationship between all the inhabitants as in more stable houses where there existed a strong sense of community. And with increasing residential mobility there were more and more houses where the inhabitants did not know each other.

Ultimately this would lead to a redefinition of the term 'neighbour'. As we saw in chapter 1, it was positively charged with connotations of contact and familiarity, mutual obligations and shared experience. These were precisely the qualities that were lost when there was high residential mobility, and the word *voisin* became restricted to its basic meaning of someone who lived nearby.

Residential mobility, however, was not the only sort. Even more drastic in its effects on the community was the influx of people who lived or lodged in another part of the city entirely, and who passed through the quarter, perhaps in the course of their work, but more conspicuously in pursuit of pleasure. The clearing of the streets, the increase in traffic, and the breaking down of the physical and psychological barriers between quarters encouraged this sort of movement. So too did the development of the boulevards at the expense of more local amusements. All these factors further stimulated the development of that wandering group, largely composed of young men, whose mobility put them largely outside the local community.

The effect of this sort of mobility may be illustrated by two incidents reported by the *garde*, both of which occurred near the Place de Grève. The first concerned a group of musicians whose performance in the extremely narrow rue Jean Pain Mollet had attracted a crowd. Three domestic servants, all living some distance away in the Temple, began to call out abuse, and when rebuked by the onlookers reacted violently. They attacked the other people in the street, apparently quite indiscriminately, including a student and an *ouvrier miroitier* (who made mirrors) both locals.[65] In the second example, the wife of a master metal-founder was standing at the door of her house in the rue des Arcis waiting for her husband to return when a man propositioned her. He was a little drunk, and presumably took her for a prostitute. He had, he said, 'had the misfortune to look at the said woman, who slapped him across the face'. This had provoked retaliation on his part and when a number of witnesses intervened he attacked them too. He turned out to be a pastry-cook from the Faubourg St Antoine. The

<hr>

[64] Y15100, 2 Sept., wit. 1, 2.   [65] Y15350, 8 May.

two witnesses who accompanied the *garde* to the *commissaire*, both also from other parts of the city and neither of whom had actually intervened, knew neither of the participants and were able to state only that 'several people' had taken the woman's part, saying that they knew her to be an *honnête femme*.[66]

There is no problem of immigrants here. In both of these cases the conflict results from the presence of men from other parts of the city, mobile individuals with time on their hands. The violence is haphazard, not the predictable violence of neighbours of whom one knew what to expect and on whom it was relatively easy to have revenge. The more strangers there were (and the more of this variety), the less well-defined were the rules of social intercourse and the less complete the control of the local community over the public thoroughfare itself. The passers-by and the public generally were not necessarily, or primarily, those who lived there, and the pressure of local opinion was therefore less effective. Intervention was potentially costly, for the actors were less likely to conform to what was expected of them and to accept public judgment on their actions. At worst, the public space was dominated by strangers and did not really belong to the local population at all.

Transience, therefore, rather than immigration, was the greatest threat to the local community. It combined with the street-clearing measures taken by the authorities to drive the locals out of the public spaces and into the houses, the courtyards, the alleyways. The end of the eighteenth century was the period when the network of passages, often known only to the locals, began to develop rapidly, reaching its peak in about the 1830s. This was partly an official move to relieve traffic congestion and to create commercial outlets off the street, but it was also a spontaneous development, a system of public footpaths recognized by custom.[67] It was a response by the locals to the increasing traffic, anonymity, and danger of the street.

As with other developments of the period, the local community may initially have been strengthened. In the courtyards and passages, as in the new markets, it was protected from the influx of strangers. It lost the street, but gained new areas of sovereignty, became more concentrated. In the long term however, as both its social composition and its geographic scope narrowed, it lost much of the regulatory power which depended on unanimity.

This was the general long-term pattern, but it did not necessarily proceed in the same way or at the same rate throughout the city. I have referred frequently to differences between the quarters. The effects of urbanization, of the withdrawal of the elites, or of the expansion of the police and of centralized authority could be attenuated or aggravated by the character of each area. Topography, social composition, location in the city, the nature and strength of the local community and of the bonds underlying it, were all factors which determined the relevance of new models to the inhabitants and the resistance of

[66] Y15350, 18 May.   [67] Boudon *et al.*, vol. 1, pp. 385–6.

the community to the general changes which were taking place. This can be illustrated by a glance at three very different areas of the city: the Grève and the neighbouring central quarters; the Faubourg St Antoine, in many ways typical of the northern and eastern *faubourgs*; and the Halles, admittedly unique, yet providing an alternative model for inner-city development.

The central quarters generally were victim to the most vigorous urbanization. They had the tallest houses, the high facades concealing a confusion of secondary buildings and a labyrinth of courtyards and passages. They had the highest population density, the narrowest streets and the worst traffic problems, all of which in turn made them the focus for much official attention. They suffered more than any other area the physical desertion of the elites. In the 1760s we find the *curé* of St Gervais complaining about the loss of revenue caused by the exodus of rich people from his parish (which covered much of the Ste Avoie area and of the Marais, as well as the streets behind the Hôtel de Ville):

The opulent world is abandoning it and moving to the fashionable districts. You will see neither Prince nor Chancellor, no Dukes or Peers, no Maréchaux de France, Intendants des Finances or Fermiers généraux, such as were once to be seen there.[68]

The central quarters were left, not just to the poor, but increasingly to a highly mobile, floating population.

Nowhere was this more marked than in the quarter of the Grève and in those adjoining it. Situated at the crossroads of the city, they were to Paris what Paris was to much of the rest of France: a precarious refuge in hard times, a melting-pot for the most diverse elements of the population. Although certain provincial groups and people from the nearby countryside tended to cluster on the side of the city closest to their place of origin, many of those who did not belong to cohesive groups like the Savoyards or the Auvergnats, or who had no links with family or *pays* already in Paris, made their way towards the lodging-houses in the rue de la Vannerie, the rue de la Mortellerie and in the tiny, cramped streets adjoining the ports. Anyone who came by water from Auxerre would land at the Quai St Paul, a couple of minutes' walk from the rue de la Mortellerie.[69] This area also, naturally enough, sheltered men in the river trades: the boatmen who brought from the Vexin, the Brie, and the other supply areas the huge quantities of grain which the city consumed every day; the men who manned the boats bringing hay and coal to the Quai de Grève; the *flotteurs* who steered the wood-trains as far as the same Quai de Grève, there to be broken up and the timber stacked to dry. Some of these trades were seasonal and the men would often stop to work in the capital for a few months, like Nicolas

[68] A.N. S7493.
[69] Cobb, *Police*, pp. 23–4. Roche, *Peuple*, p. 123. Mercier, *Tableau*, vol. 6, p. 66. Restif de la Bretonne, *Nuits*, 359e Nuit. 'Le port St Paul', reproduced in F. Bournon, *Paris Atlas* (Paris, Larousse, 1900), p. viii. Y10994, 12 June.

PLAN DU QUARTIER DE LA GRÈVE

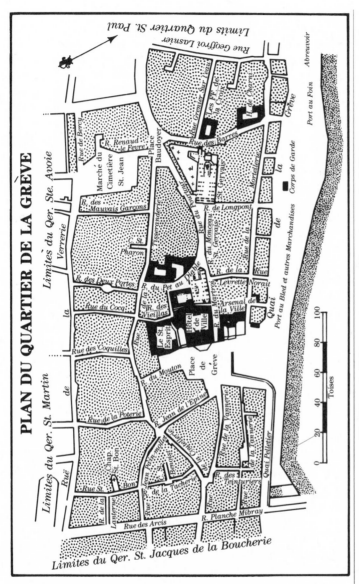

17. The Place de Grève quarter, 1773 (from the map by Jaillot)

Guénot and his two cousins, all *flotteurs*. Some would end up staying, as did Guénot himself.[70]

The lodging-houses also catered to people looking for work. The Place de Grève was the recruiting-ground for building workers, so many of them stayed in the vicinity. Other men sought work on and around the ports, doing the jobs which were not the monopoly of any of the organized bands of porters. There were also women, like Louise Des Vaux, born in Nantes and for several years in Paris where 'she has followed different callings which have led her to live in several quarters'. In May 1752 we find her living in the rue de Long Pont near St Gervais, where she had gone to escape from a former boyfriend, son of a master button-maker, whom she had met some seven or eight months earlier when she was living in a *chambre garnie* in the rue de la Juiverie.[71] Similarly, domestic servants, often laid off at a moment's notice, would take refuge in the *garnis* of the city centre, a convenient and cheap place to use as a base while they looked for another employer.[72]

All this made the Grève area one of considerable residential mobility, quite apart from the normal movement of those who were forced to change quarters for financial or family reasons. People shifted in and out of the centre very easily, and the papers of the *commissaires* provide many examples of frequent changes of domicile. But the city centre was also the area most affected by the day-to-day flow of traffic and people. The official quarter of the Grève lay right where the main north–south axis of the rue St Martin–rue St Jacques met the ancient east–west route along the north bank of the river. The rue du Temple, the rue St Antoine, and what is now the rue Beaubourg fed into the rue de la Verrerie, the northern limit of the quarter. The Pont Notre Dame allowed easy access from the Ile de la Cité, and the Seine itself was of course a highway. Anyone who crossed the city was likely to pass, if not through the Grève itself, at least close by: across the Pont Neuf or the Pont-au-Change, along the *quais* or the main roads. The documents are full of mentions of people from other parts of the city, witnesses and victims of accidents, of fights, of thefts. The widow of a glazier was crossing the Pont Notre Dame, perhaps on her way to her home near St Nicolas des Champs, when she was hit by a carriage. A master harness-maker complained that his son's hat had been stolen while they were on their way from having dinner with the boy's mother, a lottery-seller in the Faubourg St Martin, back to their lodging in the Faubourg St Germain.[73] Even if it did not necessarily lie on their route, people were drawn into the city centre by the very line of the streets and the direction of the traffic. For example, a porcelain-maker returning from Chaillot to his home in the rue du Grand Hurleur, near St Nicolas des

---

[70] R. Cobb, *Paris and its Provinces* (Oxford, O.U.P., 1975), p. 76. Cobb, *Police*, p. 229, n. 1.
[71] Y15350, early May. See also 23 Dec. wit. 5.
[72] Cobb, *Police*, p. 230. Roche, *Peuple*, p. 126. Botlan, 'Domestiques', p. 204. J. Kaplow, 'Sur la population flottante de Paris à la fin de l'ancien régime', *A.H.R.F.*, 39 (1967), 1–4.
[73] Y15350, 10 Jan., 16 Jan.

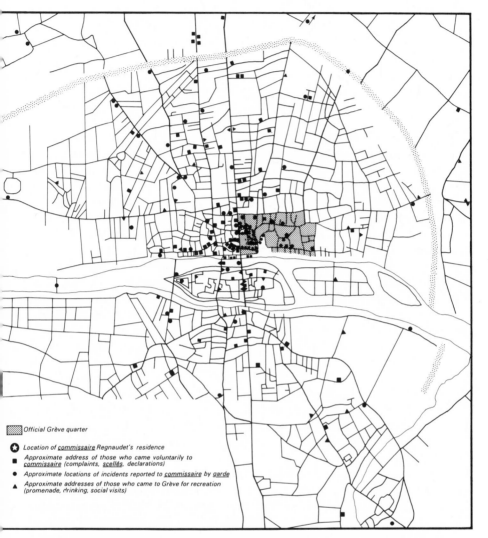

Official Grève quarter

⊛ Location of <u>commissaire</u> Regnaudet's residence

■ Approximate address of those who came voluntarily to <u>commissaire</u> (complaints, <u>scellés</u>, declarations)

● Approximate locations of incidents reported to <u>commissaire</u> by <u>garde</u>

▲ Approximate addresses of those who came to Grève for recreation (promenade, drinking, social visits)

18. Distribution of the 'clients' of *commissaire* Regnaudet, Grève, 1752

Champs, came along the Quai de la Mégisserie. It was easier to take the main roads rather than cutting directly through, along quieter but less familiar streets.[74] The movement of the *garde* betrays the same habit. The incidents reported to the *commissaire* of the Grève took place in many different parts of the city, and were certainly not restricted to his official jurisdiction. It is clear that in

[74] YI5350, 2 Oct., wit. 2.

235

many cases the *garde* headed for the centre instead of across the axes of the city to a *commissaire* who was perhaps nearer (see figure 18). Distances along the major roads seemed shorter; the flow of traffic and general habits of movement around the city led in that direction.

There were good reasons why they did, quite apart from the fact that the central area was on the way to many other parts of the city. Many official and administrative buildings were sited there: the Hôtel de Ville and the Arsenal de la Ville; further over the Châtelet and the Grenier à Sel. The Monnaie and the Ferme du Tabac were near St Germain l'Auxerrois, and the Hôtel des Postes was a bit further north, just off the rue St Honoré. The offices of many of the trades corporations were also to be found in this part of Paris: those of the *maîtresses lingères* and of the *épiciers* were next to Ste Opportune; that of the goldsmiths was in the rue des Lavandières adjoining the Grenier à Sel. In the early 1750s the curriers and the *tabletiers* both had theirs in the Place de Grève, the iron-merchants met above a wineshop in the rue de la Vannerie, the joiners assembled on the Quai de la Mégisserie, and the pin-makers had their *bureau* in the rue St Germain l'Auxerrois.[75] The commercial role of the city centre also brought in many people. Both wholesalers and individual customers came to get coal from the ports. The Quai de la Mégisserie was the main centre for ironware, and flowers were sold there on Wednesdays. The meat trade was concentrated near the Châtelet. The Cimetière St Jean was the site of an important market, and every Monday the Place de Grève was crowded with stalls selling old clothes.[76]

All this brought much traffic into the city centre. The crowds were further swollen by the entertainments which were on offer. There were some of very wide interest, such as the occasional executions in the Place de Grève and the firework displays in front of the Hôtel de Ville or on the *quais*. Others were on a smaller scale: puppet shows on the *quais* and in the Place de Grève: billiard-rooms and wineshops. Along the ports and the nearby streets, too, were concentrations of prostitutes.[77] And of course the crowds and the animation were in themselves an attraction, especially on holidays and in the evenings.

The streets of the city centre, therefore, more than any other area of eighteenth-century Paris, were always full of people, many of them visitors or short-term residents. These streets remained animated late into the night, all year round, as is clear from the reports of the *garde* and the activities of the *commissaire* himself, which continued into the early hours of the morning. This is quite different from the Faubourg St Antoine or the Luxembourg quarter, where there were few calls after eleven o'clock. Disputes in the central quarters

[75] Y15363. Y15350, 12 Oct., 31 July, 24 Aug., 2 Dec.
[76] B.N. Ms. Fr. 6687, f. 157, 28 Nov. 1788. *Mémoires des intendants*, vol. 1, pp. 671–2. Mercier, *Tableau*, vol. 2, pp. 266–8.
[77] Y15350, 21 Oct. Y14484, 25 May, interr. 2. Restif, *Tableau de la vie et des moeurs*, quoted in Cobb, *Reactions*, p. 141.

Table 8. *Disputes in Grève quarter, 1752: relationships and locations*

	Master–Journeyman/Apprentice		Neighbours		Same occupation only	Seller–Client		Strangers	Other?	TOTAL	%
	Family	Apprentice	same occupation only	and same occupation			and neighbour				
Workplace of both parties (interior)		6								6	5.6
Apartment or shop of one or both (interior)	6	1	7	1	1	3	1	4	1	25	23.1
Courtyard or stair (house of one or both)			7	1				2		10	9.3
Street: near house or workplace of one or both		2	8		2	5	1	2	1	21	19.4
street elsewhere	1	1		1	3	7				13	12.0
Wineshop				2	6	13	4	2	3	30	27.8
Other					2	1				3	2.8
Total										108	100.0

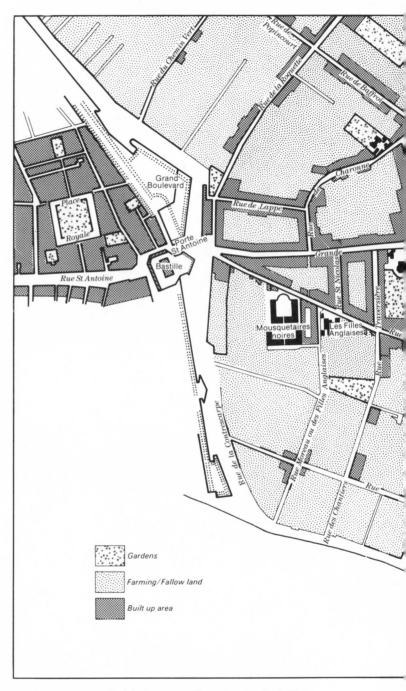

19. The Faubourg St Antoine, 1773 (from the map by Jaillot)

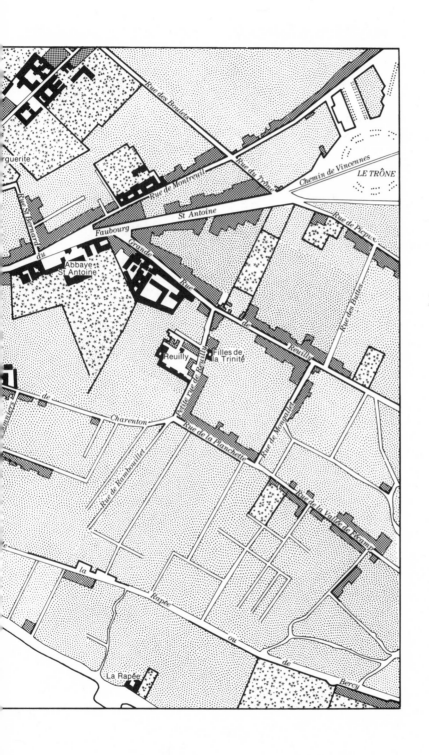

and in the major roads leading to them occurred up to midnight and as late as two in the morning, whereas in the more peripheral areas there were once again few after eleven (see graphs 1, 2 and 3, pp. 150–2). In the morning, on the other hand, the situation is reversed, with proportionately fewer disputes, fewer mentions of people in the wineshops, and fewer reports of the *garde*, a reflection of the different type of people with whom the police had to deal. Much of the city centre belonged as much to outsiders as to the local population. This is also visible in the types of disputes reported. Of those which took place in the street, a fifth were between people who were strangers both to each other and to the quarter (table 8). Almost as many again involved both locals and outsiders. Disputes between neighbours, on the other hand, took place mostly within the house, and where they did happen in the street it was invariably right outside. There are only one or two cases of *tapage* (the word *bacchanale* does not seem to have been used in this area), which as we have seen was a device used exclusively within the neighbourhood. There are, needless to say, no *charivaris*. The same relative poverty of neighbourhood sociability emerges if we look at the people who are mentioned in the wineshops of the city centre. Of seventy-six individuals who appear in the *cabarets* in and around the Grève quarter, and whose addresses are given, a third lived locally: in the quarters of the Luxembourg, the Faubourg St Antoine, and the Place Maubert (which included the Faubourg St Marcel), the figure is two-thirds. The locals who did go to the wineshops of the central area were not normally with neighbours or family but overwhelmingly with friends or workmates. There were also fewer women than in the other areas of the city looked at: eight out of one hundred and sixty-six people mentioned. As I have suggested, women went to wineshops largely in a family or neighbourhood context. In much of the city centre the local community was not sovereign, unlike in other areas of the city where it dominated street and wineshop alike.

In marked contrast to the city centre is the Faubourg St Antoine, thanks to its location, topography, and social composition. A *faubourg* was by definition outside the city proper, and the Faubourg St Antoine was particularly distinct. The bird's-eye-view maps of the eighteenth century, which mark buildings and physical features, show it branching off from the Porte St Antoine and otherwise almost entirely cut off from the built-up area. The wide boulevards marked it off from the quarters of the Marais and St Paul, while the remains of the ramparts and the ditches of the Arsenal continued to defend the eastern side of the city. The Bastille guarded the narrow gateway at the end of the rue St Antoine. To the south lay the river, with no bridges before the Ile St Louis; and north of the rue des Amandiers the green fields and gardens reached in to the backs of the newly constructed town houses along the boulevard. Unlike most areas of the city the Faubourg St Antoine had clear limits: it was certainly not possible to enter it from Paris without realizing that one had left one quarter and come into another.

This distinctness was maintained in its legal and administrative status. It lay almost entirely within the one vast parish of Ste Marguerite. The Châtelet, while formally attaching it to the St Antoine quarter, in practice recognized its independence by assigning it a *commissaire* of its own. The activities of a section of the *garde* stationed at the entrance to the Grande Rue were also confined to the *faubourg*. Only the Hôtel de Ville refused to recognize it as a unit, dividing it between the Place Royale and Hôtel de Ville quarters. When the electoral boundaries were being decided in 1789, however, the frontiers of the *faubourg* were respected and it was divided into two districts, north and south of the Grande Rue.

The Faubourg St Antoine also had a peculiar legal status. Louis XIV had allowed all artisans and merchants living in the Grande Rue du Faubourg to set up shops without having the *maîtrise* (master's certificate), except for those of the *Six Corps*, and permission was required from the *lieutenant général* before the corporations could conduct their normal inspections in company of a *commissaire* anywhere in the *faubourg*.[78] This gave its boundaries real legal significance.

Exemption from the *maîtrise* also added to the relative social homogeneity common to all areas outside the ring of the boulevards. The social elite of Paris lived in the city proper, very few people of any importance having more than a country house in any of the northern or eastern *faubourgs*. Among the marriage contracts of 1749, eighty-seven per cent of those for the Faubourg St Antoine involved men in artisanal production or commerce, as against fifty-one per cent in the parish of St Eustache, forty-six per cent in that of St Paul, and thirty-one per cent in St Roch. Male and female domestic servants alike, whose distribution and number are a good guide to levels of wealth and ostentation, were fewer than in any other quarter of the city. So were families employing servants, although the number paying the *capitation* tax was similar to other areas.[79] There was a little cluster of well-off people in the streets nearest the Porte St Antoine, as if in exile but camped outside the gates. It is an expression of their feeling of isolation (although perhaps also of the availability of suitable accommodation) that the three *commissaires* appointed to the quarter in the second half of the century all lived at the very western end of their domain: two in the rue St Nicolas, and one in the Place St Antoine itself.[80] The Faubourg St Antoine was economically and socially the most homogeneous of the quarters of eighteenth-century Paris.

These characteristics of geographic distinctness and of relative social homogeneity had important consequences for the evolution of the local community in the Faubourg St Antoine. It was insulated from many of the developments which in other areas of the city were weakening or changing it. The sense of quarter

[78] Gobert, 'Enfants trouvés', 6 (1936), 134–48, and 15 (1938), 260–81 (p. 144). Y13728, de Sartine to *syndics*, 7 Oct. 1767.

[79] Gobert, 'Enfants trouvés', 6 (1936), 144. Daumard and Furet, *Structures*, p. 53. Expilly, *Dictionnaire*, vol. 5, pp. 401–2.

[80] *Almanach Royal*. Y10994, 21 Sept., wit. 5.

and of belonging to a particular area was facilitated by the easily definable physical limits of the *faubourg*. The inhabitants thought of it as a unit, distinct from the rest of the city, to the extent that one man living in the rue de Lappe could say that when the incident of which he was a witness had occurred he had been 'returning from Paris'. Some stolen asparagus was offered for sale 'in the Faubourg St Antoine'; a young woman is described as an 'inhabitant of the Faubourg St Antoine'.[81] The same idea of the *faubourg* as a distinct unit appears in police correspondence during the Réveillon riots of 1789. 'There is considerable tumult in the Faubourg St Antoine', directed against two 'citizens of the *faubourg*', wrote the *commissaire* Le Rat.[82]

The Faubourg St Antoine was thought of not only as a physical unit but also a social one. During the Revolution the taking of the Bastille came to be regarded as the work of a somehow unanimous *faubourg*, and pamphlets abound with titles like *Les Lauriers du faubourg St-Antoine ou le Prix de la Bastille renversée*; *Les Casques de Ségovie. Eloge des habitants des faubourgs St-Antoine et St-Marcel*; *Réponse du faubourg St-Antoine à la dénonciation qui lui a été addressée ... par le faubourg St-Marceau*.[83] *Faubourg* was therefore used in a similar way to *quartier* – a term which was also quite current there – but was distinct from the rest of the city in a way that the central quarters could not be. (As the above examples show, this also applied to the Faubourg St Marcel.)

The maintenance of a sense of quarter was thus facilitated by its having a physical basis which did not exist in the city centre. I should emphasize, in making this point, that it by no means implies the existence of only one local community in the entire *faubourg*. It was like a small town, a geographic and social whole, but containing a series of overlapping neighbourhoods, each street, cluster of houses, or perhaps each wineshop or bakery lying at the heart of its own local community. Within the *faubourg* people identified with 'La Croix Faubin', with 'La Rapée', with the old house and village at Reuilly, or with their own street. But they were all *faubouriens*, and the clear distinction between the city within and without the walls, preserved in the election arrangements of 1789, gave them an added sense of local identity.

Relative social homogeneity also meant that the withdrawal of the local elites was both later and less immediately damaging than in other parts of the city. The social elite of the *faubourgs* was not composed of magistrates or nobles but of well-to-do merchants, people whose rejection of community values and sociability was as we have seen largely an eighteenth-century phenomenon. There was thus greater and more enduring unanimity, less conflict with elite values, fewer

---

[81] Y10994, 21 Sept., wit. 5. Y14436, 12 Jan., interr. and wit. 1, 10 June, 18 Dec.
[82] B.N. J. de F. 1103, ff. 141–6.
[83] *Les Lauriers* [n.d.] July 1789. *Les Casques*, Paris, 1789 (B.N. 8° Lb³⁹ 3914). *Réponse* (B.N. 8° Lb³⁹ 9023). *Liste*, Paris, 1791 (B.N. 8° Lb³⁹ 5505).

and less powerful people to exert direct control or indirect influence against popular celebrations and boisterous collective sanctions.

The other forces of change also had less effect on the outskirts of the city than in the centre. Further from the centres of power and authority, these areas could at times escape the attention of government and police, and in any case concerned them less. The streets of the *faubourgs* were less congested than those of the city proper, both because they were on the whole wider and because there was less traffic. As far as public order went, the central market and the ports were seen as the major trouble-spots and it was these that occupied official attention.[84] The inhabitants of the Faubourg St Antoine, the only *faubourg* to have a *commissaire* of its own, nevertheless had to seek him at the extremity nearest the city. For much of the century the only section of the *garde* in the area was at the city entrance to the Grande Rue du Faubourg, hardly in a convenient place to intervene quickly throughout the vast suburb it was in theory patrolling. The *faubourgs* were less policed than most other parts of the city and in the case of the Faubourg St Antoine this may even have extended to the corporations. Less police presence in turn meant that greater community self-regulation was necessary and possible. It is no coincidence that all the examples of *charivaris* which I have found came from the *faubourgs*.

Not only was it protected from the authorities, but the location of the *faubourg* somewhat shielded it from invasion by a transient, highly mobile population. Residential mobility remained very high, but there are some indications that it may not have equalled that in other parts of the city, or have been of the same character. The figures for intra-urban mobility given by F. Rousseau-Vigneron in his study of the Section of the Place des Fédérés adjoining the Faubourg St Antoine show an unexpectedly low rate of movement from the *faubourg* into the city. Of 1,666 men whose *cartes de sûreté* bear a previous address in another part of Paris 10.6 per cent came from the Arsenal and 7.5 per cent from the Mont-de-Piété (Homme Armé?) Sections, those adjoining to the south and west, but only 9 per cent from the three populous Sections of the Faubourg St Antoine put together. This evidence is far from conclusive, but we do know that a very high proportion of residential mobility took place within the *faubourg* itself.[85] In the absence of a detailed breakdown by occupation we can only guess at its nature. The *faubourg* was certainly an important job-market for journeymen, particularly in the furniture trades, but not for the unskilled and semi-skilled workers or the domestic servants who made up much of the floating population of the city. There was seasonal work for sawyers in the timber yards along the river and for agricultural labourers in the fields and vineyards, particularly to the north and east of the *faubourg*. There were a couple of lodging houses in the rue Ste Marguerite and some more scattered along the Grande

---

[84] Cobb, *Police*, pp. 16, 18.
[85] Rousseau-Vigneron, 'Place des Fédérés', p. 204. Sévegrand, 'Popincourt', p. 64.

Rue, but nothing like the concentrations to be found near the ports and the Place de Grève or around the Halles. The most mobile residential groups in the Faubourg St Antoine were the seasonal agricultural workers and the *gagne deniers* who came, presumably mostly from the country, to spend a year or so there before moving on in search of more secure employment.[86]

But more important still for the local community was protection from people just passing through. This too was afforded by the location and character of the Faubourg St Antoine, and to a lesser extent by those of the other *faubourgs*. Most of the city's traffic was of course commercial, and on working days there was certainly much coming and going to and from the city. The major manufactories of the Faubourg St Antoine supplied retailers all over Paris and beyond: most notably the *manufacture des glaces* (mirrors) of the rue de Reuilly but also the *manufacture de vernis* (polish), the *manufacture de velours* (velvet), and the *manufacture des terres d'Angleterre* (porcelain), all in the rue de Charenton. Beer, textiles, and of course furniture of all kinds were produced by numerous smaller enterprises and sold to merchants and distributers throughout Paris. In addition, a number of artisans who had shops in the central business areas had their workshops in the *faubourg*: in my sample there is a rope-maker with a shop in the rue St Denis, a potter whose main retail outlet was at the Halle aux Poissons, and numerous bakers who took their bread to the central market.[87] Market gardeners and florists sold their wares in and around the Halles. There were also some trades which depended on goods brought from other quarters. The textile industry of the *faubourg* used ribbons and buttons made in the St Denis area north of the Halles. Some raw materials came from the Faubourg St Marcel: clay and possibly charcoal.[88] Most foodstuffs, of course, came from the central market.

There was therefore extensive commercial contact with other parts of the city. The *faubourg* was familiar to a wide range of merchants and their employees, certainly to errand-boys and to those involved in transport. Yet it differed from the more central areas in that those who came were essentially those who had business there. Except for long-distance waggoners and travellers it was not on the way to anywhere else (and people and goods travelling along the Seine or Marne valleys for any distance were more likely to come by water than by road anyway). Like the other *faubourgs* it had little to offer tourists, of either the foreign or the Parisian variety. For Mercier's chapter on the Faubourg St Antoine we must wait until volume nine of his *Tableau*, and even then most of the two pages he devotes to it are taken up with his reflections on the Fronde.[89] The Faubourg St Marcel makes it into volume one, where we are told that it is a place of refuge for

---

[86] Sévegrand, 'Popincourt', pp. 47, 60, 63.
[87] Y10994, 19 Dec. Y11239, 19 Dec. Y10994, 5 Apr., 14 May.
[88] Y10994, 19 Jan., 5 Apr., 9 Apr.   [89] Mercier, *Tableau*, vol. 9, pp. 258–60.

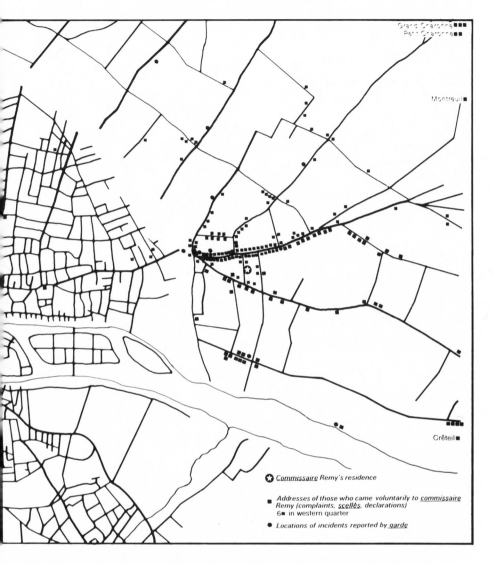

Grand Charonne ■■■
Petit Charonne ■■

Montreuil ■

Créteil ■

✪ *Commissaire* Remy's residence

■ Addresses of those who came voluntarily to *commissaire* Remy (complaints, *scellés*, declarations) 6■ in western quarter

● Locations of incidents reported by *garde*

20. Distribution of the 'clients' of *commissaire* Remy, Faubourg St Antoine, 1752

ruined men, misanthropes, alchemists, madmen, people of independent means but limited horizons, and also a few studious wise men ... who prefer to live totally unknown and separated from the noisy quarters full of entertainments. No one will ever go in search of them in this extremity of the city: if one makes the journey into that country it is through curiosity; nothing obliges you to go there; there is not a single monument to see there; the people bear no similarity to the Parisians.[90]

Despite some exaggeration Mercier is essentially right. The eastern *faubourgs* were out of the way, distinct from the rest of the city. The centres of business and of leisure were situated elsewhere. Mercier does ignore the *guinguettes*, which drew large crowds, although many of their customers came from the *faubourgs*. Nevertheless, our documents also suggest the relative isolation of the Faubourg St Antoine. The 'clientele' of the *commissaire* Remy – those who came to him or who were brought by the *garde* or the *inspecteur* – were overwhelmingly from within the *faubourg* (figure 20, p. 245). Even in the wineshops, the most likely places for passers-by to stop, there were few outsiders.

The Faubourg St Antoine, and to some extent the other *faubourgs*, was somewhat protected from the influx of passers-by and strangers which assailed the city during the eighteenth century. But the maintenance of a strong local community was also encouraged by certain aspects of the internal topography of the area, shared by nearly all the *faubourgs*. One of the typical features of pre-industrial suburbs is the branch-like network of major streets – in this case the rues de Charonne, de Charenton, de la Roquette, de Montreuil, de Reuilly, and of course the Grande Rue du Faubourg – all running in roughly the same direction and all eventually leading up to the city gate: the Porte St Antoine. There are a number of streets running north and south, but none of them crosses the Grande Rue. The rue Traversière is the only one which does not stop at the rue de Charenton; and to the north only two streets; the rue de Popincourt/de Baffroi/St Bernard and the rue de la Muette/des Boulets, lead directly across the major east–west thoroughfares. It was therefore impossible to go very far without taking, for some distance, one of these main streets. To go into the city the normal route from anywhere in the *faubourg* was through the Place St Antoine.

This had a number of important social effects. It contributed to the unity of the *faubourg* by giving all its inhabitants, to some degree, a shared physical space, although this was significant only as long as the population remained small enough for people to know each other. The Porte St Antoine was particularly important as a centre of sociability, for the *revendeuses* and stall-keepers who clustered around it saw everyone. An eloquent example is provided by a case of theft and a subsequent interrogation. A man living in the Grande Rue du Faubourg, returning home for a bite to eat at about two in the afternoon, found his door forced and a number of things stolen. His wife, having to go into the city that afternoon, naturally went through the Porte St Antoine where she stopped to tell the story to a flower-seller, 'la nommée St Germain'. Returning 'from the city' at about five she again chatted to the flower-seller, who in the meantime had seen a

---

[90] Mercier, *Tableau*, vol. 1, pp. 268–9.

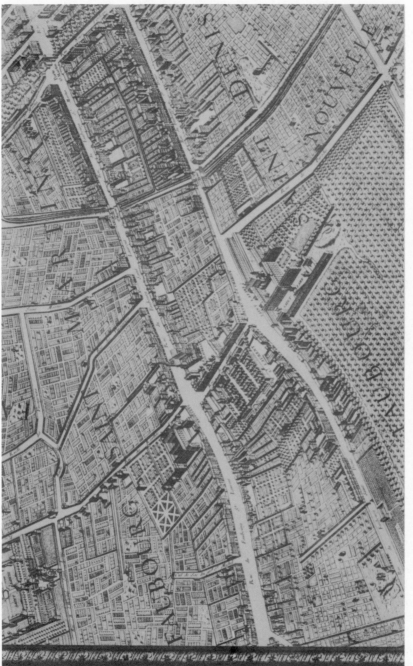

21. The Faubourg St Denis, from Plan Turgot (1739), showing low scattered houses of *faubourgs*

22. Houses in the *faubourgs*: corner of the rue du Pot de Fer and the rue Neuve Ste Geneviève, Faubourg St Marcel

man go past with a bulging sack which he had said was full of goods he had just bought very cheaply. Having found out the man's address the following day, whether from the same street-seller or from someone else is not indicated, the woman traced him to a nearby beer-shop. When she saw him she immediately recognized him as having on at least one occasion sold some things to her husband, a fact which confirmed her suspicions. Only then did she have recourse to the police. The man, arrested by the *garde* and brought before the *commissaire*, turned out to be a rag-merchant, a native of the Faubourg St Antoine. He in turn described his movements the previous day. Together with

23. Houses in the *faubourgs*: corner of the rue des Postes and the rue Neuve Ste Geneviève, Faubourg St Marcel

his wife he had taken a waggon to Villeneuve St George, outside Paris, to collect some rags, returning by 9 a.m. via Bercy. He had then sold the rags near the Temple, before going to the Halle where he had bought some clothes. Passing through the Porte St Antoine on his way home he had been hailed by the flower-seller, who asked him why he didn't bring her goods any more, to which he replied that she didn't pay him well enough.[91] This incident, which ended with the release of the rag-merchant, gives us an inkling of the network of acquaintances which a humble street-seller stationed at a key point in the city could develop. The Porte St Antoine was a particularly important spot because everyone went through at one time or another, and, because it was a bottleneck, people were often forced to stop.

Other topographic characteristics of this and of most other *faubourgs* also contributed to creating and maintaining a strong local community. The houses were on the whole much smaller and more spread out than in the city centre,

[91] Y10994, 10 Aug.

249

24. Older houses in the Faubourg St Marcel, dwarfed by later buildings: rue Broca
(formerly rue de Loursine)

making it easier to get to know everyone in a given street or neighbourhood. In the Popincourt and Quinze Vingt Sections, the population density was about eighty inhabitants to the hectare, as against 500 to 1,300 for the city centre.[92] According to the Plan Turgot, even in the most built-up area of the Faubourg St Antoine ninety per cent of the houses were of three storeys or less, sixty per cent of two storeys or less; whereas in the Section des Lombards, in the city centre, only some thirteen per cent were of three storeys or less.[93] Eighteenth- and nineteenth-century engravings of the Faubourg St Antoine show houses of two,

---

[92] Roche, *Peuple*, p. 35.   [93] Sévegrand, 'Popincourt', p. 25. Perrin, 'Entassement', p. 69.

The evolution of the local community

three, and four storeys, the latter more common in the longer-urbanized and more commercial parts of the Grande Rue du Faubourg. Elsewhere, space and cheaper land allowed lower, longer constructions, many of rural type.[94] The Plan Turgot also shows that there were rarely residential buildings behind those on the street except in the area closest to the Porte St Antoine. Behind were gardens and fields, which in places came right up to the street. The buildings were therefore more spread out: the whole Popincourt Section contained fewer houses in the Year II than did the tiny inner-city Section des Lombards. The whole rue de Charonne, a little longer than the rue St Denis, then contained eighty-four houses: the stretch of the rue St Denis between the rue aux Ours and the rue St Jacques de la Boucherie, less than half its total length, had one hundred and seven houses on one side alone.[95]

The impression of openness and space that this gives is a little misleading, for some thirty per cent of the population of the Popincourt Section was concentrated in its south-west corner. The houses in this area were just as crowded as those in the worst sectors of the inner city. The rue de Lappe, with its twenty-five low houses, sheltered 900 people in the Year II, almost the same number as lived in the forty-nine or so houses of the central rue de la Vieille Monnaie.[96] It was nevertheless over twice as long. Crowded the houses may have been, but the population of the *faubourg* was distributed, even in its most cramped sector, over a far larger area. Most importantly for the local community, there were fewer people in any given stretch of street, in any given neighbourhood, making it possible to know more of the locals.

Furthermore, the structure of the houses actually pushed people into the street. The absence of secondary dwellings behind the first line of houses meant that there was no significant population living off the street, no series of courtyards and passages to compete with the public thoroughfare as a focus of neighbourhood sociability. A high proportion of the inhabitants overlooked the thoroughfare, rather than some dingy courtyard. In many streets of the *faubourgs*, too, the ground floors were not taken up with shops: people lived right on the street. The large number of one- and two-storey houses in any case brought people closer to the street than was possible in the city centre, where an increasing number of the inhabitants lived under the rooftops.[97]

The street therefore remained the forum for neighbourhood sociability much longer in the *faubourgs* than in the busy roads of the centre. Even in the

[94] *Attaque du faubourg St Antoine*, engraving by Berthault from a drawing by Girardet, [1789]. *Fusillade au fauxbourg St Antoine, le 28 avril 1789*, engraved by Pélicier and Niguet, both B.N. Est. Va 295 fol., t. 3. *La Barrière de Vincennes*, engraved by Mercier, B.N. Est. Va 295, fol., t. 3.
[95] Sévegrand, 'Popincourt', p. 24. Perrin, 'Entassement', pp. 66–7, 69.
[96] Sévegrand, 'Popincourt', p. 25. Perrin, 'Entassement', p. 75.
[97] Roche, *Peuple*, p. 116; R. Arnette, 'Les Classes inférieures parisiennes d'après les inventaires après décès au XVIIIe siècle', unpub. *maîtrise* thesis, Paris VII, 1977, cited in Roche, *Peuple*, p. 114, n. 36.

Table 9. *Disputes in Faubourg St Antoine, 1752: relationships and locations*

		Master-Journeyman/	Neighbours			Same workplace (different trade)	Seller-Client						
	Family	Apprentice	only occupation	and same occupation	same occupation		only neighbour	and neighbour	Strangers	Other	?	TOTAL	%
Workplace of both parties (interior)	1	3			3							7	6.4
Apartment or shop of one or both (interior)	5	1	1				1					8	7.3
Courtyard or stair (house of one or both)	1	1	10	5			1					17	15.5
Street: near house or workplace of one or both	2	3	17	5	5	2	1	1	3	4	1	44	40.0
street elsewhere	2	1	3	2				1	3			12	10.9
Church			1									1	0.9
Wineshop		3	3	3	2			1		1		13	11.8
Other (fields, country, garden, friend's house)	1		2	1			1		3			8	7.3
Total												110	100.1[a]

[a] Percentages do not add up to 100 because rounded off to one decimal place.

252

much-frequented Grande Rue du Faubourg St Antoine the enormous width of the street made it safer and more pleasant to stand and talk there. In my sample of disputes from the Faubourg St Antoine about half take place in the street, the vast majority between neighbours (table 9). This contrasts with the central quarters of the Right Bank, where most disputes between neighbours take place in the courtyards and stairways, the street being more commonly the location of altercations between strangers (table 8).

In the Faubourg St Antoine and to some extent in the other areas outside the city proper, everything conspired to maintain the local community: physical isolation, social homogeneity, the shape and size of the streets and of the houses. In the city centre, on the other hand, urbanization was most advanced, the police most active, and the effects on the community most marked.

But there does exist another model for the evolution of social organization in the city centre. So far I have considered local communities based primarily on neighbourhood, but we have seen that in certain areas and streets work ties combined with those of locality, and very often of family as well, to create a particularly strong sense of community. The place where this happened on the largest scale was the central market, and the example of the Halles shows how this kind of community could for a long time survive the changes I have described.

The central market was indisputably in the city centre. It was well and truly within the ancient walls built by Philippe-Auguste, and by the mid sixteenth century, if not before, was as heavily built up as any part of Paris.[98] It lay at the junction of two major roads, the rue Montmartre and the rue Montorgueil, with the rue St Denis and the rue St Honoré framing two sides of the quarter. In the eighteenth century it had many houses of six and seven storeys, although also many lower buildings of an older style. Because of its position in the city, but above all because of its commercial function, it drew large numbers of people from all over Paris and from the countryside as well, so that on market days the streets were crowded from early in the morning. Many of those who came, however, were not strangers but regular clients and suppliers, people who were well known and who in a sense formed part of the local community.

I argued in chapter 3 that the Halles contained a series of overlapping and very strong communities based both on occupation and on locality. The Dames de la Halle, the *forts*, the *fruitier-orangers* and the *fripiers* were all extremely close-knit groups, very often bound by ties of family and *pays* as well as by work, all of them at the same time closely connected with all of the others. This is reflected in the papers of the senior *commissaire* of the quarter. His clientele was very largely composed of people who were attached to or who depended on the market. A third of all the disputes brought to him took place in the Halle itself and their timetable is influenced by that of the market. They begin at four in the

[98] Plan dit 'de la Tapisserie', *c.* 1540–60.

morning, unlike the Grève where on the whole they take place later (graphs 1, 2 and 3, pp. 150–2). Two-thirds of the people mentioned in the wineshops of the quarter lived or worked within a couple of blocks. Unlike those of the Grève and the riverside quarters, the wineshops of the Halles area catered primarily to a local clientele.

The Halles area provides the most prominent and best-documented example of a local community strongly based on work and family ties, as well as on neighbourhood, but it is not the only one. There were the other market communities in the Place Maubert, at St Germain des Prés, La Vallée, the Marché Neuf, the market next to the abbey of St Antoine, and a number of others. There were the riverside communities, although because the ports and river-banks came into the jurisdiction of the Hôtel de Ville they appear less in the papers of the *commissaires au Châtelet*. Another was centred on the Grande Boucherie and the Vieille Place aux Veaux where the butchers congregated; and further afield the community based on the Gobelins factory in the Faubourg St Marcel. Even those in the most urbanized, most policed parts of the city retained much of their character, largely because they were not solely based on the relatively fragile tie of neighbourhood, which could be undermined by high residential and day-to-day mobility, but on a combination of overlapping social bonds.

It was not only because of these multiple bonds that they remained strong, however. Many of them were not dependent on the street: I have pointed out that the shift of stalls from the street to more enclosed market-places strengthened the market communities, at least in the short term, by protecting them from the traffic and by concentrating particular occupational groups. The local community could dominate the market-place long after the streets of the city centre had been lost to it. Furthermore, where it was largely based on work and family it was all along more socially homogeneous than the community of an ordinary street. The Halles and the ports had never really known the active participation of the urban elites, except perhaps for the occasional wealthy merchant: the popularity of the *poissarde* literature among the upper classes indicates just what a foreign world it was to them in the eighteenth century. The withdrawal of the elites therefore did not greatly affect these groups. They were protected, on several counts, from developments which elsewhere were transforming the local community.

We are now in a position to analyse the effects of the various changes which were taking place and to trace the general evolution of the local community through the eighteenth century and beyond. Urbanization did profoundly affect it: a rapid influx of newcomers and the presence of large numbers of strangers – associated with population growth – changed the patterns of sociability, particularly in the central districts. But it was ultimately not population growth alone which had the most devastating effects. It was the growth in residential mobility and in the quantity of traffic, both pedestrian and vehicular, which had the most dramatic impact. These were characteristics of a particular form of urbanization. Paris had long been a big city, but it was the breaking-down of the barriers between the quarters, improvements in transport and communication, the formation of wider markets, and the decline in the importance of the quarter which to a very great extent underlay increasing mobility. All of these things were associated with the rise of the state, itself inseparable from the growing separation between elite and popular sociability. Population growth and economic change, each to some extent a product of the other, also helped to create a need for a centralized state system, but were in turn facilitated by it. The development of the state and especially of the police not only encouraged immigration by improving roads, communication and supply, but also increased the traffic flow by changing the physical structure of the city. The police intervened to clear the streets and to suppress the more boisterous forms of popular celebration and of collective sanctions disapproved of by an elite which appealed to different models and different values. The withdrawal of the elites also had a direct effect by narrowing the social basis of the community and thus breaking the effective unanimity on which collective sanctions and community self-regulation depended.

All these factors are thus interconnected, each touching the community directly but at the same time influencing the way that other developments affected it. All of them created new conditions to which it had to adapt. Some of its functions were taken over by the police or by other organs of the state. It gradually lost its role of mainstream socialization and culture transmission, and its central part in maintaining order, but took on new social functions: the integration of newcomers, psychological protection against the increasing anonymity of the urban environment. As in other places it became an instrument for the defence of local interests against central government.[99] What had once been at the heart of local 'government' was becoming a source of conservatism, opposed to mainstream values.

But, if the community represented local interests, it no longer spoke for all local interests. The progressive moral and subsequently physical withdrawal of the elites, followed in the eighteenth century by the gradual distancing of the better-off shopkeepers and tradesmen, made the local community ever more socially restricted and homogeneous. We have seen that even in the mid eighteenth century it remained strongest in the areas where there was already a high level of social and occupational homogeneity. With the spread of new individualistic ideals of privacy and delicacy in family and social behaviour, and of competition in business, the collective values of the local community, no longer dominant, became a sort of 'sub-culture'. With geographic segregation the gap widened still further, its extent apparent in the 'discovery' by the late

[99] Bercé, *Fête*, p. 190.

nineteenth-century middle and upper classes of the strange and alien world of the lower orders, through the work of men like Zola (or Mayhew in London). Parts of the *Tableau* painted by Mercier were already foreign to some of his readers. The working-class communities of the nineteenth and twentieth centuries, recently rediscovered by historians and sociologists, were the heirs of the local communities of the eighteenth century. Bethnal Green was a direct descendant.[100] So, too, were the quarter-based communities of Paris which in 1871 proved incapable of co-operating to resist the invasion of the Versaillais, withdrawing to their home territory – in some cases eighteenth-century suburbs – where one by one their barricades fell. In the new areas and the new cities there was no such direct link, but immigrant communities, just like those of eighteenth-century Paris, developed in response to the same conditions.

The continued existence of local communities in working-class areas may also help to explain the development of class consciousness. Geographic social segregation led to a clear separation between *beaux quartiers* and working-class areas, and during the nineteenth century neighbourhood identity took on a social content which it had not had in the eighteenth century. The socially restricted local community, which could become a unifying force against outside authority, could similarly unify working people against outsiders of another class. The debt owed by nineteenth-century co-operatives and trade organizations to the corporate trade institutions of the eighteenth century is obvious and has claimed much attention. The role of the local community is perhaps less evident, yet it too was based on collective values and played an important part in maintaining them.

The pre-industrial local community has a long history, as have its *fêtes* and its 'popular' culture. Can we speak, as Y-M. Bercé does of these, of its decline because of lack of intellectual support; of its 'marginalization', its becoming restricted to 'marginal' social groups and 'islands forgotten by modernization'?[101] It is true that locally based, self-regulating communities are not a form of social organization that is normally found in a highly centralized modern state. Nor do collective forms and norms match the highly individualistic values that most of the Western world espouses. Non-geographic communities, with their own systems of constraints and social pressure, have with technological and economic, political, and social change replaced those of the neighbourhood. But the definition of 'modernity' changes with the times. It may be that the dwindling of the world's resources and the reaction against an anonymous, centralized state will ensure the continued survival and evolution of an urban local community.

---

100 The local communities of the East End of London before the First World War were strikingly similar to those of the Faubourg St Antoine in the eighteenth century: E. Ross, 'Survival Networks'. On working-class communities in twentieth-century Paris see A. Vieille, 'Relations parentales et relations de voisinage chez les ménages ouvriers de la Seine', *Cahiers internationaux de sociologie*, new series, 17 (July–Dec. 1954), 140–53.

101 Bercé, *Fête*, p. 190.

Conclusion

From the point of view of neighbourhood ties Parisian society was not, as it is so often portrayed in the works of contemporary observers and of historians, chaotic, unstructured, and anonymous. It was relatively easy for provincials to become part of the city, and not simply through forming communities of their own. Nor did its behavioural norms escape them. Parisian society was very open to those who wanted to belong and who were not prevented from doing so by their work or mobility. It was this very openness, in fact, which gave contemporaries, accustomed to a more closed village society, the impression of anonymity and lack of structure.

The presence of local communities must be taken into account if the history of eighteenth-century Paris is to make sense. They were what enabled many people to survive from day to day, in the absence of welfare services and of any adequate system of poor relief. In a city where a significant proportion of the population could read only with difficulty, and where the press was heavily censored, the existence of neighbourhood communities helps to explain the rapid spread of news and rumour. The court records make more sense if it is recognized that the bulk of the accused found themselves on trial precisely because they did not benefit from the assistance of neighbours: the majority of those judged by the Châtelet lived in lodging-houses or in *chambres garnies*, moved frequently, often changed jobs. They owed their arrest partly to this very fact, and were sure to be imprisoned if there were no one to speak for them before the *commissaire*. Similarly, the presence of the local community helps to explain the pattern of abandonments of children, clearly related to poverty, yet far more common in the city centre than in the equally poor areas of the *faubourgs*.[1]

There are also implications for the major political events of the period. There has not been space here to examine the role of the local community in the Revolution, or even in the *guerre des farines* of 1775. Other research has shown, however, that those who took part in 1775 and in the great revolutionary insurrections were nearly all well established in the city, quite distinct from the unfortunates who normally appeared before the courts. The local solidarity and

---

[1] Petrovitch, in Abbiateci *et al.*, *Criminalité*, pp. 241–3. Farge, *Délinquance*, pp. 78, 123, 126, 152–88. C. Delasselle, 'Les Enfants abandonnés à Paris au dix-huitième siècle', *Annales: E.S.C.*, 30 (1975), 187–218 (pp. 208–12).

the norms of behaviour which mobilized people against *huissiers* or against the police were also to a great extent what mobilized them in the years of the Revolution. Even the Sections, larger and more formal political institutions, were for the most part based on local ties and displayed a highly parochial mentality.[2]

It would be interesting to look at other eighteenth-century cities in the same light. Paris was of course larger than most, and the pattern of urbanization was in some respects peculiar: the style of architecture made for very high population density and conditioned the locations of neighbourhood sociability. It had its own cultural traditions, embodied in the roles accorded to men and women, in the absence of organized sports, and in the precocious development of the police. Yet in general terms the conditions of life were probably typical of most eighteenth-century European cities, and people probably responded in similar ways.

In so far as Paris was typical, therefore, the presence of the local community has clear implications for the study of social organization in the eighteenth-century city. Historians generally assume that social ties in a place like Paris were 'horizontal'. That is, the population can be divided into status groups, generally defined by income or by rank, whose members throughout the city had more in common with each other than with people belonging to any other group. However in terms of everyday sociability and solidarity, as we have seen, the primary distinctions were not between employers and employees, between skilled and unskilled, or between particular trade sectors. The division here is between those who belonged to the local community and those who did not. It is a difference in the way of life, in attitudes and in forms of behaviour. This is not to say that other elements of social discrimination were unimportant, or that they conflicted with the local community. Family, work, and place of origin could all be important avenues of integration into the neighbourhood, and indeed could form primary foci of loyalty within the community.

There are further implications in the way people became part of the local community, and in the way it evolved during the eighteenth century: implications for social mobility, for class formation, and for culture transmission. People adopted ideas and values which were relevant to their social and economic situation, while remaining true to inherited traditions. Imitation certainly did play a part: it is possible to trace the diffusion of ideas and of models – just as of card games or bowls – from one part of society to another.[3] But it is not quite as simple as that. When models and forms of behaviour were adopted by individuals and groups, they were at the same time adapted. The model of 'quality', which provided an alternative to birth as a source of social prestige, was

[2] Petrovitch, in Abbiateci *et al.*, *Criminalité*, pp. 259–61. Rudé, *Crowd*, pp. 180–5. Cobb, *Police*, pp. 122, 198–200, and *Reactions*, pp. 116–21.

[3] Agulhon, *Sociabilité*, p. 422.

itself a modification of a noble model. It was by no means a rejection of aristocratic values or status, but rather a marriage of the socially dominant values with other qualities, a redefinition of terms (like *qualité* or *honnêteté*) in which some elements of the noble model were stressed more than others. But nor was it one-way, from the 'superior' social groups to the 'inferior' ones, for a form of the new 'quality' model was eventually adopted by the nobility themselves.

In order to contrast them I have emphasized the features of the 'quality' and of the 'community' value systems which were most opposed. In practice, of course, the two existed side by side. Groups and individuals blended them, taking those elements from each which were relevant to their experience. People could aspire to one model but act according to another. Or they could appeal to different models in different social contexts, adopting one at work and another at home; one with the neighbours and another before the *commissaire*.

The idea of alternative models helps us to understand how social mobility took place, both for groups and for individuals. We have seen that the availability of new models allowed certain elements of Parisian society to withdraw from the local community by giving them alternative values which they could use to justify their actions. The new models involved different forms of sociability, based on the family and the home rather than on the street, between the same sorts of people in different parts of the city rather than within a heterogeneous neighbourhood. People moved socially, both as individuals and as groups, by rejecting or loosening old contacts and ties, while forming and strengthening new ones. For a time both remained, just as people could continue to appeal to different models of behaviour in different contexts. But the nature of the relationships changed: not only did the distribution of people's social network evolve, but so did the obligations and loyalties that each relationship involved.

Finally, the evolution of the local community helps to explain class formation in the city. The successive withdrawal of the upper classes, and during the eighteenth century of the wealthier merchants and master artisans, was more and more reflected in geographic social segregation and helped to transform local solidarity into class solidarity. The potential conflict between landlord and tenant or between employer and worker, no longer tempered by personal contact and neighbourhood solidarity, would come to be perceived as the dominant element in the relationship.

And if the local community did thus play a part in class formation, then the distinction between 'vertical' ties, associated with the locality, and 'horizontal' ones, considered characteristic of a class society, is a false one. For neighbourhood ties could themselves be a source of class consciousness, uniting La Butte Rouge or Belleville–Ménilmontant against the *beaux quartiers*. This was not something that the eighteenth century was to see, although the process was under way, as it had been since the sixteenth century or before. The Revolution was to hasten it dramatically: through legal and institutional change; through the political victory of the city-wide elite over the locally based Sections; and through the bitter social antagonisms which the events of the 1790s created.

The local community, therefore, was not a static and unchanging element in an immobile 'traditional' society, 'marginalized' or destroyed by urbanization and by the rise of the state. It was a dynamic and extremely flexible social form which evolved with, and had its part to play in, a long-term process of historical change which is still under way.

Select Bibliography

A. MANUSCRIPT SOURCES

1. Archives Nationales

F⁷*2502 Census of Place Royale Section, 1791
H747² Papers concerning the municipality of Paris
H1951 Bureau de la Ville de Paris, 1774
H1956 Bureau de la Ville de Paris, 1785
LL836 Deliberations of *fabrique* of Ste Marguerite, 1759–88
LL837 Deliberations of administrators of Confraternity of St Sacrement at Ste Marguerite, 1724–91
LL838 Deliberations of administrators of Confraternity of Ste Marguerite at Ste Marguerite, 1717–86
S7493 Papers concerning finances of Paris parish churches (eighteenth century)
Y9508 Register of people in non-corporate trades, 1767
Y9525 Chambre de Police: Proceedings against journeymen, 1762–6
Y9529 Chambre de Police: Trial dossiers, various years
Y9532–5 Chambre de Police: Trial dossiers, various years
Y9538 Reports of *commissaires* on infringements of police regulations, 1719–25, 1755–7
Y9893 Grand Criminel, September 1780
Y9949 Grand Criminel, May 1785
Y10558 Enquiry into 1775 riots
Y10719–Y16022 Papers of the *commissaires au Châtelet*
y10944 Account-book of commissaire Thiérion, 1756–9
Y10986 Remy, Faubourg St Antoine, 1739
Y10994 Remy, Faubourg St Antoine, 1752
Y11037 Letters and papers, Hugues, Montmartre, *c.* 1779–85
Y11092 Formel, St André des Arts, 1776
Y11239 De Courcy, Halles, 1752
Y11243B Thierry, Cité, June 1756–7
Y11265A Thierry, Cité, January–March 1775
Y11265bisB Thierry, Cité, October–December 1775
Y11267A Thierry, Cité, April–December 1776
Y11283 Carré, Palais Royal, 1788

Y11288 Inventory of papers of de Courcy, 1723–76
Y11440 Papers, Chénon père, Louvre, *c.* 1775–90
Y11468 Doublon, St André des Arts, 1752
Y11585A Chenu, Luxembourg, January–April 1768
Y11705–Y11706 Desormeaux, Place Maubert, 1775
Y11735 Papers of the Bourse Commune, *c.* 1650–1780
Y11745 Inventory of papers of Daminois, 1692–5, 1725–7, 1741–4. Odd papers
Y11952 Bourgeois, St Jacques de la Boucherie, 1764
Y11963 Bourgeois, St Jacques de la Boucherie, 1775
Y12469 Dorival, Cité, 1774
Y12481 Dorival, Cité, 1779–80
Y12596–Y12597 De Machurin, Place Maubert, 1752
Y12612 De Machurin, Halles, 1763
Y12791 Roland, St Benoît, 1775
Y12793 Dupuy, St Benoît, July–December 1776
Y12816 Dupuy, St Benoît, 1786
Y12826 Letters and papers, Doublon, Dupuy
Y12830 Letters and papers, Roland, Dupuy, Gillet
Y13103 Bricogne, Montmartre, 1750–3
Y13163 Letters and papers, Fontaine, St Eustache, *c.* 1756–79
Y13290 Foucart, Place Maubert, 1788
Y13377 Grimperel, St Denis, January–June 1752
Y13419A Gruter des Rosiers, Ste Avoie, January–June 1789
Y13454A Gueullette, St Antoine, January–June 1789
Y13728 Letters and Papers, Chastelus, Coquelin, Doublon, Gillet
Y13750 Delavergée, Palais Royal, 1745
Y13751 Delavergée, Palais Royal, 1746
Y13760 Delavergée, Palais Royal, 1752
Y13816 Thiot, St Germain des Prés, 1788
Y13819 Complaints to Thiot, St Germain des Prés, 1770–89
Y14078 Crespy, Luxembourg, 1752
Y14391 Dubuisson, Marais, 1746
Y14436 LeRat, Faubourg St Antoine, 1788
Y14437A LeRat, Faubourg St Antoine, January–May 1789
Y14483 LeRoux, Halles, 1788
Y14484 LeRoux, Halles, 1789
Y14560 Leseigneur, St Germain des Prés, March–December 1775
Y14692 Michel, St Eustache, 1774–5
Y14701–Y14701^{bis} Inventory of archives of Dudoigt and Michel
Y14935 De Prémontval, Place Maubert, 1724
Y14950 De Prémontval, Place Maubert, 1735
Y14994 Du Ruisseau, St André des Arts, 1775
Y15099–Y15100 Desmarest, Grève, 1788
Y15101 Desmarest, Grève, January–June 1789
Y15114A Letters and papers, Menier, de la Jarie, Trudon, de Laubeypie
Y15114B Letters and papers, Ninnin

Select bibliography

YI5115A   Letters and papers, Ninnin, *c.* 1780–8
YI5115B   Letters and papers, Ninnin, Desmarest, *c.* 1788–90
YI5117   Reports of *garde* to Ninnin and Desmarest, 1778–90
YI5118   'Agendas' of Ninnin, Desmarest, 1778–89
YI5310   Inventory of papers of Regnard le jeune and Duchesne, October 1712–December 1772
YI5350   Regnaudet, Grève, 1752
YI5363–YI5365   Regnaudet, *procès-verbaux* with corporations, *c.* 1741–60
YI5384   Serreau, St Martin, 1775
YI5402   Serreau, Halles, 1788
YI5682   Sirebeau, Palais Royal, 1788
YI5707   Enquiry into accident of 30 May 1770
YI5747   Thomin, Place Maubert, 1700
YI6003   Vanglenne, Temple, January–June 1788
YI6022C–YI6022D   Papers of Company of *commissaires*, *c.* 1760–90
YI8580   Chambre civile, 1780–90
YI8795   Prévoté de Paris et de l'Ile de France, register of arrests, July 1780–January 1791
AD I 26   Police ordinances on eighteenth-century Paris

2. Archives de la Préfecture de Police

A^A173   *Procès-verbaux* of *commissaires de police* of Sections, 1791–Year IX
A^B405   Register of reports of *inspecteur* Santerre, St Denis, to *lieutenant général*, 1779–86
Fonds Lamoignon, collection of police ordinances, vols. 39–41 (1749–63)

3. Archives de la Seine

D5 B6 472   Account book of *marchand de vin*

4. Bibliothèque de l'Arsenal, MSS Bastille

10846   Reports on journeymen silk-weavers, 1724
11556   Dossier on Potel
11727   Letters and papers, 1750
12127   Letters and papers, 1761
12202   Reports on journeymen hatters, 1764–5
12369   Reports on journeymen painters and gilders 1769
12399   Dossier on Tilloy Desnoyette, former *commissaire*
12436   Dossier on *inspecteur* Troussey

5. Bibliothèque historique de la Ville de Paris

MS 678   Memoirs of J-L. Ménétra
MS 696   Household accounts of a 'bourgeoise', 1781–93

Select bibliography

MS 704 *Mémoires* and pamphlets, 1769–71
MS Côte provisoire 1753, 'Documents sur la police de Paris telle qu'elle existait en 1789'
MS Côte provisoire 4725, 'Affaires générales de police'

6. Bibliothèque municipale d'Orléans

MSS 1421–3 Memoirs of Lenoir, former *lieutenant général de police de Paris*

7. Bibliothèque nationale

MSS français 6680–7, S. P. Hardy, 'Mes Loisirs, ou Journal d'événemens tels qu'ils parviennent à ma connoissance'
MS français 8090, collection of police ordinances, 1742–56
MS Joly de Fleury 1103, papers concerning the riots of 1788–9
MS Joly de Fleury 1590, confraternities and religious associations

B. PRINTED SOURCES
(place of publication is Paris unless otherwise indicated)

1. Primary material

I. ENGRAVINGS:
Bibliothèque Nationale, Département des Estampes
Va 247d fol ⎫
Va 294–5   ⎬ Engravings of eighteenth-century Paris
II. MAPS:
Atlas des anciens plans de Paris, fascsimile reproduction, 1880
Bretez, Louis. *Plan de Paris* ('Plan Turgot'), 1739
Brion de la Tour. *Nouveau plan de Paris*, 1783
Jaillot. Maps of the twenty quarters of Paris, in Archives Nationales N IV Seine 64
Junié. *Plan des paroisses de Paris*, 1786
Rittmann and Junié. *Atlas des plans de la censive de l'Archevêché dans Paris*, 1786. Facsimile edition, Paris, 1906
Verniquet. *Plan de la Ville de Paris*, 1791
III. BOOKS:
Alletz, P. A. *Tableau de l'humanité et de la bienfaisance, ou précis historique des charités qui se font dans Paris*, 1769
Almanach Royal, 1750–89
Barbier, E. J. F. *Journal historique et anecdotique du règne de Louis XV*, edited by A. de la Villegille, 1851–7
Brice, G. *Description de la ville de Paris et de tout ce qu'elle contient de plus remarquable*, 9th edition, 1752
Encyclopédie, ou dictionnaire raisonné des sciences, des arts et des métiers, 35 vols., 1751–60
Expilly, J-J. *Dictionnaire géographique, historique et politique des Gaules et de la France*, 6 vols., Amsterdam, 1762–70

Select bibliography

Fréminville, E. de la Poix de. *Dictionnaire ou traité de police générale des villes, bourgs, paroisses et seigneuries de la campagne,* new edition, 1771

Gazier, A., ed. 'La Police de Paris en 1770, mémoire rédigé par les ordres de M. de Sartine, par J-B. C. Lemaire', *Mémoires de la Société de l'histoire de Paris et de l'Ile de France,* 5 (1879), 1–131

Guyot, P. *Répertoire universel et raisonné de jurisprudence civile, criminelle, canonique et bénéficiale,* 81 vols., 1775–86

Hardy, S. P. *Mes Loisirs,* edited by M. Tourneux and M. Vitrac, 1912

Jousse, D. *Traité des fonctions, droits et privilèges des commissaires-enqueteurs-examinateurs au Châtelet de Paris,* 2 vols., 1759

Lamare, N. de. *Traité de la police,* 4 vols., 1705–38. Fourth volume by Le Cler du Brillet
Mémoires des intendants sur l'état des généralités. Vol. 1, *Mémoire de la généralité de Paris* (drawn up *c.* 1700), 1881

Mercier, L. S. *Tableau de Paris,* new edition, 12 vols., Amsterdam, 1782–8

Nouveau coutumier général, ou Corps des coutumes générales et particulières de France, 1724, vol. 3, pp. 29–87, *Nouvelle coutume de Paris*

Peuchet, J. *Collection des lois, ordonnances et règlements de police,* 2nd series, *Police moderne de 1667 à 1789,* 8 vols., 1818–19

Restif de la Bretonne, E. *Les Nuits de Paris,* 14 vols., 1788–9

Savary des Bruslons, J. *Dictionnaire universel de commerce,* 2 vols., 1723

Talleyrand, C. M. de, *Mémoires,* ed. Couchoud, 2 vols., Plon, 1957

2. Secondary material

Abbiateci, A., Billaçois, F., Bongert, Y., Castan, N., Castan, Y., Petrovitch, P., *Crimes et criminalité en France sous l'ancien régime, XVIIe–XVIIIe siècle,* Armand Colin, 1971

Agulhon, M. *La Sociabilité méridionale,* Aix-en-Provence, La Pensée universitaire, 1966

Anderson, M. *Approaches to the History of the Western Family, 1500–1914,* London, Macmillan, 1980
Family Structure in Nineteenth-Century Lancashire, Cambridge, C.U.P., 1971

Andrews, R. 'The Justices of the Peace of Revolutionary Paris, Sept. 1792–Nov. 1794 (Frimaire Year III)', *Past and Present,* 52 (1971), 56–105
'Political Elites and Social Conflicts in the Sections of Revolutionary Paris: 1792–Year III', unpublished D.Phil. thesis, Oxford University, 1970

Apollo, vol. 101, no. 158 (April 1975). Issue on 'Musée Carnavalet, Paris of the Ancien Régime'

Apollo, vol. 101, no. 160 (June 1975). Issue on 'French Eighteenth-Century Art in the Hermitage Museum'

Ariès, P. *L'Enfant et la vie familiale sous l'ancien régime,* Plon, 1960
'The Family and the City', *Daedalus,* 106 (1977), 227–35

Aubry, G. *La Jurisprudence criminelle du Châtelet de Paris sous le règne de Louis XVI,* Librairie générale de droit et de jurisprudence, 1971

Bardet, J-P., Chaunu, P., Desert, G., Gouhier, P., Neveux, H. *Le Bâtiment. Enquête d'histoire économique, XIVe–XIXe siècle,* Mouton, 1971

Baulant, M. 'La Famille en miettes: sur un aspect de la démographie du XVIIe siècle', *Annales: E.S.C.,* 27 (1972), 959–68

Bédarida, F. 'La Vie de quartier en Angleterre: enquêtes empiriques et approches théoriques', *Le Mouvement social*, 118 (Jan.–March 1982), 9–21

Bercé, Y-M. *Fête et révolte. Des mentalités populaires du XVIe au XVIIe siècle*, Hachette, 1976

Bertrand, M. *Architecture de l'habitat urbain. La maison, le quartier, la ville*, Dunod, 1980

Bloch, C. *L'Assistance et l'état en France à la veille de la Révolution*, Picard, 1908

Bluche, F. *Les Magistrats du Parlement de Paris au XVIIIe siècle (1715–1771)*, Les Belles Lettres, 1960

Bois, J. P. 'Les Soldats invalides au XVIIIe siècle: perspectives nouvelles', *Histoire, économie et société*, 2 (1982), 237–58

Botlan, M. 'Domesticité et domestiques à Paris dans la crise (1770–1790)', unpublished thesis, Ecole des Chartes, 1976.
Abstract in *Positions de Thèses de l'Ecole des Chartes*, 1976, pp. 27–35

Bouchard, G. *Le Village immobile. Sennely-en-Sologne au XVIIIe siècle*, Plon, 1971

Boudon, F., Chastel, A., Couzy, H., Hamon, F., *Système de l'architecture urbaine: le quartier des Halles à Paris*, 2 vols., C.N.R.S., 1977

Braesch, F. 'Essai de statistique de la population ouvrière de Paris vers 1791', *La Révolution française*, 32 (1912), 289–321

Brennan, T. 'Cabarets and Labouring Class Communities in Eighteenth-Century Paris', unpub. Ph.D thesis, Johns Hopkins University, 1981
'Beyond the Barriers: Popular Culture and Parisian *Guinguettes*', *Eighteenth-Century Studies*, 18 (1984–5), 153–69

Brongniart, M. *La Paroisse St Médard au faubourg St Marceau*, A. et J. Picard, 1951

Burstin, H. 'Le Faubourg St Marcel à l'époque révolutionnaire: structure économique et composition sociale', unpub. doctoral thesis, Université de Paris I, 1977. Summary in *A.H.R.F.* 50 (1978), 117–26

Calhoun, C. 'Community: Toward a Variable Conceptualization for Comparative Research', *Social History*, 5 (1980), 105–29

Castan, N. *Les Criminels de Languedoc*, Toulouse, Université de Toulouse-Le Mirail, 1980

Castan, Y. *Honnêteté et relations sociales en Languedoc, 1715–1780*, Plon, 1974
'Pères et fils en Languedoc à l'époque classique', *Dix-septième siècle*, 102–3 (1974), 31–43
'Les Procès criminels, sources d'étude des mentalités rurales'. *Bulletin du Centre pour l'histoire économique et sociale de la région lyonnaise*, 4 (1978), 1–5

Chagniot, J. 'La Criminalité militaire à Paris au XVIIIe siècle', in *Criminalité et répression (XIVe–XIXe siècles)*, in *Annales de Bretagne et des Pays de l'Ouest*, 88 (1981), 327–45
'Le Guet et la garde de Paris à la fin de l'ancien régime', *Revue d'histoire moderne et contemporaine*, 20 (1973), 58–71

Chassaigne, M. *La Lieutenance générale de police de Paris*, A. Rousseau, 1906

Chassin, C. *Les Elections et les cahiers de Paris en 1789*, 4 vols., Jouaust et Sigaux, 1888–9

Chatelain, A. 'Complexité des migrations temporaires et définitives à Paris et dans le Bassin parisien (XVIIIe–XXe siècle)', *Etudes de la région parisienne*, 44th year, new series, 27 (July 1970), 27–39

Chaytor, M. 'Household and Kinship: Ryton in the late sixteenth and early seventeenth centuries', *History Workshop Journal*, 10 (Autumn 1980), 25–60

Select bibliography

Chevalier, L. *Classes laborieuses et classes dangereuses à Paris pendant la première moitié du dix-neuvième siècle*, Plon, 1958

Cobb, R. *Paris and its Provinces*, Oxford, O.U.P., 1975

The Police and the People, Oxford, O.U.P., 1970

Reactions to the French Revolution, Oxford, O.U.P., 1972

Collett, P., ed. *Social Rules and Social Behaviour*, Oxford, Blackwell, 1977

Contat, N. *Anecdotes typographiques: où l'on voit la description des coutumes, moeurs et usages singuliers des compagnons imprimeurs*, edited by G. Barber, Oxford, Oxford Bibliographical Society, 1980

Coornaert, E. *Les Compagnonnages en France du moyen âge à nos jours*, Editions ouvrières, 1966

Les Corporations en France avant 1789, Editions ouvrières, 1941

Darnton, R. *The Great Cat Massacre*, London, Allen Lane, 1984

'The High Enlightenment and the Low Life of Literature in Pre-Revolutionary France', *Past and Present*, 51 (1971), 81–115

Darrow, M. H., 'French Noblewomen and the New Domesticity, 1750–1850', *Feminist Studies*, 5 (Spring 1979), 41–65

Daumard, A. 'Une référence pour l'étude des sociétiés urbaines en France aux XVIIIe et XIXe siècles. Projet de code socio-professionnel', *Revue d'histoire moderne et contemporaine*, 10 (1963), 185–210

Daumard, A., and F. Furet, 'Problèmes de méthode en histoire sociale. Réflexions sur une note critique', *Revue d'histoire moderne et contemporaine*, 11 (1964), 291–8

Structures et relations sociales à Paris au milieu du XVIIIe siècle, Armand Colin, 1961

Davis, N. Z., 'Ghosts, Kin, and Progeny: Some Features of Family Life in Early Modern France', *Daedalus*, 106 (1977) 87–114

'The Reasons of Misrule: Youth Groups and Charivaris in Sixteenth-Century France', *Past and Present*, 50 (Feb. 1971), 41–75

'The Rites of Violence: Religious Riot in Sixteenth-Century France', *Past and Present*, 59 (May 1973), 51–91

'The Sacred and the Body Social in Sixteenth-Century Lyon', *Past and Present*, 90 (Feb. 1981), 40–70

Society and Culture in Early Modern France, Stanford, Stanford University Press, 1975

'Some Tasks and Themes in the Study of Popular Religion', in C. Trinkaus and H. O. Oberman, eds., *The Pursuit of Holiness in Late Medieval and Renaissance Religion*, Leiden, Brill, 1974, pp. 307–36

'Women in the *Arts mécaniques* in Sixteenth-Century Lyon', in *Lyon et l'Europe. Hommes et sociétés. Mélanges d'histoire offerts à Richard Gascon*, 2 vols., Lyon, Presses universitaires de Lyon, 1981, vol. 1, pp. 139–67

Delasselle, C. 'Les Enfants abandonnés à Paris au dix-huitième siècle', *Annales: E.S.C.*, 30 (1975), 187–218

Dennis, R. 'Community and Interaction in a Victorian City: Huddersfield 1850–1880', unpublished Ph.D. thesis, Cambridge University, 1975

Dennis, R., and S. Daniels, '"Community" and the Social Geography of Victorian Cities', *Urban History Yearbook 1981*, Leicester, 1981, 7–23

Depauw, J. 'Amour illégitime et société à Nantes au XVIIIe siècle', *Annales: E.S.C.*, 27 (1972), 1155–82

Select bibliography

Desmaze, C. *Le Châtelet de Paris, son organisation, ses privilèges, prévôts, conseillers, chevaliers du guet, notaires, procureurs, commissaires, huissiers, registres, prisons et supplices (1060–1862)*, 1863

Dinaux, A. *Les Sociétés badines, bachiques, littéraires et chantantes, leur histoire et leurs travaux*, 2 vols., 1867

Donzelet, J. *La Police des familles*, Editions de Minuit, 1977 (English translation, *The Policing of Families*, London, Hutchinson, 1977)

Durand, Y. *Les Fermiers généraux au XVIIIe siècle*, Presses universitaires, 1971
'Recherches sur les salaires des maçons à Paris au XVIIIe siècle', *Revue d'histoire économique et sociale*, 44 (1966), 468–80
'Répartition de la noblesse dans les quartiers de Paris', in M. Reinhard, ed., *Contributions à l'histoire démographique de la Révolution française*, 2nd series, Bibliothèque Nationale, 1965, pp. 21–4

Elias, N. *The Civilizing Process*, 2 vols., London, Blackwell, 1978–82. First pub. 1939

Farge, A. *Délinquance et criminalité: le vol d'aliments à Paris au XVIIIe siècle*, Plon, 1974
'Le Mendiant, un marginal? Les résistances aux archers de l'hôpital dans le Paris du XVIIIe siècle', in *Les Marginaux et les exclus dans l'histoire*, Union Générale d'Editions, 1979, pp. 312–29
Vivre dans la rue à Paris au XVIIIe siècle, Gallimard/Julliard, 1979

Faure, A. *Paris Carême-prenant*, Hachette, 1978

Ferrand, L. 'Les Confréries et leurs images', *Le Vieux Papier*, 28 (Oct. 1979), 557–63

Flammermont, J. 'Les gardes-françaises en juillet 1789', *La Révolution française*, 36 (1899), 12–24

Flandrin, J-L. *Familles, parenté, maison, sexualité dans l'ancienne société*, Hachette, 1976 (English translation, *Families in Former Times*, Cambridge University Press, 1979)

Fleury, M., and L. Henry. *Nouveau manuel de dépouillement et d'exploitation de l'état civil ancien*, Editions de l'Institut national d'études démographiques, 1965

Fossoyeux, M. 'Les Ecoles de charité à Paris sous l'ancien régime et dans la première partie du XIXe siècle', *Mémoires de la Société de l'histoire de Paris et de l'Ile de France*, 39 (1912), 225–366

Furet, F. 'Pour une définition des classes inférieures à l'époque moderne', *Annales: E.S.C.*, 18 (1963), 459–74
'Structures sociales parisiennes au XVIIIe siècle. L'Apport d'une série "fiscale" (le Grand Bureau des Pauvres et la taxe des pauvres)', *Annales: E.S.C.*, 16 (1961), 939–58

Galliano, P. 'La Mortalité infantile (indigènes et nourrissons) dans la banlieue sud de Paris à la fin du XVIIIe siècle, 1774–1794', *Annales de démographie historique*, 1966, 139–77

Ganiage, J. 'Nourrissons parisiens en Beauvaisis', in *Sur la population française au XVIIIe et au XIXe siècle. Hommage à M. Reinhard*, Société de démographie historique, 1973, pp. 271–90

Garden, M., *Lyon et les Lyonnais au XVIIIe siècle*, Université de Lyon, 1970
'Ouvriers et artisans au XVIIIe siècle: l'exemple lyonnais et les problèmes de classification', *Revue d'histoire économique et sociale*, 48 (1970), 28–54
'La Vie de quartier', *Bulletin du Centre pour l'histoire économique et sociale de la région lyonnaise*, 3 (1977), 17–28

Select bibliography

Garrioch, D. 'Verbal Insults in Eighteenth-Century Paris', in P. Burke and R. Porter (eds.), *Essays in the Social History of Language*, New York, C.U.P., forthcoming

Gaston, J. *Images des confréries parisiennes avant la Révolution*, A. Marty, 1910

George, D. *London Life in the Eighteenth Century*, Harmondsworth, Penguin, 1966. First published 1925

Gobert, A. 'Le District des Enfants trouvés au faubourg St Antoine en 1789', *La Révolution française*, new series, 6 (1936), 134–48; and 15 (1938), 260–81

Godechot, J. *La Prise de la Bastille, 14 juillet 1789*, Gallimard, 1965

Goeury, A. 'La Section Grange-Batelière pendant la Révolution française', in M. Reinhard, ed., *Contributions à l'histoire démographique de la Révolution française*, 3rd series, *Etudes sur la population parisienne*, Bibliothèque Nationale, 1970, pp. 93–153

Goeury, J-C. 'Evolution démographique et sociale du faubourg St Germain', in M. Reinhard, ed., *Contributions à l'histoire démographique de la Révolution française*, 2nd series, Bibliothèque Nationale, 1965, p. 25–60

Groppi, A. 'Le Travail des femmes à Paris à l'époque de la Révolution française', *Bulletin d'histoire économique et sociale de la Révolution française*, 1979, 27–46

Gutton, J-P. *Domestiques et serviteurs dans la France de l'ancien régime*, Aubier Montaigne, 1981

La Sociabilité villageoise dans l'ancienne France, Hachette, 1979

Hannerz, U. *Soulside. Enquiries into Ghetto Culture and Community*, New York, Columbia University Press 1969

Harris, O. 'Households and their Boundaries', *History Workshop Journal*, 13 (Spring 1982), 143–52

Hufton, O. *The Poor of Eighteenth-Century France, 1750–1789*, Oxford, O.U.P., 1974

'Women and the Family Economy in Eighteenth-Century France', *French Historical Studies*, 9 (1975), 1–22

Ibanès, J. 'La Population de la Place des Vosges et de ses environs en 1791', in M. Reinhard, ed., *Contributions à l'histoire démographique de la Révolution française*. 1st series, Bibliothèque Nationale, 1962, pp. 71–97

Jones, P. M. 'Parish, Seigneurie, and the Community of Inhabitants in Southern Central France during the Eighteenth and Nineteenth Centuries', *Past and Present*, 91 (May 1981), 74–108

Jurgens, M.. and P. Couperie. 'Le Logement à Paris aux XVIe et XVIIe siècles', *Annales: E.S.C.*, 17 (1962), 488–500

Kaiser, C. 'Les Cours souveraines au XVIe siècle: morale et contre-réforme', *Annales: E.S.C.*, 37 (1982), 15–31

Kaplan, S. *Bread, Politics and Political Economy in the Reign of Louis XV*, 2 vols., The Hague, Martinus Nijhoff, 1976

'Note sur les commissaires de police de Paris au XVIIIe siècle', *Revue d'histoire moderne et contemporaine*, 28 (1981), 669–86

'Réflexions sur la police du monde de travail, 1700–1815', *Revue historique*, 529 (Jan.–Mar. 1979), 17–77

'Religion, Subsistence, and Social Control: The Uses of St Genevieve', *Eighteenth-Century Studies*, 13 (1979–80), 142–68

Kaplow, J. *The Names of Kings: the Parisian Laboring Poor in the Eighteenth Century*, New York, Basic Books, 1972

Select bibliography

'Sur la population flottante de Paris à la fin de l'ancien régime', *A.H.R.F.*, 39 (1967), 1–14

Labrousse, E., Léon, P., Goubert, P., Bouvier, J., Carrière, C., Harsin, P. *Des Derniers Temps de l'âge seigneurial aux préludes de l'âge industriel (1660–1789)*, 1970, vol. 2 of E. Labrousse and F. Braudel, eds., *Histoire économique et sociale de la France*, P.U.F.

Laslett, P. and Wall, R., eds. *Household and Family in Past Time*, Cambridge, C.U.P., 1972

Lautman, F. 'Différences ou changement dans l'organisation familiale', *Annales: E.S.C.*, 27 (1972), 1190–6

Le Bihan, A. *Francs-maçons et ateliers parisiens de la Grande Loge de France au XVIIIe siècle (1760–1795)*, Bibliothèque Nationale, 1973

Lebrun, F. *La Vie conjugale sous l'ancien régime*, Colin, 1975

Lefebvre, G. 'Foules révolutionnaires', *A.H.R.F.*, 9 (1934), 1–26

Le Roy Ladurie, E. 'Système de la coutume. Structures familiales et coutume d'héritage en France au XVIe siècle', *Annales: E.S.C.*, 27 (1972), 825–46

Levy, C., and L. Henry. 'Ducs et pairs sous l'ancien régime, caractéristiques d'une caste', *Population*, 15 (1960), 807–30

Macfarlane, A. *Reconstructing Historical Communities*, Cambridge, C.U.P., 1977

Mann, P. H. *An Approach to Urban Sociology*, London, Routledge and Kegan Paul, 1965

Martin, G. *Les Associations ouvrières au XVIIIe siècle, 1700–1792*, A. Rousseau, 1900

Monin, H. *L'Etat de Paris en 1789*, D. Jouaust, 1889

Monnier, R. 'L'Evolution de l'industrie et le travail des femmes à Paris sous l'Empire', *Bulletin d'histoire économique et sociale de la Révolution française*, 1979, 47–60

Mounier, N. 'Le Quartier des Porcherons (1720–1789): description d'un processus d'urbanisation d'un faubourg de Paris', unpub. thesis, summary in *Positions de Thèses de l'Ecole des Chartes*, 1978, 121–31

Ozouf, M. 'Le Cortège et la ville: les itinéraires parisiens des cortèges révolutionnaires', *Annales: E.S.C.*, 26 (1971), 889–916

Perrin, G. 'L'Entassement de la population dans le Paris de la Révolution. La Section des Lombards', in M. Reinhard, ed., *Contributions à l'histoire démographique de la Révolution française*, 2nd series, Bibliothèque Nationale, 1965, pp. 61–76

Phillips, R. *Family Breakdown in Late Eighteenth-Century France. Divorces in Rouen, 1792–1803*, Oxford, Clarendon, 1980

Pillorget, R., and J. de Viguerie. 'Les Quartiers de Paris aux XVIIe et XVIIIe siècles', *Revue d'histoire moderne et contemporaine*, 17 (1970), 253–77

Poplin, D. E., *Communities: A Survey of Theories and Methods of Research*, New York, Macmillan, 1972

Pronteau, J. *Les Numérotages des maisons de Paris du XVe siècle à nos jours*, Préfecture de la Seine, 1966

Quéniart, J. *Culture et société urbaine dans la France de l'Ouest au XVIIIe siècle*, Klincksieck, 1978

Raison-Jourde, F. *La Colonie auvergnate à Paris au XIXe siècle*, Ville de Paris, Commission des travaux historiques, 1976

Ranum, O. 'Courtesy, Absolutism, and the Rise of the French State, 1630–1660', *Journal of Modern History*, 52 (1980), 426–51

Reinhard, M., ed., *Contributions à l'histoire démographique de la Révolution française*. 1st series, Bibliothèque Nationale, 1962. 2nd series, 1965. 3rd series: *Etudes sur*

Select bibliography

la population parisienne, 1970. Published by the Commission d'histoire économique et sociale de la Révolution française, *Mémoires et Documents*, vols. 14, 18, 25

Nouvelle Histoire de Paris. La Révolution, 1789–1799, Hachette, 1971

Reiter, R. 'Men and Women in the South of France: Public and Private Domains', in R. Reiter, ed., *Toward an Anthropology of Women*, New York, Monthly Review Press, 1975, pp. 252–82

Roche, D. *Le Peuple de Paris*, Aubier, 1981

'Recherches sur la noblesse parisienne au milieu du XVIIIe siècle: la noblesse du Marais', *Actes du 86e Congrès national des Sociétés savantes, Montpellier, 1961*, 1962, pp. 541–78

Le Siècle des lumières en province: académies et académiciens provinciaux, 1680–1789, 2 vols., Mouton/De Gruyter, 1978

Rochefoucauld, F. de la, *La Vie en Angleterre; ou Mélanges sur l'Angleterre*, 1784, edited by J. Marchand, 1945

Romon, C. 'Mendiants et policiers à Paris au XVIIIe siècle', *Histoire, économie, société*, 2 (2e trimestre 1982), 259–95

Ross, E. '"Fierce Questions and Taunts": Married Life in Working-Class London, 1870–1914', *Feminist Studies*, 8 (1982), 575–602

'Survival Networks: Women's Neighbourhood Sharing in London before World War I', *History Workshop Journal*, 15 (Spring 1983), 4–27

Roubin, L. *Chambrettes des Provençaux*, Plon, 1970

Rouff, M. 'Une Grève de gagne-deniers en 1786 à Paris', *Revue historique*, 105 (1910), 332–47

Rousseau-Vigneron, F. 'La Section de la Place des Fédérés pendant la Révolution', in M. Reinhard, ed., *Contributions à l'histoire démographique de la Révolution française*, 3rd series, Bibliothèque Nationale, 1970, *Etudes sur la population parisienne*, pp. 155–216

Rudé, G. *The Crowd in the French Revolution*, Oxford, O.U.P., 1959

'The Parisian Wage-Earning Population and the Insurrectionary Movements of 1789–91', 2 vols., Ph.D. thesis, London University, 1950

'La Taxation populaire de mai 1775', *A.H.R.F.*, 28 (1956), 139–79

Schlumbohm, J. '"Traditional" Collectivity and "Modern" Individuality: Some Questions and Suggestions for the Historical Study of Socialization. The Examples of the German Lower and Upper Bourgeoisies around 1800', *Social History*, 5 (1980), 71–103

Sévegrand, M. 'La Section de Popincourt pendant la Révolution française', in M. Reinhard, ed., *Contributions à l'histoire démographique de la Révolution française*, 3rd series, Bibliothèque Nationale, 1970, pp. 9–91

Sewell, W. Jr. *Work and Revolution in France*, Cambridge, C.U.P., 1980

Shorter, E. *The Making of the Modern Family*, New York, Basic Books, 1975

Smith, S. R. 'The London Apprentices as Seventeenth-Century Adolescents', *Past and Present*, 61 (1975), 149–61

Soboul, A. *La France à la veille de la Révolution*, 2 vols., Centre de documentation universitaire, 1964–9

Sonenscher, M., and Garrioch, D. '*Compagnonnages*, Confraternities and Associations of Journeymen in Eighteenth-Century Paris', *European History Quarterly*, 16 (1986), 25–45

Select bibliography

Stone, L. *The Family, Sex and Marriage in England, 1500–1800*, London, Weidenfeld and Nicolson, 1977

Sutcliffe, A. *The Autumn of Central Paris*, London, Edward Arnold, 1970

Thibaut-Payen, J. 'Pot de fleur et jambe de bois: la voirie parisienne à la fin du XVIIe siècle (d'après les registres du bureau des finances)', *Dix-septième siècle*, 126 (Jan.–Mar. 1980), 59–76

Thompson, E. P. *The Making of the English Working Class*, London, Victor Gollancz, 1963
  'The Moral Economy of the English Crowd in the Eighteenth Century', *Past and Present*, 50 (1971), 76–136
  '"Rough Music": le charivari anglais', *Annales: E.S.C.*, 27 (1972), 285–312

Tilly, L. 'Individual Lives and Family Strategies in the French Proletariat', *Journal of Family History*, 4 (1979), 137–52

Vieille, A. 'Relations parentales et relations de voisinage chez les ménages ouvriers de la Seine', *Cahiers internationaux de sociologie*, new series, 17 (July–Dec. 1954), 140–53

Vie quotidienne à Paris dans la seconde moitié du XVIIIe siècle. Catalogue of the exhibition at the Musée de l'histoire de France, 1973

Vovelle, M. *Les Métamorphoses de la fête en Provence de 1750 à 1820*, Aubier/Flammarion, 1976
  'Le Tournant des mentalités en France 1750–1789: la "sensibilité" pré-révolutionnaire', *Social History*, 5 (1977), 605–29

Watson, F. J. B. *The Wrightsman Collection*, 6 vols., New York, Metropolitan Museum of Art, vol. 1, 1970

Williams, A. *The Police of Paris*, Baton Rouge, Louisiana State University Press, 1979

Wrigley, E. A. 'Reflections on the History of the Family', *Daedalus*, 106 (1977), 71–85

Young, M., and P. Willmott. *Family and Kinship in East London*, Harmondsworth, Penguin, 1957

Index/Glossary

Note: Individual trades are listed under trade corporations.